*Sixth*
EDITION

D0223486

# COMMUNICATION & HUMAN BEHAVIOR

BRENT D. RUBEN    LEA P. STEWART

*Rutgers University*

Kendall Hunt
publishing company

**Book Team**
Chairman and Chief Executive Officer   Mark C. Falb
President and Chief Operating Officer   Chad M. Chandlee
Vice President, Higher Education   David L. Tart
Director of Publishing Partnerships   Paul B. Carty
Senior Developmental Coordinator   Angela Willenbring
Vice President, Operations   Timothy J. Beitzel
Senior Production Editor   Sheri Hosek
Permissions Editor Tammy Hunt
Cover Designer   Suzanne Millius

Cover image © Shutterstock, Inc.

# Kendall Hunt
publishing company

www.kendallhunt.com
*Send all inquiries to:*
4050 Westmark Drive
Dubuque, IA  52004-1840

# BRIEF CONTENTS

# CONTENTS

# CHAPTER 2: Communication Past and Present 21

# CHAPTER 3: Communication as a Basic Life Process 45

## CHAPTER 4: Nonverbal Communication  69

# CHAPTER 6: Perception & Information Processing  137

## CHAPTER 7: Mediated Communication  169

## CHAPTER 10: Group Communication  247

## CHAPTER 13: Public Communication  329

# PREFACE

As society evolves, each generation is faced with new challenges as well as new opportunities. In today's world, we encounter the rapid development of new communication technologies, evolving models of health care, changing concepts of marriage and family, and the benefits and conflicts associated with globalization.

We also face a variety of smaller, but no less significant, challenges on a daily basis: a relationship conflict that can't be reconciled, a lower grade than we expected to receive, a friend who doesn't seem to understand, a job that doesn't work out, or a child who disappoints us.

Whether approached from the perspective of communication or psychology, political science or art, literature or sociology, a knowledge of human behavior can be of great value in our efforts to comprehend and deal with the circumstances we encounter every day. It can also help us understand ourselves, our actions, our motives, our feelings, and our aspirations.

Perhaps the greatest value comes from approaches that draw on a number of disciplinary perspectives. This sixth edition of *Communication and Human Behavior* aims to provide this kind of framework. In this edition, we have remained true to our basic belief that communication is a fundamental life process that is necessary to our lives as individuals and to our relationships, groups, organizations, cultures, and societies. We have endeavored to clarify the meaning, importance, and implications of this perspective with up-to-date examples and research findings.

Communication is a topic that, in certain cases, is extremely basic, involving daily activities that we all take for granted—speaking, writing, and listening. At the same time, it is a complex phenomenon that plays a pivotal and far-reaching role in all human affairs. The challenge for authors of an introductory text is to capture, explain, and illustrate the more familiar facets of communication and then to integrate them into a more extensive framework for understanding the complexity and pervasiveness of human communication processes.

*Communication and Human Behavior*, 6th edition, addresses these challenges by providing a book that is expansive yet integrated, rigorous yet readable, and that links theory and practice.

# ACKNOWLEDGMENTS

A great many people have contributed to the formation and expression of the ideas presented in this book. In some cases, the contributions have been in written form. In other instances, valued assistance has come through personal contact both recently and over the years. We want to express our sincere thanks to the many colleagues, friends, and students who have contributed to this book and to our thinking about communication and human behavior.

Many people have assisted us with the development of this edition. We received invaluable assistance from our Rutgers colleagues Jenny Mandelbaum, who provided helpful suggestions about the scope of the material presented in this book, Itzhak Yanovitzky, who provided material in Chapter 5 on Persuasion, Jen Theiss, who provided material on interpersonal relationships for Chapter 9, Susan Lawrence, who provided material on 21st century careers for Chapter 1, and Ralph Gigliotti who provided material on organizational communication and leadership for Chapter 10. Rutgers graduate student Sally Abdul Wahab contributed a very helpful literature review on media influences for Chapter 7. We also acknowledge the helpful comments and suggestions we received from other colleagues in the Rutgers Department of Communication. In addition, we owe our gratitude to Abdulmanan Nur, Manager of Institutional Effectiveness at the College of North Atlantic-Qatar, for useful information about Middle Eastern culture found in Chapter 12.

This edition would not have been possible without the work of Nikolaos Linardopoulos who developed the learning objectives for each chapter, chapter summaries, and extensive material on public communication, political communication, and public relations. In addition, he provided a thorough revision of all of the web-based material that accompanies this text.

Throughout the revision process, the Center for Communication and Health Issues "family" supported the preparation of the manuscript in innumerable ways. Special thanks are owed to Alexander Nelson, Marcus Curtis, and Joseph Bae for their diligent research assistance. In addition to being willing to make uncountable trips to the library, they offered suggestions for examples used throughout the text, had provocative conversations about theoretical concepts in communication as they relate to today's college student population, and generally reminded us that students really do care about communication and its influence on their lives. In particular, Alex used his considerable editing skills to prepare references and other scholarly materials for the text. Anna Goldin and Matthew Suh read the 5th edition and offered many helpful suggestions for the revision. Larry McAllister II provided perceptive insights on contemporary social media use. Yvonne Dayan and Deepanjali Tiwari where always there when the second author was about to "stress out" too much. Their assistance, support, and cheerfulness are truly appreciated. And Marie Haverfield brought joy (aka Ainsley) into all of our lives.

We also want to acknowledge Paul Carty, Kendall Hunt's Director of Publishing Partnerships, who encouraged us to take on the task of another edition of this book. Angela Willenbring, KH Senior Development Coordinator, was massively helpful throughout the preparation of the manuscript and helped us bring our vision to life. Kara McArthur did a wonderful job copyediting and providing perceptive comments along with helpful edits.

# ABOUT THE AUTHORS

## DR. BRENT D. RUBEN

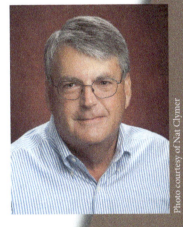

Photo courtesy of Nat Clymer

(Ph.D.—University of Iowa) is Distinguished Professor of Communication and Executive Director of the University Center for Organizational Development and Leadership at Rutgers University-New Brunswick. He is also a member of the faculties of the Rutgers Graduate School of Education/ Ph.D. Program in Higher Education and the Department of Family Medicine and Community Health/Robert Wood Johnson School of Medicine. His scholarly work focuses on developing and applying communication theory in organizational, intercultural, health, educational, and leadership contexts. He is the author of 50 books and several hundred book chapters and articles. His books include: *What Leaders Need to Know and Do*; *The Excellence in Higher Education Guide: A Framework for the Design, Assessment, and Continuous Improvement of Institutions, Departments and Programs, 8th ed.*; and *A Guide for Leaders in Higher Education: Core Concepts, Competencies and Tools* (with R. De Lisi and R. A. Gigliotti, forthcoming). He was founder and first editor of the

International Communication Association *Communication Yearbook* series and has received awards, recognizing his scholarly and professional contributions, from Rutgers, National Communication Association (NCA), National Association of College and University Business Officers (NACUBO), and National Consortium for Change and Innovation in Higher Education (NCCI). He is a frequent adviser to colleges and universities nationally and internationally in the areas of leadership, planning, organizational assessment, change, continuous improvement, and communication. Dr. Ruben also serves as Director of the Rutgers Leadership Academy, Coordinator of the PreDoctoral Leadership Development Institute (PLDI), and Rutgers' Liaison to the Consortium for Institutional Cooperation (B1G/CIC) Officers' group.

## DR. LEA P. STEWART

Photo courtesy of Albert Chau

(Ph.D.—Purdue University) is Professor of Communication and Director of the Center for Communication and Health Issues, Rutgers University-New Brunswick. She also serves as the Livingston Campus Dean and is an associate member of the Rutgers Center of Alcohol Studies. Her current research focuses on issues of dangerous drinking prevention among college students. She has written numerous scholarly journal articles and book chapters as well as five books including *Changing the Culture of College Drinking: A Socially Situated Health Communication Campaign* (with Linda Lederman). She was co-designer of the RU SURE Campaign, which won a Model Program award from the U.S. Department of Education's Safe and Drug-free Schools Program in 2000. She has consulted on health communication and education in the United States and abroad (including Lebanon and the Republic of Moldova). Her extensive grant experience includes serving as principal investigator on more than $2 million of projects related to communication and health issues among college students funded by the U.S. Department of Education, NJ Department of Human Services Division of Mental Health and Addiction Services, NJ Higher Education Consortium, and National Council on Alcoholism and Drug Dependence of Middlesex County, among others. She served as co-principal investigator on a $6 million award from the National Institute on Drug Abuse (NIDA) to form the Rutgers Transdisciplinary Prevention Research Center. In 2003, she received the Warren I. Susman Award for Excellence in Teaching, Rutgers' highest honor for teaching excellence, and in 2007 she received the Rutgers Board of Trustees Award for Excellence in Research.

# CHAPTER 1

# WHY WE STUDY
# COMMUNICATION

**In this chapter, you will learn about:**

- The multiple approaches to defining communication
- The complex nature of communication
- The ways that communication is fundamental to everyday life
- The differences between the academic and personal approaches to studying communication

## IMPORTANCE OF COMMUNICATION

- Communication is Complex
- Communication is Vital to Occupational Effectiveness
- Education Does Not Ensure Communication Competence
- Communication is a Popular and Vibrant Field of Study

## THEORIES: GUIDES FOR ANALYSIS AND ACTION

- Personal Theories
- Scholarly Theories
- Combining Personal and Scholarly Theories

## DEFINING COMMUNICATION

- Level of Observation
- The Question of Intent
- Point of View
- The Issue of Outcomes

## FUNDAMENTALS OF COMMUNICATION

- Communication is a Process
- Communication is Essential for Individuals, Relationships, Groups, Organizations, and Societies
- Communication Involves Responding to and Creating Messages
- Communication Involves Adapting to People and the Environment

## COMMUNICATION: OUR DEFINITION

## GOALS OF COMMUNICATION AND HUMAN BEHAVIOR

## CONCLUSION

## KEY POINTS

## IMPORTANCE OF COMMUNICATION

In nearly every circumstance that confronts us, the process of communication is absolutely fundamental. No activity is more basic to our lives—personally, socially, or occupationally. Indeed, communication is so essential that we often take it for granted, much as we do breathing.

If communication is as natural as breathing, why is it necessary to study and learn more about the process? Good question. The short answer is that we make a number of decisions as we engage in communication. We are aware of some of these decisions; many are not as apparent to us. The better we understand communication, the more we can be aware of our decision-making process, and the better those decisions can be. The way we understand communication influences the way we think about and react to situations and people, and the way we act and relate to others, in turn, can make a major difference in how they respond to us. And, over the short- and long-term, the consequences of these actions and reactions will have significant implications for the kinds of relationships we form, who we become as people, and the way we contribute as members of families, groups, communities, organizations, and the societies in which we live.

A more detailed answer to the question, "Why should we study communication?," includes a consideration of the following points.

## COMMUNICATION IS COMPLEX

The realization that communication is a *basic* process does not, in any way, imply that it is easily understood or controlled. To the contrary, communication is exceedingly complex and multifaceted. Examples abound in personal, family, community, professional, technological, national, and international settings. Whether we think of the goal as improving intercultural or global understanding, avoiding divorce, or reducing teenage smoking and substance abuse, the communication challenges are daunting.

The communication understanding and skills necessary to be more successful in the many complex situations we face as human beings are not simply a matter of common sense. If they were, would these problems emerge in the first place? In fact, competence in communication requires what might be called *uncommon* sense. Common sense, for instance, suggests that when individuals talk or email one another, they *exchange* information. As we will explain later in this book, the process is not nearly as simple, rational, or predictable as this view implies. For example, common sense tells us that a public speaker's presentation is very important to the outcomes in a speech setting; however, it is "uncommon sense" that helps us understand why it is often the audience members who are most critical in determining the outcomes of this type of public communication. Common sense also leads us to the conclusion that most people have largely the same communication needs and outlooks that we do, and so we believe that our own approaches to communication are likely to work well in dealing with others. While this may sometimes be a workable assumption, often it is not. In this regard, "uncommon sense" leads us to continually question our own assumptions and to become more attentive to others' needs and perspectives. It is also "uncommon sense" that guides us to carefully assess the communication situations in which we find

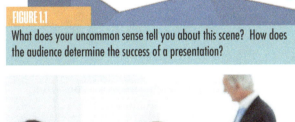

**FIGURE 1.1**

What does your uncommon sense tell you about this scene? How does the audience determine the success of a presentation?

© wavebreakmedia/Shutterstock.com

ourselves, to become more aware of our own and others' goals, and to recognize the need to develop an ever-broadening array of communication understanding and skills (see Figure 1.1). We'll examine these and other challenges of communication in more detail in the pages ahead.

We all face challenges in our personal, family, and workplace relationships. Even when we look carefully at the situations that we assume are going well, we almost always find that there are opportunities for improvement that are possible if we become more aware of how communication works. Whether we think of relationships with roommates, romantic partners, parents, colleagues at work, or acquaintances from another culture, in face-to-face or mediated settings, an understanding of communication is essential to achieving the outcomes we desire.

## COMMUNICATION IS VITAL TO OCCUPATIONAL EFFECTIVENESS

Effectiveness in any field of endeavor requires communication knowledge and skill. We need the ability to analyze communication situations, understand the people we're dealing with, develop productive communication strategies, receive and present ideas effectively through various communication channels, and collaborate successfully.

Studies of the needs of various occupations consistently reaffirm the importance of specific communication competencies in the workplace as among the most critical to success (Hart Research Associates, 2009; Jones, 2012). One extensive study of college recruiting professionals found that 10 skills and traits, ranked in the following order, were regarded as the most important qualities that employers want (NACE, 2013):

1. Ability to work in a team structure
2. Ability to make decisions and solve problems
3. Ability to plan, organize, and prioritize work
4. Ability to verbally communicate with persons inside and outside the organization
5. Ability to obtain and process information
6. Ability to analyze quantitative data
7. Technical knowledge related to the job
8. Proficiency with computer software programs
9. Ability to create and/or edit written reports
10. Ability to sell or influence others

Clearly, communication is critical in at least half of these qualities.

In a number of jobs, such as those listed in Figure 1.2, communication is the primary capability required. For more information, the New Jersey Communication Association has an excellent online resource about careers in communication (http://njca.rutgers.edu/resources/communication-careers.html).

FIGURE 1.2
Selected Communication Careers

## Managing Communication
(Integrating communication operations, programs, and services to support the mission of an organization)

Advertising Account Manager
Communication Analyst
Creative Director
Corporate and Community Relations
Crisis Communication Manager
Employee Communication and Training
External Communications Manager
Health Communication Director
Human Resources Manager
Marketing Specialist

Media Manager
Media Buyer
Media Relations Specialist
Newsletter Editor
Organizational Communication Manager
Promotions Manager
Public Information Officer
Public Relations Director
Sales Manager

## Creating Communication Products and Services
(Preparing, packaging, or repackaging communication products or services for use by others)

Advertising Copywriter
Art Director
Consumer Advocate
Customer Relations Specialist
Editing
Film Producer
Health Communication Writer
Marketing Specialist
Photojournalist

Public Information Officer
Public Relations Specialist
Reporter
Science and Technical Writer
Special Events Coordinator
Speech Writer
Website Designer
Writer

## Analyzing Communication
(Studying the foundations and theories related to communication systems, processes, programs, and services, and/or assessing their functioning)

Audience Analyst
Customer Satisfaction Analyst
Health Communication Analyst
Information Specialist

Market Researcher
Public Opinion Researcher
Social Scientist
Web Analysis

## Communication Education and Training
(Providing instruction or training in communication)

Admissions Counselor
Communication Trainer
Drama Coach
Health Communication Education

Human Resource Development
Media Training
Training and Development Specialist
Trainer for Communication Technology

In other occupations, communication expertise complements specific technical and disciplinary knowledge and ability. This is the case in fields like teaching, management, health care, international business, human resource management, counseling, politics, sales, computer applications, library and information science, and speech pathology. To perform competently, a teacher, a counselor, or a politician needs *technical* ability plus *communication* ability.

Leadership—whether in workplace, club, or community contexts—also requires a number of core competencies of which communication is one (Ruben, 2006). Focusing specifically on leadership communication skills, Conrad and Newberry (2012) identify the following specific skills (p. 115) as being important to communicating the mission, vision, and values of an organization:

- Arousing enthusiasm
- Being a change agent
- Creating group synergy
- Building team bonds
- Expressing encouragement
- Providing motivation
- Being persuasive
- Building optimism

Although the many studies of desirable communication competencies vary somewhat in their specifics, we believe that the following communication competencies, drawn from various writers (Conrad & Newberry, 2012; Stahl, 1989) and our own observations, are essential to success in many contexts including in the workplace:

- Writing
- Active listening
- Building relationships
- Making convincing presentations
- Motivating and encouraging others
- Networking
- Teamwork and collaboration
- Meeting management
- Communication/information technology skills
- Intercultural sensitivity and skills
- Social media skills
- Media literacy
- Conflict resolution
- Negotiation
- Persuasive skills
- Demonstrating respect

FIGURE 1.3

## 21st Century Communication Career Skills

### Skill Component:  Communication (Verbal and Face-to-Face)

Converses easily one-on-one and in small group settings inside and outside the organization; understands and can apply basic principles of client interaction, customer service, and sales appropriately

Presents to groups inside and outside the organization—both with preparation and spontaneously

Listens effectively and conveys to the speaker that s/he has been heard

Negotiates, bargains, persuades, debates, disagrees without being unpleasant, abrasive, or arrogant

Respects the rights of all individuals and strives to understand their point of view and concerns; understands how other cultures (of all types) differ

### Skill Component:  Communication (Written)

Effectively and professionally conveys in writing knowledge gained through analysis; summarizes complex information concisely and effectively; adapts writing to fit workplace norms (e.g., letters, professional emails, memos, executive summaries, complex reports, talking points, user manuals, etc.);  incorporates visual displays, such as graphs, as appropriate

Checks and edits documents to ensure information is correct and complete, tone and emphasis fit audience, and grammar, spelling, and punctuation are error-free

Uses word processing tools and other computer-based tools to create, edit, and format documents, build graphs, and send information electronically

### Skill Component:  Teamwork, Leadership, and Project Management

Builds collaborative relationships with colleagues and clients; interacts appropriately and effectively with peers, superiors, and assistants including those representing diverse cultures, races, gender, religions, lifestyles, and viewpoints.

Teamwork: works cooperatively with others; contributes ideas; completes necessary tasks; listens to and supports others on the team; resolves conflict and motivates others toward the accomplishment of a common goal or vision

Leadership:  motivates; assigns responsibilities effectively and coaches others as needed; sets a good example for the team; resolves disputes fairly and effectively.

Understands and applies project management principles to manage own work and the work of teams (sets realistic goals, breaks project down into component steps, prioritizes tasks, links dependent tasks, etc.)

### Skill Component: Information Gathering, IT Literacy, and Office Technology

Finds the *most relevant* information from multiple sources using the web and other tools, including social media, to identify and share current research and trends in fields of interest, determine the answers to key questions, and find the causes of and solutions to key problems

Uses commonly accepted standards to evaluate the reliability, accuracy, and usefulness of information; recognizes flawed logic and false accounts (and/or "baloney")

Identifies and learns to use the core functions of a wide range of software programs typically used in office settings (Word, Excel, etc.) and those relevant to particular areas of interest (e.g., Photoshop for publishing, design, etc.); has at least an intermediate or advanced skill level in one or more programs

Components of skills needed for success in the 21st century workforce adapted from Lawrence (2011).

# EDUCATION DOES NOT ENSURE COMMUNICATION COMPETENCE

It's all too often the case that education does not ensure competence in communication. One reason is that many aspects of communication are rarely addressed in most PreK–12 academic programs and often insufficiently in colleges and universities. For example, schools place little formal emphasis on listening concepts and practices, perhaps because educators feel that it's just common sense or everyone knows how to do it. Both assumptions are obviously unjustified.

Another important aspect of communication that receives little attention in school is nonverbal communication, though research demonstrates that some of the most significant messages in human communication are created and conveyed through nonverbal behaviors. Interpersonal and group communication skills that are necessary to effective collaboration with members of a workgroup, family, club, or community group also are often not taught in schools. This is also often the case when it comes to persuasion, relationships, organizations, leadership, intercultural and health communication—each a critical area in successful personal, social, and occupational activity. Ironically, in some instances, advanced education and training can actually be an impediment to competent communication. This sometimes happens with physicians, scientists, engineers, and others with technical training who become so programmed to communicate with individuals with an educational background similar to their own that they are much less successful when interacting with people who lack their expertise and training.

# COMMUNICATION IS A POPULAR AND VIBRANT FIELD OF STUDY

As we will discuss in Chapter 2, the study of communication is relatively new as a discipline but, at the same time, is one of the oldest fields of study. Historians generally trace the beginnings of the study of communication and human behavior to the early Greeks. Ancient Greece was an oral culture and affairs of business and government were conducted through spoken communication. It was, therefore, not surprising that an interest in understanding the theory and practice of communication would emerge during this era. Interest in communication study grew primarily out of philosophy at a time when that discipline was concerned with all aspects of the pursuit of knowledge.

The scientific revolution and the growing trend toward specialization in the pursuit of knowledge led to the development of separate disciplines for the study of behavior, and communication was among these. August Comte (1798–1857) gave the name *sociology* to the study of society and social existence, whose founders included Emile Durkheim (1858–1917), Max Weber (1864–1920), and Karl Marx (1818–1883). A decade later the psychological laboratories of Wilhelm Wundt (1832–1920) and William James (1842–1910) were established. The origins of anthropology also date to the middle of the 19th century and the work of British scholars Sir Henry James Sumner Maine (1822–1888), Sir Edward Burnett Tylor (1832–1917), and Sir James George Frazer (1854–1941). In the 20th century, political science and communication, two other fields of study with an ancient heritage, took on contemporary identities as disciplines in their own right. Communication emerged as a behavioral discipline in the 1950s to join the growing list of social sciences, each of which approaches the study of human behavior from a particular vantage point.

As a discipline, communication has also maintained intellectual ties with the humanities—especially philosophy, literature, religion, cultural studies, and art. There are also significant connections between communication and professional fields such as law, education, medicine, business, information science, cognitive science, counseling, social work, computer science, and library science. Communication has always been essential to education and, more recently, the Internet and other communication and information tools have brought new methods and new flexibility to teaching and learning. In the medical, counseling, social work, and other helping professions, researchers and health practitioners have long recognized that communication processes are critical to effectively analyzing and addressing the challenges of maintaining health and wellness. The role of communication in leadership and organizations is also an area of growing interest. Scholars in the fields of information science, information technology, journalism and media studies, and others whose work relates to the creation, storage, retrieval, and dissemination of information have very strong linkages to communication.

Today, communication is considered to be a behavioral or social science and an applied liberal art. The discipline shares with psychology, sociology, anthropology, and political science the pursuit of knowledge about human individuals and social activity. Communication also draws on the traditions of the humanities as well as professional studies. Thus, another of the attractions of being a student of communication is the opportunity to study a single discipline that integrates and applies knowledge from social sciences, humanities, and professional practice.

So the answer to the question "Why study communication?" comes down to this: whether you are interested in the social sciences, the arts, or the professions; whether your interests are primarily occupational or mainly academic; whether your interests reside in better understanding yourself, relationships, groups, organizations, cultures, or international relations; whether your focus is more applied or more theoretical; communication is an extremely important and useful area of study.

# THEORIES: GUIDES FOR ANALYSIS AND ACTION

*Communication and Human Behavior* is a book about thinking—thinking about communication. That makes it a book that emphasizes *theory* not skills. This is not to say that communication skills are unimportant. As we discussed earlier in this chapter, we believe they are critical. But we also believe that success in the practice of communication requires, first and foremost, a solid theoretical understanding of the communication process. Such an understanding provides the foundation for successfully employing communication skills. Providing this foundation is the primary goal of this book.

## Personal Theories

Essentially, theories are guides to understanding. It has often been said that there's nothing as practical as a good theory (Van de Ven, 1989) and that certainly applies to theories of communication (Lewin, 1951 cited in Cartwright, 1975, p. 169). Theories help us to describe, explain, predict, and sometimes control phenomena and circumstances we encounter.

We all have *personal theories* about a range of things—about relationships, doors, friends, and weather, for instance. Our personal theories, which are sometimes called *native theories* by social scientists (see Mokros, 1993), allow us to navigate in our physical and social environment. For example, our personal theories help us describe particular places and things, explain how to develop close relationships, predict the weather, or control the volume of a television set using a remote control. If we didn't have these theories, we would have to approach each situation we encounter as completely new and unique. We would be unable to think about new situations in more general terms and would be unable to draw on previous experiences in our efforts to describe, explain, predict, or control them. We usually give little conscious thought to the nature of our native theories, how they were developed, or how we are using them. They are based on everyday experience, tend to be taken for granted, are private, and are fairly stable over time.

BASED ON EVERYDAY EXPERIENCE. Personal theories develop over time in response to the situations and people we encounter. For example, our theories about relationships are based on our individual experiences with acquaintances, friends, colleagues, and family members over the course of our lifetime.

TAKEN FOR GRANTED. Most of us do not think very much about our personal theories, the manner in which they are formed, or the way we use them. Once developed, we generally accept them on faith. For instance, we each have our own theories about doors, and we take these theories for granted. We don't think about how we formed these theories and give little conscious attention to our theories when we approach a door, locate the door knob, and turn the knob. We push or pull a door with full confidence that it will open, and we do all this without much thought about the "theory" we are applying, nor the fact that it has emerged over time based on our experiences.

PRIVATE. Personal theories are based on experiences which are to some extent unique for each of us. We often do not discuss our theories or the experiences on which they were based. Our theories about friends are based on our unique experiences, for example, and we generally discuss them only in a limited range of circumstances. There are some instances where we might discuss the way we think about "friends" or "friendship," but it's difficult to imagine many situations where we would be sharing our theories about doors.

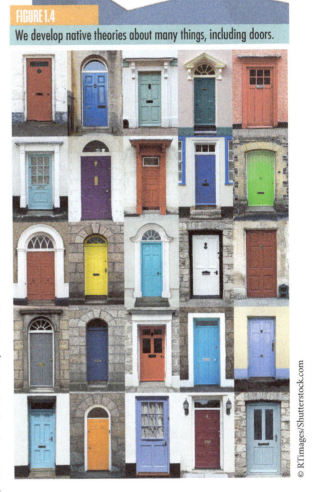

**FIGURE 1.4**
We develop native theories about many things, including doors.

© RTimages/Shutterstock.com

STABLE. Once formed, personal theories are generally quite resistant to change. Our personal theories tend to guide us to see and interpret what we observe in particular ways. Often we ignore or unintentionally distort observations that don't fit in with our personal theories. We are likely to cling to our theories about friends even after we have encountered evidence which seems to contradict our theories. For instance, if a friend has told us something that we know to be untrue, we are likely to tell ourselves he or she probably believed it was true or else altered the facts for a very good reason. Most likely, this kind of "contradictory" event could occur any number of times before we would conclude that the person is purposely lying and no longer worthy of being thought of as a friend. Or, to return to the case of our "doors," our native theory can present a challenge when we are confronted with what turns out to be an electronically controlled sliding door (see Figure 1.4).

## Scholarly Theories

Theories of a scholarly or scientific nature are similar to personal theories in terms of their basic functions: they, too, are used to describe, explain, predict, and sometimes control objects, people, and events. However, in contrast to personal theories, they are based on systematic observation and testing. They are also questioned, public, and because of this they are subject to modification.

BASED ON SYSTEMATIC OBSERVATION AND TESTING. Scholarly theories are developed through research involving systematic observation, information gathering, and analysis. Studies may be conducted in experimental laboratories or in natural settings. Data are gathered purposefully by means of interviews, questionnaires, or careful observations; and the results are systematically analyzed. For example, a theory about relationships may be based on the analysis of information derived from direct observations or videos. Or a theory could result from an analysis of interviews or surveys of a cross-section of individuals in varying types of relationships.

QUESTIONED. Unlike personal theories, which tend to be accepted on faith and quite stable once they are formed, scholarly theories are continually questioned. Scientific theories are regarded as tentative and may be reexamined through follow-up studies and analyses. Consider our example of doors and door knobs: We have personal theories that allow us to predict that when we turn the door knob and push or pull, a door will open. Rather than be content with a personal theory about doors and door knobs, a scientific theory would be continually and methodically tested to ensure predictability. Thus, engineers in a corporation that manufactures door entry and lock systems would test and retest their products to determine precisely how likely it is that the door knob mechanism will operate as intended or when push, pull, or sliding doors are most appropriate. They might want to determine the average number of uses a sample of door entry mechanisms can tolerate before they fail to function or the relative reliability of push/pull versus sliding doors. Then they would want to study how and why malfunctions occur, and then develop and test theories about how to correct the problem.

PUBLIC. The methods and results of scholarly and scientific theories are disseminated to other scholars and scientists. The goal is to allow others to evaluate particular theories in terms of at least three standards:

- Validity—accuracy
- Reliability—consistency and dependability
- Utility—usefulness and applicability

A scholarly theory will be reported at scholarly conferences or meetings and in journals, book chapters, and books so that other scholars and students can test and apply the ideas. (Exceptions to the public nature of research may occur in the case of studies that are done within a proprietary context, such as those funded by certain profit-making organizations, where findings are purposely not shared for reasons of security or confidentiality.)

SUBJECT TO MODIFICATION. Because scholarly and scientific theories are public—and generally published in print or online—they are available, accessible, and subject to refutation or modification based on new information. Thus, scientific theories can be modified and improved as findings from new research emerge.

## Combining Personal and Scholarly Theories

We all have personal theories of communication and human behavior. Like other such theories, our views of communication are based on a lifetime of experience. They are personal. We take them for granted, and they tend to be fairly stable. There are also many scholarly and scientific theories regarding communication and human behavior.

In this book, we will be examining a number of these scholarly and scientific theories. A familiarity with these theories has great value in its own right in helping us to become more aware of the nature and dynamics of communication. Exploring these theories can have the additional value of encouraging and providing tools to help us more critically evaluate our personal theories. That is, we can begin to subject our own theories to some of the more rigorous standards associated with scholarly theory development and testing. Do our personal theories hold up in light of more systematic observation and testing? Are they valid, reliable, and useful? Can we benefit from making our personal theories public and discussing them with other people to see where they converge and where they differ? Are we able to modify our personal theories when evidence warrants? By comparing our personal theories with scholarly theories, we can better understand each and narrow the gap between the two and, in the process, also enrich our understanding of human behavior—and of ourselves.

## DEFINING COMMUNICATION

Few words are used in as many different ways, by as many different people, as the word *communication*. To some, the term *communication* brings to mind an image of a speaker addressing an audience from behind a podium, the lively discussion among colleagues at a meeting, or an exchange of glances between lovers. But communication can be a debate, a sermon, a posting on social media, a memorable night at the theater, the efforts of a child trying to overcome a speech disorder, texting, email, a roadside sign, or a thoughtful walk on the beach. Communication is what we think of when we see two friends conversing over coffee, a tear, an outstretched arm, a knowing smile, people using sign language, a kiss, an obscenity scrawled on a restroom wall, even an individual engaged in a silent protest.

The multiple uses of the term *communication* can be confusing. People who are unfamiliar with the discipline may wonder whether the term has any limits. Is everything communication? How does being interested in communication differ from being interested in life?

To address the issue, it is important to understand that:

- *Communication* is the name of a discipline, as well as the label for a phenomenon. That is, the term refers both to an academic area and a focus of study.
- *Communication* has popular, professional, and technical meanings.

The term is commonly used in a very general way by the general public, in a more focused occupational framework in professional circumstances, and in a still more specialized manner in technical and academic settings.

Quite obviously, there are a number of different meanings of the word *communication*. In fact, in one classic study, communication scholars Frank Dance and Carl Larson (1976) identified 126 published definitions. The *Oxford English Dictionary*, often considered the definitive record of the English language, alone lists over 15 definitions.

Definitions of communication have elements in common; they also have a number of differences in terms of the level of observation, the question of intent, the point of view, and the issue of outcome. [The discussion of levels of analysis, the question of intent, and normative judgment is based, in part, on Dance and Larson (1976) and Peters (1999).]

## Level of Observation

One can study communication on any number of levels—at the level of cells, individuals, relationships, organizations, a particular culture or society, or even the global level. Definitions may focus on any one, several, or all of these levels. We will explore specific applications of those definitions throughout the book.

## The Question of Intent

Scholars often disagree about whether messages have to be intentionally created to be considered communication. Virtually all communication theorists agree that intentional acts that are noted and reacted to should be considered communication (Litttlejohn & Foss, 2010). Thus, if an individual asks another person a question and the person answers, it seems clear that communication has occurred because we can presume that the speaker intended to convey a message. Some scholars would limit their definition of communication only to these acts (e.g., Motley, 1990). These scholars believe that communication refers solely to those events in which there are purposely created messages. They might well exclude from the definition of communication those situations in which it is unclear that an individual meant to create or convey a message to others—even if the behavior had meaning to others.

Other scholars argue that communication occurs any time behavior is attended to and interpreted, whether it was intentional or not (Andersen, 1991). Unintentional behavior that has meaning might include a yawn in class being perceived by others as boredom or an email accidentally forwarded to an unintended recipient. The yawner or the email initiator was not intending to communicate to others, but other recipients of these messages may well have attached a specific meaning to the behaviors, nonetheless (see Figure 1.5).

FIGURE 1.5

Unintentional messages can be as meaningful to communication as messages that are intentionally created.

© A and N photography/Shutterstock.com

© djedzura/Shutterstock.com

© A and N photography/Shutterstock.com

© michaeljung/Shutterstock.com

## Point of View

Communication can be thought about from a speaker's or writer's point of view or from the viewpoint of a listener or reader. Most commonly communication is talked about in terms of the activities and efforts of a person who initiates messages—his or her goals, message approach, style, and so forth. But, communication can also be considered from the perspective of a listener or reader, with particular focus on a recipient's needs, goals, reactions, or styles.

## The Issue of Outcomes

Some definitions of communication include only situations in which a particular outcome occurs, for example, situations in which understanding, acceptance, and agreement seem to result from an interaction. Such a definition might not see communication as having occurred if misunderstanding, disagreement, or some other unintended outcome resulted from a situation. Other definitions focus on whether the process has taken place, more than upon whether specific outcomes have resulted.

# FUNDAMENTALS OF COMMUNICATION

To make sense of these many distinctions, to explain the field to others, and to organize our study of the field, we need a comprehensive and unifying definition of communication. A definition that meets these goals should include and integrate the following fundamentals of communication.

## Communication Is a Process

Communication is a *process*—an activity that has many separate but interrelated steps that occur over time.

When we prepare for and deliver a public presentation, for instance, we are not engaged in a single, static act. We move, instead, through a sequence of interrelated activities as we plan, gather materials, rehearse, perform, and perhaps adjust the presentation as we're giving it based on the audience's reaction to it.

The communication that occurs in a conversation is, similarly, an activity composed of a number of interrelated steps occurring over time. Consider the following:

> "Hi, how are you?"
> "Good.  What about you?"

Even in such a simple exchange, a number of steps are involved as messages are created, sent, received, interpreted, and responded to.

## Communication Is Essential for Individuals, Relationships, Groups, Organizations, and Societies

As individuals, communication is our link to the world, our means of making impressions, expressing ourselves, influencing others, and giving of ourselves. It is also our means of learning about the world and other people, becoming who we are, being entertained, persuaded, amused, deceived, or informed.

It is through communication that we form relationships of all kinds—from the casual exchanges that take place between a customer and a store employee or between strangers on social media or waiting in line at a movie theater, to the intimate conversations or texts between lovers or members of a family. For friends, acquaintances, family, or colleagues at school or work, communication is the means of pursuing joint activities, relating to each other, and sharing ideas.

In groups, organizations, and societies, communication is the means through which we coordinate our own needs and goals with those of others. Within larger organizations, societies, and the global community, communication provides the web of connections that allows for collective action, the establishment of a common identity, and the development of leadership.

## Communication Involves Responding to and Creating Messages

It is through the process of creating and responding to messages that we interact with our surroundings and one another. As we will discuss in greater detail later, a *message* is any symbol or collection of symbols that has meaning or utility. Messages may involve verbal codes—such as spoken or written language—or nonverbal codes, involving appearance, gestures, touch, or other means. Examples include a speech, emoticon or emoji, letter, wink, flag, poem, advertisement, or painting.

Responding to messages involves attending to them, interpreting and using them in some way—as individuals and in relationships, groups, organizations, or societies.

We engage in message creation through verbal and nonverbal behavior. For example, we create messages when we introduce ourselves to someone, since we are in the process of constructing a meaningful message—at least, it is meaningful to us. The person we are meeting is engaged in message interpretation when he or she notices, attaches meaning to, and makes use of our introductory comments (see Figure 1.6).

**FIGURE 1.6**

Introductions are important opportunities for message creation and interpretation.

In face-to-face settings, messages are conveyed from person to person or place to place verbally and nonverbally. In other situations, communication technology—or *media*—play an important role by extending our "natural" capabilities for communication. In these instances, communication between the individuals, groups, organizations, or societies is *mediated*.

## Communication Involves Adapting to People and the Environment

We create and interpret messages—as individuals, and in relationships, groups, organizations, and societies—to relate to the environment and to the people around us. In some cases, the process consists primarily of adjusting to the circumstances in which we find ourselves. More often,

© kurhan/Shutterstock.com

communication involves actively creating situations and coordinating our actions with others. As we shall see, the same basic dynamics occur in groups, organizations, and societies, but on a progressively larger scale.

## COMMUNICATION: OUR DEFINITION

Communication focuses on the way people create, convey, select, and interpret the messages that inform and shape their lives. More specifically, communication can be defined as *the process through which individuals in relationships, groups, organizations, and societies create and respond to messages in order to relate to the environment and one another.*

This definition is helpful for thinking about the nature of communication and for explaining it in fairly straightforward terms to others. It also provides a useful framework for organizing the ideas presented in this book.

## GOALS OF COMMUNICATION AND HUMAN BEHAVIOR

The sixth edition of *Communication and Human Behavior* is a book designed to help students learn to think cogently and systematically about communication and its relationship to human behavior. It is based on the assumption that the way we think about communication makes an important difference in the way we understand what is going on around us and in the way we conduct our lives.

This book has three goals:

1. To introduce communication as an area of study. *Communication and Human Behavior* provides an overview and explanation of communication theories, basic concepts, key scholars, issues, and applications.
2. To provide a framework that helps make connections between communication theory and communication processes in action. The objective is to help students develop a communication-oriented perspective on events taking place around them—personally, socially, in work situations, nationally, and internationally.
3. To provide tools to help students use this communication-oriented perspective to analyze, better understand, and be more competent in their own communication behavior.

## CONCLUSION

In a broad range of settings and contexts, communication plays a basic and fundamental role. So essential is the role of communication that it is easily taken for granted and thought to be common sense. When one considers the many problems that result from poor communication, however, the complexity and challenges associated with the process make it clear that this is not the case.

Popular and scholarly writings speak to the importance of communication in our personal and occupational lives. The process is fundamental in many jobs and more generally contributes to professional effectiveness in nearly every field. Communication theory and skills are not assured by one's education, as many of the critical aspects of the phenomenon are underemphasized in formal education. Because of its relevance, its importance, and its many challenges as a topic and field, communication is an extremely popular field.

Theories are the building blocks of understanding. Theories of behavior provide guides to understanding and action. They help to describe, explain, predict, and sometimes control human affairs. Over the course of our lifetimes we each develop personal theories based on our experiences that are quite stable once developed. We typically spend little time analyzing or discussing these theories. In contrast, scholarly and scientific theories are systematically developed, publicly shared, and carefully tested with the goal of achieving validity, reliability, and utility. The two types of theories can be quite complementary and mutually informative.

Communication theories and definitions are numerous and sometimes contradictory. They vary depending on their level of observation, assumptions relative to intention, point of view implied, and perspective on the issue of outcomes. The definition that serves as the foundation for this book is: Human communication is the process through which individuals in relationships, groups, organizations, and societies create and use information to relate to the environment and one another.

## KEY POINTS

After reading this chapter, you should be able to:

- Explain how communication is a pervasive part of contemporary life with relevance to our lives as individuals, family members, professionals, and members of communities and society
- Describe the different approaches to defining and studying communication
- Analyze the ways that individuals develop personal (native) theories of communication based on their life experiences
- Identify examples of how the study of communication theory can help us better understand human behavior, more fully appreciate the skills and techniques that are important to achieving communication goals, and improve our ability to reflect upon and make sense of our own behavior

# REFERENCES

Andersen, P. A. (1991). When one cannot communicate: A challenge to Motley's traditional communication postulates. *Communication Studies, 42,* 309-325.

Cartwright, D. (Ed.). (1975). *Field theory in social science: Selected theoretical papers by Kurt Lewin* (1951). Westport, CT: Greenwood Press.

Conrad, D., & Newberry, R. (2012). Identification and instruction of important business communication skills for graduate business education. *Journal of Education for Business, 87,* 112-120.

Dance, F. E. X., & Larson, C. (1976). *The functions of human communication: A theoretical approach.* New York, NY: Holt, Rinehart, Winston.

Hart Research Associates. (2010). *Raising the bar: Employers' views on college learning in the wake of the economic downturn.* Retrieved from https://aacu.org/sites/default/files/files/LEAP/2009_EmployerSurvey.pdf

Jones, L. K. (2012) *The foundational skills.* (Job skills for the 21st century: A guide for students). Retrieved from http://www.careerkey.org/pdf/TheFoundation JobSkills.pdf

Lawrence, S. E. (2011). Composite list of 21st century career readiness skills and competencies. Unpublished ms.

Littlejohn, S. W., & Foss, K. A. (2010). *Theories of human communication* (10th ed.). Long Grove, IL: Longwood Press.

Motley, M. T. (1990). On whether one can(not) communicate: An examination via traditional communication postulates. *Western Journal of Speech Communication, 54,* 1-10.

Mokros, H. B. (1993). The impact of native theory of information on two privileged accounts of personhood. In J. R. Schement & B. D. Ruben (Eds.), *Between communication and information: Information and behavior* (Vol. 4, pp. 57-79). New Brunswick, NJ: Transaction.

NACE. (2013). *Job outlook 2014.* Bethlehem, PA: National Association of Colleges and Employers.

Peters, J. D. (1999). *Speaking into air: A history of the idea of communication.* Chicago, IL: University of Chicago Press.

Ruben, B. D. (2006). *What leaders need to know and do: A leadership competencies scorecard.* Washington, DC: National Association of College and University Business Officers.

Stahl, D. (1989, March). Managing in the 1990s: Versatility, flexibility and a wide range of skills: A new study outlines the requirements for managerial success in a complex and fast-changing business world. *AT&T Journal,* pp. 8–10.

Van de Ven, A. H. (1989). Nothing is quite so practical as a good theory. *Academy of Management Review, 14*(4), 486-489.

# CHAPTER 2

# COMMUNICATION
## PAST AND PRESENT

**In this chapter, you will learn about:**

- How communication is considered to be one of the oldest yet newest disciplines
- Why early Greeks saw communication theory and practice as critical
- Why the popularity of communication is a mixed blessing
- Communication as an activity, a social science, a liberal art, and a profession

## ANCIENT ROOTS OF COMMUNICATION STUDY

- Rhetoric and Speech
- Origins of Communication Theory: Early Greece

## 17TH–19TH CENTURIES

## JOURNALISM

## EARLY 20TH CENTURY: DEVELOPMENT OF SPEECH AND JOURNALISM

## THE 1940S–1960S: INTERDISCIPLINARITY

- Lasswell's View of Communication
- Shannon and Weaver's Model
- Katz and Lazarsfeld's Model
- Westley and MacLean's Model

## THE 1970S–1980S: GROWTH AND SPECIALIZATION

## THE LATE 1980'S–2000: THE INFORMATION AGE

- Information as a Commodity
- Converging Media

## THE 21ST CENTURY: COMMUNICATION STUDY TODAY

- Ancient and Newly Emergent
- Discipline and Interdisciplinary Link
- Personal and Professional Applicability
- Old and New Technology
- Problem and Solution
- Practical Skill and Fundamental Life Process

## THE EVOLUTION OF THEORY

- Communication Theory Today

## CONCLUSION

## KEY POINTS

## ANCIENT ROOTS OF COMMUNICATION STUDY

It is difficult to determine precisely when and how communication first came to be regarded as a significant factor in human life. According to historians, considerable concern about communication and its role in human affairs was expressed prior to the 5th century BCE, in classical Babylonian and Egyptian writings and in Homer's Iliad (for a detailed summary of the early history of speech and rhetorical communication study see Harper, 1979). An essay written in about 3,000 BCE offers advice on how to speak effectively, while *The Precepts*, composed in Egypt about 2,675 BCE, provides guidance on effective communication including the importance of listening as well as speaking the truth.

As with other disciplines that have sought to explain human behavior, the beginning of systematic theory development in communication can be traced to the Greeks. Their initial interest sprang from the practical concerns of day-to-day life. Greece had a democratic form of government, and virtually all facets of business, government, law, and education were carried on orally. Greek citizens also had to be their own lawyers. Accused and accuser alike presented their cases before a jury of several hundred people who had to be convinced of the rightness of a position. Lawsuits were common in Athens, and, as a result, public speaking in legal contexts became a preoccupation.

## Rhetoric and Speech

What might be considered as the first theory of communication was developed in Greece by Corax and later refined by his student Tisias. The theory dealt with courtroom speaking, which was considered the craft of persuasion. Tisias became convinced that persuasion could be taught as an art and provided encouragement for instructors of what was called rhetoric. Corax and Tisias developed the concept of message organization, suggesting that a message should have three parts corresponding to contemporary concepts of introduction, body, and conclusion.

The sophists were a group of itinerant teachers in Athens in the 5th century BCE who set up small schools and charged their pupils for tutoring. Protagoras of Abdera (490–420 BCE) taught concepts that are embodied in the modern idea of debate. He taught that a good speaker should be able to argue both sides of a proposition. In addition, he encouraged students to write short messages that did not refer to a particular occasion to be used whenever they were called upon to speak in public.

Gorgias of Leontini (485–380 BCE) was a contemporary of Protagoras and was one of the first to advocate the use of emotional appeals in persuasive speeches. Gorgias was especially concerned about style and the use of appropriate figures of speech.

Isocrates (436–338 BCE), another famous Greek sophist, wrote speeches for others to deliver and was very influential in his time. He is known for his belief that an orator should be trained in the liberal arts and should be a good person.

The writings of two other scholars—Cicero (106–43 BCE) and Quintilian (35–100 CE)—also contributed to the broadening theory of communication. Like Plato and Aristotle, Cicero developed rhetorical theories and saw communication as both an academic and a practical matter. His view of communication was so comprehensive that it included all of what is now considered the domain of the social sciences. He believed a successful speaker was a knowledgeable person. Quintilian is remembered primarily as an educator and synthesizer, bringing together in his writing the previous 500 years' thinking about communication (Harper, 1979). His practical guidelines demonstrate how a good communicator should be educated.

The view that communication was critical to virtually all aspects of human life was widely held during the Classical period—4th and 5th centuries BCE (for a more detailed discussion see Peters, 1999). However, the comprehensive perspective that characterized communication during this era was largely reversed in the medieval (5th to 15th centuries) and renaissance (14th to 17th centuries) periods. With the decline of the oral tradition and democracy, much of the interest in communication also waned, and the study of rhetoric was dispersed among several different fields.

## Origins of Communication Theory: Early Greece

**FIGURE 2.1**

In Greek mythology, Athena was considered to be the goddess of wisdom, courage, mathematics, and war strategy.

© Sergey Rusakov/Shutterstock.com

Aristotle (384–322 BCE) and his teacher Plato (428–347 BCE) were the most central figures in early communication study. Both regarded communication as an art or craft to be practiced and as an area of study. As Aristotle noted in the opening paragraph of his classic work on rhetoric:

> [T]o a certain extent all men attempt to discuss statements and to maintain them, to defend themselves and to attack others. Ordinary people do this either at random or through practice and from acquired habit. Both ways being possible, the subject can plainly be handled systematically, for it is possible to inquire the reason why some speakers succeed through practice and others spontaneously; and everyone will at once agree that such an inquiry is the function of art. (Aristotle, *Rhetoric,* Roberts trans. published 1954, p. 19)

Not surprisingly, given the history of the field, most of the earliest perspectives on communication focused on public settings in which an orator spoke to a listener or group of listeners with the goal of persuading them of the correctness of a particular point of view (Peters, 1999).

Aristotle (see Figure 2.2) saw communication as the means through which citizens participated in democracy. He described communication in terms of an orator or speaker constructing an argument to be presented in a speech to hearers—an audience as depicted in Figure 2.3. The speaker's goal was to inspire a positive image of himself or herself and to encourage the members of the audience to be receptive to the message. As Aristotle (see Roberts trans., 1954) wrote:

> [R]hetoric exists to affect the giving of decisions . . . the *orator* must not only try to make the argument of his *speech* demonstrative and worthy of belief; he must also make his own character look right and put his *hearers,* who are to decide, in the right frame of mind. (p. 90) (Emphasis added)

FIGURE 2.2
Aristotle

© Panos Karas/Shutterstock.com

For Aristotle, communication was primarily a verbal activity through which speakers tried to persuade—to achieve their own purposes with a listener through skillful construction of an argument and delivery of a speech.

Eventually, the work of Augustine (354–430 BCE) led to a rediscovery of classical Greek theory. His writings applied communication to the interpretation of the Bible and other religious writings and to the art of preaching. In so doing, Augustine united the practical and theoretical aspects of communication study.

## FIGURE 2.3
### Aristotelian View

| Speaker | → | Argument | → | Speech | → | Listener(s) |

## FIGURE 2.4
### Sir Francis Bacon

© Georgios Kollidas/Shutterstock.com

# 17TH – 19TH CENTURIES

Early in the 17th century, Sir Francis Bacon (1561–1626) included both speechmaking and writing that was designed for more practical purposes in his theories (see Figure 2.4). He proposed an ethical basis for communication and argued that the function of true rhetoric was the furtherance of good. His ideas had a major influence on later writers.

During the 18th and 19th centuries, emphasis in communication study was placed on written argument and literature.

George Campbell (1719–1796), a Scottish philosopher and professor of divinity, wrote on the philosophical aspects of rhetoric. He maintained that rhetoric had four purposes: to enlighten, to please the imagination, to move the passions, or to influence the will. Another 18th century Scottish writer, Hugh Blair, proposed theories that could be applied either to writing or to speaking. His book, *Lectures on Rhetoric and Belles Lettres*, was a guide to composition and was very influential at the time.

There was also great interest in speaking style, articulation, and gesture, leading to the formation of the National Association of Elocutionists in 1892. The elocutionists were a powerful force at this time and produced a very stylized mode of delivery that included vocal manipulation and physical gestures. A *New York Times* article on July 3, 1892 about their first convention noted that it was "an extraordinary gathering of men and women, its proceedings were interesting and picturesque and we may scarcely doubt that its beneficent influence will be exerted more or less vigorously all over the land. The formation of a dignified national association of elocutionists should not be considered a commonplace event in a nation of careless talkers" (p. 4).

By the end of the 19th century, most colleges and universities were organized into departments, and rhetoric and speech were often taught within departments of English.

## JOURNALISM

The other field that contributed significantly to the heritage of communication study is journalism. Like rhetoric and speech, journalism also dates back several thousand years. The practice of journalism began some 3,700 years ago in Egypt, when a record of the events of the time was transcribed on the tomb of an Egyptian king. Years later, Julius Caesar (100–4 BCE) had an official record of the news of the day posted in a public place, and copies of it were made and sold (Frank, 1961, p. 2)

Early newspapers were a mixture of newsletters, ballads, proclamations, political tracts, and pamphlets describing various events. Like speech and rhetoric, they were forms of public communication. The mid-17th century saw the emergence of the newspaper in its modern form; and the first paper published in the United States, *Publick Occurrences Both Foreign and Domestick,* appeared in 1690 in Boston, but only lasted for one issue. The second newspaper, *The Boston News-letter,* wasn't published until 1704 (Brown, 2015).

**FIGURE 2.5**

Elizabeth Jane Cochran (1862–1922) was a journalist who wrote investigative articles about the plight of women factory workers, the lives and customs of people in Mexico, and the mistreatment of women in a mental hospital, as well as chronicling her adventurous round-the-world trip. At a time when women did not use their own names as bylines, she adopted the pen name Nellie Bly.

© Neftali/Shutterstock.com

# EARLY 20TH CENTURY: DEVELOPMENT OF SPEECH AND JOURNALISM

In the early 20th century, speech emerged as a discipline in its own right. In 1909, the Eastern States Speech Association—now the Eastern Communication Association—was formed and, in 1910, held its first annual conference. The National Association of Academic Teachers of Public Speaking, which became the Speech Association of America and the Speech Communication Association—now, the National Communication Association—was formed in 1914 (Cohen, 1994). In 1915, the *Quarterly Journal of Public Speaking* was first published, followed soon after by the *Quarterly Journal of Speech. Communication Monographs* began publication in 1934. Unlike previous publications, which emphasized speech practices, the new journal stressed research. Most of the studies published in the early volumes dealt with speech phonetics and phonology, physiology, and pathology (Bormann, 1965). By 1935, the speech association had 1700 members, and speech was well established as a field.

Although the practice of journalism dates back many years, formalized study in the area did not progress rapidly until the early 1900s. In 1905, the University of Wisconsin offered what were perhaps the first courses in journalism, at a time when there were few, if any, books on the topic. By 1910, there were half a dozen volumes available, and between 1910 and 1920 some 25 works on journalism and newspaper work were compiled, signaling a pattern of continued growth (Hyde, 1937).

The advent of radio in the 1920s and television in the early 1940s resulted in the wider application of journalistic concepts. These new (at the time) media contributed to the development of an expanded view of the nature of journalism.

Interest in communication was not limited to speech and journalism. In philosophy, scholars wrote about the nature of communication and its role in human life. Anthropologists, psychologists, and sociologists focused on communication and its role in individual and social processes; and writers in the area of language also contributed to the advancement of communication study.

# THE 1940S – 1960S: INTERDISCIPLINARITY

In the 1940s and early 1950s, the scope of the study of communication broadened substantially. A number of scholars from the various behavioral and social science disciplines began to develop theories of communication which extended beyond the boundaries of their own fields. In anthropology, for example, research concerned with body positioning and gestures in particular cultures laid the groundwork for more general studies of nonverbal communication. In psychology, interest focused on persuasion, social influence, and, specifically, attitudes—how they form, how they change, their impact on behavior, and the role of communication in these dynamics. Researchers were especially concerned with issues of persuasion, including how propaganda persuaded individuals, how public opinion was created, and how the developing media contributed to persuasive efforts (Delia, 1987). Kurt Lewin (1890–1947) and his colleagues conducted a major research program on group dynamics. Carl Hovland (1912–1961) and Paul Lazarsfeld (1901–1976) conducted early research on mass communication.

Sociologists and political scientists studied the nature of mass media in various political and social activities, such as voting behavior, and other facets of life. In zoology, communication among animals began to receive considerable attention among researchers. During these same years, scholars in linguistics, general semantics, and semiotics, fields that focused on the nature of language and its role in human activity, also contributed to the advancement of communication study.

By the end of the 1950s a number of writings had appeared that paved the way for the development of more integrated views of communication. It was during these years that the National Society for the Study of Communication (now the International Communication Association) was established with the stated goal of bringing greater unity to the study of communication by exploring the relationships among speech, language, and media (Weaver, 1977).

These developments set the stage for the rapid growth of communication as an independent discipline. In the 1960s, scholars synthesized thinking from rhetoric and speech, journalism and mass media, and the other social science disciplines. The term communication became linked to speech and rhetoric in basic books on the field during these years.

Communication was of interest in many disciplines during the 1960s, including sociology, psychology, political science, anthropology, linguistics, and administrative studies.

During this period, a number of very influential models of communication were published by scholars. Among the most influential were those of Harold Lasswell, Claude Shannon and Warren Weaver, Elihu Katz and Paul Lazarsfeld, and Bruce Westley and Malcolm MacLean. Each of these scholars offered perspectives on the nature of communication that built on the earliest concepts of the phenomenon.

## Lasswell's View of Communication

One of the most often cited characterizations of communication was advanced by political scientist Harold Lasswell (1902–1978) in 1948 as an outgrowth of his work in the area of political propaganda. Lasswell provided a general view of communication that extended well beyond the boundaries of political science. He said that an act of communication could best be explained by the answers to the following questions:

Who
Says What
In Which Context
To Whom
With What Effect?  (Lasswell, 1960, p. 117)

Lasswell's view of communication, as had Aristotle's some 2000 years earlier, emphasized the elements of speaker, message, and audience, but used different terminology (see Figure 2.6). Both scholars viewed communication as a one-way process in which one individual influenced others through messages.

Lasswell offered an expanded definition of *channel* that included mass media along with speech as part of the communication process. His approach also provided a more generalized view of the *goal* or *effect* of communication than did the Aristotelian perspective.  Lasswell's work suggested that there could be a variety of outcomes or effects of communication, such as to inform, to entertain, to aggravate, as well as to persuade.

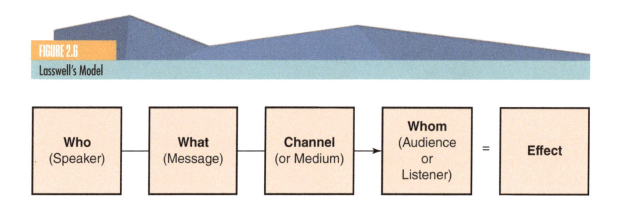

**FIGURE 2.6**
Lasswell's Model

## Shannon and Weaver's Model

The model developed by Claude Shannon (1916–2001) and Warren Weaver (1894–1978) described the communication process in this way:

> Communication include[s] all the procedures by which one mind may affect another. This, of course, involves not only written and oral speech, but also music, the pictorial arts, the theatre, the ballet, and in fact all human behavior. (Shannon & Weaver, 1949, p. 3)

Like Lasswell, Shannon and Weaver saw communication in terms of a one-way process by which a message was sent from a source through a channel to a receiver. Their model (see Figure 2.7) was somewhat more detailed, however, because they made several distinctions that the other models had not. Specifically, they differentiated between a signal and a message, an information source and a transmitter, and a receiver and destination. They described the workings of the model as follows:

> The information source selects a desired message out of a set of possible messages. . . .
> The selected message may consist of written or spoken words, or of pictures, music, etc.
> . . . The transmitter changes the message into the signal which is actually sent over the
> communication channel from the transmitter to the receiver. (Shannon & Weaver, 1949,
> p. 7)

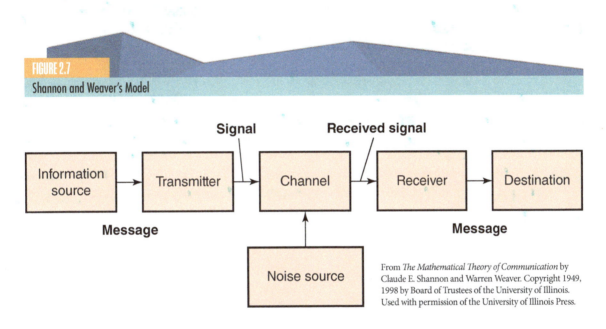

**FIGURE 2.7**

**Shannon and Weaver's Model**

From *The Mathematical Theory of Communication* by Claude E. Shannon and Warren Weaver. Copyright 1949, 1998 by Board of Trustees of the University of Illinois. Used with permission of the University of Illinois Press.

If one considers the example of a dramatic series carried on "cable television," the channel is the cable; the signal is the varying electrical current carried by the cable; the information source is the performers, their backdrop, and so on; the transmitter is the set of devices (camera, audio and video amplification system, and so on) that converts the visual and vocal images of the performers into electrical current. In this example, the receiver is the television set and cable converter equipment. The receiver's purpose is to change the signal back into a message that can be received and interpreted at the destination (a viewer, in this case).

Shannon and Weaver introduced the term noise as the label for any distortion that interferes with the transmission of a signal from the source to the destination. In this example, an illustration of noise would be electrical interference, leading to audio or video distortion, in the cable line. They also advanced the concept of correction channel, which they regarded as a means of overcoming problems created by noise. The correction channel was operated by an observer who compared the initial signal that was sent with that received; when the two didn't match, additional signals would be transmitted to correct the error.

## Katz and Lazarsfeld's Model

In 1955, political scientists Elihu Katz (1926–) and Paul Lazarsfeld (1901–1976) presented a two-step flow concept of communication in their book *Personal Influence* (Katz & Lazarsfeld, 1955). The model was based on earlier research in which they found that information presented in the mass media did not reach and have an impact on individuals as previous views of communication seemed to suggest it would. Specifically, their research found that political radio and print messages had a negligible effect on individuals' voting decisions.

In searching for an explanation for this lack of effect, they developed a view that linked interpersonal dynamics to mass communication. They determined that undecided voters were influenced more by people around them than by information provided by the mass media; husbands and wives were influenced by their spouses, club members by other club members, workers by their colleagues, children by their parents, and so on. Their research also indicated that some people were consistently more influential than others, leading them to conclude that "ideas often seem to flow from radio and print to opinion leaders and from them to the less active sections of the population"—in a two-step flow (see Figure 2.8).

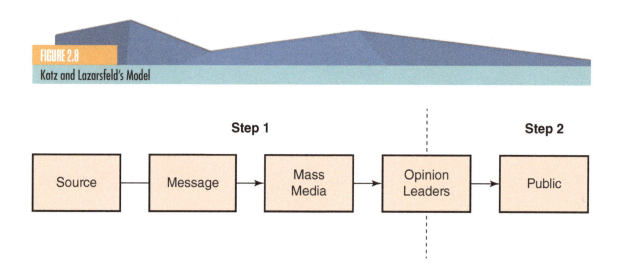

**FIGURE 2.8**

Katz and Lazarsfeld's Model

Step 1 | Step 2

Source → Message → Mass Media → Opinion Leaders → Public

Although research has since suggested that the two-step concept is only applicable in some situations, this formulation has been very influential over the years. It served to link face-to-face and mass communication, and also introduced the idea of opinion leaders. It also has served as the basis for the development of diffusion theory, which describes the process by which new ideas and technological innovations are introduced and adopted within a group, organization, or community.

## Westley and MacLean's Model

A somewhat different approach to communication was developed by Bruce Westley (1915–1990) and Malcolm S. MacLean, Jr. (1913–2001). They suggested that the communication process begins with receiving messages, rather than sending them. To be more precise, Westley and MacLean's view indicates that the process actually begins with a series of signals or potential messages. As depicted in Figure 2.9, there are a large number of signals—potential messages—in a communicator's environment, which are referred to as "Xs" in their model.

Signals may involve a single sense modality such as sight or sound (X), or they may involve a combination of several modalities, for instance, sight, sound, and touch. The designation for such a signal would be $X_{3m}$—the "3m" indicating that three modalities are involved.

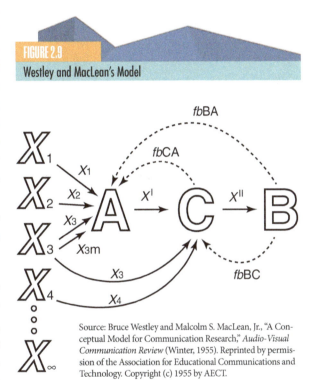

**FIGURE 2.9**

Westley and MacLean's Model

Source: Bruce Westley and Malcolm S. MacLean, Jr., "A Conceptual Model for Communication Research," *Audio-Visual Communication Review* (Winter, 1955). Reprinted by permission of the Association for Educational Communications and Technology. Copyright (c) 1955 by AECT.

The model indicates that in a given situation only some of the many signals (Xs) in one's environment at any point in time are attended to by an individual (A). When individual A processes these signals and interprets them, what is, in effect, a new message ($X^I$) results. It is this new message—A's personal representation of the sum of all the Xs—that is passed along when individual A describes what he or she saw or heard to a second individual (C).

# THE 1970S – 1980S: GROWTH AND SPECIALIZATION

The expansion and specialization that began in the late 1960s reached new heights in the 1970s. Interpersonal communication became an increasingly popular area, as did the study of nonverbal interaction. Information science, information theory, and information and communication systems were other topics of increasing interest. During these same years, group, organizational, political, international, and intercultural communication emerged as distinct areas of study.

Interest in communication was apparent in the popular, as well as the academic, realm. In 1975, the *Harper Dictionary of Contemporary Usage* listed communication as a "vogue word—a word . . . that suddenly or inexplicably crops up . . . in speeches of bureaucrats, comments of columnists . . . and in radio and television broadcasts."

One factor that contributed to the widespread usage of the term communication, but also some ambiguity, was the use of a single term to refer to a field of study, a set of activities, and a profession. People study communication, people communicate (or, more accurately, engage in communication), and people earn their livelihood creating communication products and services. The use of a single term in these three ways was, and is, fairly unique among disciplines.

Another factor adding to both the broad usage but also some confusion was the use of communication and communications. Traditionally, communications had been used to refer to media or to specific messages being transmitted through these media. Communication has historically been used to refer to the activity of sending and receiving messages (through media or face-to-face) and to the discipline as a whole. With the increasing interest in communication technology, the term communications began to be used interchangeably with communication in popular—and sometimes academic—contexts, blurring what had originally been a useful technical distinction.

# THE LATE 1980S – 2000: THE INFORMATION AGE

The Information Age is a popular term used to refer to the period beginning in the late 1990s, and in many senses continuing to the present time. This has been a period in which communication and information technology came to play an increasingly important role in our society. So pervasive are the impacts of these new media and the communication and information services they have created that it is difficult to find an aspect of our personal and professional lives that has not in some way been affected (see Figure 2.10).

## Information as a Commodity

During the 1980s and 1990s, there was an increasing interest in information communicated via messages as an economic good or commodity—something that can be bought and sold—and in the technologies by which this commodity is created, distributed, stored, retrieved, and used. In the United States communication and information companies have emerged as some of our largest businesses.

Communication and information became central in the tele-communication, publishing, Internet, and computer industries, as well as in banking, insurance, leisure and travel, and research. People in these fields spent an increasing amount of their time packaging information into products and services that could be sold in domestic and foreign markets. In the United States, Japan, Sweden, England, and a number of other countries at least half of the society's labor force was engaged in communication and information-related work.

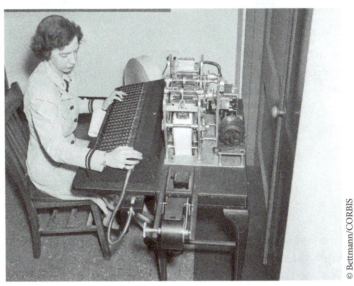

**FIGURE 2.10**

Grace Hopper (1906–1992), one of the earliest computer programmers, popularized the term "debugging" to refer to fixing computer code.

© Bettmann/CORBIS

## Converging Media

New and converging media were a fundamental feature of the landscape of the period. Certainly the most obvious change during this period was the growth of the Internet, and other information storage, transmission, and retrieval systems using computers.

During these years, media were brought together to form hybrid technologies that permitted communication sources and receivers to carry out functions that were once difficult, time-consuming, or even impossible. In earlier periods, specific technologies had more or less specific uses. Television was a medium for viewing mass-produced and mass-distributed programs that reached a "television set" via the airwaves. During the Information Age, television became not only a medium for the mass distribution of standardized programs but also a device for use with the Internet, DVDs, video games, cable systems, and a display for print as well as visual computer output. The telephone underwent a similar transformation. Designed for one-to-one conversation, telephones and telephone lines were used not only in this way but also in conjunction with computers and FAX machines for the transmission of text and graphics as well as voice. Typewriters, once used exclusively for print correspondence and report preparation, were combined with the telephone and television screen to form new, hybrid telecommunication systems.

Thus, the infamous "Information Age" brought new labels, new and hybrid media, extended concepts of communication and information, changing economic realities, and new jobs for an increasing number of communication and information workers. During these years our perspective broadened to include newer media and the nature and function of communication technology in general. The Information Age greatly heightened attention to the pervasive role of technology in our lives and its impact on human behavior.

# THE 21ST CENTURY: COMMUNICATION STUDY TODAY

The preceding sections of this chapter have traced the development of the communication discipline from its early beginnings, through periods marked by interdisciplinary development, through its emergence and growth as a discipline in its own right through the end of the 20th century. From this overview, we can draw a number of conclusions about the present period that are helpful in understanding communication study as it exists today.

## Ancient and Newly Emergent

The core of modern communication study has its origins in the work of the early Greek philosophers. The 1900s, however, brought a number of changes to the discipline, including a new name. Within the last 50 years, the scope of the field has broadened, its structure has changed, and every facet of it has grown substantially. In this respect, communication can be viewed as a newly emergent field, the newest of the disciplines concerned with the study of human behavior.

## Discipline and Interdisciplinary Link

As has been the case for at least the past half century, communication in the present period is a strong discipline in its own right. At the same time, interest in communication extends well beyond the boundaries of the communication field.

This duality attests to the central role of communication in human affairs. And, at a time when the boundaries between these and other fields are becoming less rigid, communication serves as an important intellectual link among scholars of various persuasions and points of view.

In communication studies, we approach issues such as these from the perspective of the creation, transmission, interpretation, and use of information by individuals in relationships, groups, organizations, cultures, and societies. The value of integrating our efforts with the works of scholars in other disciplines has become increasingly apparent in the years since.

## Personal and Professional Applicability

The importance attached to communication in contemporary life can also be seen in the extent to which the phenomenon is regarded as essential to our personal as well as our occupational roles. The shelves of libraries and bookstores are filled with writings emphasizing the importance of communication to the establishment and maintenance of meaningful interpersonal and family relationships. And, but a few rows away, are an equal number of books describing the importance of communication to successful professional and organizational functioning. Such publications address the importance of communication for individual leaders, team collaboration, organizational effectiveness, and marketplace competitiveness, among other topics.

## Old and New Technology

Speaking and listening are as basic to communication and human behavior at the early years of a new millennium as they were at the time of the ancient Greeks. And yet, in the present period, we benefit from any number of technologically enhanced forms of communication, which give permanence and portability to the messages of face-to-face communication. Beyond taken-for-granted media such as newspapers, radio, television, and magazines are a broad array of new technologies that find their way to the market every year. Whether one thinks of smart-phones, tablets, wireless local networks, global positioning systems, high definition televisions, video games, or the many other emerging tools, toys, and technologies, the possibilities for new forms of communication are quite remarkable. And yet as we shall discuss in greater detail later, for all the new forms of communication, many if not most of the basic communication challenges and functions remain.

Inquiring minds might legitimately ask if all the new communication forms that fill our pockets, briefcases, homes, and offices have improved the quality of our lives. Are we better informed than we were 50 years ago? Are we better entertained? Is world understanding improving? Are our personal and family relationships better, more meaningful? These are good questions, we think, and are precisely the kind of questions that should increasingly be addressed by those interested in communication study in the 21st century and beyond.

## Problem and Solution

Few topics are as pervasive in the popular culture as communication. We have become so accustomed to hearing and reading commentaries on the challenges we face in crossing social, demographic, political, gender, cultural, lifestyle, religious, or occupational boundaries that it is easy to overlook the central role communication is perceived to play in these matters. In such conversations, communication—or, more precisely, the lack thereof—is seen as the fundamental problem. And yet, as Peters (1999) has pointed out, communication is also seen as the essential solution. Paradoxically, communication is seen as both a chasm and a bridge. The significance afforded to the phenomenon in our time is quite remarkable, and a factor that contributes to the vitality and importance of communication study and communication practice.

## Practical Skill and Fundamental Life Process

Another interesting contrast regarding communication study today is its breadth. In many communication courses, the primary emphasis on communication continues to be as a skill and, more specifically, on the set of techniques associated with creating and disseminating messages, orally or in written form, in face-to-face or technologically mediated settings. There are other courses, however—more often the type that would make use of a book such as this—that approach communication theoretically, viewing it as a fundamental life process, one that is basic to our physical, personal, social, political, and cultural existence. The fact that communication study encompasses such a broad range of interests is a source of some confusion and frequently requires definitional clarification in discussions. At the same time, as in previous periods, this breadth also creates what is a useful tension for the field—a tension between the search for practical technique and the quest for theoretical understanding. Each makes a useful and complementary contribution to the field in its effort to advance human knowledge and capability.

# THE EVOLUTION OF THEORY

The earliest perspectives on communication were concerned with public speaking with the goal of persuasion. Orientations broadened to include communication in private as well as public settings; nonverbal and technologically mediated as well as verbal messages; multiple as well as single sources and receivers; and a broad array of purposes, functions, and outcomes.

Amidst many of the obvious changes in form, certain underlying themes have remained relatively constant for most of the 2,500-year history of the field. Perhaps the most fundamental of these traditional themes is the view that communication consists of a source constructing and transmitting a message to one or more receivers in order to bring about a particular effect. In this way of thinking, as depicted in Figure 2.11, communication is a one-way event consisting of a one-way transfer of information from source to receiver(s). This $S \rightarrow M \rightarrow R = E$ characterization of communication has been so pervasive in the thinking of the field that it represents what philosopher Thomas Kuhn (1922-1996) and others refer to as a paradigm. Paradigms are broad theoretical orientations that guide the work of scholars in a field over a substantial period of time. They are pervasive and highly influential, and shape and are reflected in scholars' theories, research, and practice.

Eventually, the paradigms of a field change. Although there is no simple explanation as to how and why this happens, it is often the case that change is stimulated by new observations and evidence that cannot be accommodated by the prevailing paradigm. Research findings, observations, or events that cannot be explained by, or are inconsistent with, existing paradigms are termed anomalies. Often, then, anomalies are the stimulant for discarding one paradigm and searching for an alternative (Kuhn, 1970).

From our review of the recent history of communication models, it is evident that this kind of change has been occurring in communication. Further examination reveals that the anomaly that has given impetus to this transition is relatively simple: message sent is not equal to message received: $MS \neq MR$.

Even as Aristotle advanced his orator-to-listener view of communication, he and his contemporaries acknowledged that the persuasive efforts of the speaker were not always successful. It was presumed that the match between the message sent and that received could be made more predictable if sources learned more about how to construct and deliver messages effectively.

The idea of opinion leaders and the two-step flow, first suggested in the work of Katz and Lazarsfeld (1955), again reflected an awareness of the fundamental anomaly. The two-step concept provided an explanation for the lack of predictive value of the classical paradigm.

The work of Westley and MacLean dealt with the $MS \neq MR$ anomaly by creating a model that did not begin with the sending of messages, but rather with an individual surrounded by Xs—information sources—some of which were intentionally provided by other people and some not. This way of

**FIGURE 2.11**

One-Way Transfer of Information

$$S \rightarrow M \rightarrow R = E$$

Paradigm

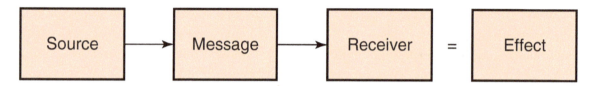

| Source | → | Message | → | Receiver | = | Effect |

thinking provided a logical and expanded explanation as to why the message as interpreted by a receiver often had little in common with the message as intended by a particular source.

## Communication Theory Today

Whereas the S → M → R = E paradigm predominated during much of the history of the field, the past 50 years have brought a number of changes to this perspective. As you can see from Table 2.1, the evolution of the concept of communication has been:

- From source- and message-centered *to* receiver- and meaning-centered
- From one-way *to* interactive and transactional
- From event- *to* process-oriented
- From an exclusive emphasis on information transmission *to* an emphasis on interpretation and relationships, as well as information transmission
- From public speaking *to* a framework that takes account of communication in a variety of contexts including the individual, relationships, families, groups, organizations, societies, and media

**TABLE 2.1**

Models of Communication:  An Overview

| Model | How Communication Works | Major Factors Stressed in Explaining Communication Outcomes | Direction Flow |
|---|---|---|---|
| Aristotle | Speaker constructs messages that bring about persuasive effects among listeners | Source and Message | One-way |
| Lasswell | Speaker constructs messages, selects a channel, and thereby brings about a range of effects among listeners | Source, Message, and Channel | One-way |
| Shannon and Weaver | Source encodes message and transmits through channel to receiver | Source, Message, Noise | One-way with feedback |
| Katz and Lazarsfeld | Source encodes messages and transmits information through mass media to opinion leaders who relay it to public | Channel, Message, Receiver, Opinion Leader | One-way (mediated) |
| Westley and MacLean | Source selectively encodes messages and transmits information in modified form to receiver who decodes, encodes, and transmits information in modified form to other individual(s) with feedback at every step | Receiver, Meaning, Feedback | Circular (through feedback) |

# CONCLUSION

Communication has a rich and lengthy history, which can be traced back to Babylonian and Egyptian writings prior to the 5th century BCE. The initial contributions to communication study came from scholars in what was termed rhetoric. They viewed communication as the practical art of persuasion. Aristotle and Plato, who were particularly significant to early communication study, saw rhetoric and the practice of public speaking not only as an art but also as a legitimate area of study.

Along with rhetoric and speech, journalism also contributed to the heritage of communication study. As with rhetoric, journalism initially was concerned primarily with practical rather than theoretical matters. By the beginning of the 20ᵗʰ century, rhetoric and speech were clearly established as disciplines in their own right, and journalism began to take shape as a field of study as well.

During the early 20ᵗʰ century, interest in communication continued in rhetoric and speech, and the advent of radio and later television led to the wider application of journalistic concepts and the development of more theories of the overall process. The 1940s and 1950s were years of interdisciplinary growth, as scholars from various disciplines advanced theories of communication that extended beyond the boundaries of their own fields.

The 1960s were a period of integration. A good deal was done to synthesize the writings of rhetoric and speech, journalism and mass media, as well as other disciplines. A number of landmark books appeared within the discipline.

During this time, additional models of the communication process were advanced, extending the work of earlier scholars.

The 1970s and early 1980s were a time of unprecedented growth within the field. It was also a period in which much specialization occurred, giving rise to progress in our understanding of interpersonal, group, organizational, political, international, and intercultural communication.

Continuing growth and interdisciplinary advancement distinguished the communication field in the late 1980s and 1990s, and developments of the Information Age were important influences. Converging media, along with economic and marketplace developments, underscored the pervasive impact of communication and communication media on our lives.

At the beginning of the 21ˢᵗ century, the discipline of communication and the phenomena it studies are center stage in human affairs. The subject is at once ancient and newly emergent, a discipline in its own right and an interdisciplinary crossroad for scholars from a wide variety of fields. Communication is as relevant to personal as it is to professional affairs, and the role of new and old technology continues to be a focus of the times and the discipline. As Peters (1999) has noted, communication study is concerned with both the major problem and most hopeful solution of contemporary life, and the focus of the field of communication is at once on some of the most practical of skills and on the most fundamental of life processes.

This overview of the history of communication reveals a number of changes during the 2,500-year heritage of the field—changes both in the theory of the communication process and in the discipline in which it is studied.  We have seen that the communication field is both ancient as well as a product of the 20ᵗʰ century, interdisciplinary in heritage, the home of scholars and professionals, a discipline which benefits from the approaches of both the humanities and behavioral sciences, and an area in which media are of continuing concern.

# KEY POINTS

After reading this chapter, you should be able to:

- Describe the ways that communication has long been regarded as important to the practice and understanding of human affairs and, in the past half century, an increasingly popular academic subject
- Explain the development and evolution of the key communication models
- Identify how the communication discipline is the basis for linkages between scholars and practitioners from many other fields
- Articulate the paradox of communication and how it is both the basis for many of the problems of human affairs and also the potential solution

# REFERENCES

Aristotle. *Rhetoric*. (1954). Published in *Aristotle: Rhetoric and Poetics* (W. R. Roberts, Trans.). New York: The Modern Library.

Bormann, E. G. (1965). *Theory and research in the communicative arts*. New York: Holt.

Brown, R. J. (Ed.). (2015). HistoryBuff.com. Retrieved June 14, 2015, from http://www.historybuff.com/library/reffirstten.html.

Cohen, H. (1994). *The history of speech communication: The emergence of a discipline, 1914-1945*. Annandale, VA: National Communication Association.

Delia, J. G. (1987). Communication research: A history. In C. R. Berger & S. H. Chaffee (Eds.), *Handbook of communication science* (pp. 25-30). Newbury Park, CA: Sage.

Frank, J. F. (1961). *The beginnings of the English newspaper 1620-1660*. Cambridge, MA: Harvard University Press.

Harper, N. L. (1979). *Human communication theory: History of a paradigm*. Rochelle Park, NJ: Hayden.

Hyde, G. M. (1937). *Foreword*. In G. F. Mott (Ed.), *Survey of journalism* (p. vii-viii). New York: Barnes & Noble, Inc.

Katz, E., & Lazarsfeld, P. F. (1955). *Personal influence: The part played by people in the flow of mass communications*. New York: The Free Press.

Kuhn, T. S. (1970). *The structure of scientific revolutions* (2nd ed.). Chicago: University of Chicago Press.

Lasswell, H. D. (1960). The structure and function of communication in society. In W. Schramm (Ed.), *Mass communications* (pp. 117-130). Urbana, IL: University of Illinois Press.

Peters, J. D. (1999). *Speaking into air: A history of the idea of communication.* Chicago: University of Chicago Press.

Shannon, C. E., & Weaver, W. (1949). *The mathematical theory of communication.* Urbana, IL: University of Illinois Press.

Weaver, C. H. (1977). A history of the International Communication Association. In B. D. Ruben (Ed.), *Communication Yearbook I* (pp. 607-609). New Brunswick, NJ: Transaction.

# CHAPTER 3

# COMMUNICATION
## AS A BASIC LIFE PROCESS

**In this chapter, you will learn about:**

- The ways that communication is a basic life process
- The similarities and differences between human and animal communication
- The primary modes of communication
- The symbolic meaning of communication

## BEYOND S → M → R = E: THE ADAPTATION PERSPECTIVE

## COMMUNICATION PROCESSES IN ANIMALS AND HUMANS

## COMMUNICATION MODES

- Visual Messages
- Tactile Messages
- Olfactory and Gustatory Messages
- Auditory Messages

## BASIC LIFE FUNCTIONS OF COMMUNICATION

- Courtship and Mating
- Reproduction
- Parent-Offspring Relations and Socialization
- Navigation
- Self-Defense
- Territoriality

## THE COMMUNICATION ICEBERG

- The Visibility and Invisibility of Human Communication

## VISIBLE ASPECTS OF COMMUNICATION

- People
- Symbols
- Permanence and Portability

## INVISIBLE ASPECTS OF COMMUNICATION

- Meaning
- Learning
- Subjectivity
- Negotiation
- Culture
- Interacting Contexts and Levels
- Self-Reference
- Self-Reflexivity
- Ethics
- Inevitability

## CONCLUSION

## KEY POINTS

# BEYOND S → M → R = E: THE ADAPTATION PERSPECTIVE

In this chapter we will present a view of communication that builds upon and substantially extends the "transmissional" view of communication that was so important to the history of communication thinking.

The traditional S → M → R = E approach viewed communication primarily from the perspective of message transmission, where the goal is presumed to be sending messages to establish a commonness between source and receiver. The framework presented in this chapter and throughout this book envisions communication more broadly as the process whereby humans and animals process messages in order to adapt—to cope with and shape the demands and challenges of life. It is the process through which living beings create, transform, and use information in order to relate to their environment and one another.

The model of communication provided in Figure 3.1 illustratives a systems view of the communication process. Rather than view communication as involving the purposeful sending of messages from a source to a receiver, a systems model characterizes the process as one in which individuals are bombarded by a large number of messages as they go about their daily routines within their environments. Some of these messages are sent intentionally by others through language, writing, and conscious expression; some are accidental such as nervous gestures, unintentional choices of clothing, unplanned facial expressions and movements; and some of the messages which may make a difference to individuals may have their source in the physical environment—a sunset, a tree, the wind, or a twinkling star. We will talk more about the nature of the dynamics involved in the perception and reception of messages in later chapters. For now, the key point is that in a systems view, communication is recognized to be multidimensional, multidirectional, and extremely complex—involving messages which are created and transmitted and others that are not.

FIGURE 3.1

A Systems Perspective on Communication. A multiplicity of factors are at play in even the most basic situation, and the net result is that the communication process is multidimensional, multidirectional, and extremely complex—involving messages that are intentionally created and others that are not.

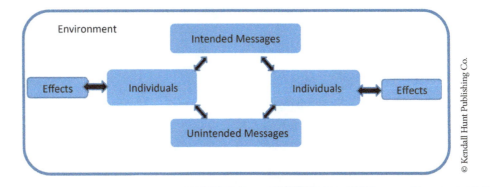

© Kendall Hunt Publishing Co.

While animal communication is clearly not the focus of this book, an appreciation of the role communication plays in activities of all living systems is very helpful as a foundation for better understanding the role this process plays in human affairs.

## COMMUNICATION PROCESSES IN ANIMALS AND HUMANS

All animals and humans are *open systems,* which is to say they participate in continual give-and-take transactions with their environment. These transactions are essential to life. The basic process is one in which a living system takes in, uses, and in the process transforms materials that are necessary to its life functioning.

As one moves from plants to animals, the nature of the system-environment transactions becomes increasingly complex. Animals not only depend for their survival on chemical and physical exchanges but also on communication. Through communication animals and humans create, gather, and use information to interact with and adapt to their environment and its inhabitants.

Just as animal and human systems take in oxygen and foodstuffs and transform them into materials necessary to their functioning, they also transform and use information. In this most basic sense, *communication is the essential life process through which animals and humans create, acquire, transform, and use information to carry out the activities of their lives.*

## COMMUNICATION MODES

For any living system, information used to guide behavior is derived by processing messages in the environment. The world in which animals and humans exist is filled with a vast array of such messages. Some of these (such as the words exchanged between friends or the mating call of a bird) are purposefully created by living things. Other cues (such as a flash of lightning or the sound of a falling tree) are not. Both purposeful and nonpurposeful cues are vital as potential sources of the information that shapes behavior.

### Visual Messages

For humans, visual messages are particularly important. A wave and a smile from a friend, a blush of embarrassment, a tear, new clothes or a new car, a text, or the subject line on an email, are all

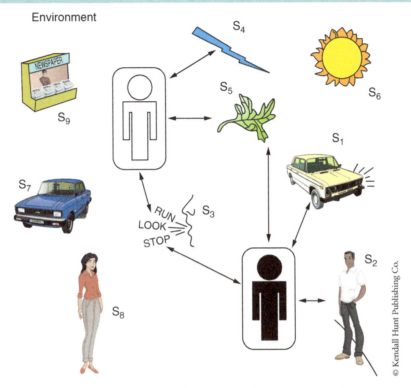

potential sources of information that can hold great significance for us when they are noticed and attended to, as illustrated in Figure 3.2.

Some animals also make substantial use of visual cues. The color and calls of birds, the alluring colored wings of a butterfly, the rhythmic light of a firefly, and the movement of head, ears, or tail by primates all serve as valuable information sources.

As significant as sight is for humans and some animals, it is generally not as crucial as other communication modes in most species. Many animals lack the visual capacities necessary for processing light and depend instead on touch, sound, smell, or taste as primary modalities for relating to their environment or to one another. See Table 3.1 for a listing of some of these communication modes.

**TABLE 3.1**

Communication Modes

| Modality | Form of Message |
|---|---|
| **Visual** | **Sight** |
| | Facial Displays |
| | Movement of Body Parts |
| | Distance and Spacing |
| | Position |
| | Dress |
| | Other Symbols, Adornment, and Emblems |
| **Tactile** | **Touch** |
| | Vibration |
| | Stroking |
| | Rubbing |
| | Pressure |
| | Pain |
| | Temperature |
| **Olfactory and Gustatory** | **Smell and Taste (Pheromones)** |
| | Body Odors |
| | Special Chemicals |
| | Food Sources, Fragrances, and Taste |
| **Auditory** | **Sound** |
| | Incidental Sounds |
| | Vibrations |
| | Whistling |
| | Drumming |
| | Rubbing |
| | Vocalization |

## Tactile Messages

For animals and human beings, touch, bumping, vibration, and other types of tactile messages are important. From before birth through the first months and years of life, physical contact plays a critical role in the biological and social development of human infants, as well as the young of other species. Tactile messages remain crucial throughout the lives of many animals, in parent–young relations, courtship and intimate relations, social greetings, play, and aggression and combat. These cues also play a vital role in self-defense and self-preservation.

## Olfactory and Gustatory Messages

Many animals also use olfactory and gustatory information to relate to their environment and to one another. *Pheromones* is the technical term used to refer to these chemical messages. Pheromones are carried through water or air. Vertebrates receive these messages through a nose, fish through a nose or odor-sensitive cells on the body, and insects by means of sensors located in their antennae. As with other modes, the brain and nervous system filter out irrelevant cues and guide the system to respond only to those signals to which the animal is attuned or to which it has learned to attend.

## Auditory Messages

For humans and many animals, auditory messages provide critical links to the environment and to one another. Some sounds—thunder, an earthquake, or the surf splashing against the shore—have inanimate sources. Other auditory messages are produced by living things through speaking, whistling, honking a horn, drumming, or striking a part of the body against an object, the ground, or another part of the body.

In order for auditory signals to be useful, the vibrations must be detected, received, and processed by means of a special organ which converts the data into electrical impulses that can be interpreted by the brain. Lower-order animals generally respond to sound either by approaching or moving away from the source; most higher-order animals and humans are able to act on auditory messages in a number of ways due to prior learning. Auditory messages are important in the lives of a wide range of species, including birds, insects, and primates, in addition to humans—all of which depend on these cues in caring for their young, learning, courtship and mating, and "language" acquisition and use (Baker, 2001; Slater, 2003; Stumpf, 2001).

# BASIC LIFE FUNCTIONS OF COMMUNICATION

The significance of communication and the various information-processing modes is clearest when one considers some of the basic life functions they serve. See Table 3.2 for a list of basic life functions.

| TABLE 3.2 | |
| --- | --- |
| **Basic Life Functions of Communication** | |
| Courtship and Mating | |
| Reproduction | |
| Parent–Offspring Relations and Socialization | |
| Navigation | |
| Self-Defense | |
| Territoriality | |

## Courtship and Mating

Although differences exist in the specific courtship and mating practices of various species, all involve communication. Humans and other animals must be able to identify other individuals of their own species. Also, individuals must attract and sometimes persuade one another, and the mating activity must be synchronized.

As with other species, human courtship involves the identification and attraction of mates. These processes occur primarily through visual, auditory, and tactile modes, although some studies suggest that chemical cues may also play a role. Human courtship and mating involve persuasion and negotiation.

The songs of grasshoppers and crickets serve this purpose, as does the odor of moths and the light flashing of fireflies. With birds, mating involves the creation and reception of auditory messages ranging from a simple, repetitive, and not necessarily musical call to complex song-and-dance presentations, acrobatics, and rituals.

## Reproduction

Offspring of any species, as they reach adulthood, bear a strong physical resemblance to their parents. A bear cub grows up to look and act like a bear, not a cat or a dog. Physiologically, structurally, in general appearance, and in a number of behavioral patterns, the young of any species replicate or reproduce their parents. This reproduction comes about through a biological communication process in which the sperm cell of a male and egg cell of a female merge to provide a blueprint for the growth and development of the offspring.

DNA, located within cells, is the molecular basis of heredity. The general pattern of growth of living things is through division of cells. A single cell divides to produce two, each of which divides to produce two more, and so on. In some organisms, this continues until thousands, millions, or billions of cells are produced. Division, growth, and development proceed according to the blueprint, as the cells form into layers and masses that fold together and intermesh to form tissues, organs, and more complex structures.

Reproduction of human offspring by their parents begins after a sperm and egg join. The egg cell, most of which is filled with food, is about one two-hundredth of an inch across. In this space are all the instructions that represent the mother's contribution to the inherited characteristics of the child. The sperm cell, which is only about 1/80,000 the size of the egg, carries only the messages necessary to the father's contribution to the developmental blueprint. Through the union of these two cells, all the information needed for the continuity of the species is transmitted in what is undoubtedly life's most fundamental communication process.

## Parent–Offspring Relations and Socialization

Children's survival depends on relations with adults. Human infants, in fact, are dependent on others of their species longer than are other creatures. In lower-order animals, the survival of a species and the communication capabilities necessary to this end are largely assured through inheritance.

With many social animals, extended contact between parent and young is required. When this contact does not occur, the important role of communication in the survival of a species is underscored. Some birds that are raised without interaction with others of their kind become totally confused about their identity. Zoologist Konrad Lorenz (1903–1989) was the first to study the processes by which birds and other animals learn or imprint their identity in early social interaction. Simon (1977) recalls one of Lorenz's most famous observations:

> One of the most striking as well as pathetically comical instances [of "identity confusion"] concerned an albino peacock in an Australian zoo, the lone survivor of a brood that had succumbed to a spell of bad weather. The peafowl chick was placed in the only warm room available, . . . the one in which the giant tortoises were housed. Although the young peacock flourished in these surroundings, the peculiar effect of its reptilian roommates on the bird became apparent not long after it had attained sexual maturity and grown its first train: beginning then and forever after, the peacock displayed his magnificent plumes in the amorous "wheel" position *only* to giant tortoises, eagerly if vainly courting these reptiles while ignoring even the most handsome peahens with which the zoo supplied him. (p. 23)

# Navigation

The term *navigation* refers to the purposeful movement of an animal through space, from one location to another. Goal-directed movement of this kind is necessary for nearly all of life's activities, including mating, food location, and self-defense.

In each of these activities, sound, sight, odor, temperature, or other messages must be used. Information must also be processed to determine present location and also to guide movement in a desired direction.

Many animals have highly developed navigation capabilities and can travel great distances with precision. The skills of cats, horses, and homing pigeons are well known in this regard, as are those of ducks and geese, who may maintain two seasonal homes several thousand miles apart. Apparently, some animals orient themselves by processing data about landmarks, the sun, or stars. Other animals use a sonarlike system of sounds and echoes for navigation. The echolocation skills of bats are so well developed that in total darkness they can pass between two black silk threads placed less than a foot apart without touching them. And, the dolphin's echo system has such sensitivity that the animal can distinguish two different fish at a distance of 15 to 18 feet (Méry, 1975).

One of the most elaborate navigation processes is that used by social bees in locating and securing food. Nobel Prize recipient Karl von Frisch (1886–1982) found that when a worker bee locates a desirable source of food, it announces the find to other bees in the hive by a dance (Lindauer, 1961; Wilson, 1971), as shown in Figure 3.3.

Navigation processes are also essential for humans, although the communication forms and modalities involved differ. In a basic sense, a person striding along a busy sidewalk at rush hour or driving on a crowded highway has a great deal in common with the navigation activities of an ant,

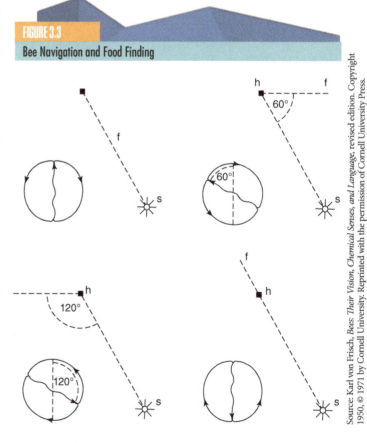

**FIGURE 3.3**

**Bee Navigation and Food Finding**

Source: Karl von Frisch, *Bees: Their Vision, Chemical Senses, and Language,* revised edition. Copyright 1950, © 1971 by Cornell University. Reprinted with the permission of Cornell University Press.

bat, dolphin, or songbird. Each must analyze an immense quantity of information in order to arrive safely at the intended destination.

**FIGURE 3.4**
Fight or Flight?

## Self-Defense

Communication plays an important role in the processes through which living systems identify and respond to potential threats to their safety and well-being. If an animal senses the presence of a danger—a predator, a falling tree, the headlights of a car, and so on—it prepares instinctively to defend itself or to flee as illustrated in Figure 3.4. As a part of what has been called the *stress response,* hormonal and muscular systems are activated, readying the animal for maximum physical output (Selye, 1956; Schusterman, Reichmuth, & Kastak, 2000).

The outlet for this stress energy—the act of fighting or retreating—is often the basis for information used by other animals. This is so, for instance, when the alarm response of one bird evokes a reaction in others that in turn produce their own distress calls.

Among humans, the natural fight-or-flight response is often constrained or channeled into other culturally sanctioned actions. When this occurs, communication also plays a central role in ways that will become clear in later discussion.

## Territoriality

The establishment and maintenance of a home or territory is another activity in which communication is essential. Humans and most other animals become attached to particular places, often to those locations where they were born, spent their youth, or mated; and many living creatures mark and even defend these territories.

Territories also play an important role in the lives of social insects. Many species go to great lengths to construct their dwellings and to compete for prime housing sites. Often insects can determine the presence of a foreigner and will often attack if an individual violates the territory. Animals also establish and maintain what might be thought of as *mobile* or *transitory territories,* and these, too, involve communication. Some fish and birds, for example, travel or rest in groups, and a stranger that violates the boundary may well meet with considerable resistance.

Territoriality is as important to human life as it is to the lives of many other animals, although often less obviously so. In many situations, humans maintain *personal space*—portable or transitory territories—in a manner similar to other animals. Face-to-face interaction provides another example. In such contexts, interactants become uncomfortable unless a customary amount of personal space is maintained between the individuals. The specifics depend on the situation, culture, and relationship among them. A coat or backpack on an empty seat in a library, or a towel or umbrella on a beach, may also serve to mark transitory territories, in much the same way as a bird's song claims a section of a forest.

Humans also use communication to mark their territories in more permanent ways. Over the years a great deal of human effort has been directed toward acquiring, dividing, and maintaining space of one kind or another—countries, states, counties, municipalities, and personal properties. The use of fences as territorial boundary markers is an interesting human invention to accomplish this goal.

# THE COMMUNICATION ICEBERG

As we have seen, humans have a good deal in common with other animals in terms of the basics of communication, and yet human communication is also unique in many respects. In this section we examine the unique and differentiating aspects of human communication.

## The Visibility and Invisibility of Human Communication

When a person without a background in communication theory listens to two people engaged in conversation, watches a group standing to salute a flag, observes a small group decision-making session, or orders products through the Internet, the communication process appears to be rather simple and straightforward. Messages are sent, messages are received, people behave accordingly, and that's that.

Or so it seems. Actually, in the case of human communication, the aspects of the process that can be easily observed are really only the tip of the communication iceberg, as suggested by Figure 3.5.

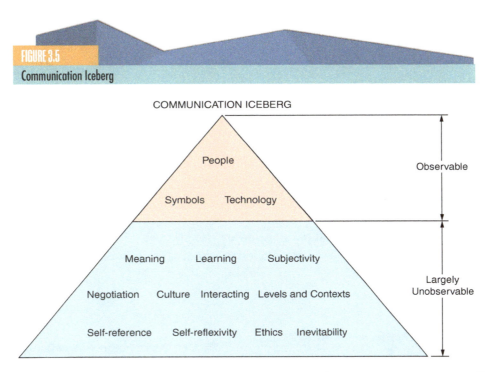

FIGURE 3.5
Communication Iceberg

COMMUNICATION ICEBERG

People

Symbols     Technology

Observable

Meaning        Learning        Subjectivity

Negotiation    Culture    Interacting    Levels and Contexts

Self-reference    Self-reflexivity    Ethics    Inevitability

Largely
Unobservable

Most of the operations and functions that are necessary to make the communication process "work" are invisible to the untrained eye. Consider the following situation. Jamal says: "Casey, please pass the salt." Casey picks up a salt shaker and passes it to Jamal. In this circumstance as in others, it seems that meaning has been transferred from Jamal to Casey through a verbalized message. However, even in an elementary situation like passing salt, the communication process is far more complex than it appears. And most of that complexity is invisible.

In this simple example, a number of elements are involved in the communication process, and each affects the outcome. First, Jamal must decide to engage in communication. Then, he must formulate a message that he believes will convey a desire for the salt. Next, the message must be sent. At this point, Casey has to "decide" to attend to the message, must interpret it appropriately, and must choose to act on it in accordance with Jamal's intent.

In order for either party to be able to use language in this transaction, substantial learning is required; "pass" and "salt" are useful symbols only because their meanings have come to be standardized through a complex process of social communication. Given all this, a simple communication event that begins with a verbal request for salt and ends up with the salt being passed is no small accomplishment.

To appreciate fully the complexities of communication, it is necessary to have an understanding of both the "visible" and "invisible" characteristics of human communication.

# VISIBLE ASPECTS OF COMMUNICATION

When we observe communication taking place, three important components of the process are readily observable: people, symbols, and media.

## People

In this context, when we refer to *people* we are thinking in terms of individuals functioning as message senders and/or receivers. We include in this category public speakers, as well as individuals speaking to one other person, a group, or an organization. Individuals engaged in writing, electronic messaging, or other forms of message creation and transmission are also included. We also include individuals who are the recipients of messages in a communication situation, either as listeners, readers, or observers.

## Symbols

What do we mean by the term *symbols*? *Symbols* are characters, letters, numbers, words, objects, people, or actions that stand for or represent something besides themselves. There have been many attempts to identify precisely what it is that makes us different from other living things. A number of writers have pointed to our social nature. However, many animals depend for their survival on other members of their species. Other scholars have suggested that our capacity for communication might be the distinguishing characteristic. As we know, however, the production, transmission, and reception of messages is essential to the social lives of many species; and communication in one form or another is necessary to the adaptation and survival of all animals. As humans, we *do* have a unique communication capability; we can create and use symbols and symbolic language, and it is this skill and the many consequences of it that perhaps best highlight the special nature of the human animal (Rapoport, 1973).

What exactly does it mean to say that humans create and use symbolic language? A *language,* in the most general sense, is a set of characters, or elements, and rules for their use in relation to one another. There are many types of languages. Most familiar are spoken and written languages, such as English, Spanish, or Swahili. The Morse code, Braille, genetic code, and various computer "languages" are less obvious examples. See Figure 3.6 for an illustration of this concept.

With language, we code and transmit messages from one point to another using one or more communication modes. Oral, spoken, and other acoustically coded languages make use of the auditory mode. Written or light-utilizing languages utilize the visual channel.

Most languages are based on arbitrary symbolization. While letters and words are the most obvious elements in our symbolic language, there are many others that are important to human life. An illuminated red light located on a pole near an intersection is a symbol, as is George Washington, the Eiffel Tower, or a rectangular piece of cloth with thirteen red and white stripes and fifty white stars on a blue field in the upper corner.

Symbols represent things or ideas about things. Words are symbols because they represent objects, ideas, relationships, people, places, and feelings—to name just a few of the concepts or objects that are referenced by words.

FIGURE 3.6

The English alphabet, Morse Code, sign language, Braille, and the ASCII (American Standard Code for Information Interchange) computer code are among our most used languages. Each has evolved to meet a specialized set of human needs. The languages differ from one another in their form, yet in terms of the more basic functions served, they have much in common.

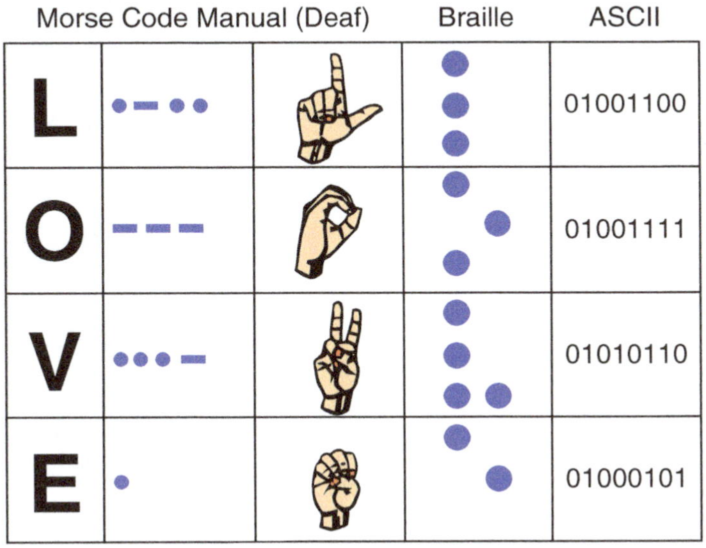

| | Morse Code | Manual (Deaf) | Braille | ASCII |
|---|---|---|---|---|
| **L** | • — • • | | ● ● ● | 01001100 |
| **O** | — — — | | ● ● ● | 01001111 |
| **V** | • • • — | | ● ● ● ● | 01010110 |
| **E** | • | | ● ● | 01000101 |

Artwork © Kendall Hunt Publishing Co.

The symbols (words) in a language that represent concepts and objects are arbitrary. In most cases, there is no direct or obvious connection between the symbol and the referent (the thing the symbol stands for). Individuals in a society have to learn which words represent which things. For example, we learn that "window" is the appropriate word for the pane of glass that is in the middle of a wall. This symbol may refer to other objects, too. All windows are not the same size and shape, but we continue to use the word "window" to label them. In fact, some windows may even be opaque. Problems in communication often result when we forget that the symbol is not the referent and that many symbols have more than one referent.

Another fundamental, but easily overlooked, illustration of symbolic language is our monetary system. We think little about the communication process that occurs when we go into a store, pick out an item priced at $15, go to the cashier, hand over a ten- and a five-dollar bill, and leave the store with a "thank you" and the item in a bag. This exchange is very much a communication event, one in which symbolic language plays a crucial role. When we give the clerk a ten- and a five-dollar bill, in effect, we are only handing over two pieces of high-quality paper. They have no inherent value, other than the expense of the paper and ink. They are symbols and as such their value to us comes about as a consequence of the meanings we have learned to attach to them—but more about that later. We live, quite literally, in an environment filled with symbols of various kinds (see Figure 3.7 for one example of important symbols).

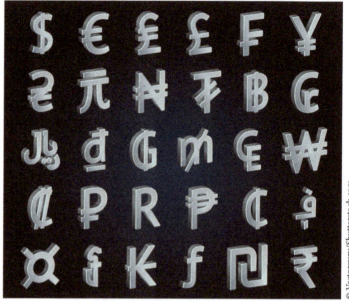

**FIGURE 3.7**

How many of these currency symbols can you identify?

### PERMANENCE AND PORTABILITY.

For most animals, visual, tactile, olfactory, gustatory, and auditory signals are transitory in nature, and, in most cases, animals must be within sight or hearing range in order to respond to messages from another individual; even olfactory cues used to mark a territory or provide a trail are generally fleeting.

For humans, through the use of technology, symbols can have permanence and significance apart from the situation in which they were originally used. Information provided in a letter sent to a friend, a book, a poem, a scientific formula, the blueprint for a building, or signs along a highway is not transitory in nature. Such messages may have a virtually unending existence and use. In fact, their life is limited only by our human capacity for preserving the physical materials on which they are recorded.

Technology makes it possible for us to accumulate and transmit information from one generation to the next. This enables us to "bridge" or "bind" time—to use records of the past, as well as the present, and to create messages today that will be a part of the environment of future generations.

Because of technology, human communication also has the capacity for "portability"—for bridging space. The objects or people to which particular symbols refer need not be present in order for the symbol to be useful in communication. Information coded and packaged in one geographic location can be transmitted to people in a distant location, for example. Communication technologies extend and provide an alternative to face-to-face communication as a means of sending and receiving messages.

# INVISIBLE ASPECTS OF COMMUNICATION

Ten other aspects of communication are critical but invisible to the untrained eye. These include: meaning, learning, subjectivity, negotiation, culture, interacting contexts and levels, self-reference, self-reflexivity, ethics, and inevitability.

## Meaning

We invent symbols. In order to use them in communication, we also have to invent their meanings and the responses we make to them. To illustrate the point, consider the word *bird*. *Bird* has no inherent, intrinsic meaning or significance. It is simply a particular pattern of auditory vibrations that comes about by the manipulation of the vocal cords, lips, tongue, and mouth, or a configuration of ink on paper in the case of written language. The characteristics of the word and sounds of its spoken pronunciation comprise a symbolic code that is useful only to those who are able to decipher it. The word is arbitrary in the sense that it has no relation to the animal to which it refers, other than that which we have invented and accepted. Any word could have been chosen in its place.

As another illustration, let's return to the example of a red light at an intersection. In casual conversation, we may say that the light "means" stop. Actually, however, the light means nothing in and of itself. It is a symbol. Its meaning was invented. Through custom and habitual use—and, in this case, legislation—people have come to interpret the symbol as a guide to behavior: to stop. Similarly, the red, white, and blue cloth that we know as the American flag has no intrinsic meaning other than that which we have created and accepted.

As humans, we are not only capable of creating events, but also the significance and meaning those events will have for us. Even matters as basic as determining what and how to eat are not solely matters of biology and genetic programming. While some people, for example, look forward with enthusiasm to celebrating a summer holiday with a juicy barbecued steak, a vegan would find that thought revolting. In a similar sense, decisions as to whether to eat with fingers, fork and knife, or chopsticks, and whether to use one's left hand to eat (as would be acceptable in some cultures) or only one's right hand, as is customary in many Muslim cultures, depend on the meanings we have invented and attached to life's circumstances.

## Learning

A bird is born knowing how to build the nest necessary for mating and survival; the instructions are inscribed on the chromosomes of the fertilized egg cell from which it developed. Lightning bugs inherit the knowledge needed to emit and respond to luminescent messages of a potential mate, and bees are apparently born programmed with the information needed to create and interpret the waggle dance. Human beings have to actively learn much of the physical and communication skill that is "natural" for many other animals. As Vickers (1967) has noted, "Insofar as I can be regarded as human, it is because I was claimed at birth as a member of a communication network, which programmed me for participation in itself" (p. 272).

Analytical reflection will remind us of the underlying complexity of human communication. Whether we consider interactions between scientists using mathematical equations, the "value" of the money we carry around in our pockets, the significance we attach to our flag, a spoken exchange between acquaintances, or facial expressions and gestures between colleagues at work, the symbols and their meanings have to be created, agreed upon, and learned to be useful for communication. Their significance is created by us, and they are useful for communication only to the extent that we learn and are able to use them appropriately.

## Subjectivity

The symbols we use in human communication will not necessarily mean the same things to all of us. We relate to messages in a particular way as a product of our experiences. No two of us have precisely the same experiences, and, therefore, no two of us attach precisely the same meaning to the messages around us. To put it differently, we do not all encode and decode messages in the same way. (See Chapter 5 for a more extensive discussion of these concepts.) Furthermore, even one individual may not attach exactly the same meaning to a particular message at different points in time or in different circumstances.

The subjective aspect of human communication extends to all types of symbols—words, art, money, flags, and so on. When two people look at a work of art, for instance, the meanings it will have for them are in part personal, reflecting their own experience. Consider the illustration in Figure 3.8. Some may see an attractive flag hanging in front of a building and not attach any meaning to it beyond admiring its colors. Others may see it as a

**FIGURE 3.8**

What does this symbol mean to you?

© Boumen Japet/Shutterstock.com

symbol of gay pride while others may believe that it signals something about the feelings of the owners of the business in the building. The meanings one attaches to this picture as a whole provide a further illustration of the subjectivity of communication.

Monetary symbols also illustrate the personal nature of human communication. The value of money is subjective. While a child walking in a crowd may bend down to pick up a penny, many adults will not. To some people, a birthday gift of twenty dollars is regarded as generous; for others it may be seen as insignificant.

A recognition that much of communication is subjective and personal has led to the observation that the amazing thing about human communication is not that it sometimes seems to *fail* but, rather, that it ever seems to *succeed.* Is it any wonder that two lovers, colleagues, or countries come away with very different interpretations of who is to blame in a conflict?

## Negotiation

As unique as we and our meanings may be, communication between people generally seems to work pretty well. How can this be? For symbols to work in our efforts to relate effectively to others, our meanings must mesh with the meanings of others. As we engage in communication, we take part in a process of negotiation through which we reconcile our meanings with those of others.

Unlike efforts by management and representatives of a labor union to arrive at terms for a contract, this negotiation process is essentially invisible. It involves individuals adjusting and readjusting the messages they send and the interpretations they attach to the messages of others, in an effort to make sense of, cope with, and adapt to the demands and opportunities that present themselves.

## Culture

The fact that our meanings often seem to mesh reasonably well with others' meanings is no accident, nor is it simply the result of the negotiation that takes place within a given interaction. Rather, we are influenced through our participation in groups, organizations, and as members of society. Through this participation, we establish a commonness of cultural experience with other people through social communication. Our symbols and their meanings become shared and standardized (or *intersubjectified)* and take on an objective quality; that is to say, our symbols come to seem real. Thus, we seldom question whether our money has value or if our words have meaning. With continued use, symbols and their meanings become part of the cultural environment we take for granted.

Through human communication, we create a common culture and a shared view of reality and come to be able to understand one another—to coordinate the meanings for the symbols we use. The more we develop common meanings for symbols with another person, the better the communication process will "work." Store owners who trade pieces of high-quality green paper for goods or services do so because they have learned to attach a similar meaning to the pieces of paper as customers do. Merchants also operate in the belief that the bank and creditors will attach a similar significance to them. When those pieces of paper are "checks," the effectiveness of the communication may dissolve, as the problems of subjective meaning loom large.

Artist Ben Shahn (1972) makes this point very eloquently:

> It is the images we hold in common, the characteristics of novels and plays, the great buildings, the complex pictorial images and their meanings, and the symbolized concepts, principles, and great ideas of philosophy and religion that have created the human community. The incidental items of reality remain without value or common recognition until they are symbolized, recreated, and imbued with value. (pp. 130-131)

## Interacting Contexts and Levels

Human communication operates in various contexts and at various levels. It is the lifeblood of individuals, relationships, groups, organizations, and societies. Intrapersonal, interpersonal, group, organizational, public, mass, and societal communication do not operate in isolation. There is interplay among all levels. The relationships in which we are involved, the groups of which we are members, the organizations we work for, and the society and world community in which we live, all have an impact on our individual communication activities. In turn, intrapersonal communication and the ways we feel and think about ourselves influence our interactions in relationships, groups, organizations, and society, as well as public and mediated communication. Human communication is the web that unites and gives mutuality to the various forms and levels of human activity.

## Self-Reference

The meanings we learn to attach to the symbols we use—and the symbols others use—always reflect our own experiences. As a result, the things we say and do and the way we interpret others' words and actions are a reflection of—and a statement about—our meanings, experiences, needs, and expectations. When people say, "It certainly is cold outside today," "Kimchi is spicy," "That movie was exciting," or "That course is really hard," they are talking as much about their own feelings, meanings, and experiences as about the temperature, Korean food, a movie, or a course.

It is in this sense that human communication is self-referencing and autobiographical: What we see in and say about other people, messages, and events in the environment always says as much about us as it does about them.

## Self-Reflexivity

Another related characteristic of human communication is our capacity for self-reflexiveness or self-consciousness. This human capacity which allows individuals to view themselves as "self," as a part of and apart from their environment, is the core of the communication process (Budd & Ruben, 1987). Because of *self-reflexiveness,* we are able to think about our encounters and our existence, about communication and human behavior. This capability enables us to set goals and measure our progress toward them, to have expectations of ourselves, and to recognize when we have met them. On the other hand, it is also through self-reflexiveness that we recognize our failures, expectations we do not meet, and qualities we admire but do not possess.

It is our capacity for self-reflexiveness that allows us to theorize about ourselves and our experiences— to "get outside ourselves" in order to look at ourselves. In effect, we enter into a relationship with ourselves that is similar in many ways to the relationships we have with others. We talk to ourselves, think about ourselves in particular ways, and "act" in particular ways toward ourselves. Our patterns of self-reflexive communication have great implications for how we talk to, think about, and act toward others. These behaviors, in turn, have consequences for how we relate to ourselves.

## Ethics

Up to this point, we have discussed various approaches to the communication process without acknowledging that there are some very individual choices embedded within this process. Models of communication deal with an idealized process. In real life, however, individuals often have to make some very difficult choices when communicating with others. For example, most societies value honesty as a fundamental principle. But if a friend who has been seriously ill asks "How do I look?" what is an appropriate response? Truthfully, the friend may look very weak, but if we care about our friend's well-being, is it right to be totally honest and say "You look terrible"? In this instance, many well-meaning individuals might try to cheer up the friend by telling the person he or she looks fine even though this response is a lie.

Deciding when or if it is acceptable to deceive others and what type of deception is acceptable is only one instance of the ethical choices we make every day as communicators. Ethical issues arise in all types of communication situations including interpersonal communication, organizational communication, political communication, advertising, and the news media (Johannesen, 1996).

## Inevitability

"We cannot not communicate." This is a phrase coined by Watzlawick, Beavin, and Jackson (1967) to emphasize the point that we are inevitably engaged in the process of creating and processing messages during every waking moment. Our verbal and nonverbal behaviors are ongoing sources of information for others, and, in turn, we are continually and unavoidably processing messages created by the people, circumstances, and objects in our environment, and about ourselves.

From this perspective, we can see the technical inaccuracy of concepts such as "communication breakdown" or "failure to communicate." Communication is always taking place. Messages are inevitably being created and processed. Most often, what are termed "breakdowns" and "failures" result not from the lack of message sending and receiving but, instead, from differing interpretations of messages, expectations, intentions, or outcomes.

## CONCLUSION

In this chapter we have examined visible and invisible characteristics that are fundamental to human communication. Visible characteristics include people, symbols, and media. We create and use symbols and symbolic language. A language, in the most general sense, is a set of characters or elements, and rules for their use in relation to one another. Symbols are characters, letters, numbers, words, objects, people, or actions that stand for or represent something besides themselves. Through the use of technology, symbols have the potential for permanence and portability. For most animals, visual, tactile, olfactory, gustatory, and auditory signals are transitory in nature. Human symbols have significance apart from the situation in which they were originally used and may have a virtually unending existence and use.

Invisible characteristics include meaning, learning, subjectivity, culture, interacting levels and contexts, negotiation, self-reference, self-reflexivity, ethics, and inevitability. Human communication involves meaning. In order to use symbols in communication, their significance and the responses to them must be created. Learning is another characteristic. Animals are born with the knowledge of the meanings to attach to the signals necessary for their survival; humans must learn communication patterns and meanings. The characteristics of words and the sounds of their spoken pronunciation comprise a symbolic code that is useful only to those who have learned to decipher it.

Human communication is subjective. The symbols used in human communication will not necessarily mean the same things to those who create and send messages as they do to those who receive them. People relate to messages in a particular way as a product of their experiences. No two individuals have precisely the same experiences, and no two people attach precisely the same meaning to the messages in the environment.

Negotiation is another characteristic of human communication. When we engage in communication with others, we negotiate a shared culture. Generally, our meanings mesh reasonably well with others' meanings, because others' meanings are learned through social interaction. In this social communication process, symbols and their meanings become shared and standardized—intersubjectified.

Human communication operates in various contexts and at various levels. It is the lifeblood of individuals, relationships, groups, organizations, and societies, and there is interplay between contexts and between levels.

Self-reference is another characteristic of human communication. The meanings we learn to attach to the symbols we use reflect our own experiences. As a result, things that we see in or say about other people, messages, and events in the environment are always autobiographical—they say as much about the person offering the description as they do about the objects being described.

Another related characteristic of human communication is our capacity for self-reflexiveness. Because of our symbol-using capacity we are able to reflect upon ourselves and our actions, to set goals and priorities, to have expectations.

Ethical choices are a very fundamental aspect of everyday communication dynamics. Key ethical considerations include fostering dialogue, valuing diversity, tolerating disagreements, and valuing integrity. Finally, human communication is inevitable. "We cannot not communicate." Our verbal and nonverbal behaviors are ongoing sources of information for others; and, in turn, we are continually and unavoidably processing information about the people, circumstances, and objects in our environment, and about ourselves.

# KEY POINTS

After reading this chapter, you should be able to:
- Analyze the significance of symbols in our daily interaction
- Explain the largely invisible nature of communication and how it differs from commonly observable aspects
- Identify the multiple modes of communication and their related effects
- Describe the main characteristics of the communication process

# REFERENCES

Baker, M. C. (2001). Bird song research: The past 100 years. *Bird Behavior, 14*, 3-50.

Budd, R. W., & Ruben, B. D. (1987). *Beyond media* (2nd ed.). New Brunswick, NJ: Transaction Books.

Johannesen, R. L. (1996). *Ethics in human communication* (2nd ed.). Prospect Heights, IL: Waveland.

Lindauer, M. (1961). *Communication among social bees*. Cambridge, MA: Harvard University Press.

Linden, E. (2002). *The octopus and the orangutan*. New York, NY: Dutton.

Méry, F. (1975). *Animal languages* (M. Ross, Trans.). Westmead, UK: Saxon House.

Rapoport, A. (1973). Man, the symbol user. In L. Thayer (Ed.), *Communication: Ethical and moral issues*. New York, NY: Gordon and Breach.

Schusterman, R. J., Reichmuth, C. J., & Kastak, D. (2000). How animals classify friends and foes. *Current Directions in Psychological Science, 9*, 1-6.

Selve, H. (1956). *The stress of life*. New York, NY: McGraw-Hill.

Shahn, B. (1972). *The shape of content*. Cambridge, MA: Harvard University Press.

Simon, H. (1977). *The courtship of birds*. New York, NY: Dodd, Mead, & Co.

Slater, P.J. B. (2003). Fifty years of bird song research: A case study in animal behavior. *Animal Behavior, 65*, 633-640.

Stumpf, M. P.H. (2001). Language's place in nature. *Trends in Ecology & Evolution, 16*, 475-476.

Vickers, G. (1967). The multivalued choice. In L. O. Thayer (Ed.), *Communication: Concepts and perspectives* (pp. 259-278). Washington, DC: Spartan Books.

Watzlawick, P., Beavin, J. H., & Jackson, D. D. (1967). *Pragmatics of human communication: A study of interactional patterns, pathologies, and paradoxes*. New York, NY: Norton.

Wilson, E. O. (1971). *The insect societies*. Cambridge, MA: Belknap Press.

# CHAPTER 4

# NONVERBAL
# COMMUNICATION

**In this chapter, you will learn about:**

- The definition and components of nonverbal communication
- The differences and similarities between nonverbal and verbal communication
- The importance of nonverbal communication in our daily interactions

## SIMILARITIES BETWEEN NONVERBAL AND VERBAL COMMUNICATION

- Rule-Governed
- Intentionality
- Common Message Functions
- Persuasion and Social Influence

## DIFFERENCES BETWEEN NONVERBAL AND VERBAL COMMUNICATION

- Awareness and Attention
- Overt and Covert Rules
- Control
- Public versus Private Status
- Hemispheric Specialization

## PARALANGUAGE

- Vocalic Forms
- Written Forms

## THE FACE

- Eye Gaze
- Pupil Dilation

## THE BODY

- Hair
- Physique
- Dress and Adornment
- Artifacts

## GESTURES (KINESICS)

- Inherited, Discovered, Imitated, and Trained Actions
- Types of Gestures

## TOUCH (HAPTICS)

## USE OF SPACE (PROXEMICS)

- The Physical Environment

## TIME (CHRONEMICS)

- Timing
- Timeliness

## MESSSAGES AND MEANINGS: MS ≠ MR

## CONCLUSION

## KEY POINTS

Consider the following scenario:

> Chang is wearing a business suit and freshly shined leather shoes. He goes through airport security and walks down the concourse toward the seating area for Gate 14. He walks over to a row of unoccupied chairs, places the briefcase he is carrying on the seat to his right, puts a shopping bag with a Target logo near him on the floor, and sits down. He begins to scan pages of *The Wall Street Journal* on an iPad, glancing periodically at his watch and the screen listing incoming flights.

> After about five minutes have passed, a middle-aged woman dressed in a casual outfit and carrying a large purse walks over and takes a seat directly across from him and begins checking her smart-phone before opening up a book.

> Chang glances up, and his eyes catch hers. She smiles, and he looks away. Chang concentrates his attention on the iPad, but senses that the woman is still looking at him. Finally, he glances up and confirms that she is continuing to stare at him.

> At this point, the woman gets up and walks away. Several minutes later she reappears, walks over to the seat two seats away from Chang and sits down without saying a word. At this point, Chang picks up his briefcase and shopping bag and walks quickly toward a coffee shop near Gate 16. Shortly thereafter, the woman gets up and heads off in the same direction.

Though no words were spoken in this scenario, the individuals' appearances, facial expressions, dress, actions, as well as use of space and time provide important cues that are interpreted and acted upon. Based on the woman's smile, eye contact, and physical movement, Chang concludes that the onlooker may be taking more than a casual interest in him, and he removes himself from the situation.

You probably also formed initial impressions of the two individuals based on nothing more than the sparse description of their nonverbal behavior. For instance, you may have concluded that Chang is:

- A business person or professional
- Waiting for a plane
- Carrying items purchased at Target
- Conscious of the time
- Disinterested in engaging with a stranger

You may assume the woman is:

- Traveling for pleasure not business
- A reader
- Interested in initiating contact with Chang

The formation of your reactions to the characters in this scenario—and theirs to one another—based primarily on nonverbal cues is not unique to this situation. Manusov and Patterson (2006) define nonverbal communication as the process of sending and receiving information through appearance, objects, the environment, and behavior in social settings.

Particularly in circumstances where we are forming first impressions, or where there are conflicts between words and actions, nonverbal messages are often far more influential than verbal ones. In fact, researcher Albert Mehrabian suggests that when we are trying to understand a speaker's intent (e.g., is the word *love* meant sincerely or sarcastically?), the verbal message (the word) accounts for only 7% of our overall impression and the rest is accounted for by nonverbal factors such as tone of voice and facial expression (Mehrabian, 1971; 1972).

Although there are questions as to the exact percentage and questions about the methodologies in some of these studies, it is clear that nonverbal cues are very influential in interpreting meaning. A great many nonverbal factors contribute to the global impressions people form. Sometimes impressions are accurate; often they are incorrect, exaggerated, or incomplete. In the situation described at the beginning of this chapter, our first impressions may be correct. However, a number of other interpretations are possible. The Target shopping bag may have been given to Chang to carry several reports from his office, presents for his family, or items that wouldn't fit in the suitcase he checked earlier. The frequent glances at his watch could have simply been a nervous gesture, and he may have been looking through *The Wall Street Journal* in order to have something to talk to his boss about when he returned home. He might have been passing time before going to work at one of the shops in the airport, waiting for a passenger who would need help with her wheelchair when she arrived on an incoming flight, or was a plainclothes TSA security officer.

The woman in the casual outfit may have been interested in establishing a personal relationship or simply a friendly person with no intentions that involved Chang. Her actions may have been a response to his or any apparent connection could have been coincidental. Or, *she* may have been a member of the security staff with questions about the contents of the shopping bag and growing suspicions about Chang's nervous behavior.

Even from this simple example, three important characteristics of nonverbal communication are apparent:

1. A number of factors influence nonverbal communication.
2. Nonverbal messages generally have any number of potential meanings.
3. The interpretation of nonverbal communication depends on the nonverbal messages themselves and also on the circumstance and the observer.

# SIMILARITIES BETWEEN NONVERBAL AND VERBAL COMMUNICATION

## Rule-Governed

"Rules" might be placed in quotation marks, because these are generally not the sort of guidelines that are written down, formally taught, or officially enforced. Nonetheless, rules and regularities do operate in nonverbal communication, as they can in verbal messages, which we will discuss in the next chapter. Some of these rules pertain to the production of nonverbal messages, and others serve to guide us in interpreting the significance of these messages. To illustrate, there are taken-for-granted rules that we learn to follow when we initiate nonverbal behaviors such as shaking hands when meeting people for the first time in a business context.

**FIGURE 4.1**

Nonverbal cues may have special significance within a particular culture.

© Pikoso/Shutterstock.com

As with verbal messages, some nonverbal patterns are common to the behavior of all individuals. In facial expressions, for instance, studies suggest that there is a predictable relationship among emotions such as happiness, sadness, anger, disgust, surprise, or fear, and distinctive movements of facial muscles regardless of a person's personal and cultural background (Ekman, 1972; Ekman, Friesen & Ellsworth, 1972; Harper, Wiens & Matarazzo, 1978). Gestures, such as head nodding, that we associate with "yes" and "no," as well as crying or laughing also seem to be universal, although their precise meanings may not be. But there are a great many more patterns that are unique to particular individuals, groups, regions, occupations, circumstances, and cultures (see Figure 4.1).

## Intentionality

Unlike verbal messages, which are generally consciously used by people for the purpose of sending specific messages, nonverbal communication is often a more subtle and unintentional process.

While we may consciously use particular facial expressions, gestures, and dress on a first date, job interview, or a group meeting, with the intention of creating a desired effect, there will be many additional unintentional nonverbal messages created in these situations. Unintentional cues might include lowering your eyebrows and tightening your lips in anger, nervousness, or frustration in a particular situation, even when you are trying to appear calm, relaxed, and accepting.

## Common Message Functions

Nonverbal and verbal behavior may have any one of several relationships to one another (Burgoon & Saine, 1978):

- *Redundancy*:  Nonverbal behavior can be used to say the same thing that is being said verbally.  For example, a person says "I am going to sit down" and then walks over to a chair and sits in it.
- *Substitution*:  Signalling something nonverbally rather than saying it.  For example, a handshake may substitute for saying "Hello, it's nice to meet you."
- *Complementation*:  Using nonverbal behavior to supplement or modify what is being transmitted verbally.  For example, smiling and saying, "Come in, I'm glad to see you."
- *Emphasis*:  Using nonverbal behavior to accentuate or punctuate what we are saying verbally. For example, making a fist or shaking your finger to underscore a point being made verbally.
- *Contradiction*:  Using nonverbal behavior to send messages that conflict with the verbal one. For example, saying "Nothing is the matter" in a tone of voice that makes it clear to the hearer that something is wrong.
- *Regulation*: Using nonverbal behavior to regulate communication interactions determining who will speak, for how long, and even when a change in topic will occur.  (adapted from pp. 10-13)

## Persuasion and Social Influence

Like language and verbal communication, nonverbal communication can play a role in the dynamics of persuasion and social influence.  To the extent that people are able to use nonverbal behavior to appear authoritative, credible, or attractive they may also be able to achieve their persuasive goals (Gass & Seiter, 2014).  Burgoon, Guerrero, and Manusov (2011) identify several reasons why nonverbal communication can be an important factor in social influence. For example:

- We can use intentionally provided nonverbal messages such as expressions, gestures, or dress to create positive impressions of ourselves.
- Nonverbal communication including touch, the use of personal space, and eye contact can play an important role in the establishment of rapport and intimacy.

- Nonverbal behavior including gestures or expressions can be used to heighten or detract attention from persuasive verbal messages.
- Nonverbal messages can encourage others to imitate our behaviors.
- Nonverbal messages such as disapproving or encouraging glances can reinforce or discourage others' actions.

# DIFFERENCES BETWEEN NONVERBAL AND VERBAL COMMUNICATION

## Awareness and Attention

During the last several decades, nonverbal communication has emerged as an area of extensive scholarly study and a topic of popular articles and books. Nonetheless, verbal communication continues to receive more formalized attention.

This emphasis is most apparent when we consider the manner in which training in the two areas is handled in schools. Proficiency in verbal communication is, in fact, considered to be so important that it is regarded as one of "the basic skills" and great effort is expended to ensure that we are taught rules of pronunciation, syntax, semantics, and pragmatics as a part of our formal education. Theory and practice in the written and oral use of language are provided at virtually all educational levels.

By comparison, nonverbal skills receive little attention in most schools. Music, dance, art, and physical education are generally included as part of the curriculum. However, no proficiency training comparable to composition, literature, or public speaking is provided for the nonverbal competencies that are so vital to human communication. Often, activities that centrally involve nonverbal communication are before- or after-school or optional activities.

## Overt and Covert Rules

One of the explanations for the relatively greater emphasis placed on verbal communication is that in all cultures there are *overt rules* and structures for language and language use. As a result, guidelines for language use are available from various sources. Nothing comparable exists for nonverbal communication. There are no nonverbal dictionaries or style manuals. And, other than books on etiquette, fashion, and body language, there are no guides to nonverbal usage.

We learn the *covert rules* of nonverbal communication more indirectly, through observation, and subtle—and sometimes not so subtle—patterns of reward and punishment (V. Manusov, personal communication, 2005). Thus, we "know the rules" for greeting and expressing affection to others nonverbally—when to shake hands, for how long, how hard to squeeze the other person's hand, and when hugs and kisses are appropriate—but these rules are covert and not as universally agreed on (see Figure 4.2). Few of us are conscious of their role in governing our behavior or are able to articulate the rules involved.

**FIGURE 4.2**

How to shake hands "correctly" is a learned behavior.

## Control

While we devote considerable attention to managing our nonverbal communication in some situations, we are often more successful in controlling our verbal messages. If the goal is to convey our competence or grasp of a situation, for example, most of us are better able to control the impression we create verbally than nonverbally. Through planning and rehearsal, we will probably be able to gain predictability regarding the messages we will send verbally. However, despite our best efforts to manage our nonverbal behavior, nervousness or embarrassment may be quite apparent through *nonverbal leakage* (nonverbal behavior that contradicts our verbal messages)—a trembling voice or sweaty palm, for instance (Ekman & Friesen, 1969a).

## Public versus Private Status

Language usage patterns have long been regarded as a topic that is appropriate for public discussion and scrutiny. Teachers, parents, or friends are generally quite willing to ask us questions when they don't understand what is being said or to comment when they disagree with what we have said. However, matters relating to our appearance, gestures, mannerisms, and body positions are often considered private, personal, and even taboo topics, and are therefore far less likely topics of open discussion, analysis, or critique.

## Hemispheric Specialization

Another major difference and a topic of scholarly interest is the location in the brain in which nonverbal activities are centered. The left hemisphere of the brain is thought to play a predominant role in language processes (Geschwind, 1982; Ornstein, 1977; Springer & Deutsch, 1981). Other activities that require the sequential processing of information, such as mathematics, also seem to rely heavily on the left hemisphere. The right hemisphere is of special significance in the recognition of faces and body images, art, music, and other endeavors where integration, creativity, or imagination are involved (Springer & Deutsch, 1981).

Studies show that some individuals with damage to the right hemisphere of their brains have difficulty with location and spatial relationships, recognition of familiar faces, or recognition of scenes or objects. Other research, which argues convincingly in favor of right-hemisphere specialization, has shown that even where damage to the language centers in the left hemisphere is so severe that the patients may have difficulty speaking, the ability to sing is often unaffected (Springer & Deutsch, 1981). People with severe stutters can often sing without difficulty, too.

## PARALANGUAGE

We've all heard the phrase, "It's not what you said, but how you said it." What we say—using words, phrases, and sentences—is obviously important to communication. However, the way we use language can be even more important than our words as sources of information. *Paralanguage* refers to any message that accompanies and supplements language. Technically speaking, any supplemental nonverbal message can be viewed as an instance of paralanguage.

## Vocalic Forms

*Vocalics* are auditory messages, other than words, created in the process of speaking (Burgoon & Saine, 1978). Vocalics, which include pitch, rate of speech, rhythm, coughs, giggles, nasality, pauses, and even silence, are very significant sources of impressions in face-to-face communication (Burgoon & Saine, 1978). Recall that Mehrabian found that when an individual is trying to determine his or her feelings about another person, vocalics accounts for nearly 40% of the impression that is formed (Mehrabian, 1972).

Long before children develop skill in language use, they acquire a familiarity with the tonal pattern of the language they hear in their surroundings. Studies suggest that from the tonal contours of their babbling, it is possible to identify the language environment in which children live, even as early as their second year of life (Wang, 1982). In other words, the paralinguistic patterns acquired by children reflect not only the language patterns of the region in which they are being raised (see below), but also the unique patterns of their family and friends.

Accompanying spoken language, paralinguistic cues such as loudness, rate of speaking, tone, interjections, pitch variation, and use of pauses can have a major influence on whether and how one reacts to a person and his or her verbalizations. On the basis of pitch, for example, we are able to determine whether a particular utterance is a statement or a question, a serious comment, or a sarcastic barb. Whether the word *Really* spoken out loud is interpreted as *Really?* or *Really!* is determined through paralanguage rather than through the word itself. In the same way, we decide whether "That's just wonderful" is to be taken literally or to mean quite the opposite.

Pitch is also the difference between whether "Can I help you?" creates a positive or negative impression. Spoken with a raised pitch at the end of the sentence, the sense is one of politeness and genuine interest. The same words spoken in a monotone are likely to be taken as rudeness or disinterest.

Interjections (*nonfluencies*)—such as *like, um, huh,* or *you know*—and stuttering may also have an impact on the way an utterance is interpreted. Remember the teacher who inserted *um* between every other word? Consider the potential difference in the impressions and likely impact created by each of the following:

> *Sam:* Um, like do you want to go like now or later?
> *Bonita:* Do you want to go now or later?

Although the words are essentially the same, the meanings we might attach to these two messages, and the inferences we would draw about their sources, can be quite different. Based on first impressions, would you rather hire Sam or Bonita to represent your company to the public? Who would you prefer to date?

As suggested by previous examples, paralanguage provides a basis for inferences about a speaker, as well as having a potential influence on the impact of the content of the message. Rate of speed and accent, for example, can provide the basis for inferences as to nationality, the region of the country in which the person was raised, and other characteristics associated with stereotypes about the geographic locale. The stereotypical linguistic patterns of the "fast-talking Easterner" or "the slow-speaking Southerner," are often associated with behavioral, as well as geographic, characteristics. Paralanguage can also provide the basis for assumptions about the speaker's educational level, interest in the topic, and mood. Moreover, tone, pitch, rate of speech, and volume provide clues as to an individual's emotional state.

In some languages, paralanguage is even more essential to communication than it is in English. In Chinese, for example, tones determine the meaning of words. Standard Chinese has only four tones:

falling, rising, level, and dipping (or falling and then rising) (Wang, 1982). Changing the tone has the same kind of effect on the meaning of a word as changing a vowel or a consonant would in English.

## Written Forms

Up to this point we have been discussing paralanguage as it relates to *spoken* language. The form of a word or statement is also important to interpretation in *written* language use. The visual appearance of written materials, in terms of punctuation, spelling, neatness, the use of space for margins and between words, whether the document is printed or handwritten, and even the color of ink are likely to influence a reader's reaction to the words and its source (see Figure 4.3).

In written language, paralinguistic cues serve as a basis for generalized inferences as to how educated, careful, respectful, or serious a person is, and may provide clues as to his or her mood or emotions at the time of writing. These, in turn, may affect the way others think about and relate to the author.

**FIGURE 4.3**

In the early 20th century, proper penmanship was such an important part of any correspondence that students in elementary school were taught a particular form of cursive writing called the Palmer Method.

© RG-vc/Shutterstock.com

The use of paralinguistic cues is evident in the conventions developed for communication via email. For example, using capital letters is usually considered SHOUTING. Emoticons or emojis are useful in email and text messaging, but of course can create negative impressions if misused or overused.

## THE FACE

Generally speaking, we react to a person's face holistically (see Figure 4.4). That is, when we look at someone's face, we get an overall impression and seldom think of the face in terms of its distinctive features. Yet as Knapp and Hall (2006) explain:

The human face comes in many sizes and shapes. Faces may be triangular, square, or round; foreheads may be high and wide, high and narrow, low and wide, or protruding; complexions may be light, dark, smooth, wrinkled, or blemished; eyes may be close or far apart, or bulging; noses may be short, long, flat, crooked, "humpbacked," or a "ski slope"; mouths may be large or small with thin or thick lips; and cheeks can bulge or appear sunken. (p. 295)

Beyond their significance in contributing to one's overall appearance, facial expressions serve as message sources in their own right, providing probably the best source of information as to an individual's emotional state—happiness, fear, surprise, sadness, anger, disgust, contempt, and interest (Knapp & Hall, 2006). Our feelings are often, as the adage suggests, "written all over our faces" (see Figure 4.5). It has been estimated that our faces are capable of creating 250,000 expressions. Nevertheless, we don't actually show that many. Researchers estimate there are only about 44 distinct ways in which facial muscles move.

**FIGURE 4.4**

Our holistic understanding of expressions tells us these children are happy.

© Rawpixel/Shutterstock.com

Researchers also believe that the role of the face in relation to emotion is common to all humans. Describing what has been called a "neurocultural theory of facial expression," Ekman, Friesen and Ellsworth (1972) explain: "What is universal in facial expressions of emotion is the particular set of facial muscular movements when a given emotion is elicited" (p. 50). The specific events and circumstances that *trigger* emotions vary from one individual and culture to another (Ekman, 1972), and the customs and rules guiding the *display rules* of particular emotions also may vary from person to person and from culture to culture. Yet, for any emotion, exaggeration, understatement, and masking (deception) may occur (Harper, Weins & Matarazzo, 1978). An employee who needs to keep a job might exaggerate or mask an emotion of disappointment with a smile, for example, when learning that a promised "generous raise" only amounts to 75 cents an hour.

FIGURE 4.5

In addition to contributing to overall appearance, one's face provides the basis for inferences as to one's emotional state, age, mood, interest level, personality, and reaction to events and people.

© Piotr Marcinski, 2014. Shutterstock, Inc.

© Ivy Photos, 2014. Shutterstock, Inc.

© ollyy, 2014. Shutterstock, Inc.

© ollyy, 2014. Shutterstock, Inc.

© ollyy, 2014. Shutterstock, Inc.

© ArtFamily, 2014. Shutterstock, Inc.

© Daniel M. Ernst, 2014. Shutterstock, Inc.

There is also a potential source of messages related to physical attraction and to inferences about age—both reasons why cosmetic products, botox, and plastic surgery have become increasingly popular ways by which people try to take control over the nonverbal messages created through their facial appearance.  In addition, dilated pupils and frequent blinking have been associated with evidence of being less truthful (Riggio & Freeman, 1983).

## Eye Gaze

Probably the most influential features of the face in terms of communication are the eyes. As Ellsworth (1975) notes:

> Unlike many nonverbal behaviors having a potential cue-value that is rarely realized, such as foot movements, [or] subtle facial or postural changes, a direct gaze has a high

probability of being noticed. For a behavior that involves no noise and little movement, it has a remarkable capacity to draw attention to itself even at a distance. (p. 56)

As significant as eye behavior is to human communication, most of us are relatively unsophisticated in our awareness of eye behavior and our ability to describe eye movements with any precision. Among those who study this facet of our nonverbal behavior, a number of terms have been advanced that assist in precise descriptions (Harper, Weins & Matarazzo, 1978).

- *Onesided look:* Gaze by one person in direction of another's face
- *Face-gaze:* Directing of one person's gaze at another's face
- *Eye-gaze:* Directing of one person's gaze at another's eyes
- *Mutual look:* Two persons gaze at each other's face
- *Eye contact:* Two persons look into each other's eyes and are aware of each other's eye gaze
- *Gaze avoidance:* Avoidance of another's eye gaze
- *Gaze omission*: Failure to look at another without intention to avoid eye contact. (p. 173)

In U.S. culture, children are told that "it's not polite to stare" and, as adults, we see frequent reminders of this "rule." If a person in a car stops at a traffic light, and the person in the next car looks interesting in some way, the person may "steal a glance," but must be careful not to appear to stare which could be taken as a sign of an inappropriate level of interest or, in some instances, as a challenging "glare." Similarly, while waiting in a line at a grocery store or sitting in a restaurant or other public place, we may casually glance at the people around us, but at the same time we generally try to avoid "getting caught looking"—and often try to appear as if we are not looking at the other people at all.

Actually, the rule that many adults apply may be stated as, "It's not polite to stare at people you don't know very well, unless you can do so without having them notice you." When and if we are noticed, we pretend not to have been looking, unless the intent is to violate the other's expectations or get them to notice us.

The rules for eye contact with friends and acquaintances are quite different from those for strangers. When conversing verbally with even a casual acquaintance, some degree of mutual eye gaze is customary in U.S. culture. "Looking" may help us grasp the ideas being discussed and is an indication of attention and interest among people in many but not all cultures. Among close friends, extended eye contact is not only acceptable in many cultures, but is expected. In the case of intimate friends and lovers, prolonged glances may be exchanged periodically even when no accompanying words are spoken.

There are a number of other situations where eye glances are optional. For instance, when a speaker such as a teacher asks a question of a large audience, each member of the group may choose to engage with or avoid the glance of the speaker. Generally, students believe that the likelihood of being called on to answer a question is considerably greater if they look at the teacher than if they look away. Depending on the instructor, this may or may not be true.

At what and whom we look, for how long, under what circumstances, whether the gaze is one-sided or mutual, and whether we are engaged in gaze omission or gaze avoidance, provide the basis for inferences as to our focus of attention, interests, intentions, and even attitudes. Looking may be a matter of observing, orienting, inspecting, concealing, avoiding, or searching for pacification (Nielsen, 1962).

Researchers have demonstrated that a primary function of eye gaze, or the lack thereof, is to regulate interaction. Eye contact serves as a signal of readiness to interact, and the absence of such contact, whether intended or accidental, tends to reduce the likelihood of such interaction (Harper, Weins & Matarazzo, 1978). Other studies suggest that eye gaze also plays an important role in personal attraction. In general, in U.S. culture, positive feelings toward an individual and a high degree of eye contact go together. Perhaps for this reason we often assume that people who look in our direction are attracted to us.

A number of factors have been shown in research to be related to the extent of eye gaze, including distance, physical characteristics, personality, topic, situation, and cultural background (Knapp & Hall, 2006). Based on this research, we can predict that, generally, more eye contact will occur when a person is physically more distant from another, when the topic being discussed is impersonal, and when there is a high degree of interest in the other person's reactions. Greater eye contact also occurs when one is trying to dominate or influence others, comes from a culture that emphasizes eye contact during conversation, is generally outgoing, is striving to be included, is listening rather than talking, or is dependent on the other person (Knapp & Hall, 2006).

One would expect less eye gaze between people who are physically close, when intimate topics are being discussed, when there are other relevant objects or people nearby, or when someone is not particularly interested in the other person's reactions or is embarrassed. Similarly, if an individual is submissive, shy, sad, ashamed, attempting to hide something, or of higher status than the person with whom he or she is talking, less eye contact is also likely (Knapp & Hall, 2006). Obviously, these are generalities which may not apply in a given circumstance and, of course, are culturally dependent.

Eye gaze is one area of nonverbal communication in which there are many cultural differences. For example, a student from Greece commented that in his culture it is considered polite to maintain direct eye contact while listening to someone talk. His North American friends continually asked him if something was wrong because they felt that he was "staring at them." In some cultures, it is considered respectful to look down when a person in authority is speaking. In North America, however, parents often criticize children for not listening—a conclusion they reach if children are not making eye contact with them or looking in an appropriate direction while others are speaking to them.

## Pupil Dilation

The pupils of the eye can be an indication of interest or attraction (see Figure 4.6). As we look at people or objects that are seen as appealing, the pupils tend to enlarge; and, in at least some experimental settings, there is evidence that pupil size can be a factor in judgments of a person's attractiveness. In these studies, pictures of females with enlarged pupils were consistently rated as more attractive by males than were those of women with small pupils (Hess, 1975).

The extent to which pupil size is actually a useful source of information

**FIGURE 4.6**

Research suggests that when we look at an individual or object that is of interest to us or is seen as attractive our pupils dilate.

is still a question. Particularly in a culture such as the United States, in which most people stand so far apart during conversations, it is difficult to discern the size of another person's pupils, even when making an effort to do so. In Middle Eastern cultures, however, where the standard distance separating people during conversations is much smaller, information based on pupil size may be more usable by the interactants (Hall, 1979).

## THE BODY

It is said that "Beauty is only skin-deep," and "You can't judge a book by its cover." However, there is little doubt that, particularly when other sources of information are lacking, "surface-level" information plays a critical role in human communication.

Appearance is probably the single most important information source in the formation of initial impressions. Perhaps the most dramatic evidence of the importance of appearance comes from studies of dating preferences, in which perceived attractiveness was more important than such factors as religion, race, self-esteem, academic achievement, aptitude, personality, or popularity, in determining how well individuals would like one another. Evidence from other studies suggests that physical attractiveness is not only important to dating preferences but also is often a predictor of how successful, popular, sociable, sexually attractive, credible, and even how happy people are (Knapp & Hall, 2006). And, of course, what is considered attractive varies by culture.

A number of factors contribute to appearance, among them one's *hair, physique, dress, adornment,* and *artifacts.*

## Hair

Hair style (including facial hair), length, and color are important nonverbal message sources (see Figure 4.7). These factors contribute to what is perceived as overall attractiveness and may also serve as the basis of inferences about a person's personality, age, occupation, attitudes, beliefs, and values.

## Physique

Physique includes body type, size, and shape. Studies have suggested, for example, that inferences may be drawn about personality based on *somatype*—body shape and size. People who appear to be softer or rounder (endomorphs) may be assumed by some people to be affectionate, calm, cheerful, extroverted, forgiving, kind, soft-hearted, or warm. People who appear to be muscular, bony, and athletic-looking (mesomorphs) may

**FIGURE 4.7**
Hair color, length, and style contribute to our perceptions of others.

© mania-room/Shutterstock.com

be stereotyped as active, argumentative, assertive, competitive, confident, dominant, optimistic, or reckless; and people who are tall and thin in appearance (ectomorphs) may be perceived as aloof, anxious, cautious, cool, introspective, meticulous, sensitive, or shy. Although most studies find a match between particular physical traits and people's *perceptions,* there is little correlation between somatypes and actual behavioral characteristics (Knapp & Hall, 2006).

A person's height alone also may provide the basis for negative stereotyping. For males in North American culture, greater height may be associated with positive qualities, while, beyond a certain point, the opposite is the case for females (see Figure 4.8). As Hopper (2012) has pointed out, shorter people are unfairly often portrayed in popular media as villains, liars, or annoying neighbors.

As noted previously, the popularity of cosmetic surgery procedures that enhance or minimize certain physical characteristics speaks quite clearly to the perceived importance of physique in nonverbal communication.

© Okssi/Shutterstock.com

**FIGURE 4.8**
Artifacts may be used to change our perceived height. What would you conclude about the people who choose to wear these shoes?

## Dress and Adornment

Dress fulfills a number of functions for us as human beings, including decoration, physical and psychological protection, sexual attraction, self-assertion, self-denial, concealment, group identification, and display of status or role (Knapp & Hall, 2006). Cosmetics, jewelry, eyeglasses, tattoos, hair weaves, false eyelashes, and body piercings serve many of these same purposes.

As Leathers (1976) has observed: "Our social identity and image is defined, sustained and positively or negatively modified by communication through appearance" (p. 96). Dress is the major facet of appearance through which we can exercise control over the messages we create. We generally assume that people make conscious choices about what they wear and, therefore, take their dress to be an important source of information about them (Manusov, 1991).

The styles and color of dress and adornment also play a noteworthy role in nonverbal communication and may be chosen quite intentionally. Regardless of whether they are intentional or not, our dress often contributes to others' impressions and judgments about our gender identity, age, approachability, financial well-being, social class, tastes, values, cultural background, and other characteristics. For example, do you perceive your professors differently if they wear business attire or more casual outfits like shorts? Are business suits appropriate attire in some classes rather than others, and why?

Badges of various kinds also provide information about a person's identity, status, or affiliations. Dress often serves as an occupational badge, as is generally the case with police officers, nurses, doctors,

FIGURE 4.9

In addition to providing a source of basic information such as age, gender, occupation, and group affiliation, dress also often plays a critical role in first impressions.

© mimagephotography, 2014. Shutterstock, Inc.

© auremar, 2014. Shutterstock, Inc.

© Paul Hakimata Photography, 2014. Shutterstock, Inc.

clergy, military personnel, and members of particular athletic teams. In such instances, the uniforms people wear are designed, standardized, and worn with the intention of sending a particular set of messages. The "uniforms" of college students, business-people, or factory workers may serve much the same function, though they are not necessarily intended to do so (see Figure 4.9).

Other badges are hats, shirts, sweatshirts, or jackets that bear the name of an individual, school, employer, manufacturer, favorite motorcycle or car, concert or musical performer. Specialized jewelry such as wedding or engagement rings, or a necklace with a name or religious symbol, may also serve to provide information about someone's identity, status, group, or organizational affiliation.

## Artifacts

We surround ourselves with artifacts—toys, technology, furniture, decorative items, and so on. Our cars and homes are also artifacts (or objects) that provide additional messages from which others may draw inferences about our financial resources, aesthetic preferences, personality, status, or occupation. Business cards, briefcases, a particular brand of cellphone, laptop, or car, may serve as artifactual cues to which others react as they form impressions (see Figure 4.10).

**FIGURE 4.10**

Some people like to surround themselves with artifacts while working, yet others would perceive this environment as totally disorganized.

© bikeriderlondon/Shutterstock.com

# GESTURES (KINESICS)

Movements of body, head, arms, legs, or feet—technically labeled *kinesics*—play a very critical role in human communication. Gestures, as well as other cues, may either be *purposeful*—messages which are intended to achieve a particular purpose—or *incidental* and *unintended*. Some gestures may be used as complements for language, such as shaking your head back and forth while saying the word *no* when asked a question. In other instances, we use gestures in place of words. In U.S. culture, a shrug of the shoulders, for instance, is used to indicate confusion or uncertainty, a frown and slow horizontal back-and-forth motion of the head to indicate frustration or annoyance, or the circle sign made by the thumb and the forefinger to mean "OK."

Studies suggest that we progress in the development of our capacity for gesturing through four basic stages (Wood, 1976).  In the first stage, from birth to three months, irregular, jerky movements of an infant's body indicate excitement and distress. In the next stage, three to five months, infants are able to move their bodies more rhythmically in patterns associated with anger and delight. In the third stage, five to 14 months, children develop specialized gestures such as making faces, head turning, and poking. Between the ages of 14 and 24 months, children are able to express affection for particular people, as well as joy and jealousy, through contact movements such as poking, hitting, and caressing.

## Inherited, Discovered, Imitated, and Trained Actions

Anthropologist Desmond Morris (1977) suggests that people acquire their gestures through *inheritance, discovery, imitation,* and *training*.

*Inherited* (inborn) gestures include include the sucking response of a baby and the use of body contact gestures as a part of courtship.

Some gestures we *discover* as we identify the limitations and capabilities of our bodies. The way people cross their arms is an example. There is little variation from one culture to another, but there are differences between individuals within any one culture, and each individual tends to be fairly consistent over time. Some of us fold left hand over right, and others right over left. Regardless of which we have become accustomed to, it is difficult to reverse the pattern without considerable effort (Morris, 1977), as shown in Figure 4.11.

We acquire many of our gestures unknowingly from the people around us as we grow up. The typical handshake, for instance, is acquired through *imitation*, as are many other greeting forms and cultural and subcultural mannerisms.

Actions such as winking, playing tennis, jumping on one foot, whistling, or walking on your hands, require active *training* in order to master. The wink, for example, taken so much for granted by an adult, is a formidable challenge for a child. Like other trained actions, substantial observation and systematic effort is required to master it.

**FIGURE 4.11**

We develop a pattern for crossing our arms. Try this experiment: cross your arms and then reverse them. How does that feel?

© Gelpi JM/Shutterstock.com

## Types of Gestures

There are many ways of classifying gestures. An extensive list provided by Morris (1977) includes the following:

**BATON SIGNALS AND GUIDE SIGNS.** One type of gesture, the *baton signal,* is used to underscore or emphasize a particular point being made verbally. Examples of baton signals include a downward clipping motion of the hand, a forward jabbing movement of the fingers and hand, and the raised forefinger. Another similar kind of gesture is the *guide sign,* by means of which we indicate directions to others, as when we point, direct, or beckon another person nonverbally.

**YES/NO SIGNALS.** *Yes/no signals* are a category of gesture created primarily by movements of the head. While many gestures are unique to one or several cultures, the vertical "yes" head nod appears to be fairly universal.  While the gesture may be universal, the meaning may differ.  Even though we might assume that the meaning of the "yes" nod is fairly specific, there are a number of variations:

> *The acknowledging nod:* "Yes, I am still listening."
> *The encouraging nod:* "Yes, how fascinating."
> *The understanding nod:* "Yes, I see what you mean."
> *The agreeing nod*: "Yes, I will."
> *The factual nod:* "Yes, that is correct." (Morris, 1977, p. 68)

In North American culture, the "no" gesture consists of a horizontal movement of the head. In many other parts of the world a side-to-side swaying of the head is also used to say "maybe yes, maybe no." In addition to the head, the hand and fingers can also be used to express yes–no signals. For instance, in North American culture a shaking of the forefinger from side to side is a way of saying "no." Again it is important to recognize the existence of cultural differences. For example, a quick upward nod of the head can mean "no" in Greece.

**GREETINGS AND SALUTATION DISPLAYS.** The most familiar greeting forms are the handshake, embrace, and kiss by which people signal their pleasure at someone's arrival or the significance of their departure.

There are several stages in the greeting or salutation process (Morris, 1977). The first phase is the *inconvenience display.* To show the strength of our friendliness, we "put ourselves out" to varying degrees. Such gestures may involve standing to welcome a guest, "dressing up," or other preparations in anticipation of the guest's arrival. For the guest it may mean a long journey. If this is the case, the host may make an effort to meet a guest at a train station or airport—as when a members of a family drive to the airport to greet a family member returning from a trip.

The second stage is the *distant display.* From the moment the guest and host see each other, they can indicate the other's presence by several other gestures including a smile, eyebrow flash, head tilt, wave, and sometimes an outstretching of arms indicating an upcoming embrace. As the two individuals approach one another, they may signify pleasure at the other's presence by hugging, squeezing, patting, kissing, or pressing their checks together, perhaps with extended eye contact, laughing, smiling, or even crying. The particular greeting used depends on a number of factors including the nature of the relationship, the situation in which they are meeting one another, the length of time that has passed since they have seen one another, and the extent of change in either person's status since they were together.

**TIE SIGNS.** The *bonding* or *tie sign* is a category of gesture through which individuals indicate that they are in a relationship. In much the same way that wedding rings or matching clothing signal a relationship between two or more people, certain gestures may serve the same purpose. As illustrated in Figure 4.12, gestures such as handholding, linked arms, two people sharing food from the same plate, and close physical proximity when sitting or walking provide the basis for impressions about the individuals and the nature of their relationship even in the absence of verbal messages.

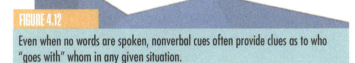

**FIGURE 4.12**

Even when no words are spoken, nonverbal cues often provide clues as to who "goes with" whom in any given situation.

© Blend Images/Shutterstock.com

**ISOLATION GESTURES.** Other common gestures include body positioning, such as crossing arms or legs, which can conceal or block portions of the body from view. In some instances, *isolating gestures* may serve as intentional messages, though more often they are less purposeful. These and other gestures called barrier signals or auto-contact behaviors include hugging yourself, supporting your chin or cheek with a hand or arm, and touching your mouth, and may signal discomfort or anxiety even though we may be unaware of these feelings (Morris, 1977). According to Ekman and Friesen (1969b), these kinds of gestures—which they term adaptors or manipulators—tend to increase with anxiety.

**OTHER GESTURES.** Gestures also play a major role in courtship, mating, and sexual contact. Hand holding, kissing, stroking, and forms of sexual contact often serve these functions, as does *preening behavior*—for instance, stroking or flipping your hair, adjusting makeup or clothing, or stroking your own arms or legs to call attention to yourself or increase your attractiveness (Knapp & Hall, 2006).

In some religious practices, gestures of various kinds also have significant functions. Kneeling, standing at appropriate times, bowing, and folding or extending your hands in prayer are symbolic means through which people may participate in the central rituals of a faith.

# TOUCH (HAPTICS)

When a gesture is extended to the point where physical contact is involved, tactile messages are created. For human beings, the significance of tactile messages, also known as *haptics,* begins well before birth in the prenatal contact between mother and infant. From the first moments of life, touch is the primary means by which children and parents relate to one another. Through this tactile mode, feeding takes place and affection is expressed.

During the early years of our development, touch continues to be the central means for expressions of warmth and caring among family members and close friends. Beginning with the preschool and elementary years, physical contact also takes on a role in play and sports. During this period, we also learn the significance of tactile messages in greeting rituals such as handshakes, hugs, or kisses.

In the teenage and preadult years, touching takes on increasing significance in expressions of warmth, love, and intimacy. Tactile messages are important in athletic endeavors, in the actual activity of the sport and in the pats and slaps of assurance and encouragement among players and coaches.

Two of the interesting facets of tactile messages are their range of uses. Among adults, most physical contact is associated with informal greetings and gestures of departure between friends and colleagues. Tactical messages are also associated with expressions of intimacy and sexual activities, and with expressions of hostility and aggression. Because of their multiple uses, tactile messages can be sources of ambiguity and potential discomfort, and translating the meaning of specific tactile behavior can be a challenge. The situations in which these messages occur often provide additional cues that help with the interpretive process.

In health care settings, for example, one of the sources of discomfort for some patients is the fact that examinations and treatment involve being touched by relative strangers in a manner that we normally associate with intimate relations. Depending on the circumstance, people involved, and the culture, touch may lead us to react more intensely than we normally would to verbal or other nonverbal cues. Touching another person without his or her consent is regarded in many societies as far more disturbing than verbal abuse or obscene gestures.

That said, levels of contact and comfort with touching vary to some extent from one culture to another. In some Asian or African cultures, for example, male friends may walk down the street hand-in-hand as they talk. In Middle Eastern cultures, casual acquaintances stand so close together when talking that North Americans may assume they are intimates. By comparison, North Americans typically go to great lengths to avoid unnecessary touching in public settings whenever possible. In an elevator or crowded shopping mall, for instance, North Americans touch strangers only when necessary and often experience discomfort while doing so (Knapp & Hall, 2006).

# USE OF SPACE (PROXEMICS)

The use of space, *proxemics,* plays an important role in human communication in its own right and in conjuction with other modes of nonverbal and verbal behavior. To some extent the discomfort and intensity of reactions sometimes associated with tactile messages, as discussed above, occur because we each have well-defined expectations as to how much personal space we will have around us, though we are often less than fully aware of these expectations.

It can feel uncomfortable when our *personal space,* the "portable territory" we carry with us from place to place, is "invaded." Being bumped unnecessarily in an elevator, having our beach towel stepped on by someone we don't know, or being unnecessarily crowded while shopping generally cause us discomfort for this reason. A typical response is to readjust our own position to regain the amount of space we think we need. Research suggests that in some instances the extreme violation of personal space over time, such as occurs in extremely large crowds and very high density neighborhoods, contributes to frustration, intense reactions, and sometimes aggression.

Edward Hall (1959) has done much to broaden our understanding of the way space is used during face-to-face conversations. He found that the distance between North American interactants varied predictably depending on the setting and the content of conversation:

- *Public conversations:* 12 feet to the limits of visibility
- *Informal and business conversations:* 4 to 12 feet
- *Casual conversations:* 1½ to 4 feet
- *Intimate conversations:* 0 to 18 inches

Fluctuations in each category depend on a number of factors: the culture in which the conversation takes place, the ages of the interactants, topic being discussed, setting, nature of the relationship, attitudes and feelings of the individuals, and so on (Knapp & Hall, 2006).

The use of space and position is also important in seating (see Figure 4.13). In a group situation,

**FIGURE 4.13**

Body positioning and the way space is used play important roles in human interaction.

© Rawpixel/Shutterstock.com

for instance, certain positions are more often associated with high levels of activity and leadership than others. Being in front of a group, separated more from the group as a whole than are any of the individual members from one another, affords the isolated individual a position of distance, insularity, and authority. Examples are a teacher in front of a class, a judge in front of the court, a religious leader at the front of the church, and so on.

A person's position within a large room—a classroom, for example—can also have an influence on verbal behavior. In typical classes, over 50% of the comments are initiated by class members located in the front and center positions within the room, referred to as the "participation zone." For many individuals, position is the most influential factor explaining their participation (Knapp & Hall, 2006). In smaller groups, particularly where furniture is involved, the head of the table is traditionally a position of leadership, honor, respect, and power.

In a conference room, a similar association often exists with the person sitting at the head of a table. Some researchers have found, for instance, that in experimental jury deliberations, the person sitting at the head of the table was chosen much more often as leader than people in other positions (Strodtbeck & Hook, 1961).

Thus, our use of space and positions relative to others, whether in silence or active conversation, and how, when, and where we stand or sit can be significant factors that contribute to others' impressions of us and ours of them, and in shaping communication behavior more generally.

## The Physical Environment

Our buildings, furniture, decor, lighting, and color schemes are the result of human decision making (see Figure 4.14). In addition to providing shelter and housing, and facilitating our various activities, the man-made elements of our physical environment also serve a number of informational functions—some intentionally, many by accident.

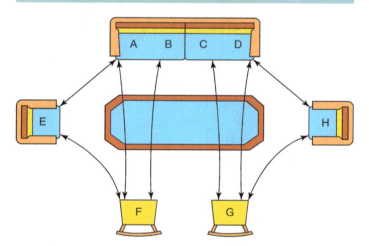

**FIGURE 4.14**

The arrangement of furniture and seating patterns play an important role in the level and direction of conversation. All other things being equal, the pairs marked by arrows would engage in the most frequent conversation. Those persons seated on the couch would be least likely to engage in interaction.

From *Public Places and Private Spaces: The Psychology of Work, Play and Living Environment* by Albert Mehrabian. Copyright © 1976 by Basic Books, Inc. Reprinted by permission of Basic Books, a member of the Perseus Book Group.

Whether we think of the arrangement of furniture and the selection of wall hangings in our homes, the design and furnishing of an elegant restaurant, the layout of a shopping mall, or the architecture of a massive airport complex, all have much in common in terms of communication.

DIRECTING BEHAVIOR. Each environment with its furniture, decor, and colors serves as a source of information that may have an impact on the people present. Some of the information is "designed-in" by the architect or designer to shape the way the environment or its parts are used. Sidewalks in a park, for example, direct our movement as we walk about. Similarly, chairs used in some fast-food restaurants are designed to be comfortable for only a fixed period of time and may well influence our decisions about how long to remain in the environment.

PROVIDE SYMBOLIC VALUE. Structures and their contents, by virtue of their size, shape, use of space, and decor, may also have symbolic significance for us. Religious buildings and their contents are often symbolic by their very nature. Large rooms with high ceilings, stained glass windows, dimly lit interiors, deep colors, and sacred books and objects, each have information value to those who use the environment.

The symbolic properties of houses of worship have their parallels in shopping malls, parks, restaurants, as well as in the structure and decor of homes and apartments. The differences, for instance, between being invited to dine in a candlelit room with elegantly upholstered armchairs and soft music compared to the experience of having dinner at the counter of a truck stop or diner are quite substantial.

REGULATING INTERACTION. Environments may also provide the basis for information that regulates—encourages or discourages—interaction. The private study carrels in a library, for example, serve to separate and isolate their users, discouraging interaction, while a business office with no private offices or partitions encourages interchange. In a similar sense, a classroom with permanently attached chairs contributes to "one-way" message flow (Sommer, 1969).

# TIME (CHRONEMICS)

The use of time and timing—*chronemics,* as it is technically called—is another critical, and often overlooked, factor in communication. In fact, the reactions to our words and deeds may depend far more on *when* we speak or act than on the content of the interaction.

# Timing

Timing plays a role in interaction at two levels of analysis: (1) micro and (2) macro. Micro-conversational time-use characteristics include the speed at which we talk, the number and extent of pauses and interruptions, our "talk-to-silence" ratio, and our patterns of conversational turn taking. These factors can be important in terms of message transmission, reception, and interpretation; and each also serves as a basis for the formation of impressions about the people involved in the interaction. Too little talking, for instance, can be perceived as disinterest, shyness, or boredom; whereas too much talking can be construed as aggressiveness, self-assuredness, presumptuousness, overconfidence, self-preoccupation, or rudeness.

At the macrolevel are our more general decisions as to whether to even engage in conversation at a particular point in time. The decisions we make about when to speak and when to be silent, when we have said too much and when too little, when to "speak our piece," and when to "suck it up" and "keep it to ourselves" are some of the most critical decisions we make relative to communication.

# Timeliness

Individuals and cultures vary in the extent to which they think of time as a commodity. Sayings like "Time is money," "Never put off until tomorrow what you can do today," and "The sooner the better" reflect a view that time is a scarce commodity that needs to be carefully managed. "Haste makes waste" and "Take time to smell the roses" emphasize the importance of taking time to appreciate and enjoy experiences.

Given the significance of time in the daily lives of many individuals, it is not surprising that the way time is used can have an important impact on nonverbal communication and behavior. Being "early" or "late" is a message—the significance of which depends largely on the way those involved think about time. The meaning provided by such messages also varies depending on a number of factors, including the amount of time we are early or late, the purpose of an appointment, the length of the relationship between the people involved, the relative status of the parties involved, or the culture in which the communication takes place, for example.

Being 15 minutes late for a job interview can lead to the cancellation of the appointment, while being 15 minutes late for the start of a party may result in being embarrassingly "early." Being late for a business meeting carries different consequences than being late for a social engagement. Arriving an hour late—even with a good reason—for a first date will probably be reacted to differently than being late for dinner with one's spouse. In such circumstances, timeliness and the use of time—being on time, late, or early—may be as significant a source of information to other people as whatever one does or says after arriving.

In addition to individual differences, there are also significant intercultural differences in the use of time. Viewing time as a scarce commodity to be carefully managed is common to many North Americans. The faster things get done, the less time is "wasted." In Latin America and the Middle East, "rushing" to get things done is often less of a preoccupation. Arriving at a social engagement at a time that a Canadian would consider "late" would be considered "on time" or even "early" in Ecuador.

Individual and cultural differences in the meaning of time, along with other cultural differences relative to nonverbal communication, are extremely important to learn about, understand, and respect.

# MESSAGES AND MEANINGS: MS ≠ MR

We have seen how nonverbal behaviors play a pervasive role in human communication. Nonverbal message-making is natural, inevitable, and constant. Individuals create any number of nonverbal messages that can and often do become significant to others. Sometimes the behaviors are intentional, like wearing team-related clothing to a sporting event or waving your hand in greeting. Often they are accidental, like blushing or catching the eye of a stranger while waiting in a line.

The nonverbal behaviors of any one individual contribute to the vast array of messages in the environment that surround us at any point in time and compete for our attention and interest.

It is important to keep in mind that the presence of particular nonverbal messages in the environment provides little or no assurance that they will be attended to or interpreted in a particular way. Eye contact intended as a sign of interest by one person may be read as aggressiveness by another; a gesture interpreted as an isolation gesture by one person may be regarded as a way of keeping warm in a cold room to others. Verbal and nonverbal behaviors are *sources* of meaning, but they are not, in and of themselves, *meaningful*, with the possible exception of facial expressions that accompany universal emotions.

The meanings of verbal and nonverbal messages depend not only on the messages that are available, but also on our individual ways of processing information and on our social interactions with others. Whether we regard a particular person as attractive or intelligent will depend minimally on: (1) the nonverbal and verbal behaviors of the person; (2) the way we personally attend to and interpret those behaviors; and (3) the social interactions with our peers and other members of our society that have helped to define and shape our notion of what constitutes attractiveness or intelligence.

To determine the meanings of particular messages, we have to look beyond the nonverbal and verbal messages to the processes involved in information reception. We must look also to the relationships, groups, organizations, cultures, and societies which provide the contexts in which nonverbal and verbal messages are created, shared, and interpreted. Each of these topics will be examined in detail in subsequent chapters.

# CONCLUSION

Nonverbal behavior plays an important role in human communication. There are a number of similarities between verbal and nonverbal communication. They: (1) are rule-governed; (2) make possible the production of unintended, as well as purposeful, messages; and (3) share a variety of message functions in common.

There are also key differences: (1) Compared to language, there has been a lack of awareness and attention to nonverbal cues and their impact on behavior; (2) nonverbal communication involves rules that are primarily covert rather than overt; and (3) verbal message processing is thought to occur primarily in the left hemisphere of the brain, while the right hemisphere is essential for processing information related to nonverbal activity.

Paralanguage, appearance, gestures, touch, space, and time are six primary sources of nonverbal messages. Appearance plays an important role in interpersonal relations, particularly in initial impressions. Dress, adornment, and physique are facets of appearance that serve as potential information sources. The face is a central aspect of one's appearance, providing the primary source of information as to one's emotional state. Hair also can be an important message source.

The eyes are perhaps the most important component of the facial system in terms of communication. Based on direction and duration of eye gaze, or the absence thereof, cues are provided that serve as the basis of inferences as to interest, readiness to interact, and attraction. Pupil size may also be important.

Gestures are potential sources of information. Among the most common types of gestures are: baton signals and guide signs, yes/no signals, greetings and salutation displays, tie signs, and isolation gestures.

Touch is another source of messages that plays a central role in greetings, the expression of intimacy, and acts of aggression. The intensity of reactions to tactile cues is suggestive of the importance of space in communication. When our personal space is invaded in other than intimate relationships, discomfort—and often a "fight or flight" reaction—results.

The significance of spatial cues is also apparent in seating patterns. Certain seating positions may be associated with high levels of participation and leadership. The nature and placement of elements in the physical environment—furniture, decor, lighting, and color schemes—also generate messages that are potentially significant to behavior. They often provide cues that influence their use, symbolic value, and interaction patterns.

Time, timing, and timeliness can also be significant in the communication process. The way time is shared in conversations, for instance, can be a source of information that is even more influential than the content of those discussions. Timeliness—being considered "late" or "early"—can itself be a potential information source. Substantial cultural variations exist.

Our verbal and nonverbal behaviors—some intentionally enacted—create a pool of messages that is part of the environment that surrounds us. The presence of verbal and nonverbal messages provides no assurance that they will be attended to or be of particular significance to individuals within that environment. Messages sent (intentionally or not) do not equal messages received.

## KEY POINTS

After reading this chapter, you should be able to:

- Define nonverbal commnunication
- Explain the differences between verbal and nonverbal communication
- Analyze the significance of the components of nonverbal communication and their effect in our daily interactions
- Assess the impact of nonverbal messages in the communication process

## REFERENCES

Burgoon, J. K., Guerrero, L. K., & Manusov, V. (2011). Nonverbal signals. In M. L. Knapp & J. A. Daly (Eds.), *Handbook of interpersonal communication* (4th ed., pp. 239-286). Thousand Oaks, CA: Sage.

Burgoon, J. K., & Saine, T. (1978). *The unspoken dialogue: An introduction to nonverbal communication.* Boston, MA: Houghton Mifflin.

Ekman, P. (1972). Universal and cultural differences in facial expressions of emotions. In J. K. Cole (Ed.), *Nebraska symposium on motivation* (Vol. 20, pp. 207-283). Lincoln, NE: University of Nebraska Press.

Ekman, P., & Friesen, W. V. (1969a). Nonverbal leakage and clues to deception. *Psychiatry, 32*(1), 88-106.

Ekman, P., & Friesen, W. V. (1969b). The repertoire of nonverbal behavior: Categories, origins, usage, and coding. *Semiotica, 1*(1), 49-98.

Ekman, P., Friesen, W. V., & Ellsworth, P. C. (1972). *Emotion in the human face: Guidelines for research and an integration of the findings.* New York, NY: Pergamon Press.

Ellsworth, P. C. (1975). Direct gaze as a social stimulus: The example of aggression. In P. Pliner, L. Krames, & T. Alloway (Eds.), *Nonverbal communication of aggression* (pp. 5-6). New York, NY: Plenum.

Gass, R. H., & Seiter, J. S. (2014). *Persuasion: Social influence and compliance gaining* (5th ed.). Boston, MA: Pearson/Allyn & Bacon.

Geschwind, N. (1982). Specializations of the human brain. In W. S.-Y. Wang (Ed.), *Human communication: Language and its psychobiological bases* (pp. 110-119). San Francisco, CA: W. H. Freeman.

Hall, E. T. (1979, August). Learning the Arabs' silent language. *Psychology Today,* 47-48.

Hall, E. T. (1959). *The silent language.* New York: Doubleday.

Harper, R. G., Wiens, A. N., & Matarazzo, J. D. (Eds.). (1978). *Nonverbal communication: The state of the art.* New York, NY: Wiley.

Hess, E. H. (1975). *The tell-tale eye.* New York, NY: Van Nostrand Reinhold.

Hopper, T. (2012, September 7). A diminutive history of height: How being short has its disadvantages. Retrieved from http://news.nationalpost.com/news/canada/a-diminutive-history-of-height-how-being-short-has-its-disadvantages

Knapp, M. L., & Hall, J. A. (2006). *Nonverbal communication in human interaction* (6th ed.). Belmont, CA: Thomson Wadsworth.

Leathers, D. G. (1976). *Nonverbal communication systems.* Boston, MA: Allyn and Bacon.

Manusov, V. (1991). Unpublished notes on nonverbal communication.

Manusov, V., & Patterson M. L. (Eds.). (2006). *The Sage handbook of nonverbal communication.* Thousand Oaks, CA: Sage.

Mehrabian, A. (1971). *Silent messages.* Belmont, CA: Wadsworth.

Mehrabian, A. (1972). *Nonverbal communication.* Chicago, IL: Aldine-Atherton.

Morris, D. (1977). *MANWATCHING: A field guide to human behavior.* New York, NY: Harry N. Abrams.

Nielsen, G. (1962). *Studies of self-confrontation.* Copenhagen, DK: Munksgaard.

Ornstein, R. E. (1977). *The psychology of consciousness.* San Francisco, CA: Freeman.

Riggio, G. R. & Freeman, H. S. (1983). Individual differences and cues to deception. *Journal of Personality and Social Psychology, 45,* 899-915.

Sommer, R. (1969). *Personal space.* Englewood Cliffs, NJ: Prentice Hall.

Springer, S. P., & Deutsch, G. (1981). *Left brain, right brain.* San Francisco, CA: Freeman.

Strodtbeck, F., & Hook, L. (1961). The social dimensions of a twelve man jury table. *Sociometry, 24,* 397-415.

Wang, W. S.-Y. (1982). The Chinese language. In W. S.Y. Wang (Ed.), *Human communication: Language and its psychobiological bases* (pp. 52-62). San Francisco, CA: W. H. Freeman.

Wood, B. S. (1976). *Children and communication.* Englewood Cliffs, NJ: Prentice Hall.

# CHAPTER 5

# VERBAL
# COMMUNICATION

**In this chapter, you will learn about:**

- The significance of verbal communication in our daily lives
- The stages through which language develops and is interpreted
- The connection between language and reality
- The ways that verbal messages are used to construct meaning in our everyday interactions.

## MESSAGE PRODUCTION

## ENCODING AND DECODING

## MESSAGE- VERSUS MEANING-CENTERED MODELS OF COMMUNICATION

## THE NATURE OF LANGUAGE

- Cognitive Factors
- Acquiring Our Language Capability

## REPRESENTATION

- Language and Reality
- Limitations of Language for Representation

## CONVERSATION

- Negotiation of Meanings
- Rules and Rituals
- Language and Gender
- Content and Relationship
- Metacommunication
- Microaggressions

## PERSUASION AND SOCIAL INFLUENCE

- Compliance-Gaining
- Social Influence

## CONCLUSION

## KEY POINTS

## MESSAGE PRODUCTION

As we have seen, nonverbal communication is a fundamental aspect of human behavior. The same is true for verbal communication and perhaps even more obviously so. As a way to open our discussion of language and verbal communication, consider the following scenario that involves a number of facets of communication. Consider the following description of a job interview:

It's job search time. A friend texts you about a job that is available in your area. You exchange more details via email, and then you check the organization's website for more details. You update your resume, prepare a cover letter, create pdfs of both of them, and upload them to the company's site.

Several weeks later you get an email expressing interest in your application, and a preliminary phone interview is scheduled.

You didn't do particularly well on your last interview so you know that it's critical to spend time preparing. You go online to gather information about the organization and then plan what you'll say if you're asked why you want the position and why you aren't working right now. You also make up a list of questions you would like to ask the recruiter and give some thought to the kind of impression you would like to create.

When the day of the interview arrives, you receive a call from a person who identifies himself as a preliminary screener from the Human Resources department.

All seems to go well, and a week later you receive a call to schedule an in-person interview. You review your notes from the phone interview, ask your friends and family what they know about the organization, and review your responses to questions you anticipate being asked. Because you learned in an interviewing class that you are expectd to show interest in the organization when you are interviewed, you develop a longer list of questions you would plan to ask.

On the interview day, you give some thought to your dress, make decisions you think would be appropriate, and plan to arrive about 10 minutes early. You feel well-prepared and are ready to make a good impression. When the interviewer appears, you greet her enthusiastically with "Hello. How are you?," shake her hand, and take a seat next to the desk.

As the questioning begins, you try to respond in a way that will lead the interviewer to see you as comfortable yet not too informal, interested but not overly assertive, composed yet spontaneous, self-assured but not arrogant, interested in the job but not desperate.

After about an hour, the interviewer says that she has no more questions and asks if you do. You ask about starting salary, opportunities for advancement, benefits, and when she anticipates that a hiring decision will be made—questions you selected because they would yield information you need and also reinforce the impression of your competence and experience.

After brief responses, the interviewer thanks you for coming in and indicates that she will be in touch with you as soon as all the applicants for the position have been considered. You respond, "Thanks," stand, shake her hand, and depart.

Now let's examine this situation from the organization's point of view. The task of finding a qualified person was initiated long before the interview, with the collection of information and the preparation of the job description and posting of the job advertisement. While the job ad is the message of most immediate relevance, in a more general sense, the firm's recruitment process actually began with the advertising and public relations efforts they have engaged in over the years—all designed to enhance their visibility and positive reputation.

After screening many applications, the list of people to be interviewed by phone, and then in-person, was finalized. Their goals for the interview itself were to create a positive, yet realistic, impression of the organization and the job and to evaluate candidates' suitability for the position.

Questions were asked from a standardized interview guide that was developed for use with all applicants. They were designed to help probe candidates' technical qualifications, while giving the interviewer a sense of how much "homework" applicants had done to prepare for the interview, what relevant experience candidates had, how composed and confident they were, how they approached problems, and how they dealt with people. Typical interview questions include:

- How did you learn about this position?
- Are you familiar with our company?
- Why did you apply for this position? What made it of particular interest to you?
- Can you tell me a bit about the university you attended and your major? Why did you select that school? That field?
- What extracurricular activities have you participated in?
- Did you hold any leadership positions in student organizations?
- How do you believe your experiences in school prepared you for this position?
- What work experiences have you had that are relevant to this job?
- What would you describe as your greatest strengths and weaknesses?
- What are your long-term career objectives?

# ENCODING AND DECODING

In a situation such as the one described, each party is putting forth a good deal of effort to provide information, to create particular kinds of impressions, and also to gather information that will be helpful to decision-making.

Each of the individuals involved have specific goals in mind and communicate in ways designed to achieve them. This message-sending process—converting an idea into a message—is termed *encoding*. Each person is also hoping that the messages they are creating will be *decoded*—translated into an idea—that is more or less as they intended.

In the interview example, each person is seeking to inform and also, to a certain extent, persuade the other. The interviewer is seeking to share relevant information about the company and job; and the candidate, in turn, wants to share pertinent information about his or her experience and qualifications. At the same time, each party hopes to convince the other of their interest in the situation and one another. And assuming each sees that the potential fit of the candidate with the job is good, additional effort is put forth—by the HR representative to promote the virtues of the company and job, and by the interviewee to promote his or her own qualities, capabilities, and potential for contributing to the company.

Even in circumstances like the job interview—where participants have a clear idea of the meaning they want to convey through their messages—they are also likely to communicate information that is unintended. This happens no matter how well we plan or rehearse. An inappropriate greeting, uncertainty in responding to a question, a shaky voice, an abrupt change of topic, a poorly constructed phrase, the lack of eye contact, misspelled words on a resume, a misused word in responding to a question, talking too much or too little, or "overselling," can easily have as much—or more—impact as the messages we try to encode intentionally (see Figure 5.1).

**FIGURE 5.1**

An accurate and carefully proofread resume is essential.

"Everything on your resume is true ... right?"

© Cartoonresource/Shutterstock.com

## MESSAGE- VERSUS MEANING-CENTERED MODELS OF COMMUNICATION

As we discussed in Chapter 2, many of the classic models of communication emphasized *message transmission* and were concerned with the flow of messages from a sender through a channel to a receiver. Looking at communication in this way had several advantages when those models were developed, and they continue to be popular, particularly among those who have not studied communication academically. What we refer to as "transmission models" are helpful for thinking about how communication *ideally* works if you look at the process solely from the perspective of a sender—a person who has particular goals and a clear idea of what he or she is intending to convey through a message. However, the process often works in a less than ideal way. Once that message is created and "sent" it may get lost or distorted as it flows through channels, and receivers may miss or distort the message the sender was hoping to convey.

For example, a statement like, "Look at that new BMW SUV hybrid" might be a clear message from the perspective of a person who is knowledgeable about cars. Someone with interest or knowledge in this area may have no problem visually differentiating a "BMW" from other types of vehicles, a "new" model from older ones, and a "hybrid SUV" from other types of cars. A person without this knowledge or interest would be quite clueless when it comes to receiving the intended message and might simply respond with a blank expression. We could describe this situation as ineffective communication or a breakdown in communication if we were thinking of communication as the effective transmission of an intended message from a sender to a receiver.

Another view of communication focuses on communication as the *generation of meaning*. Fiske (1982) describes this perspective in this way:

> For communication to take place I have to create a message out of signs. This message stimulates you to create a meaning for yourself that relates in some way to the meaning that I generated in my message in the first place. The more we share the same codes, the more we use the same sign systems, the closer our two "meanings" of the message will approximate. (p. 43)

Note that this definition relies on concepts such as signs, codes, and meaning. In this view, messages are constructed of signs which produce meaning through interaction with receivers (Fiske, 1982). This view emphasizes the creation and negotiation of meaning while transmission models emphasize the movement of messages—assuming that meanings are contained in, and automatically transmitted through, the message.

In thinking about communication, then, we can choose to focus primarily on message senders and receivers and the flow of messages between them or we can devote our attention more to issues related to the meanings that parties attach to messages. In the example above, for instance, the "BMW hybrid" message was important to the message initiator—it was quite rich with meanings about the car, the individual's interests and knowledge, and his or her point of attention at a particular moment in time. To the message recipient who is not interested in cars, the meaning of the message likely had little to do with "BMW" or "hybrid" and more to do with his or her disinterest. Instead the message may have been interpreted as a reminder of their lack of shared knowledge and interest in cars, and perhaps even of deeper differences and priorities between the two. So, the two views of communication (the transmission-oriented view and the meaning-oriented perspective) lead to very different ways of understanding the process and its outcomes.

Meaning-centered views are generally more complex and nuanced. They go beyond a focus on messages and message transmission to emphasize the ways in which individuals think about and react to the messages they create. Meaning-centered perspectives are particularly helpful when it comes to understanding why messages may lead to one or more responses that are not what a sender had intended. Generally, the deeper, meaning-centered perspectives direct our attention to the differing ways meanings are attached to messages by senders and receivers, a topic that will be examined in detail in Chapter 6. Both the transmission-oriented and meaning-centered perspectives contribute to our understanding of the phenomenon of communication, and, as we shall see, there is value in being able to apply both to analyzing the dynamics of human communication.

# THE NATURE OF LANGUAGE

Verbal messages make use of alphanumeric language, one of humanity's most impressive accomplishments. About 10,000 distinct languages and dialects are in use today, and each is unique in some respects (Wang, 1982). There are also a number of commonalities among languages. All spoken languages, for instance, make use of a distinction between vowels and consonants, and in nearly all languages the subject precedes the object in declarative sentences (Wang, 1982). Every language has an identifiable pattern and set of rules relative to:

- *Phonology:* The way sounds are combined to form words
- *Syntax:* The way words are combined into sentences
- *Semantics:* The meanings of words on the basis of their relationship to one another and to elements in the environment
- *Pragmatics:* The way in which language is used in practice

## *Cognitive Factors*

Human physiology (such as our vocal cords and larynx) explains how sounds can be produced but not the workings of the communication process. These mechanisms are controlled by the brain and nervous system, which enable us to sense, make sense of, and relate to our environment and to one another. Here, the differences between humans and other animals are striking.

One example will help to illustrate this point. Studies of chimps and gorillas who have been taught American Sign Language indicate clearly that primates can be taught to use language. However, the total vocabulary of the most successful of these "students" was 400 words. In contrast, the average human has a vocabulary of nearly 200 times that many words (Hunt, 1982).

Findings from neurophysiological research have pointed to the importance of particular areas of the brain for linguistic functioning. Especially important in this regard are *Broca's area* and *Wernicke's area* (see Figure 5.2), both of which are located in the left half or hemisphere of the brain (Buck, 1982; Springer & Deutsch, 1989). Research suggests that ideas or feelings that an individual wishes to vocalize are translated into an appropriate auditory pattern in Wernicke's area and then transmitted to Broca's area, which activates the electrical impulses needed to mobilize the voice-producing mechanisms and to create the intended vocalization (Geschwind, 1991). This conclusion is supported by studies that have shown that damage to Broca's area of the brain disturbs the production of speech but has much less impact on comprehension, whereas damage to Wernicke's area disrupts all aspects of language use (Geschwind, 1991).

## Acquiring Our Language Capability

A good deal of attention has been devoted to determining precisely how and when we first develop competency in the use of language. Some linguists contend that the basic structure of language is innate in humans and that a child needs to learn only the surface details of the language spoken in his or her environment. Others see language acquisition as a part of the general development of the individual (Moskowitz, 1991). Both groups agree that interaction between the individual and the environment is essential to linguistic competence. Studies have demonstrated that without the capacity and opportunity to talk with others, no language capability develops (Moskowitz, 1991).

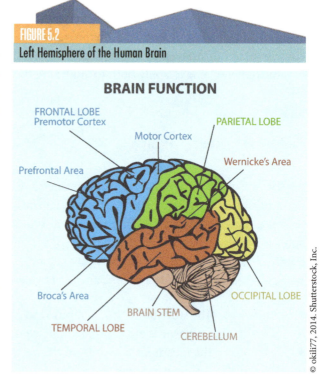

**FIGURE 5.2**
Left Hemisphere of the Human Brain

**BRAIN FUNCTION**

FRONTAL LOBE
Premotor Cortex

Motor Cortex

PARIETAL LOBE

Prefrontal Area

Wernicke's Area

Broca's Area

OCCIPITAL LOBE

BRAIN STEM

TEMPORAL LOBE

CEREBELLUM

© okili77, 2014. Shutterstock, Inc.

There are two broad perspectives on language acquisition—the psycholinguistic approach and the sociolinguistic approach (O'Kane & Goldbart, 1998):

1. *The psycholinguistic approach.* Early utterances—*protowords* (the forerunners of words) and words themselves—are based on a child's personalized understanding of the world. Language is a means for the expression of meanings he or she has learned.
2. *The sociolinguistic approach.* Language development occurs when a child has a reason to communicate. Language is learned through social interaction and is a means for accommodating the demands of social life. (pp. 2–3)

Studies of the first few months of life suggest that language acquisition begins with random "coos" and "giggles" in the presence of family members and other familiar persons, as illustrated in Figure 5.3. At age six to nine months, the "coos" and "giggles" are replaced by babbling sounds; and by 18 months, most children can form a few simple words—*dada*, *papa*, *mama*, or *nana* (Wood, 1976; Linnenberg, 1968).

**FIGURE 5.3**

The Development of Language Skills

| Child's Age | Coordination | | Language |
|---|---|---|---|
| 4 months | | 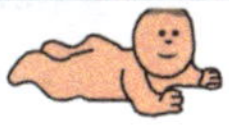 Holds head up. | Coos and chuckles when people play with him/her |
| 6 to 9 months | |  Can sit alone and pull himself/herself up into a standing position. | Babbles continually, sounding like this: "gagagag; yayayaya; dadadada." |
| 12 to 18 months | |  First stands alone, then walks along furniture, and, finally, walks alone. | Uses a few words, follows simple commands, and knows what "no" means. |
| 18 to 21 months | |  Walking looks stiff and jerky, sits in a chair, can crawl down stairs, and throw a ball (clumsily). | Understands simple questions and begins to put two or three words together in sentences. |
| 24 to 27 months | |  Runs well, but falls when making a quick turn. Can also walk up and down stairs. | Uses short sentences composed of words from a 300–400 word vocabulary. |
| 30 to 33 months | |  Has good hand and finger coordination and can manipulate objects well. | Vocabulary increases in size, and three and four word sentences are prevalent; language begins to sound adult like. |
| 36 to 39 months | |  Runs smoothly and negotiates sharp turns; walks stairs by alternating feet; can ride a tricycle, and stand on one foot for a few seconds. | Talks in well-formed sentences, following rather complex grammatical rules; others can generally understand what he/she is talking about. |

Source: *The Genesis of Language: A Psycholinguistic Approach*, edited by Frank Smith and George A. Miller. © 1966 Massachusetts Institute of Technology. Reprinted by permission of The MIT Press.
Artwork © Kendall Hunt Publishing Co.

The speech patterns of others in the environment are important during this stage and throughout language acquisition. Generally, the speech of those who care for and speak to a child differs from adult language use. Vocabulary is simplified; intonation patterns are exaggerated; sentences are simple; frequent questions are asked by mothers; and frequent assertions are made by fathers (Moskowitz, 1991). This phenomenon is known as child-directed speech (Gleason, 1987).

During the earliest stages of language development children use single words to label, assert, or question (Wood, 1976). In addition to describing an important person, for example, the word *mama* may be used as an assertion. *Mama!* may mean, "I want you!" or "I need you, now!" Posed as a question, *Mama?* is a way of saying, "Where are you?" or "Will you come help me?" or "Is that you?"

As seen in Figure 5.3, when most children reach the age of two, they begin to form two-word messages which may have a variety of meanings. As Moskowitz (1991) has observed: "The two-word stage is a time for experimenting with many binary semantic-syntactic relations such as possessor-possessed ('Mommy sock'), actor-action ('Cat sleeping'), and action-object ('Drink soup')" (p. 138).

Although the child's vocabulary is growing, words are being used primarily to define specific, concrete actions and objects. The word *car* may be understood as "a way to go to the store" and a *jack-in-the-box* is "what plays music and pops up." From this point on, a child's vocabulary and ability to form sentences progresses rapidly. Before youngsters are three, most are able to use their 300 to 400 word vocabularies to create well-formed sentences of three, four, and more words (Wood, 1976).

As children grow older, their phonetic, syntactic, semantic, and pragmatic skills develop. Words are used in increasingly abstract ways. Whereas *dog* means "my dog Spot" to a toddler, to a youngster it may refer to "my dog Spot and Paulina's dog Rusty." And in later stages of development, *dog* becomes "a kind of pet" and later "a specific kind of four-legged animal."

What began as the use of words and sentences to refer to things that are immediate and tangible gradually evolves to a capability for referring to ideas and objects that are abstract or distant. Thus, as a child develops increasing skill in the use of language, the linkage between his or her words and the particular events of the immediate surroundings becomes progressively more remote. For an adult, the meanings words have are abstractions based on a lifetime of experiences.

Language is an incredibly powerful tool for message making. We use language not only in vocal but also in written form, not only in single sentences but also in lengthy documents and databases, not only face-to-face but also in situations involving communication technologies. We can classify the major everyday uses of language into three categories: (1) Representation; (2) Conversation; and (3) Persuasion and Social Influence.

# REPRESENTATION

## Language and Reality

At the most basic level, language enables us to name and symbolically represent elements in our world. Ferdinand de Saussure, a noted linguist, maintains that the relationship between the word (the "signifier") and the object it represents ("the signified") is an arbitrary one. With the exception of a few onomatopoeic words like *whoosh* and *clang*, there is no intrinsic connection between the objects and the "signs" we use to refer to them. Some labels refer to the tangible and concrete—friends, teachers, books, courses, reading,

FIGURE 5.4

An early "prescription" for curing a fever involved wearing an amulet with the word *abracadabra* in the form of a triangle. Perhaps that's why we think of *abracadabra* as a magical word today.

```
A - B - R - A - C - A - D - A - B - R - A
A - B - R - A - C - A - D - A - B - R
A - B - R - A - C - A - D - A - B
A - B - R - A - C - A - D - A
A - B - R - A - C - A - D
A - B - R - A - C - A
A - B - R - A - C
A - B - R - A
A - B - R
A - B
A
```

and writing. Language also provides the means through which we represent abstract concepts—friendship, learning, love, knowledge, freedom. Through language, we are able to manipulate symbols in our thinking. We can create, test, and refine our theories or understandings of the world.

The relationship between language and the "reality" it represents is complex. In the 3$^{rd}$ century, for example, the word *abracadabra* was believed to be capable of curing malaria. A Roman physician named Quintus Serenus Sammonicus wrote a "prescription" instructing his patients who had a fever to wear an amulet with the word inscribed on it (see Figure 5.4) for nine days and then throw it over their shoulders into a river (Hempelmann & Krafts, 2013).

The words and concepts we have available to represent experience guide us toward particular ways of understanding reality. In English, a common arrangement of nouns and verbs is:

Subject → Verb → Object

An example is provided by the phrase, "Rowen's comment angered Tracey." The pattern is "one person or thing causing another person or thing." Implicit in the form is a sense of one-way causality—the subject (noun) causes (verb) the outcome in the object (noun). Patterns of representational language use are more than just ways of talking. They imply and encourage ways of thinking—in this instance, they encourage us to see things in terms of "this" (the comment) causing "that" (Tracey's anger).

According to the *Sapir–Whorf hypothesis,* language "is not merely a reproducing instrument for voicing ideas but rather is itself the shaper of ideas. . . . We dissect nature along the lines laid down by our native language" (Whorf, 1956). For example, although colors occur on a continuous spectrum without natural divisions, we classify this spectral band into discrete sections (such as blue versus green). Most people who speak the same language agree on these labels. While many languages classify colors in the same way English does, some languages divide the spectrum differently. A person's ability to remember a particular color correlates to the codeability of a word for that color in the speaker's language.

The realities which confront us have a great impact on our language and the patterns we develop and use. In a society in which people's survival depends upon fishing, for instance, the language will include many words and phrases that capture subtleties of weather, the sea, boats, and fishing. These subtleties are absent in the common language of more technologically oriented societies in which computer and electronics terminology abound. Similarly, the language used by an engineer to describe the structures of the world may be difficult to comprehend by a friend who is a lawyer or a psychologist. Although the language system available to us has a major impact on our perceptions, scholars have varying opinions as to the extent that the external reality we experience is shaped by our language (Farb, 1978; McWhorter, 1978).

The use of language is such a basic and subtle aspect of human life that its representational and "artificial" nature is often overlooked. This is especially so when particular language use patterns are widely shared. As long as others seem to share our meaning, we believe that representation and "reality" are the same; yet there are many instances where we *assume* our words are being understood and their meanings shared when they may not be.

Researchers have shown that terms like *always*, *often*, and *rarely*, when used by health care professionals in the context of laboratory reports, are subject to a wide range of interpretation. A study of physicians and health care administrators in several settings showed that estimates of the meaning of the word *always* varied from 60% to 100% of the time. For *sometimes*, estimates ranged from 0 to 90%; and for *rarely*, meanings varied from 0 to 95% (Robertson, 1983). In addition, health care professionals may use terms differently than patients. For example, imagine hearing that your test results following cancer surgery were *positive* and assuming that this was a good outcome when your physician was using the term to mean "continuing or remaining cancer cells."

Generally, language seems to work "as if it were real." Most often, when we ask someone to pass the salt, their arm extends, grasps a salt container, and, without much difficulty at all, places the salt container in front of us. But there are also a number of circumstances in life which remind the reflective person that an uncritical belief in the "reality of language" can lead to difficulties. Saying that something is or is not true, or that this or that should or should not happen, does not make it so.

Similarly, a man saying that he is "in love" may not tell us all that much about the way he feels, how he will behave, or what he really thinks about the concept and the person to whom his words refer. We may use the words *I do* or *I will*, for example, to seal the bonds of marriage. Although these two words have great symbolic value to the people involved at that moment, the stability of the marriage will depend not upon the words but upon the behaviors and personal philosophy to which they refer.

Beyond the problems that arise from confusing words with the people, behaviors, actions, or ideas to which they refer, additional complexity in language results because in actual use words seldom represent the same things to two different people. As noted earlier, the meanings each of us attaches to words and phrases depend on our experiences. As a consequence, the meanings of words are subjective and, to some extent, unique to each individual. The following exchange illustrates the point:

> *Adrian*: (9:00 AM) Devon, I need the report on the Johnson deal that you've been working on for this afternoon's meeting.
> *Devon*: Okay, Adrian, I'll get it to you right away.
> *Devon*: Sidney, that report I gave you to finish yesterday has to go out this morning.
> *Sidney*: No problem.
> *Adrian*: (4:30 PM that afternoon) Devon, where's the report you promised to get me?
> *Devon*: You should have had it this morning. I asked Sidney to send it right over to you.
> *Adrian*: Well, it's not here and you know this isn't the first time something like this has happened . . .
> *Devon*: Sidney, what happened? The report for Adrian was supposed to go out this morning.
> *Sidney*: I did what you requested, Devon. I told an intern to put it in the mail at 11:45 AM.

As a result of the day's events, Adrian has accumulated more evidence that Devon is unreliable. Devon has decided once and for all that she simply can't count on Sidney, and Sidney is convinced that Devon is a poor manager and always looking for a reason to shift blame for her own inadequacies to others. Although these conclusions may be justified, it is also quite likely that at least a partial explanation of what occurred is to be found in the words and phrases each person used and how they were interpreted. Initially, Adrian indicated to Devon that he needed the report for the afternoon meeting. Devon told Sidney that it had "to go out this morning," but what did "go out this morning" mean? To Sidney, who gave it to an intern at 11:45 AM, it meant *go out* this morning. To Adrian and Devon it meant *be delivered* this morning. The same kinds of problems arise in many if not most other settings (see Figure 5.5).

## *Limitations of Language for Representation*

Scholars of what is termed *general semantics* have identified a number characteristics that should serve as cautions as we thinking about the usefulness of language and and communication (Budd, 2003).

**THE PRINCIPLE OF NONIDENTITY (A IS NOT A).** The principle of nonidentity reminds us of a point mentioned previously, that words are not the same order of "stuff" as the "realities" to which they refer. The world is constantly changing, while the language available for making sense of it may not. The reverse may also occur when language changes but the reality it refers to doesn't.

For example: who would have imagined even 15 years ago that advances in electronics would mean that words like *smartphone, streaming, app, USB,* or *pdf* would become household terms for most of us?

© Jim Lambert, 2014. Shutterstock, Inc.

**FIGURE 5.5**
Minor differences in word choice—such as "may be" versus "is" in the signs shown—may have a substantial impact on the significance a message will have.

**THE PRINCIPLE OF NON-ALLNESS (A IS NOT ALL A).** The principle of non-allness asserts that "the map is not the territory"—our language can never represent all of the objects, events, or people to which we are referring. As Rapoport (1962) explains:

> No matter how good a map you make, you cannot represent all of the territory in it. Translated in terms of language, it means that no matter how much you say about some "thing," "event," "quality," or what not, you cannot say all about it. (pp. 19-20)

**THE PRINCIPLE OF SELF-REFLEXIVENESS.** The principle of self-reflexiveness calls attention to the problems that can arise when we use language to talk about our use of language. When we use concepts to talk about concepts, we become increasingly abstract and move progressively into the world of words and away from the world of the tangible.

For example, our self-reflexive capability allows us to label ourselves "successes" or "failures" as if these were actual characteristics that have an existence apart from our representations of them. We may easily forget that one cannot *be* a success or failure but can only be *seen* or *interpreted* as such by someone.

# CONVERSATION

## *Negotiation of Meanings*

When we create a spoken or written message, our language serves as the medium to convey our representations. It is our means of projecting ourselves and our ideas into the environment.

Language is also a tool for the negotiation of meanings between and among individuals. It is the means by which we are able to coordinate our own activities with those of others, to undertake joint projects, to discuss and solve problems, and to share in the pursuit of personal and social needs.

As we have discussed previously, the messages we create reflect our meanings—meanings influenced by our own experiences, needs, and goals. When others decode our messages, they do so in terms of the meanings our words have for them—based on their experiences, needs, goals, and capabilities. When people talk about their feelings about *dogs*, they, of course, are using the word *dog* to refer to the "dogs-of-their-experience" as they are relevant to the current conversation. When we decode the message, we do so in terms of the "dogs-of-our-experience" (see Figure 5.6).

FIGURE 5.6

In everyday usage, we speak and hear based on the meanings words have for us.

**"DOG"**

© Scorpp, 2014. Shutterstock, Inc.

"I can't think of a better companion than a dog. They are faithful, kind, affectionate. . . Sunshine is like a member of the family."

© Eric Isselee, 2014. Shutterstock, Inc.

"I'd never think of going out at night without my dog by my side."

© Erik Lam, 2014. Shutterstock, Inc.

"I've never cared much for dogs as pets."

© Charlie Bard, 2014. Shutterstock, Inc.

"I agree, dogs make great pets."

Thus, in any conversation (or written exchange), language serves as a medium through which individuals: (1) code and externalize meanings through messages and (2) decode and internalize meanings as they translate the messages of others. As the interaction continues, language serves as the channel through which the people involved may: (3) discover discrepancies and/or similarities in their meanings and (4) negotiate a mutuality of meaning appropriate to the purposes at hand. For example, Charles tells Acacia "I love you." Acacia says, "I love you, too." Each has heard the verbal message provided by the other, and the words each person is saying are the same. Can we assume the message has the same meaning for both Charles and Acacia? Not necessarily. As we discussed in the last chapter, whether we think in terms of ourselves as "senders" or "receivers" of messages in a relationship, group, organization, society, or mass audience, messages sent (intentionally or not) do not necessarily equal messages received. Common messages do not necessarily result in shared interpretation. Maybe Charles and Acacia have the same meanings in mind. Or, perhaps, Charles means he wants to get married, while Acacia means she wants to go out only with Charles. The same distinction between message and meaning is important in verbal communication just as it is in the realm of nonverbal codes.

## Rules and Rituals

Do you get out your cell phone to communicate with friends as soon as you leave class? We take our ability to converse with friends and colleagues very much for granted, so much so that it may seem like quite a simple activity. But, as with other aspects of communication, things are seldom as simple as they seem on the surface. As communication researcher Margaret McLauglin (1984) indicates, our ability to engage in conversation presupposes that we have and can use an incredible amount of knowledge:

> . . . not only what we might call *world knowledge* (that groceries cost money, that parents love their children, that dogs bite, etc.), but also more specific knowledge bases, such as the rules of grammar, syntax, etiquette, and so on, as well as specifically conversational rules such as "When someone has replied to your summons, disclose the reason for the summons," and "Before saying good-bye to a telephone caller, reach agreement that all topical talk is completed." What is fascinating about conversation is that the ordinary person rarely reflects upon the vastness of the knowledge store that is required to carry it on. (p. 14).

Like the rules for language use, conversation *rules* serve as prescriptions and guides. Some rules are obvious and explicit—like the rules of tennis, traffic regulations, or the requirements for membership in a formal group or organization. Other rules are implicit and subtle, like work etiquette, or the informal norms and practices expected of members of a group or organization. *Conversational rules* are generally implicit and subtle, and yet they are a strong force in guiding our verbal interaction. They describe how one must, should, or should not behave in interactions with others (Shiminoff, 1980).

Conversational rules facilitate cooperative effort, help to structure and regularize interaction, provide a basis for predicting patterns of communication, and guide us in interpreting the actions of others.

Scholars who study language and communication (Ashcraft & Gavansky, 2013; Grice, 1975; McLaughlin, 1984; Norman & Rumelhart, 1975; Wardhaugh, 1985) have developed an inventory of the rules that guide our behavior in conversations. We can group these rules into the following categories: cooperativeness, responsiveness, interactiveness, and conformance.

COOPERATIVENESS. Without some degree of cooperativeness and willingness to commit to interaction, conversation is impossible. H. Paul Grice, an important contributor to our understanding of conversational rules, called this general rule the *cooperative principle,* which leads to other maxims of cooperation (Grice, 1975) including:

- Make your contribution as informative as is required.
- Do not say what you believe to be false.
- Do not say that for which you lack evidence.
- Be brief.
- Avoid obscurity of expression. (pp. 45–46)

RESPONSIVENESS. The obligation to be aware of and accommodating to the needs of other interactants involves inferring and responding to others' knowledge and beliefs, responding to questions and requests for information, using a manner and tone that takes account of the needs of other interactants, being clear, being courteous, and avoiding excessive boasting and self-promotion.

INTERACTIVENESS. Interactiveness also refers to rules governing the management of the conversation. These commitments have to do with conversational sequences and rituals, including:

1. *Initiating interaction.* Initiating conversations and/or responding to the initiation efforts of others. If, for example, I say: "How are you?" the expectation is that you will participate in the initiation ritual by responding and will do so along the lines of: "Fine, and you?"
2. *Establishing a conversational agenda.* Participating in the process of setting the agenda for discussion such as in a meeting. If, for example, I say: "I guess our main topic of discussion today is how to update our social media presence," the expectation is that you will either agree with the agenda as defined and allow it to guide the conversation or disagree and take the lead in suggesting another agenda.
3. *Turn taking as the conversation progresses.* Sometimes called *interaction management.* This is the expectation that people will "take turns" in speaking as a conversation progresses, avoiding monopolizing the discussion or nonparticipation.
4. *Topic shifting.* Changing topics and/or responding to the topic changes of others. The expectation is that topic changes are suggested and agreed to or explicitly negotiated, rather than unilaterally imposed. If you are in the middle of an enthusiastic description of a recent

trip you took, it is expected that the other person will not interrupt in the middle of your story and begin talking about a something else. Rules call for the other person to work to produce a gradual, "natural" transition in the topic or to wait until a natural break in the conversation occurs or to introduce a transition that is responsive to you. Thus, he or she might say: "That sounds cool. You're lucky you get to travel. I've been learning about European history in class. Let me tell you about it."

5. *Closing.* Terminating conversations and responding to termination initiatives by others— sometimes called *leave-taking.* The expectation is that leave-taking occurs by mutual agreement. That is, it is expected that someone will not get up and walk away while you're in the middle of talking about your trip. As with openings, there are a number of conversational rituals and conventions associated with conversational closings. Thus, a closing like, "OK, then, take care," and a response, such as, "You, too!" serve to signal the desire of the initiator to terminate conversation and provide a standardized way of dealing with what would otherwise be an ambiguous and potentially awkward circumstance.

CONFORMANCE. Conformance refers to our obligation to adhere to conversation rules or to provide an explanation when a violation occurs. The expectation is that we will follow rules in our conversations. When violations occur, the consequences are frequently negative. They may include confusion, frustration, misunderstanding, a loss of trust or friendliness among conversants, or a reinterpretation of the value and goals of the conversation by one or more of the parties involved.

There are any number of circumstances in which we violate rules. We may shift a topic abruptly, get up to leave in the middle of a conversation, exaggerate or understate, or say things we don't mean. There may be good reasons for these actions. When rule violations occur, the expectation is that we will explain the reason for the violation. For instance, when you interrupt someone, change a subject quickly, take a phone call, or exit a conversation abruptly, an explanation is expected to explain and help to excuse the rule violation.

One of the most blatant examples of rule violation occurs when one interactant knowingly engages in deception. In such a circumstance, the informativeness rule and, hence, the sharing of information have been undermined. When all other rules are followed, efforts to deceive may be quite successful— even though they certainly raise ethical issues. For instance, we may find ourselves persuaded by a cooperative, responsive, and interactive salesperson, even when some of the information provided about a product is incorrect. One of the reasons this occurs, of course, is that we are often better able to make accurate judgments about whether conversational rules are being followed than whether we are being told the truth. However, if deception is detected, it is likely to have a substantial impact on the conversation and the meanings which result—as well as on the future of the relationship.

Rules and the significance of rule violations depend on the situation or context to a considerable extent. Our expectations may differ depending on whether we are talking with an intimate friend or a stranger, a child or an adult, a member of the same or other sex, a salesperson or a member of the clergy, one other person or several others. Thus, contextual, gender, ethnic, racial, and cultural differences may all have an impact on conversational protocol (see Figure 5.7).

## Language and Gender

In most cultures, individual communication behaviors are used by both men and women. For example, in North American culture men and women may smile to indicate pleasure or raise their voices to indicate anger. According to one estimate, men and women overlap in their communication actions 99% of the time (Canary & Hause, 1993). Nevertheless, there are scholars who note that men and women learn to speak differently and that men and women may internalize different norms for conversation (e.g., Coates, 1986; Hancock & Rubin, 2015; Tannen, 2007). According to this view, men tend to adopt a more competitive style in conversation while women tend to adopt a more cooperative mode. Because gender is the social construction of masculinity and femininity within a culture, these differences may vary by culture (see Chapter 8 for a more extensive discussion of this aspect of communication). The areas in which differences have been noted by some researchers include: conversational maintenance and

**FIGURE 5.7**

Conversational analyst and communication scholar Jenny Mandelbaum points out that we are so immersed in communication that it is hard for us to see it objectively or analytically. This is especially the case with everyday conversation, even though in many ways it is the "currency" of our daily lives. Once we begin to take a close look at ordinary conversation though—both the things we say, and the ways we say them with our words, voices, and bodies—we may begin to revise our taken-for-granted views of communication. Close examination of everyday conversations in a variety of settings can be accomplished by collecting audio- and videotape recordings, transcribing them in detail, and then using the transcripts as guides while analyzing the tapes in detail. Close looking and listening of this kind reveal a number of unexpected features of our everyday communication practices.

For instance, we commonly believe that we communicate in order to exchange information, and that this is a major function of our everyday encounters. It turns out, though, that even simply exchanging information (something that we rarely do, in fact) is fraught with concerns of self-presentation and identity (e.g., how do I seem to the person I am talking with? What are they making of what I'm trying to do?) and relationship (e.g., do I appear to be "acting superior" by telling them this? Am I being respectful? or respected?). That is, any communicative action that we engage in shapes, and is shaped by, identity and relational concerns. We may not always be completely aware of this, but looking closely at the interactional practices we use to "put together" different actions in conversation can help us understand, first of all, how these actions are accomplished, and, second, how concerns about identities and relationships are inextricably implicated in the ways in which we engage in everyday communication.

© Monkey Business Images/Shutterstock.com

question asking, interruptions, argumentativeness, and lexical and phonological characteristics (Stewart, Cooper, Stewart & Friedley, 2003).

**CONVERSATIONAL MAINTENANCE AND QUESTION ASKING.** Women often spend more time and effort facilitating the continuation of conversation. Consider the following dialogue from an encounter at a restaurant:

> *Marti:* What are you going to order?
> *Thomas:* The burger.
> *Marti:* That sounds good. Does it come with fries? I think I'll have the chicken salad.
> *Thomas:* I think so.
>
> (After the order is taken, and a moment of silence . . . )
>
> *Marti:* I went to the mall yesterday to look for a dress for my sister's wedding.
> *Thomas:* Yeah?
> *Marti:* But I couldn't find anything I liked. I guess I'll have to keep looking around. I wonder what my cousin is going to wear. She always comes up with something that looks better than anyone else. Maybe I'll get my hair done differently, too. What do you think?
> *Thomas:* (Looks at his phone and doesn't respond.)

Researchers have also found that when they analyzed tapes of actual conversations, 70% of the questions asked during conversations were posed by women (Fishman, 1985). Women may be more likely to contribute to a conversation by asking questions (e.g., "Are you hungry? Should we get some lunch?"), while men's contributions may be directives that tell the other person what to do (e.g., "I'm hungry. Let's get lunch") (Mulac, Weimann, Widenmann & Gibson, 1988).

Wardhaugh (1985) argues that silence is a "potent communicative weapon" and notes that silence is regarded as "speaking at least as loud as any words that might have been uttered" (pp. 71–72). It is difficult to ignore a silent response to what we have said and not to wonder what it means. Often silence causes an individual to question the nature of the interaction or, more fundamentally, the nature of the relationship.

It is interesting to note that these differences may not appear in mediated contexts. For example, Thomson and Murachver (2001) studied women's and men's email and found no differences in terms of who was more likely to ask questions, offer compliments, apologies, or opinions, and insult someone.

**INTERRUPTIONS.** Interruptions can serve a control function in conversation by taking control of the other person's turn (Stewart et al, 2003). They can also be used as confirming responses or signs of conversational involvement (jumping in to contribute something else to an interesting conversation) or just errors in turn taking (Turner, Dindia & Pearson, 1995). Research has indicated that there are no differences in the rate of interruptions based on gender (males and females seem to use interruptions at the same level), but people interrupt a woman more than they interrupt a man who is speaking (Hancock & Rubin, 2015).

ARGUMENTATIVENESS. *Argumentativeness* is defined as a stable trait that predisposes an individual in communication situations to advocate positions on controversial issues and to verbally attack the positions that other people take on these issues (Infante & Rancer, 1982). In general, men score higher on measures of argumentativeness than women (Infante, 1985). Although women are able to use this communication strategy when appropriate, they are more likely to believe that arguing is a strategy for dominating and controlling another person and, therefore, to dismiss it in many situations as rude or inappropriate (Nicotera & Rancer, 1994).

LEXICAL AND PHONOLOGICAL CHARACTERISTICS. Studies show that women use a larger vocabulary to discuss topics they have greater interest in and experience with. And, conversely, in areas where men have greater expertise, their vocabularies are more expansive. Men also tend to swear more often than women (Newman, Groom, Handelman, & Pennebaker, 2008).

There also may be differences in the adjectives used by women and men. Lakoff (1975) has noted that words like *adorable, charming, sweet,* and *lovely* are more likely to be used by women, while men are more apt to use terms such as *nice, good,* or *pretty.* Studies suggest that women use intensifying adverbs more than men—for example, "I *really* enjoyed the book," or "I'm *so* disappointed."

Newman et al. (2008) provided the following examples of lexical differences when college students were asked to write whatever they were thinking about in a "stream of consciousness" paper:

> *Female:* Okay, so I'm sitting here talking to my friends. I miss them so much. They live back home in Houston. I wish I could see them just like old times. I remember when we would all hang out together. It was great.
> *Male:* I find it amusing that in writing a stream of consciousness about what I am thinking, my mind is completely focused on what I am going to write in the stream of consciousness paper. Thus, my stream of consciousness is about my stream of consciousness about my stream of consciousness, etc.
> *Female:* Right now, I am thinking about my chemistry homework and test. I am very nervous about it and I am worried that I may not succeed to my fullest potential.
> *Male:* Stream of consciousness? How do you start something so vague? I keep a journal which I write in occasionally, but I can not remember the last time an assignment consisted solely of write your thoughts. (p. 224)

Newman et al.'s (2008) research supports Tannen's (2007) idea that women are more likely to use a "rapport" style where they discuss social topics and express internal thoughts and feelings, while men are more likely to use a "report" style where they describe the quantity and location of objects.

**GENDER MARKERS.** Spender (1995) argues that the masculine form of a word is often taken as the standard while the feminine form is derived from it. For example, men are *poets*, *princes*, and *actors*. Women are *–esses* (*poetess*, *princess*, *actress*). And we often think of the masculine form first. For example, try to say "wife and husband" instead of "husband and wife" or "queen and king" instead of "king and queen." Occupational titles are classic examples of gender-marked speech. Even with all of the changes in occupational roles recently, it is difficult to picture a woman when hearing the words "construction worker" or a man when hearing the word "nurse."

**BINARY THINKING.** The English language tends to direct our attention in binary ways. For example, it is easy to list "opposites" like light or dark, tall or short, happy or sad, fast or slow. Of course, we realize that there are many emotions "between" happy and sad but they are more difficult to label. Our language treats gender identity in the same manner. In traditional thinking, a person is considered to be either male or female, but in reality people are more complex than that. Some people are cisgender (people whose sense of personal identity corresponds to the sex and gender assigned to them at birth, according to a new entry in the *Oxford English Dictionary*) while others might identify as trans, gender fluid, genderqueer, or other non-binary identities (Anwar, 2015). For this reason and to acknowledge the complexity of gender identities, it is important not to assume that we necessarily know the most appropriate descriptive terms for others. Where we are uncertain, it is best to ask people what personal pronouns they prefer (see Figure 5.8).

**FIGURE 5.8**

People may use many pronouns to identify themselves. Be sure to tell others your preferred pronouns and ask them theirs.

she/hers/her

ze/zem/zir

ze/hir/hir

they/their/them

ey/eir/em

he/his/him

## Content and Relationship

Whether we use our words in a planned, intentional way or in a less systematic, unintentional fashion, verbal messages provide a potential source of two types of information: (1) information about *content*—the topic under discussion and (2) information about *relationships*—about the source, how the source regards the intended recipient(s), and about the relationships among the individuals involved (Watzlawick, Beavin & Jackson, 1967).

© Monkey Business Images/Shutterstock.com

**FIGURE 5.9**

All messages, including asking your neighbors to sign a petition, have a content and a relationship dimension.

Consider the situation depicted in Figure 5.9. Imagine that the "volunteer" may be asking her neighbors to sign a petition in favor of another neighbor who is running for a political office. In a circumstance like this, at the most obvious level, her verbal message would include content such as facts about the candidate's qualifications, experience, and position on particular issues. At the same time, these messages would also be likely to include subtle cues about how she views the neighbors and vice versa. For instance, the content and tone of the speaker's persuasive message might reveal whether she believes the neighbors are open-minded about the candidate and issues involved, sees them as receptive to her message, believes they are likely voters, thinks they view her as a friendly, or the opposite. As the conversation progresses, the verbal and nonverbal messages created by all of the people involved not only provide content relative to the explicit topic, but also contribute to the formation, reinforcement, or change in the relationship that exists between the people involved. So it is that even in what seem to be very straightforward situations, the communication process provides topical information and shapes relationships at the same time.

To further clarify this distinction, consider the following statement:

> *Kim:* I tell you, Trey, Jessie is an incompetent and uncaring person!

From a content point of view, Kim is indicating she has some negative views about Jessie. Beyond that, Kim's message also has relational implications. Even from this short utterance, we can infer that Kim feels quite strongly about Jessie, and we might further surmise that Kim is a quite outspoken and perhaps also a fairly judgmental person. Further, in her comments about Jessie, Kim may also be providing clues about how she feels about Trey. It seems likely that Kim sees Trey as a more intimate acquaintance than Jessie. We could also infer that she trusts Trey. But it is also possible that she is pursuing a specific personal motive by sharing her thoughts about Jessie with Trey, or that she simply doesn't care who knows how she feels about Jessie. At the least, we can safely assume that Kim has some reason for wanting to share her reactions to Jessie with Trey.

No matter what Kim's intent is, however, her message has both content and relationship components. In each of these hypothetical situations, there is a relational dimension to the comment—a dimension which is quite different from, but at least as important as, the content dimension. The implications for the relationships would vary depending on the situation, individuals involved, how well they know one another, etc. This exchange might bring Kim and Trey closer together and reinforce a distance in their relationship with Jessie. Or Trey might see this exchange as another example of Kim's judgmentalness and a reminder that he doesn't have much trust in Kim and needs to be careful how much information he shares with her. Or the exchange may have any of a number of other relational implications for the people involved or for others who try to analyze the significance of the interaction. In any case, making sense of the content element of a message is, quite obviously, much easier than interpreting the relational intentions or analyzing the relational consequences.

Here are two additional examples:

1. *Dad:* (Following the sound of breaking glass) Marco?
   *Marco:* Daddy, I didn't do it. Honest.

2. *Ali:* Mary, I want to talk to you.
   *Mary:* Ali, I know what you're going to say. I'm sorry. I never intended for you to get hurt . . . It just happened.

In all respects except the content, these two exchanges are quite similar. In each instance the first speaker is really saying very little from a topical point of view. In fact, in both cases, the individuals who initiate the conversation provide no information that identifies a topic for discussion. The second speakers, however, provide the basis for a number of inferences. Both Marco and Mary seem to assume they are being asked about a particular act, even though this is not necessarily the case. They respond *defensively*—as though they have been attacked. Their responses, perhaps motivated by guilt, fear, or both, are messages from which we could infer something about their feelings and attitudes. Their messages also provide the basis for inferences about how they feel about the other person. In both cases, it's clear that these interactions are taking place between people who have an ongoing relationship. It's also apparent that both Marco and Mary are concerned about their relationships, by necessity or choice. For whatever reasons, both seem to see themselves in a "one-down" or inferior position, in which they must justify, explain, and/or seek forgiveness or approval from Dad or Ali.

Let's examine a slightly more complicated situation:

> *Jacob:* My wife and I are really excited. We've got a chance to go to Las Vegas this weekend; I got a really great deal on the Internet. It wasn't really the time we had picked to go, but we just can't pass it up . . . Doubt we'll ever have a chance to go so cheaply again.
> *Zach:* I considered going, but with my job and the economy the way it is right now, I decided it's not smart to spend money on travel this year.

In this brief exchange, Jacob is providing information about the prospect of an upcoming trip. He's also explaining that it will cost much less than the normal amount. The fact that Jacob is talking about the trip at all may suggest that he's the type of person who enjoys sharing his excitement. Or he may be boasting; perhaps he is seeking attention or recognition.

By explaining that he got a good deal, Jacob may provide a clue that he wishes to be seen as clever, shrewd, or economical. Or, alternatively, his message may suggest that he is the kind of person who feels the need to justify or apologize for his good fortune. The decision to share his plans with Zach suggests that Jacob cares about or values Zach, or that he wants to impress him, or to solicit support or encouragement.

Zach says that he doesn't think it is a smart time for a trip. Beyond this, his response may provide a clue that he is unwilling to share in Jacob's excitement. He may be jealous. Or he may fail to detect Jacob's excitement. Zach's response also may suggest that he wishes to be seen as more rational, frugal, and/or sensitive to the global economy than Jacob. From a relationship perspective, it seems that he feels no obligation to acknowledge or contribute to Jacob's excitement and has no particular interest in providing an audience for further discussion of Jacob's trip.

While the content aspect of an utterance is generally fairly straightforward to discern, it is often much harder for interactants—or observers—to be confident about their understanding of the relationship aspect. Nonetheless, all utterances have significance at both content and relationship levels. They provide topical information while contributing to the creation, reinforcement, evolution, or change in relationships.

## *Metacommunication*

Sometimes we engage in conversations about our conversation or, to put it differently, we communicate about communication. This process is termed *metacommunication* (Watzlawick, Beavin & Jackson, 1967).

1. *Emelia:* Let's go to a movie tonight.
2. *Mateo:* Oh, I don't know.  Can we talk about it later?
3. *Emelia:* That's becoming a pattern around here, Mateo. You never want to carry a discussion through to a conclusion.
4. *Mateo:* The pattern *I see* is the one where you refuse to end a conversation until you've gotten the decision you want.
5. *Emelia:* Same old story. You can't handle any negative feedback. One small criticism and you get so defensive.

In the first exchange above—(1) and (2)—Mateo and Emelia are discussing the possibility of going to a movie. With Emelia's response (3), there is a shift from talking about the movie to talking about the way Mateo responded. In his next response (4), Mateo comments on Emelia's communication. Emelia continues the process of metacommunication as she replies (5), carrying forth a fairly common pattern of communication.

Of course, metacommunication can be used in a way that leads to more positive outcomes in a relationship, too. Consider this conversation:

1. *Genevieve:*  Let's go to a movie tonight.
2. *Chin:* Oh, I don't know. Can we talk about it later?
3. *Genevieve:* That doesn't really sound like you, Chin. Is everything okay?
4. *Chin:* I got some bad news at work today and don't feel like going out.
5. *Genevieve:* What's wrong? Can I help?

In this instance, Genevieve and Chin begin by discussing going to a movie (1) and (2), but Genevieve interprets Chin's reply as atypical and asks him about it (3). This metacommunication leads Chin to disclose his bad news (4), and then Genevieve asks for more information and offers support (5).

## Microaggressions

Microaggressions are "brief and commonplace daily verbal, behavioral, and environmental indignities, whether intentional or unintentional, that communicate hostile, derogatory, or negative racial, gender, sexual-orientation, and religious slights and insults" (Sue, 2010, p. 5).  Whether they are intentional or nonintentional, they are perceived by the members of the targeted group to be offensive.  For example, saying that someone who does something silly or stupid is "so gay," asking an Asian-looking person what country they were born in, saying that a black person "sounds so articulate," or raising your voice when speaking to a blind person are all examples of microaggressions that reinforce stereotypical thinking.  African American and LGBTQ college students often complain about being the target of microaggressions from white students who may be unaware of the impact of their language use on other people. Women report being the recipients of labeling ("she's such a bitch"), being called by their first names when men are called "Mr." or "Professor," as well as being the target of unwanted stares or remarks about their bodies.

# PERSUASION AND SOCIAL INFLUENCE

Language and verbal communication play a central role in the processes associated with persuasion and social influence. The term *persuasion* is often used to refer to intentional message-sending activities where the goal is to gain compliance.

## Compliance-Gaining

Early persuasion theories and practices were very much influenced by linear and mechanistic traditions of communication, where the idea was that a sender would bring about compliance in receivers by creating and transmitting carefully designed persuasive messages through channels appropriately selected for the desired goal. This way of thinking about persuasion was, and continues to be, useful in a number of contexts, particularly in the work of what Cialdini and Sagarin (2005) term "compliance professionals," such as salespeople, fundraisers, and political lobbyists. Cialdini and Sagarin (2005) have identified six principles of compliance: (1) reciprocity, (2) social validation, (3) commitment/consistency, (4) friendship/liking, (5) scarcity, and (6) authority. It is important to learn about these principles not only to become a successful persuader, but also to prevent others from persuading you to do something you don't really want to do.

RECIPROCITY. The "rule of reciprocity suggests that people feel obligated to give back the form of behavior they have received from others" (Gouldner, 1960). The rule suggests that, in general, anything you give (such as a gift, a favor, or a kindness) should be returned in some form to you by the recipient. One implication of this principle is that gifts given or favors shown at one point in time are likely to lead to gifts and favors returned in the future, if not at the moment—the notion that underlies the "pay it forward" idea (Cialdini & Sagarin, 2005). And you are more likely to do a favor for someone who has already done a favor for you.

No doubt each of us can think of any number of instances where this principle is strategically employed by compliance professionals as well as by others who have come to recognize how this principle can be used to our advantage. In such cases, we enhance the likelihood of achieving the outcomes we desire by "modeling" the behaviors we're hoping to elicit from others.

SOCIAL VALIDATION. It is common for people to be influenced by other people in an effort to make sense of events transpiring around them, and behaviors and ideas seem more correct if we see others practicing those behaviors or agreeing with the assertions and interpretations of others. For example, if a group of people coordinate their behavior and stand together and look skyward on a crowded street, it is likely that others who come along will look skyward, too (Milgram, Bickman & Berkowitz, 1969).

The social validation rule for compliance can be stated in this way: "One should be more willing to comply with a request or behavior if it is consistent with what similar others are thinking and doing" (Cialdini & Sagarin, 2005, p. 150).

COMMITMENT/CONSISTENCY. This principle says that after committing to a position, we should be more willing to comply with requests for behaviors that are consistent with that position (Cialdini & Sagarin, 2005, p. 152).

Both commitment and consistency can be important forces in compliance-gaining. If people commit to a particular position, it's likely that they'll stick with that position—perhaps even to the point of what might be termed stubbornness (Kiesler, 1971). Sometimes called "yes/yes appeals," persuasive strategies that use this principle might ask for small initial signs of commitment, and then build on these initial commitments to solicit larger or more extensive forms of commitment in a related area. For example, a fundraiser might ask for a small sum of money and then ask for larger and larger sums after each subsequent donation.

FRIENDSHIP/LIKING. As Cialdini and Sagarin (2005) note, it is "a fact of social interaction to which each of us can attest . . . that people are more favorably inclined toward the needs of those individuals they know and like" (p. 155). Persuasive strategies are often built around the idea of creating friendships as a first step, and *then* following up with efforts to gain compliance.

Studies suggest that when we see someone as being physically attractive or similar to us, or if an individual compliments us or cooperates with us, they are likely to have an easier time with persuasive efforts directed toward us than otherwise.

SCARCITY. Hearing that a particular item of apparel, electronic equipment, or a car is the last one to be available for some time (or from this seller) is often a quite powerful persuasive message. As Cialdini and Sagarin (2005) put it: "Opportunities seem more valuable to us when they are less available." Learning that "this is the last pack of baseball cards" or the only antique clock of its kind may suddenly enhance the desirability of the item. The scarcity principle related to compliance may be stated as: "One should try to secure those opportunities that are scarce or dwindling" (Cialdini & Sagarin, 2005, p. 159).

**AUTHORITY.** We have a tendency to value and comply with messages from authority figures we value. Consistent with this idea, advertisers often include "endorsements" or "testimonials" by authorities or experts (real or not) to help sell products or ideas. Con artists and phishing attempts on the Internet may also make use of this scheme, whereby authorities or symbols of authority are used as sources for deceptive messages and illicit compliance-gaining strategies (Cialdini & Sagarin, 2005).

**INOCULATION.** While persuasion theories and practices are most often focused on supporting, encouraging, and promoting compliance, inoculation is concerned with efforts to use messages to "inoculate" against or refute persuasive efforts. As Pfau and Szabo (2003) explain:

> The supportive approach seeks to reinforce existing beliefs and attitudes. If a person believes that a ballistic missile defense system is desirable, a supportive approach would provide arguments and evidence to bolster this position. By contrast, the refutational or inoculative approach attempts to threaten people's attitudes by warning of possible challenges to attitudes and then raises and preemptively refutes these challenges. The person who supports a ballistic missile defense system would be told that she or he can expect to encounter strong arguments opposing her or his position. The specific objections would be raised and immediately refuted. (p. 268)

Studies indicate that efforts to refute or inoculate—to create resistance to persuasive efforts that would foster a change in our thinking—are generally quite effective when messages include reference to potential threats to this way of thinking and then provide information that refutes these threats (Pfau & Szabo, 2003). Including references to threats provides a motivation for resisting persuasive efforts that advocate an alternative perspective, and refutational information content serves to strengthen previously held attitudes and to reinforce our defense against other people's efforts to change them (Pfau & Sazbo, 2003).

Inoculation strategies are applied in a variety of settings including politics, business, and health care (Pfau & Sazbo, 2003). In health contexts, for example, inoculation efforts are widely employed to create resistance to pro-smoking messages. Such persuasive efforts are often used by parents and teachers, and are core elements in health communication campaigns intended to discourage commercial or peer pressure to smoke cigarettes.

High school and college students may be taught "resistance strategies" to use in situations where they are asked to smoke cigarettes or drink alcohol. Common strategies include direct refusal (saying "no"), alternative suggestions ("No thanks, I'd like a soda),", excuse ("I have an exam tomorrow, and I have to study for it later"), and explanation ("I just don't like the taste of alcohol") (Harrington, 1995).

# Social Influence

Persuasion involves purposeful efforts to change behaviors through communication by appealing to reason and emotions (Miller, 1987). Social influence is a more general concept which may refer to either intentional or unintentional influence outcomes that occur in interpersonal, group, and public contexts.

As we noted earlier, some compliance-gaining strategies and practices have been very much influenced by linear and transmission-oriented models of communication. In some settings these models work well for explaining and guiding compliance-gaining. These frameworks are particularly applicable to settings where influence efforts are conscious, planned, and undertaken strategically.

Other perspectives on communication, particularly those which highlight the interactive, meaning-centered, and interpretive nature of communication, are also helpful for explaining more informal and naturally occurring social influence dynamics. Clark and Delia (1979) have proposed three types of goals that are present in any interaction:

1. overtly instrumental objectives, in which a response is required from one's listener(s) defining the task of the communicative situation,
2. interpersonal objectives, involving the establishment or maintenance of a relationship with the other(s), and
3. identity objectives, in which there is management of the communicative situation to the end of presenting a desired self image for the speaker and creating or maintaining a particular sense of self for the other(s). (p. 200)

Mutual influence is an ongoing and inevitable process in normal conversations and in social interaction in general. As Burgoon and Buller (2003) argue:

> [I]t is a misnomer in interpersonal interaction to separate senders from receivers. . . . In normal conversations, speakers encoding messages are simultaneously monitoring and decoding the conversational behavior of listeners . . . Likewise, listeners usually are not passive message recipients. While listening, they provide verbal and nonverbal feedback . . . and formulate their own talk. (p. 240)

Thus, conversations are dynamic, multifunctional, multidimensional, and multi-modal events in which participants must perform numerous communication tasks simultaneously in real time.

A vast literature exists exploring the nature and consequences of social influence. Among the most fundamental frameworks to emerge from this work is the two process model of influence (Turner, 1991). The framework highlights two types of influence: (1) informational influence and (2) normative influence.

*Informational influence* is described as "true influence," meaning that this type of influence results in privately held acceptance and internalization and long-lasting attitude change (Turner, 1991). By way of contrast, *normative influence* involves public compliance in which a person conforms to prevailing social pressures, but does not actually accept the position or behavior internally. In such instances, the power of others to offer rewards or punishments, or the individual's desire for approval or to avoid rejection, motivate compliance or conformity with others' views, but that compliance or conformity is not accompanied by genuine commitment (Turner, 1991).

As has been demonstrated in any number of studies, and is also often observed in everyday communication, social and peer pressure to conform is a powerful shaping force in human behavior. For example, Yanovitzky, Stewart, and Lederman (2006) discovered that perceived alcohol use by friends and best friends was a stronger predictor of personal alcohol use among college students than perceptions of alcohol use among other peers (i.e., other college students). Given our fundamental need to join and be a part of groups, the old adage "choose your friends wisely" continues to be good advice.

# CONCLUSION

Through our words, sentences, tone, appearance, actions, and other behaviors, we produce messages that are potentially significant sources of information for others. Some of the messages we encode intentionally, others more by accident. Decoding occurs when our messages are attended to and interpreted.

Most of our purposefully created messages involve the use of language. Languages are similar to one another in several respects. All have rules relative to phonology, syntax, semantics, and pragmatics. Still more basic similarities result from the physiological and cognitive capacities of humans. The physiology of human speech is more advanced than is necessary for vocalizations in other species, and the differences between human mental abilities and those of other animals are even more pronounced. Particular areas of the brain—*Broca's area* and *Wernicke's area*—both of which are located in the left hemisphere, are thought to be critical to language use.

Our capacity for language develops from the time we are infants through a progressive series of stages. As adults, we use language not only to refer to the immediate environment, as does the child, but also to record, describe, assert, express emotion, question, identify ourselves, entertain, defend, and accomplish a number of other purposes.

Language plays a central role in human interaction in terms of representation, conversation, and persuasion and social influence. At the most basic level it is our means for representing and labeling elements of our environment and one another.

By means of language we negotiate understandings through conversation. Understanding the nature of conversation requires an awareness of the influence of rules and rituals, language and gender differences, content and relationship messages, and meta-communication. Understanding the nature of persuasion and social influence requires an awareness of principles that contribute to compliance-gaining.

Language and verbal communication play a central role in the processes associated with persuasion and social influence. Persuasion involves purposeful efforts to change behaviors through communication. Social influence is a more general concept that may refer to either intentional or unintentional influence outcomes that occur in interpersonal, group, and public contexts. Some approaches to persuasion have been influenced by the linear and transmission-oriented models of communication. Other perspectives on communication, particularly those that highlight the interactive, meaning-centered, and interpretive nature of communication, are also helpful for explaining more informal and naturally occurring social influence dynamics. Mutual influence is an ongoing and inevitable process in normal conversations and in social interaction.

## KEY POINTS

After reading this chapter, you should be able to:

- Explain the process of developing language skills
- Describe how the "rules of language" are used for relationship negotiation, persuasion, and social influence
- Analyze the complex relationship between language and reality
- Articulate the use and importance of verbal codes in our daily lives

## REFERENCES

Anwar, M. (2015). "Cisgender" was just added to the Oxford English Dictionary and here are three reasons this is important. Retrieved from http://www.bustle.com/articles/94604-cisgender-was-just-added-to-the-oxford-english-dictionary-and-here-are-three-reasons-this-is

Aronson, E., Turner, J. A., & Carlsmith, J. M., (1963). Communicator credibility and communication discrepancy as a determinant of opinion change. *Journal of Abnormal and Social Psychology, 67,* 31-36.

Ashcraft, M. H., & Gavansky, G. A. (2013). *Cognition.* Boston, MA: Pearson.

Buck, R. (1982). Spontaneous and symbolic nonverbal behavior and the ontogeny of communication. In R. S. Feldman (Ed.), *Development of nonverbal behavior in children* (pp. 29-62). New York, NY: Springer-Verlag.

Budd, R. W. (2003). General semantics. In R. W. Budd & B. D. Ruben (Eds.), *Interdisciplinary approaches to human communication* (pp. 71-93). New Brunswick, NJ: Transaction.

Burgoon, J. K., & Buller, D. B. (2003). Interpersonal deception theory. In J. S. Seiter & R. H. Gass (Eds.), *Perspectives on persuasion, social influence, and compliance gaining* (pp. 239-264). Boston, MA: Pearson.

Canary, D. J., & Hause, K. S. (1993). Is there any reason to research sex difference in communication? *Communication Quarterly, 41,* 129-144.

Cialdini, R.B., & Sagarin, B. J. (2005). Principles of interpersonal influence. In T.C. Brock & M.C. Green (Eds.), *Persuasion: Psychological insights and perspectives* (pp. 143-170). Thousand Oaks, CA: Sage.

Clark, R. A., & Delia, J. G. (1979). *Topoi* and rhetorical competence. *Quarterly Journal of Speech, 65*(2), 187-206.

Coates, J. (1986). *Women, men, and language.* New York, NY: Longman.

Farb, P. (1978). *Word play.* New York, NY: Bantam Books.

Fishman, P. M. (1978). Interaction: The work women do. *Social Problems, 25,* 397-406.

Fiske, J. (1982). *Introduction to communication studies.* New York, NY: Methuen.

Geschwind, N. (1991). Specializations of the human brain. In W. S.-Y. Wang (Ed.), *The emergence of language: Development and evolution* (pp. 72-87). New York, NY: W. H. Freeman.

Gleason, J. B. (1987). Sex differences in parent-child interaction. In S. U. Philips, S. Steele, & C. Tanz (Eds.), *Language, gender, and sex in comparative perspective* (pp. 189-199). Cambridge, UK: Cambridge University Press.

Gouldner, A. W. (1960). The norm of reciprocity. *American Sociological Review, 25,* 161-178.

Grice, H. P. (1975). Logic and conversation. In P. Cole & J. L. Morgan (Eds.), *Syntax and semantics: Speech acts* (Vol. 3, pp. 41-58). New York, NY: Academic Press.

Hancock, A. B., & Rubin, B. A. (2015). Influence of communication partner's gender on language. *Journal of Language and Social Psychology, 34*(1), 46-64.

Harrington, N. G. (1995). The effects of college students' alcohol resistance strategies. *Health Communication, 7*(4), 371-391.

Hempelmann, E., & Krafts, K. (2013). Bad air, amulets and mosquitoes: 2,000 years of changing perspectives on malaria. *Malaria Journal, 12,* 232.

Hunt, M. (1982). *The universe within: A new science explores the human mind.* New York, NY: Simon & Schuster.

Infante, D. A. (1985). Inducing women to be more argumentative: Source credibility effects. *Journal of Applied Communication Research, 13,* 33-44.

Infante, D. A., & Rancer, A. S. (1982). A conceptualization and measure of argumentativeness. *Journal of Personality Assessment, 46,* 72-80.

Kiesler, C. A. (1971). *The psychology of commitment: Experiments linking behavior to belief.* New York, NY: Academic Press.

Lakoff, R. (1975). *Language and woman's place.* New York, NY: Harper & Row.

Littlejohn, S. W. (1996). *Theories of human communication* (5th ed.). Belmont, CA: Wadsworth.

McLaughlin, M. L. (1984). *Conversation: How talk is organized.* Beverly Hills, CA: Sage.

McWhorter, J. H. (2014). *The language hoax: Why the world looks the same in any language.* Oxford, UK: Oxford University Press.

Milgram, S., Bickman, L., & Berkowitz, O. (1960). Note on the drawing power of crowds of different sizes. *Journal of Personality and Social Psychology, 12,* 79-82.

Miller, G. R. (1987). Persuasion. In C.R. Berger and S.H. Chaffee (Eds.), *Handbook of communication science* (pp. 446-483). New York, NY: Sage.

Moskowitz, B. A. (1991). The acquisition of language. In W. S.-Y. Wang (Ed.), *The emergence of language: Development and evolution* (pp. 131-149). New York, NY: W. H. Freeman.

Mulac, A., Wiemann, J. M., Widenmann, S. J., & Gibson, T. W. (1988). Male/female language differences and effects in same-sex and mixed-sex dyads: The gender-linked language effect. *Communication Monographs, 55,* 315-335.

Newman, M. L., Groom, C. J., Handelman, L. D., & Pennebaker, J. W. (2008). Gender differences in language use: An analysis of 14,000 text samples. *Discourse Processes, 45,* 211-236.

Nicotera, A. M., & Rancer, A. S. (1994). The influence of sex on self-perceptions and social stereotyping of aggressive communication predispositions. *Western Journal of Communication, 58,* 283-307.

Norman, D. A., & Rumelhart, D. E. (1975). *Explorations in cognition.* San Francisco, CA: Freeman.

O'Kane, J. C., & Goldbart, J. (1998). *Communication before speech: Development and assessment* (2nd ed.). London, UK: David Fulton Publishers.

Pfau, M., & Szabo, E.A. (2003). Inoculation and resistance to persuasion. In J. S. Seiter & R. H. Gass (Eds.), *Perspectives on persuasion, social influence, and compliance gaining* (pp. 265-286). Boston, MA: Pearson.

Pfeiffer, J. (1985). Girl talk-Boy talk. *Science, 6*(1), 58-63.

Rapoport, A. (1962). What is semantics? In S. I. Hayakawa (Ed.), *The use and misuse of language* (pp. 11-25). New York, NY: Fawcett Premier.

Robertson, W. O. (1983). Quantifying the meaning of words. *JAMA: Journal of the American Medical Association, 249*(19), 2631-2632.

Shiminoff, S. (1980). *Communicative rules: Theory and research.* Beverly Hills, CA: Sage.

Spender, D. (1995). Nattering on the net: Women, power and cyberspace. Milbourne, Australia: Spiniflex.

Springer, S. P., & Deutsch, G. (1989). *Left brain, right brain* (3rd ed.). New York, NJ: W. H. Freeman.

Stewart, L. P., Cooper, P. J., Stewart, A. D., & Friedley, S. A. (2003). *Communication and gender* (4th ed.). Boston, MA: Allyn & Bacon.

Sue, D. W. (2010). *Microaggressions in everyday life: Race, gender, and sexual orientation.* Hoboken, NJ: John Wiley & Sons.

Tannen, D. (2007). *You just don't understand: Men and women in conversation.* New York, NY: Harper Collins.

Thayer, L. (1982). Communication: *Sin qua non* of the behavioral sciences. In R. W. Budd & B. D. Ruben (Eds.), *Interdisciplinary approaches to human communication* (pp. 7-31). New Brunswick, NJ: Transaction Books.

Thomson, R., & Murachver, T. (2001). Predicting gender from electronic discourse. *British Journal of Social Psychology, 40,* 193-208.

Turner, J.C. (1991). *Social influence.* Pacific Grove, CA: Brooks/Cole.

Turner, L. H., Dindia, K., & Pearson, J. (1995). An investigation of female-male verbal behaviors in same-sex and mixed-sex conversations. *Communication Reports, 8,* 86-96.

Wang, W. S.-Y. (1982). Language and derivative systems. In W. S.-Y. Wang (Ed.), *Human communication: Language and its psychobiological basis* (pp. 36-38). San Francisco, CA: W. H. Freeman.

Wardhaugh, R. (1985). *How conversation works.* Oxford, UK: Basil Blackwell.

Watzlawick, P., Beavin, J. H., & Jackson, D. D. (1967). *Pragmatics of human communication.* New York, NY: Norton.

Whitehall, H. (1964). The English language. In N. Webster (Author), *Webster's new world dictionary of the American language* (pp. xv-xxix). Cleveland, OH: World.

Whorf, B. L. (1956). *Language, thought, and reality.* Cambridge, MA: MIT Press.

Wood, B. S. (1976). *Children and communication: Verbal and nonverbal language development.* Englewood Cliffs, NJ: Prentice Hall.

Yanovitzky, I., Stewart, L. P., & Lederman, L. C. (2006). Social distance, perceived drinking by peers, and alcohol use by college students. *Health Communication, 19*(1), 1-10.

# CHAPTER 6

# PERCEPTION & INFORMATION PROCESSING

**In this chapter, you will learn about:**

- The process of perception and the implications for communication outcomes
- The variables and characteristics which influence the perception process
- The effects of the perception process on our ability to process and act on everyday messages

## SELECTION

## INTERPRETATION

## RETENTION (MEMORY)

- Short-Term and Long-Term Memory
- Semantic and Episodic Memory

## RECEIVER INFLUENCES

- Needs
- Attitudes, Beliefs, and Values
- Goals
- Capability

- Use
- Communication Style
- Experience and Habit

## MESSAGE AND INFORMATION INFLUENCES

- Origin
- Mode
- Physical Characteristics
- Organization
- Novelty

## SOURCE INFLUENCES

- Proximity
- Physical and Social Attraction and Similarity
- Credibility and Authoritativeness
- Motivation and Intent
- Delivery
- Status, Power or Authority, and Peer Pressure

## TECHNOLOGICAL AND ENVIRONMENTAL INFLUENCES

- Technology
- The Environment
- Consistency and Competition

## AN ACTIVE AND COMPLEX PROCESS

## CONCLUSION

## KEY POINTS

Perception and the processing of information involves attending to and transforming environmental messages into a form that can be used to guide behavior. This process is an active one, consisting of three elements—*selection, interpretation,* and *retention.* We will discuss each of these in detail in the pages ahead, beginning with an illustration.

Ed awoke this morning at 7:30 AM to a grey sky and light rain. He noticed the weather almost immediately, because it was a Saturday and he had looked forward all week to a chance to get outside. He chatted with his wife, Jane, about a variety of topics while he dressed and ate breakfast. He began to ponder his options as to how to spend the day, given that he was stuck inside. Ed left the breakfast table and walked down the hallway.

He glanced in the study and saw the piles of pages strewn about his desk. "I should work on the report due next week," he thought to himself. "My annual review will depend on how well my boss likes it."

He continued into the family room where he noticed his children, Ripley and Sparrow, sitting in front of the television set. He reflected to himself on how fast time goes by, and decided that he really ought to spend more time with the kids. "Maybe a board game or some sort of craft project we could work on together . . ." He exchanged a few brief words with his children, and it seemed that Sponge Bob was of more interest to the kids than he was, so he turned his attention to a stack of newspapers and magazines lying across the room on a table. As he looked at the pile of reading material, he thought about how he had spent only a few minutes with the mail, newspapers, magazines all week—and the email inbox! "I really should try to get caught up on these today," he thought. "No . . . the report has got to come first!"

He made his way back to the study, situated himself at the computer, and began to shuffle through the materials he needed for the report. He came across a book he had been using as a primary source in his report, picked it up, and began rereading sections of the text and leafing through the illustrations.

He started streaming some music on his computer but the occasional interruptions for commercials annoyed him, so began listening to a podcast he had downloaded to his phone.

As he sat at the desk, Ed glanced out the window. Incredible! The grey skies had cleared, the rain had stopped, and the sun was shining brightly. He heard the distant whine of a neighbor's lawn mower and glanced almost instinctively at his own lawn. "My yard really does need to be mowed . . . And the car is dirty," he thought to himself. "I could do both jobs tomorrow, if the weather holds."

He checked the Weather Channel: "Clearing this afternoon, highs in the low 80's."

"I'll wash the car today so it will be clean for the weekend and put off mowing the lawn until tomorrow," he decided. "The grass might still be a bit wet now, anyway . . .

But what if the weather report is wrong? *If* it's wrong? It's always wrong. If I put off mowing until tomorrow, and it rains, I might not be able to mow until next weekend; and by then the grass will be so long it would take most of two days to mow."

"How ridiculous this is!" he concluded. "The lawn is ruling my life. It's amazing how one's priorities evolve by default. Back to the report!"

This story reveals a good deal about Ed's communication habits, values, orientations, and, at the same time, helps to illustrate how perception and information processing works. For analytic purposes, let's briefly reconstruct the scenario, paying particular attention to the cues Ed attended to, the meanings he attached to them, and the manner in which these meanings guided his behavior.

There are a number of things Ed might think about upon waking on a given day. On this particular day, he was primarily concerned with the day of the week and the weather—*Saturday* and *rain*. That he chose to be interested in these particular things and not others had largely to do with the meanings each had for him. Saturday was a special day, one he had looked forward to all week. Grey clouds and rain meant it would be impossible for him to pursue some of the activities he had hoped and planned for. Together, *Saturday* and *rain* signified plans ruined, nothing more, nothing less.

**FIGURE 6.1**

Sometimes it's difficult to prioritize tasks.

Despite this reality, Ed moved through the sequence necessary to the activities he had come to think of as essential to the start of each day: taking a shower, shaving, selecting clothes, dressing, making his way to the kitchen, sitting down at the table, talking to his wife, eating breakfast, and so forth.

As he chatted with Jane, new messages were introduced into his environment. These provided an opportunity for him to overcome the "plans ruined" aura, which to that point had been the dominant theme in his information processing.

In talking to his wife—and himself— Ed determined that there was little

© iQoncept/Shutterstock.com

to be gained by thinking about his original plans. There were, after all, a number of plans one might have that *Saturday + rain* would not ruin. As he began to attach new meaning to the situation, his attention was directed toward information sources and possible interpretations he was unaware of only minutes earlier.

Because Ed was ready to consider options as to how to spend the day, the stack of documents on his desk for his report was singled out from other potential sources of information in the environment. At some level of awareness, these documents meant a variety of things to him at that point, including *job unfinished, frustration, guilt,* and *challenge.* However, none of these meanings were compelling enough to lead him to undertake work on the report at that instant.

In the family room, the sound of his children playing became prominent communication sources. They triggered a variety of meanings—*affection, enjoyment, responsibility, concern.* As with the significance of the report, these meanings were central to his self-concept and sense of what matters, and, as a result, they commanded his interest and receptivity.

In passing, he also attended momentarily to the television show they were watching. He recognized at some slightly-less-than-conscious level that the messages generated by the Sponge Bob cartoon were performing very different functions for Ripley and Sparrow than for him. In some sense, Ed was competing with Sponge Bob for his children's attention—and he was losing the competition.

The presence of the week's mail, magazines, and newspapers became additional sources of communication. In the context of his own life they signified *knowledgeability, credibility, enjoyment,* and *responsibility.* Ed was also aware of a need to be familiar with the "news" in order to be current in discussions with his friends and colleagues.

Though these meanings were also important to his definition of himself, they were not, at that instant, as critical as the meanings related to other things. Ed "decided"—again, in a less-than-wholly-aware manner—to reject these and other options in favor of returning to work on the report.

The communication process continued as he selected a particular information source—an Internet channel—and streaming content to be "background music" for his working. His unstated objective in so doing was to override competing background cues in the immediate environment.

In looking through the materials on his desk, his eyes fell upon a book that had been significant earlier in his work. It became the primary object of his attention for several minutes, as he recalled its contents and his reaction to them. Noise resulting from the commercials on the streaming music channel became another unavoidable information source, and he acted to replace those messages with others from the podcast he had stored on his phone.

On glancing out the window, the clearing skies and sun became significant cues for him. They signified "original plans OK; no need to pursue the present options, unless you want to." As his attention shifted to the environment outside, Ed noted the whine of a lawn mower, which triggered a variety of meanings, each of which required attention and resolution—the lawn, the car, and so on.

In scanning through the alternative meanings called up from memory, he inadvertently began a self-reflexive thought process. As he reflected on his own information processing, this time quite consciously, he decided to execute more control over himself and his surroundings and pursue what he had determined to be the most "logical" alternatives for use of his time.

In returning his attention to work on the report, Ed, in effect, decided to attach less value to messages related to the physical environment external to his study—the lawn, cars, and so on. He chose instead to focus on information sources that were pertinent to his report and to working on the report itself. The act of selecting the option he did also had the effect of reaffirming his priorities.

Many interesting facets of communication are illustrated in even a rather commonplace situation such as the one just described. As straightforward and natural as the events that transpired may seem, they involve an array of factors and represent active processes of information selection, interpretation, and retention.

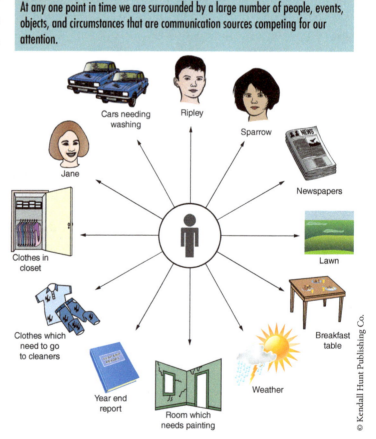

**FIGURE 6.2**

At any one point in time we are surrounded by a large number of people, events, objects, and circumstances that are communication sources competing for our attention.

Cars needing washing

Ripley

Sparrow

Jane

Newspapers

Clothes in closet

Lawn

Clothes which need to go to cleaners

Breakfast table

Year end report

Weather

Room which needs painting

© Kendall Hunt Publishing Co.

## SELECTION

At any instant in time we are surrounded in our environment by persons, objects, and circumstances that are sources of messages vying for our attention and interest. In the foregoing sequence, Ed's wife and children, the pages of his report, the computer, his phone, Sponge Bob, the outdoors, the lawnmower, and the weather were each potential communication sources that were competing for his attention, as illustrated in Figure 6.2.

Predictably, in such circumstances we select certain information sources to attend to and disregard others. Even in a simple situation we make a number of complex decisions, and we are unaware of many of them. When one analyzes the situation, it becomes apparent that Ed "decided" to give attention to the weather, the day of the week, his children, and the report rather than to other information sources in his environment—such as a room that needed painting, clothes that were to be taken to the cleaners, an unopened package on the table, the expressions on his children's faces when they exchanged words, and so on.

This selection process operates similarly in all situations. Consider a circumstance where we pause in a hallway to chat with an acquaintance. First, the very act of noticing the other person involves selection of particular communication sources. Triggered by the constellation of factors associated with the appearance of the other person, and perhaps some verbal cue like "Hi," we begin focusing ourselves on the other person and on things that we believe will be necessary to the interchange that will follow. In so doing, we ignore other potential cues—the temperature, the color of the carpeting, the appearance of other people who may pass by, the noise of a nearby copy machine, or the thunderstorm outside—through a complex selectivity process that has occupied the attention of many scholars over the years (e.g., Albert, Becker & Brock, 1970; Broadbent, 1957; Craig, 1979; Donohew & Palmgreen, 1971a, 1971b; Krippendorf, 1993; Treisman, 1969).

The classic illustration of *selective attention* is provided by large parties and similar social gatherings. During such events, we find that it is not at all difficult to carry on a series of perfectly intelligible discussions without being overly distracted by other conversations. It is even possible to tune in to an exchange among several other people a good distance away, without shifting our position and while appearing to be deeply engrossed in conversation with a person close at hand. In that same setting, we are able to tune out the entire external environment, periodically, in order to concentrate on our own feelings, decide what we ought to be doing, or think about how we are being perceived by others. It is also possible to attend to the gathering as a whole, paying attention to the level, pitch, rhythm, number of interactions, and level of activity, as a basis for making some general assessments of the gathering as a whole—whether it is sedate or wild, winding up or down, and so on (Becker, 1978). We should note, however, that in some instances our skills at communicative multi-tasking may not always be as refined as we think they are—trying to text or send email while driving representing one very notable example.

Given these examples, it may seem as though selection operates much like a filter, letting in some sounds, images, or smells, while screening out others (Broadbent, 1957). However, the process is often more complex than this way of thinking implies. For instance, we know that even when we have "tuned in" to a particular communication source and "tuned out" others, the selected-out messages may, nonetheless, be taken note of. This is the case, for instance, when a honking horn or the sound of an incoming text interrupts our attention in a discussion with a friend while crossing the street, or when the sound of our own or a friend's name is heard "through" the otherwise unintelligible din of a party (Craig, 1979). Additionally, there is evidence to suggest that it is possible to take note of and attach meaning to messages even when we are unaware of doing so (Dixon, 1981).

An understanding of the complexity of the attention process has led to the adoption of a "modified filter model" as a way of thinking about selection (Craig, 1979). It is thought that we assign priorities to competing information sources and allocate attention among them, while monitoring other messages and perhaps even attending to still other sources that are unknown even to the individuals involved.

## INTERPRETATION

*Interpretation* occurs when we assign meaning or significance to a cue or message in the environment—whether to regard it as important or trivial, serious or humorous, new or old, contradictory or consistent, amusing or alarming.

Depending on the way we select and interpret messages, very different consequences result. For example, in Figure 6.3, depending on where we focus, we may see two women talking or three white columns.

FIGURE 6.3
Interpretation—The Construction of Meaning

© Juriah Mosin, 2014. Shutterstock, Inc.

Even our reaction to a simple, "Hi, how are you?" will depend, among other things, on whether we think a person appears to us to be male or female (and the significance we attach to their perceived gender), whether we regard the individual as attractive or unattractive, whether the person is a family member or a stranger, how the person is dressed, where the encounter takes place, and how we interpret the other person's motives.

## RETENTION (MEMORY)

From the preceding discussion, it should be apparent that memory plays an indispensable role in the interpretative process. We are able to store and actively use an incredible amount of information, and we can locate and use it with an efficiency and ease of operation that is astounding (Hunt, 1982).

We have little difficulty accessing the information we need in order to go about our daily routine—to locate the bathroom, closet, and kitchen; to select appropriate clothing and to dress; to start and operate an automobile; or to find the way to the bus or train. In a split second, and with a high degree of accuracy, we can answer questions like "Who was the first president of the United States?" or "What is the name for the sound frequently heard following lightning?" These certainly seem like "simple" questions. But think how remarkable it is that we are able to retrieve this kind of information so quickly and with so little effort.

As Hunt (1982) notes:

> Although every act of thinking involves the use of images, sounds, symbols, meanings, and connections between things, all stored in memory, the organization of memory is so efficient that most of the time we are unaware of having to exert any effort to locate and use these materials. Consider the range of kinds of information you keep in, and can easily summon forth, from your own memory: the face of your closest friend . . . the words and melody of the national anthem . . . the spelling of almost every word you can think of . . . the name of every object you can see from where you are now sitting . . . the way your room looked when you were eight . . . the set of skills you need to drive a car in heavy traffic . . . and enough more to fill many shelves full of books.  (p. 86)

These are examples of *recall*—active, deliberate retrieval of information from memory, a capability that may well be unique to humans. We share with other animals the capacity to use information for *recognition*—recognizing objects, places, circumstances, and people when in their presence (Hunt, 1982).

Much effort has been directed to understanding the complex processes by which memory operates, particularly in the area concerned with identifying stages of information processing (Lindsay & Norman, 1977; Loftus & Loftus, 1976).

## Short-Term and Long-Term Memory

Information enters the system through one or several communication modes. In selecting and attending to particular messages, we begin to attach meaning to those symbols following rules we have learned and frequently used (Hunt, 1982). A good deal of sensory information can be processed within the system at any one time. If, for example, you scroll through a website to determine what movie is playing at a particular theater, not only that information but also information relative to other items on the screen, such as other movies and other theaters, or ads, would also be processed at some level of awareness. The information other than that being sought would be lost and would decay very rapidly—probably within a second or so—unless it became a particular focus of attention (Loftus & Lofus, 1976).

Information that is to be further used becomes a part of what is called *short-term memory* and is available for a relatively restricted period of time—perhaps 15 seconds (Loftus & Loftus, 1976). Our short-term memory capacity is limited under normal circumstances to a few pieces of information only—a phone number, an email address, or a string of several letters or words. Most of us have had the experience of meeting someone at a party and forgetting that person's name by the end of our conversation. This forgetting illustrates how rapidly information is lost from short-term memory. Through recitation or rehearsal, however, we can extend the time available to use information. Thus, if we repeat the person's name when we are introduced, the likelihood of remembering it greatly increases.

Some of the information is further processed and elaborated to become a part of our *long-term memory.* Generally, the longer the time that a piece of information is available to us in short-term memory, the greater the chance that it will become a part of our long-term memory. Therefore, if we call someone by name several times during our conversation we are far more likely to remember the name later. Names become a part of our long-term memory either naturally, through use, or actively, through conscious memorization.

Recall and recognition exemplify the two general classes of human memory: (1) relatively slow retrievals that require conscious processing and (2) relatively fast retrievals that require no conscious processing. Some of the other characteristics of these two retrieval processes include (Mandler, 1985):

| *Slow Retrievals* | *Fast Retrievals* |
|---|---|
| Nonautomatic | Automatic |
| Conscious | Unconscious |
| Controlled | Uncontrolled |
| Indirect access | Direct access |
| Voluntary | Involuntary |

## Semantic and Episodic Memory

Our general knowledge of the people, places, and things in the world is called *semantic memory. Episodic memories* relate to recollections and retrieval of information regarding personal happenings, particular objects, people, and events experienced by an individual at a specific time and place (Williams, Conway & Cohen, 2008). *Autobiographical memories*—memories of oneself—are considered to be episodic. While this distinction is a useful one, scholars also point out that the two types of memory are related: Semantic knowledge is derived from episodic memory, and episodic memories are organized and categorized based on semantic categories.

Cohen (2008) provides the following list of characteristics of memory:

- Memory is an overloaded system—there is more to be remembered than can possibly be managed by the brain.
- Memory must be selective—decisions must be made as to what to remember and what to ignore.
- Memory must be dynamic—adjustments must be made in response to changes in the world around us.
- Memory must link past, present, and future—memory provides for continuity of meaning across time.
- Memory must be able to construct hypothetical representations—imagination, creativity, and consideration of possibilities are necessary characteristics of memory.
- Memory must store both general and specific information—generalized and specialized knowledge are both required in human activity.
- Memory must store information implicitly—information must be easily and automatically stored and organized for retrieval. Often this is done in terms of categories, time periods, and level of generality/specificity.
- Memory processes must be complex—elaborate information sorting and organizing processes are necessary to integrate new information with past experience.
- Memory retrieval strategies are critical—retrieving information becomes more critical and difficult as memories proliferate.
- Memory retrieval must utilize spontaneous and deliberate retrieval—memories must be able to be retrieved spontaneously as well as deliberately.  (adapted from pp. 384-389)

As useful as the foregoing view of information processing is, it is important to be aware of the limitations of what has been termed the *sequential-stage model*. Researchers remind us that information processing is an extremely complex operation. It is often difficult to distinguish between its various stages. The distinction between selection, interpretation, and episodic and semantic memory can be fuzzy. Further, a sequential-stage model could imply that information processing is a passive and programmed process. Clearly this is not the case; complex interactions between the individual and environment are fundamental to the ongoing dynamics of information processing.

# RECEIVER INFLUENCES

For each of us, a complex set of influences works together to influence our decisions as to which messages we will attend to and how we will interpret and retain the information that results. Many of these have to do with the nature of the *receiver*.

As children we adapt to a world in which we are highly dependent upon parents and other adults for the satisfaction of our needs, wants, and desires. That dependence creates a particular set of information-reception tendencies for most of us, in which our parents, relatives, and, gradually, peer relations are highly significant.

## *Needs*

*Needs* are among the most crucial factors that play a role in information processing. Scholars generally agree that our most basic needs, like those of other animals, have to do with our physiological well-being—food, shelter, physical well-being, and sex (Maslow, 1954). See Figure 6.4 for an illustration. These basic needs can be potent forces in directing our behavior. When unmet, our efforts to satisfy these needs are important guiding forces in information reception and processing. To the individual who hasn't eaten for several days, for example, few message sources are likely to be as noteworthy, or *salient,* as those relating to food. The knowledge that unsatisfied needs often increases the salience of particular messages has led nutritionists to suggest that a good way to save money and eat more healthily is to shop for groceries after eating, rather than before.

The same pattern occurs with regard to our health. A headache or upset stomach or other symptoms, which are readily dismissed by people who believe themselves to be well, may become the focus of great attention and concern for people who think they may be ill.

Other needs or motives, including social contact, reality exploration and comprehension, socialization, diversion, entertainment, and play, have to do with our spiritual, psychological, social, and communicative well-being (Maslow,

FIGURE 6.4
Maslow's hierarchy of needs

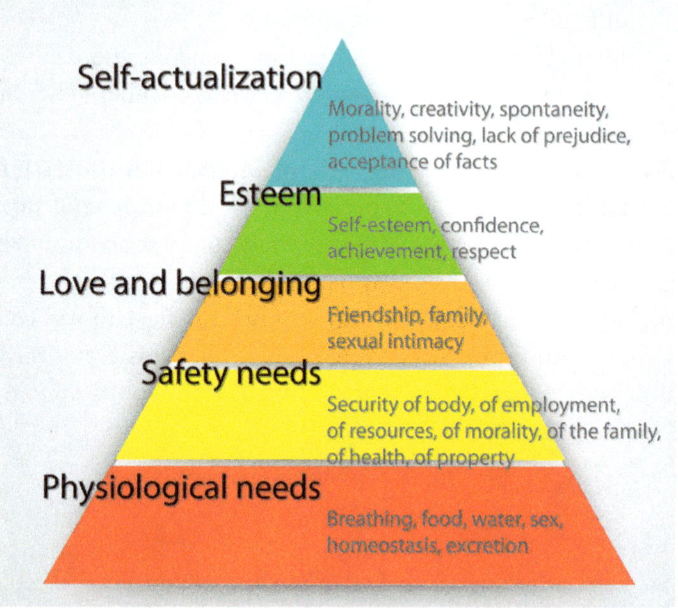

Self-actualization
Morality, creativity, spontaneity, problem solving, lack of prejudice, acceptance of facts

Esteem
Self-esteem, confidence, achievement, respect

Love and belonging
Friendship, family, sexual intimacy

Safety needs
Security of body, of employment, of resources, of morality, of the family, of health, of property

Physiological needs
Breathing, food, water, sex, homeostasis, excretion

© Anna Levtushenko/Shutterstock.com

1954). Perhaps the most basic of these needs has to do with maintaining and developing our identity and self-concept (Maslow, 1954), topics that will be addressed in more detail in Chapter 8. All of us want to be seen positively, as worthy, desirable, competent, and respectable. There are, of course, differences between us in the ways we understand these concepts and in the particular qualities for which we wish others to value us. Some of us aspire to be seen as creative, intelligent, professionally competent, and an occupational success. Being seen as religious, honest, honorable, or empathetic may be more important to others. Some of us would prefer to be admired for our leadership ability; others wish to be respected for their loyalty as followers, and so on.

Personal, social, and communicative needs play an important role in selection, interpretation, and retention. Their role has been highlighted by scholars who focus on the "uses and gratifications" of mass media (Katz, Blumler & Gurevitch, 1974; Rubin, 1993). This work helps substantiate the view that there can be a direct relationship between particular unsatisfied, or ungratified, needs and resulting patterns of exposure to mass media programs and other message sources.

## Attitudes, Beliefs, and Values

The attitudes, preferences, and predispositions one has about particular topics, persons, or situations also play a critical role in information-processing activities and outcomes. For instance, people will generally attend to and be favorably disposed toward messages, sources, and interpretations that support their present views before they consider nonsupportive messages, sources, or conclusions (Wheeless, 1974). If we favor a candidate for a particular elective office we are likely to pay more attention to sources of information about that candidate, such as articles and political advertisements, than we will to items about other candidates. We are also likely to spend time talking about politics with other people who share our views.

*Values* is a term used to refer to basic principles that we live by—our sense of what we ought and ought not to do in our relations with the environment and one another. As with attitudes and beliefs, values influence selection, interpretation, and retention.

There are instances where messages that are likely to be interpreted as inconsistent and nonsupportive of our attitudes, beliefs, or values can lead to *more,* rather than *less,* attention and interest. We may devote attention and effort to persuading people who espouse beliefs or values that differ from our own. Following a similar logic, we sometimes spend more time reflecting upon people and events that trouble us than on those that reassure and comfort us, perhaps because we have come to take the latter for granted.

## Goals

Most of us are at best only partially aware of our needs, attitudes, beliefs, and values. In contrast, we consciously set our *goals.*

When an individual decides to pursue a particular plan, career, personal relationship, or personal challenge, that goal serves to direct his or her attention toward certain information sources and away from others, as suggested in Figure 6.5.

If a woman has the goal of driving from Princeton, New Jersey, to JFK Airport in New York City to catch a specific flight, this objective plays a major role in guiding information selection, interpretation, and retention. On the way to the airport, she must process messages concerning the location, direction, and rate of speed of her car and other vehicles in the vicinity. She must also attend to, interpret, and remember the road markings and signs that provide pertinent information and those that indicate the way to the airport. The gauges, instruments, and other controls of the car must also be monitored. Additionally, she must pay attention to weather conditions, time remaining before arrival at the airport, location of the long-term parking area, the proper terminal for the flight departure, the flight number, her seat assignment, the boarding time, and so on. Until the goal is achieved and she is seated on the airplane, a substantial amount of her information-receiving effort is influenced by the commitment to the self-determined goal of taking a plane flight to another city.

**FIGURE 6.5**

At any point in time, one's goals have a direct and profound effect on information selection, interpretation, and retention.

When we set a goal of achieving a certain level of competence in an area such as sports, for example, this objective shapes not only the messages to which we attend but also the interpretations of them that we make. First, the goal increases the likelihood that we will expose ourselves to communication sources and situations that pertain to sports in general and our chosen sport in particular. Second, pursuing the goal may well increase our contact with other people interested in a similar activity, and this will have an additional influence on information reception. The demands of physical fitness may also play an important role in determining how information about food, alcohol, and cigarettes will be attended to, interpreted, and remembered.

In a similar manner, a decision to pursue a particular career—to become a physician, for instance—directs our attention toward certain messages and away from others. Pre-med students are influenced by their goal toward gaining knowledge about physiology, anatomy, and chemistry and away from information pertinent to students of engineering, business administration, or journalism. Acquiring appropriate interpretations for these information sources is a priority until the goal is achieved or revised. A change of goals often also implies a change in information processing.

## Capability

Our level of intelligence, previous experience with a particular topic area, and facility with language have an important impact on the kinds of messages we attend to and the manner in which we interpret and retain them. The probability of people who speak only English spending much time listening to Spanish radio broadcasts, watching French television programming, or reading novels in Russian is naturally very low, simply because they lack the capability of meaningfully processing the information. By the same token, it is unlikely that people who have no quantitative or research background will enjoy reading articles in technical or scholarly journals. While they may possess the intellectual potential, their lack of familiarity with research and with the technical language used in the publications affects potential interest and comprehension, not to mention retention.

## Use

We attend to and devote effort to understanding and remembering messages we think we will need or be able to use. The learning of language offers an excellent example. It is a virtual certainty that children will learn to speak the language of those around them. For the most part, this learning occurs irrespective of whether there are efforts at formal instruction. We attend to, learn to interpret, and retain messages about how to use spoken language because it is essential to our participation in most human activities.

In school we attend to and retain a large quantity of information on a variety of topics that may have no immediate personal relevance. Were it not for the opportunities and requirements to "rehearse" and "use" this retained knowledge to demonstrate course mastery on exams and quizzes, much less information would be remembered.

The same principle operates in many other domains. To the individual who is thinking about getting a new car, statistics such as safety ratings, estimated miles per gallon, and price suddenly become much more salient, more interesting, and far easier to remember than they were prior to the decision to shop for a car.

## Communication Style

Communication style can influence information reception in two ways: first, depending on our habits and preferences, we may be drawn to or may actively avoid the opportunity to deal with other people. People who are shy or apprehensive about engaging in verbal communication in a group setting, for example, may avoid such circumstances whenever possible (McCroskey, 1977; McCroskey, 1984; Phillips & Metzger, 1973). Such an individual might prefer to watch a television show on health or consult a website for information on a particular illness, rather than ask a doctor for information. Even when people with this style of communication make an effort to actively engage in interpersonal situations, they may be uncomfortable. This discomfort may well affect the way they attend to, interpret, and retain information.

A less direct influence of our communication style on information reception has to do with the manner in which we present ourselves to others. The way we "come across" to those with whom we interact can have a substantial impact on the way they react to us, and this will influence both the quality and quantity of information they make available. People who are highly talkative, for instance, often have less verbal information available to them than they otherwise might, because the people with whom they converse have limited time to share their thoughts or feelings—or because of concerns that information they provide may be shared more readily with other people than they desire (see Figure 6.6). Various aspects of

© weniworks/Shutterstock.com

our interpersonal style—our greetings, tone, word choice, level of openness, dress, and appearance—also have an impact on the messages other people make available to us, and this, in turn, has a direct bearing on our selection, interpretation, and retention.

## Experience and Habit

Many of our information reception tendencies develop as a result of our accumulated experiences. Our "communication habits" are no doubt the major guiding influence in how we select, interpret, and retain messages at any moment in time. Whether we think of watching a particular television show, exchanging pleasantries with an acquaintance on the way to work, checking email and social media sites throughout the day, or arguing with a friend or family member, our previous experiences, and the communication patterns we have developed as a result of these experiences, have a definite influence on our message reception patterns. See Figure 6.7.

## MESSAGE AND INFORMATION INFLUENCES

In addition to factors associated with *receivers,* characteristics of the information, or *message,* also have an impact on selection, interpretation, and retention. Five particularly important considerations are origin, mode, physical character, organization, and novelty.

**FIGURE 6.7**

Glance at the items in the illustration below for five to ten seconds, close the book, and list the items that you can remember on a sheet of paper. When you compare the resulting list with the picture, it is obvious that many items were forgotten and others were perhaps never noticed in the first place. Further study of those things noticed and remembered, and those not, can underscore aspects of the information reception process, the impact of memory on selection and retention of new information, and the complexity of information processing. Generally speaking, in any situation, what we notice and remember directly reflects our past experiences. Sometimes an item is taken note of precisely because we cannot relate to and identify it. In any case, those things noticed and remembered and those forgotten in any situation generally say as much or more about us—our past experiences, interests, priorities, hobbies, and so on—as they do about the actual information sources present in the environment.

© tovovan, 2014. Shutterstock, Inc.

# Origin

Some of the messages we attend to have their origins in our physical environment. When we select an item on which to sit, identify a landmark as a guide to navigation, pick out an apartment in which to live, decide whether the temperature in our room is too high, or develop a theory of why apples fall from trees, we do so using information based on objects, events, relationships, or phenomena in the physical environment.

We also make use of information we create ourselves through *intrapersonal communication.* When we listen to and think about what we have said to someone else, try to recall our knowledge about a particular topic, "talk to ourselves," or look at ourselves in a mirror before leaving for an important engagement, we are processing information of which we are the source. We also use messages we ourselves create to assess our own internal feelings. Our sense of illness, fear, happiness, frustration, confusion, excitement, pain, and anxiety result from information that originates in our own physiological functions and the attention and interpretations we derive from them.

Certainly the great majority of information of significance to us in our environment arises either directly or indirectly from the activities of other people in relationships—through *interpersonal communication.* Often these messages originate in face-to-face interaction with others. Other interpersonal messages are the product of the activities of people separated from us in either time or space or both, transported to us by means of various communication media.

In some circumstances we are limited as to which of these message sources we can use. If, for example, we wish to find out the temperature in Tokyo last night, we have little choice but to rely on messages provided by other people through technology. If we want to know how we feel about some situation facing us tomorrow, we rely on information we create ourselves. If we need to determine the exact temperature of water being heated for cooking, that information can be best derived by placing a thermometer in the water.

There are many other instances in which we can choose among these sources. We can seek an answer to the question, "Is it hot in here?" using any of these sources; we can make a determination based on our personal "feelings"; we can ask the opinion of one or several other people; or we can consult a nearby thermometer. A similar situation occurs when we undertake a project such as figuring out how to set up a new piece of technology. We may choose to tackle the chore ourselves making use of the manufacturer's instructions. We could seek the assistance of a friend. We may "dig right in" without consulting the instructions, relying on our own resources and prior experience with similar projects. Or we can use a combination of these information sources.

The availability or lack of availability of various message sources has an obvious and direct impact on the way in which we attend to, interpret, and retain information. Individuals may vary in terms of their preferences for particular types of sources; however, when there is a choice, many of us rely on "self-created" messages first. That is, if we think we already have the information necessary in a particular circumstance, we may go no further. When we feel we lack the internal resources to make sense of or handle a particular situation on our own, we turn to other sources. For instance, when we enter a grocery store to shop for particular items, we will probably go directly to the shelves where we expect to find them. If, however, the store is an unfamiliar one, or the items are not where we expected, we are likely to look around for signs to help us navigate or to ask an employee for assistance.

## Mode

Perception and information processing varies depending on whether visual, tactile, auditory, gustatory, or olfactory modes are involved. In any number of situations, a touch or reassuring embrace will be taken note of and interpreted in quite a different way than spoken words of encouragement. In such an instance, actions may speak louder than words. Likewise the smell of decaying garbage may be a much more poignant message than a newspaper story about the consequences of a sanitation workers' strike or a description of the odor from a friend who witnessed the accumulating trash. In other circumstances, however, words may be extremely important, such as in a brainstorming session, a term paper, a text to a friend, a legal brief, or a trial.

## Physical Characteristics

Physical characteristics such as size, color, brightness, movement, and intensity can also be important to information processing. In general, symbols, actions, objects, or events that are large or prominent attract more attention than those which are not. A bright light is more salient than a dim light, large type is more noticeable than small type, moving images are more captivating than stills.

Actions and circumstances that have major consequences for large numbers of people—a fire, natural disaster, or international conflict for instance—are more likely to be taken note of than less important events of less widespread impact. These events appear on the front page of the newspaper, as lead stories on the evening news, or on the opening page of a news-oriented website. The extent of their impact is a major factor in the information-reception processes of reporters, writers, and editors, who recognize that readers and viewers are also likely to attend to and be interested in these events.

Other things being equal, messages that have vivid color, brightness, motion, or intensity are more apt to be noticed and taken account of than those lacking these characteristics (see Figure 6.8). A four-color advertisement, a brightly colored dress or jacket, or a high intensity light are likely to be attended to before objects lacking these attributes. The intensity of potential visual or verbal messages can also be an important consideration in message reception.

## Organization

As will be discussed in greater detail in a later chapter, a good deal of research in the area of persuasion has been directed toward determining the way in which the ordering of ideas or opinions affects message reception. Research suggests that when we are presented with a series of items, we devote greatest attention to the items listed first. As a result, this information has the greatest likelihood of becoming a part of our long-term memory (Lofus, 1980). When asked to recall items from a list after it has been completed, individuals do best with those things presented near the beginning (*primacy*) and those near the end (*recency*). The items at the end are thought to be recalled because they are still a part of one's short-term memory, while those at the beginning are remembered because the information can be retrieved from long-term memory (Lofus, 1980).

**FIGURE 6.8**
**Bright colors attract our attention**

© Ellerslie/Shutterstock.com

The significance of organization on information reception is evident in a variety of settings. Within a picture or a report the arrangement of elements can have a substantial impact on the overall impression created. The ordering of material within a database is also an important factor in whether and how that material will be used. Even the arrangement of foods at a grocery store often has an impact on the communication process. How many times do we pick up grocery items we hadn't intended to because we noticed them while on our way to the place in the store where bread or milk were shelved?

## Novelty

Information that is novel, unfamiliar, or unusual stands out, "grabbing our attention"—if only for a moment. While we may generally devote very little attention to the color of automobiles, a bright pink or yellow car is likely to "catch the eye" of even the most preoccupied motorist.

The same principle applies in other areas such as dress, language, appearance, or greetings, to which we may devote little conscious attention unless these message sources dramatically violate what we have come to expect. For example, although we are usually only somewhat aware when we engage in a ritualistic handshake greeting, we certainly do take note when the other person squeezes our hand too firmly, too loosely, or continues to shake long after the conventional length of a handshake. For another example, see Figure 6.9.

FIGURE 6.9

An unusual friendship.

© Monkey Business Images/Shutterstock.com

# SOURCE INFLUENCES

Some of our most interesting and complex information-reception decisions involve interpersonal sources. Why do we listen to and believe some people more than others? Why are we more influenced by some people than others? Our decisions depend on a number of factors including: *proximity, attractiveness, similarity, credibility, authoritativeness, motivation, intent, delivery, status, power or authority,* and *peer pressure.*

## *Proximity*

Our distance from a source can have a major influence on the likelihood of our attending to particular messages. Other things being equal, we are more likely to be exposed to sources that are close at hand than to those that are farther away (Lin, 1973). The closer we are, the less time, effort, and money that must be expended to engage in communication.

For example, if we are near a computer or a smartphone, we are far more likely to search the Internet for an answer to a vexing question, than to wait to ask a friend later in the day. For this same reason, we are far more likely to attend to the actions and reactions of our roommate or a colleague at work in a nearby office than to those of people who live a block away or work in the next building. The knowledge of these dynamics has not been missed by architects and others who design space with the goal of increasing or decreasing communication.

The significance of distance as a factor in communication is highlighted by considering the function of technology. By means of communication technology, messages from thousands of miles away become available without leaving the comfort of our home, office, or neighborhood. For example, if we have online access to a library database, we are much more likely to look for a journal article on a computer than go into a library to speak to a librarian. It is, in fact, the ease of access to information provided by communication media of various types that has made them such a central part of our lives.

## Physical and Social Attraction and Similarity

Interpersonal communication often has a great deal to do with how attractive we believe a particular message source is. A person's general appearance is an important source for information processing, particularly when forming first impressions. If we are attracted to a person, it is likely that we will pay increased attention to, remember, and attach relatively greater significance to his or her words. In this way, attraction plays a significant, though often subtle, role in influencing the nature of message reception. Researchers have found that positive reactions to a person's physical appearance lead to a favorable perception of other characteristics such as talent, kindness, honesty, and intelligence (Cialdini & Sagrin, 2005; Dion, Berscheid &Walster, 1972; Eagly, Ashmore, Makhijani & Longo, 1991; Rich, 1975)

Though we tend to think of attractiveness primarily in physical terms, we often find people appealing for other reasons as well. An individual who appears to be friendly, warm, empathetic, and concerned, and who expresses interest in or respect for us, may be quite attractive to us as a social companion. Like physical attractiveness, *social attractiveness* also can be an important influence in information reception.

We are also generally more favorably inclined toward people we know and like, leading to what may be termed a *friendship/liking principle*. This principle suggests that we react more favorably to and are more likely to comply with requests from friends or others we like (Cialdini & Sagarin, 2005).

*Similarity* is another factor of significance in communication. The more like a source we are, or believe ourselves to be, the more likely we are to pay special attention to that person and what he or she says (Wheeless, 1974). Often similarities that increase our interest in others are basic characteristics such as gender, level of education, age, religion, ethnic background, hobbies, lifestyle, or language capacity. In other instances, we are drawn to people because they share our needs, attitudes, goals, or values. Generally speaking, the more similar we believe ourselves to be to others, the more influential their messages are (Ciadini & Sagarin, 2005).

The influence of similarity on perception and reception is vividly illustrated by the great impact of our peer group, beginning in our early school years. Our peers play a significant role in shaping our reactions to clothing, movies, music, school, books, various occupations, and also to our parents, friends, and acquaintances. For many of us, we continue to be disproportionately influenced in our communication behavior by those with whom we share similar backgrounds and preferences.

## Credibility and Authoritativeness

Legitimate authorities are extremely influential sources in information processing (Aronson, Turner & Carlsmith, 1963; Milgram, 1974). Indeed, it seems quite natural that we are likely to attend to and retain information from sources we believe to be experienced and/or knowledgeable (Hovland & Weis, 1951; McCroskey, 1986). Certain people—or groups—may be viewed as credible and authoritative, regardless of the topic. Information provided by medical doctors, clergy, or professors, for example, may be regarded as more noteworthy than messages from people with other vocations, even on topics that are outside the professional's areas of expertise.

Similarly, many of us afford actors, television personalities, politicians, and other people who are in the public eye particular attention and credibility—even without necessarily realizing that we are doing so. Thus, the actor speaking on politics or the medical doctor lecturing on religion may receive more than the usual level of attention from receivers.

In some instances, the attention and credibility accorded to a particular person very much depends on the topic in question. Other things being equal, for example, we are more likely to attend to and retain information on international affairs presented by a network news commentator than to messages on the same topic offered by our next-door neighbor. When the topic is insurance, however, we may well attach more weight to the views of a neighbor who has 25 years' experience working in that field than to reports provided on television.

## *Motivation and Intent*

The manner in which we react to a particular interpersonal message source depends on the way we interpret their actions (Seibold & Spitzberg, 1981). Langer, Blank, and Chanowitz (1978) found, for example, that when people waiting in line to do copying were asked if they minded if someone cut in line ahead of them, 60% of them consented to the request. When a person wanting to move to the front of the line explained that they would like to cut in "because they were in a rush," the number who were agreeable jumped to 94%, suggesting that even very basic information about the motive behind a request can have a major impact on the way messages are received.

Depending on what motives we attribute to an individual, our response may vary substantially. If we assume a person intends to inform or help us, we are likely to react in quite a different way than if we believe the intention is to persuade or deceive us. The way we explain behavior to ourselves is the focus of research in an area called *attribution theory*.

## Delivery

The manner in which a source delivers a message can be an important influence in information reception. Among the factors that come into play in delivery of spoken messages are volume, rate of speaking, pitch, pronunciation, and the use of pauses and other factors associated with the way messages are created and conveyed. Other nonverbal considerations, including visual factors, such as gestures, facial expressions, and eye contact may be significant, too.

## Status, Power or Authority, and Peer Pressure

The presence or lack of *status*—position or rank—can also be important in determining how likely it is that an information source or message will be selected and acted on. The *power* or *authority* of a source—the extent to which the source is capable of dispensing rewards or punishment for selecting, remembering, and interpreting messages in a particular way—is also influential in communication.

Generally speaking, parents, teachers, employers, supervisors, or others who have greater status, power, or authority relative to us have a better than average chance of obtaining our attention to their messages. The significance we attach to their role typically directs our attention to their words and actions in an effort to be aware of their opinions or to seek their favor. Even nonverbal symbols of power or status, such as a physician's white coat or stethoscope, the uniform of a security guard, or an expensive business suit, can influence information processing (Cialdini & Sagarin, 2005). To the extent that we can be rewarded or punished through grades, money, favors, or praise for interpreting their messages in particular ways, we may be especially attentive to others.

It is also well-recognized that the influence of peers and members of our reference groups is extremely significant. Members of these groups typically play a vital role in shaping, reinforcing, and validating our perceptions and interpretations of messages in specific situations, and throughout the course of our lifetimes (Cialdini & Sagarin, 2005; Turner, 1991).

## TECHNOLOGICAL AND ENVIRONMENTAL INFLUENCES

Beyond the receiver, information, and source, *technology* and the *environment* also have a substantial impact on communication.

# Technology

The technology, channel, or medium through which messages reach us can be another significant influence in information processing. Differences, such as whether messages are presented via print or electronically, film or video, or the spoken words of a friend, can have a direct, and in some cases obvious, influence. Simply in terms of availability, some technologies provide a greater likelihood of exposure to information than others. For instance, most of us are far more likely to be exposed to televised or social media messages on climate change or political philosophy—to pick just two examples—than to access the content on those topics presented in scholarly journals.

Of the various mass media, television traditionally received the most attention among scholars. This interest is not surprising given the central role of television in the lives of most Americans. In the 1950s, members of the average family watched four and a half hours of television per day. That number jumped to over eight hours in the 2000s (TVB, 2012). In terms of the dynamics of message reception, it is important to note that individual viewing varies considerably by demographic group. For example, women on average spend five and a half hours per day watching television while men spend an average of almost five hours, and teens and children spend approximately three and a half hours (TVB, 2012).

It is also the case that the definition of "TV viewing" has become increasingly blurred. Television screens have become a medium for displaying not only mass-produced broadcast and "cable" programming, but also films and Internet content. Additionally, it is possible to view "television" via computers or smartphones, further complicating efforts to isolate the relative exposure and influence of television and other techologies. As an example, an increasing number of TV viewers multi-task using other media while watching television (Cass, 2013). This may consist of *media meshing*, defined as engaging in the use of smartphones, tablets, and other mobile media on topics that are directly related to a television show being watched, or *media stacking*, which relates to media multi-tasking—viewing television while engaging in the use of other media which are unrelated to what is being viewed on a larger screen TV (Cass, 2013). Another example of the blurring definition of "TV viewing" is provided by Netflix which rebroadcasts TV and movie programming via the Internet and has nearly 30 million U.S. subscribers (Kleinman, 2013).

In 1997, 18.6% of U.S. homes had computers with active Internet connections. By 2003, that number had grown to 54.6% and to about 80% in 2008 (Ingram, 2008). Moreover, in 2013, 61% of U.S. cell phone owners were using smartphones, up from 21% in 2010 (Kleinman, 2013). According to estimates, people living in the United States will soon be spending more time on alternative digital devices than in front of their television sets (Kleinman, 2013).

Technology has always played an important role in message production, delivery, and access; that role continues today, but specific patterns continue to evolve. See Table 6.1.

# The Environment

**CONTEXT.** The manner in which a particular person or event is reacted to often depends on whether we are at home or on vacation, at work or at school, or engaged in a leisure activity. It will also depend on whether the messages are received in an office, a church, a classroom, an auditorium, or a bedroom. It is not difficult to think of examples of how the same message would be interpreted very differently depending on the context in which it was encountered. See Figure 6.10.

The presence of other people often has a very direct bearing on how we select as well as interpret and retain information. How we think other people see us, how we want to be seen, what we believe others expect from us, and what we think they think about the situation we are in are among the considerations that shape the way we react in social situations.

**TABLE 6.1**

**Average Time Spent per Day with Major Media by U.S. Adults, 2011 to 2015**

**Average Time Spent per Day with Major Media by US Adults, 2011-2015**
*hrs:mins and CAGR*

|  | 2011 | 2012 | 2013 | 2014 | 2015 | CAGR (2011-2015) |
|---|---|---|---|---|---|---|
| **Digital** | 3:40 | 4:20 | 4:51 | 5:15 | 5:38 | 11.4% |
| —Desktop/laptop* | 2:33 | 2:27 | 2:19 | 2:22 | 2:22 | -1.8% |
| —Mobile (nonvoice) | 0:48 | 1:35 | 2:16 | 2:34 | 2:51 | 37.2% |
| —Other connected devices | 0:18 | 0:18 | 0:17 | 0:19 | 0:25 | 7.8% |
| **TV**\*\* | 4:34 | 4:38 | 4:31 | 4:22 | 4:15 | -1.8% |
| **Radio**\*\* | 1:34 | 1:32 | 1:30 | 1:28 | 1:27 | -2.0% |
| **Print**\*\* | 0:44 | 0:38 | 0:32 | 0:26 | 0:21 | -17.0% |
| —Magazines | 0:18 | 0:16 | 0:14 | 0:12 | 0:10 | -13.5% |
| —Newspapers | 0:26 | 0:22 | 0:18 | 0:14 | 0:11 | -19.8% |
| **Other**\*\* | 0:39 | 0:38 | 0:31 | 0:26 | 0:24 | -11.7% |
| **Total** | **11:11** | **11:46** | **11:55** | **11:57** | **12:04** | **1.9%** |

*Note: ages 18+; time spent with each medium includes all time spent with that medium, regardless of multitasking; for example, 1 hour of multitasking on desktop/laptop while watching TV is counted as 1 hour for TV and 1 hour for desktop/laptop; \*includes all internet activities on desktop and laptop computers; \*\*excludes digital*
*Source: eMarketer, April 2015*
188127                                                  www.eMarketer.com

If we are in the company of colleagues or friends, we may pay particular attention to the people, events, and circumstances they prioritize. In our effort to decide how well we liked a particular movie, lecture, painting, or person, the reactions of other people are often of major significance to our own judgments. Sometimes, we conform our own information processing to that of others for appearances only; in many other instances the influence is more subtle, pervasive, and consequential.

**REPETITION.** We are likely to take into account and remember messages that are repeated often. Frequently repeated advertising slogans and jingles, political talking points, song lyrics, or dates stand out in our minds, simply because we have seen, heard, or read them so often. Repetition also contributes to our learning a language, our parents' and friends' opinions, the slang and jargon of our associates, and the accent of our geographic region.

# Consistency and Competition

It has long been recognized that the drive for consistency is an important influence in information processing (Cialdini & Sagarin, 2005). Efforts to achieve consistency can shape the way we perceive, receive, interpret, and recall messages in a variety of situations in the short term, and often that influence can be very long-lasting (Turner, 1991). This principle is fundamental to the classical theories of influence by Leon Festinger (cognitive dissonance theory), Fritz Heider (balance theory), Theodore Newcomb (strain toward symmetry theory), and others (Caldini & Sagarin, 2005).

When a person has been exposed over a long period of time to one religious orientation, one political philosophy, or one set of values, there is an increased likelihood that the individual will come to select and accept messages consistent with that position. *Brainwashing* is the extreme example of this sort of communication phenomenon. In such circumstances, the individual is bombarded with messages that advocate a particular position, and information supporting alternative points of view is systematically eliminated from the environment. When coupled with the promise of reward (or absence of punishment) and consistency, the lack of competitive messages becomes a powerful shaping force influencing the probability of message selection and the manner of interpretation and retention.

**FIGURE 6.10**

The context or setting in which potential information sources are encountered can be an important factor influencing whether and how messages are selected, interpreted, and remembered.

© Christin Lola/Shutterstock.com

In considerably less extreme forms, the educational process makes use of these same principles. Math, language, reading, and spelling are taught not only through repetition but also through consistency. The arrangement of classroom furniture and the use of examinations, lectures, books, and homework assignments are among the strategies typically used to minimize the influence of competing messages. Health communication campaigns designed to reduce dangerous drinking on a college campus may address these competing message (such as alcohol advertising in the student newspaper or "happy hour" specials at neighborhood bars) by communicating to students accurate information about other students' drinking (e.g., a significant number of students choose not to drink or not to drink to excess) to encourage them to follow more healthy behaviors (Lederman & Stewart, 2005).

## AN ACTIVE AND COMPLEX PROCESS

Selection, interpretation, and reception are basic to perception and information processing, and these activities are fundamental to communicating. As should be apparent from the wide array of influences discussed in this chapter, information processing is one of the most active and complex facets of human communication. Morton Hunt (1982) makes this point in discussing the opening sentence of Gibbon's *The Decline and Fall of the Roman Empire* ("In the second century of the Christian era, the Empire of Rome comprehended the fairest part of the earth, and the most civilized portion of mankind"):

> A reader who finds this sentence perfectly intelligible does so not because Gibbon was a lucid stylist but because he or she knows when the Christian era began, understands the concept of "empire," is familiar enough with history to recognize the huge sociocultural phenomenon known as "Rome," has enough information about world geography so that the phrase "the fairest part of the earth" produces a number of images in the mind, and, finally, can muster whole congeries of ideas about the kinds of civilization that then existed. What skill, to elicit that profusion of associations with those few well-chosen cues—but what a performance by the reader! One hardly knows which to admire more. (pp. 119-121)

Without doing any injustice to Hunt's intent, we could extend the point to apply equally to the impressive accomplishments of a listener in a personal, group, technologically mediated, or public setting, or to the observer of visual images in an art gallery, a baseball game, a website, or a television program.

## CONCLUSION

In this chapter, our focus has been on the nature of information reception, and the processes involved in sensing and making sense of the people, objects, and circumstances in our environment. Individuals play an active role in this process though they may have little awareness that it is taking place.

Selection, interpretation, and retention are primary facets of information reception. Collectively, they are the processes by which we create, transform, and use information to relate to our environment and one another.

Selection involves the selective attention to particular environmental information sources from all those to which a person is exposed. Interpretation consists of the transformation of those messages into a form that has value and utility for the individual. Retention involves short- and long-term, semantic, and episodic memory. In actual operation, selection, interpretation, and retention are very much interrelated activities.

A number of factors have an impact on selection, interpretation, and retention. Many of them have to do with receivers and their needs, attitudes, beliefs, values, goals, capabilities, uses, style, experience, and habits.

Other factors that influence information reception have to do with messages—their origin, mode, physical characteristics, novelty, and organization. Sources also have an impact on reception, through their proximity, attractiveness, credibility, motivation, intention, delivery, status, power, and authority. Message reception may also be affected by factors related to technology and the environment.

## KEY POINTS

After reading this chapter, you should be able to:

- Explain the significance of selection, interpretation, and retention on communication outcomes
- Identify the various environmental, receiver, and sender-based influences on the perception process and associated messages
- Analyze the complex nature of perceiving and interpreting information in our daily lives

## REFERENCES

Albert, S. M., Becker, L. A., & Brock, T. C. (1970). Familiarity, utility, and supportiveness as determinants of information receptivity. *Journal of Personality and Social Psychology, 14,* 292-301.

Aronson, E., Turner, J. A., & Carlsmith, J. M. (1963). Communicator credibility and communication discrepancy as determinants of opinion change. *Journal of Abnormal and Social Psychology, 67,* 31-36.

Becker, S. L. (1978). Visual stimuli and the construction of meaning. In B. S. Randhawa (Ed.), *Visual learning, thinking, and communication* (pp. 39-60). New York, NY: Academic Press.

Broadbent, D. E. (1957). A mechanical model for human attention and immediate memory. *Psychological Review, 64,* 205-215.

Cass, S. (2013). More viewing, less attention: TV watchers multitask with mobile devices. *IEEE Spectrum*. Retrieved from http://spectrum.ieee.org/semiconductors/devices/more-viewing-less-attention

Cialdini, R. B., & Sagarin, B. J. (2005). Principles of interpersonal influence. In T. C. Brock & M. C. Green (Eds.), *Persuasion: Psychological insights and perspectives* (pp. 143-170). Thousand Oaks, CA: Sage.

Cohen, G. (2008). Overview: Conclusions and speculations. In G. Cohen & M. A. Conway (Eds.), *Memory in the real world* (3rd ed., pp. 381-390). New York, NY: Psychology Press.

Craig, R. T. (1979). Information systems theory and research: An overview of individual information processing. In D. Nimmo (Ed.), *Communication yearbook 3* (pp. 99-120). New Brunswick, NJ: Transaction, International Communication Association.

Dion, K., Berscheid, E., & Walster, E. (1972). What is beautiful is good. *Journal of Personality*, *24*, 285-290.

Dixon, N. F. (1981). *Preconscious processing*. London, UK: Wiley.

Donohew, L., & Palmgreen, P. (1971a). An investigation of "mechanisms" of information selection. *Journalism Quarterly*, *48*, 624-639.

Donohew, L., & Palmgreen, P. (1971b). Reappraisal of dissonance and the selective exposure hypothesis. *Journalism Quarterly*, *48*, 412-420.

Eagly, A. H., Ashmore, R. D., Makhijani, M. G., & Longo, L. C. (1991). What is beautiful is good, but... *Psychological Bulletin*, *110*, 109-128.

Hovland, C. I., & Weiss, W. (1951). The influence of source credibility on communication effectiveness. *Public Opinion Quarterly*, *15*, 635-650.

Hunt, M. (1982). *The universe within*. New York, NY: Simon & Schuster.

Ingram, S. (2009, January 15). About 80% of United States homes have a computer. Retrieved from Technology Tell website: http://www.technologytell.com/gadgets/44143/about-80-of-united-states-homes-has-a-computer/.

Katz, E., Blumler, J. G., & Gurevitch, M. (1974). Utilization of mass communication by the individual. In J. G. Blumler & E. Katz (Eds.), *The uses of mass communications* (pp. 22-23). Beverly Hills, CA: Sage.

Kleinman, A. (2013, August 1). Americans will spend more time on digital devices than watching TV this year: Research. Retrieved from http://www.huffingtonpost.com/2013/08/01/tv-digital-devices_n_3691196.html.

Krippendorff, K. (1993). The past of communication's hoped-for future. *Journal of Communication*, *43*, 34-44.

Langer, E., Blank, A., & Chanowitz, B. (1978). The mindlessness of ostensibly thoughtful action: The role of "placebic" information in interpersonal interaction. *Journal of Personality and Social Psychology*, *36*, 635-642.

Lederman, L. C., & Stewart, L. P. (2005). *Changing the culture of college drinking: A socially situated health communication campaign*. Cresskill, NJ: Hampton Press.

Lin, N. (1973). *The study of communication.* New York, NY: Bobbs-Merrill.

Lindsay, P. H., & Norman, D. A. (1977). *Human information processing.* New York, NY: Academic.

Loftus, E. (1980). *Memory.* Reading, MA: Addison-Wesley.

Loftus, G. R., & Loftus, E. F. (1976). *Human memory: The processing of information.* Hillsdale, NJ: Lawrence Erlbaum.

Mandler, G. (1985). *Cognitive psychology: An essay in cognitive science.* Hillsdale, NJ: Lawrence Erlbaum.

Maslow, A. (1954). *Motivation and personality.* New York, NY: Harper.

McCroskey, J. C. (1977). Oral communication apprehension: A summary of recent theory and research. *Human Communication Research, 4,* 78-96.

McCroskey, J. C. (1984). The communication apprehension perspective. In J. A. Daly & J. C. McCroskey (Eds.), *Avoiding communication: Shyness, reticence, and communication apprehension* (pp. 12-38). Beverly Hills, CA: Sage.

McCroskey, J. C. (1986). *An introduction to rhetorical communication.* Englewood Cliffs, NJ: Prentice Hall.

Milgram, S. (1974). *Obedience to authority.* New York, NY: Harper.

Phillips, G. M., & Metzger, N. J. (1973). The reticent syndrome: Some theoretical considerations about etiology and treatment. *Speech Monographs, 40,* 220-230.

Rich, J. (1975). Effects of children's physical attractiveness on teacher's evaluations. *Journal of Educational Psychology, 67,* 599-607.

Rubin, A. M. (1993). Audience activity and media use. *Communications Monographs, 60,* 98-105.

Seibold, D. S., & Spitzberg, B. H. (1981). Attribution theory and research: Formalization, review, and implications for communication. In B. Dervin & M. J. Voight (Eds.), *Progress in communication sciences* (Vol. 3, pp. 85-125). Norwood, NJ: Ablex.

Treisman, A. M. (1969). Strategies and models of selective attention. *Psychological Review, 76,* 282-299.

Turner, J. C. (1991). *Social influence.* Pacific Grove, CA: Brooks/Cole.

TVB. (2012). *TV Basics: A report on the growth and scope of television.* New York, NY: TVB Local Media Market Solutions. Retrieved from http://www.tvb.org/media/file/TV_Basics.pdf

Wheeless, L. R. (1974). The effects of attitude, credibility, and homophily on selective exposure to information. *Speech Monographs, 41,* 329-338.

Williams, H. L., Conway, M. A., & Cohen, G. (2008). Autobiographical memory. In G. Cohen & M. A. Conway (Eds.), *Memory in the real world* (3rd ed., pp. 21-90). New York, NY: Psychology Press.

# CHAPTER 7

# MEDIATED
# COMMUNICATION

**In this chapter, you will learn about:**
- The definition and key theories of mediated communication
- The evolution and use of mediated communication tools over time
- The effects of mediated communication in our daily lives
- The characteristics of contemporary media tools

## THE TOOL-MAKING ANIMAL

## COMMUNICATION TECHNOLOGY AND ITS FUNCTIONS
- Production and Distribution
- Reception, Storage, and Retrieval

## TYPES OF MEDIA

## EVOLUTION OF COMMUNICATION MEDIA: FROM SMOKE SIGNALS TO THE INTERNET

## COMMUNICATION TECHNOLOGY IN CONTEMPORARY LIFE

## TECHNOLOGICAL CONVERGENCE

- Increasing Number of Messages and Media
- New Technology Means More Messages and New Communication Literacy Needs
- Substituting Communication for Transportation
- Evolving Concepts of Office and Home
- Increasing Value of Information as a Commodity
- Increasing Availability of Synthetic Experience

## UNDERSTANDING MEDIA INFLUENCE

- Cues-Filtered-Out Theories
- Social Influence Theory
- Adaptive Structuration Theory

## MEDIATED COMMUNICATION: A MIXED BLESSING

- Synchronicity
- Interactivity
- Control of Content
- Anonymity
- Responsibility and Accountability
- Sense of Place

## COMMUNICATION TECHNOLOGY AND THE QUALITY OF LIFE

- Media Forms

## CONCLUSION

## KEY POINTS

## THE TOOL-MAKING ANIMAL

Beyond our human capacity for creating and using messages, one of our other basic human skills is the capacity to create tools—and few tools have had as much impact on our daily lives as the tools of communication. Our tool-making facility has given us the ability to create *communication technologies* that extend our natural ability to create, transmit, receive, and process messages of various types—visual, auditory, olfactory, gustatory, and tactile. Communication technologies (including computers, mobile phones, tablets, smart watches, video game consoles, and electronic billboards) are pervasive.

In this chapter, our focus is on these technologies, or *media* as they may also be called, and *mediated communication*—communication that occurs when media intervene, or *mediate,* between message sources and receivers.

# COMMUNICATION TECHNOLOGY AND ITS FUNCTIONS

At first consideration, tools like smartphones, satellite radio, voice message systems, computers, and pens may not seem to have much in common. On further reflection, however, it becomes apparent that in one way or another each of these devices extends our ability to engage in human communication.

## Production and Distribution

When we analyze the communication media that we take so much for granted, we find that one of the most basic functions they perform is to extend our ability to produce and distribute information at great distance in space or time from the point of origin. *Production* involves the creation of messages using communication media. *Distribution* has three components:

1. *Transmission:* Moving messages
2. *Reproduction and amplification:* Duplicating, amplifying, or multiplying messages
3. *Display:* Making messages physically available once they arrive at their destination

Spoken language is our most basic means of vocal message production, but other media play an important supporting role (see Figure 7.1). Included in the long, diverse, and ever-expanding list of visual media that make message production and distribution possible are the alphabet, pens and pencils, computers, the Internet, billboards, signs, and message-bearing articles of clothing. Many media combine audio and visual capabilities, among them television, film, wireless networks, many cameras, DVRs, cable and satellite systems, and the Internet. In addition, Braille is an example of a message production and distribution technology that involves tactile codes (see Figure 7.2).

**FIGURE 7.1**

Message Production and Distribution Media

| Auditory Media | |
|---|---|
| Spoken Languages | Satellite Radio |
| Musical Instruments | Telephones |
| "Walkie-Talkies" | Pagers |
| **Visual Media** | |
| Alphabet | Bumper Stickers |
| Internet | Skywriting |
| Cave Drawings | Billboards |
| Hand and Arm Signals | Ribbons and Badges |
| Photography and Photographic Equipment | Whiteboards |
| Flags | Message-Bearing Articles of Clothing |
| **Auditory-Visual Media** | |
| Broadcast Television | Electronic Games |
| Teleconferencing | Films |
| **Tactile Media** | |
| Braille | Medical Palpation |

## Reception, Storage, and Retrieval

Many of the media that aid in message production, distribution, reproduction and/or amplification also play an important role in message reception in that they serve to make messages available and easily accessible. In addition to the communication technologies that come readily to mind, there are others such as glasses, radar, and telescopes that assist with the reception of visual information, and others such as headphones, earbuds, and hearing aids that expand our capabilities for receiving auditory messages.

Without basic communication technologies there would be no way to preserve messages over time or to transport them from one place to another. Moreover, if there were no publications, digital media, telecommunication, or Internet, it would be impossible to rapidly distribute a single message to a number of distant points around the globe more or less simultaneously. Without communication technology, our human capacity for producing, distributing, copying, organizing, storing, and retrieving information would be limited to sending and receiving messages in face-to-face settings.

# TYPES OF MEDIA

Communication media may be used to extend message-sending and message-receiving in any context or setting.

*Traditional mass media* such as newspapers, magazines, books, radio, and television multiply, duplicate, or amplify messages for distribution to large and diverse audiences. Newer digital media and message formats such as broadcast email, social networking, automated robo-calling, and public websites and apps provide an alternative to traditional media when it comes to *public* or *mass communication*—transmission of a common message to large numbers of people who may or may not know, or be known to, the message initiator.

Other digital applications such as text messaging, podcasts, and email—along with more traditional media forms like notes, letters, and phone calls—extend interpersonal communication and message sending and receiving between individuals who generally know one another. These and other media may also be used to support communication functions within and between groups or organizations.

Where it was once a simple matter to describe media based on whether they were being used in a mass, group, interpersonal, or intrapersonal context, the evolving nature of communication technology makes these distinctions increasingly less useful.  As implied in the foregoing discussion, depending on how they are configured, these media can be used to support communication in relationships, groups, organizations, communities, or societies, and in many cases the same technologies can be used for any of a number of purposes.

Media can be used to enhance message sending and message receiving aimed at informing, entertaining, educating, persuading, aggregating information, promoting community and political engagement, alerting individuals to a problem or mobilizing people, or improving health. Like other forms of communication, technology can also be used for other far less noble goals such as deceiving, alienating, manipulating, or bullying.

What all media have in common is

**FIGURE 7.2**

Reading Braille.

their capacity to enhance and extend the basic processes of message sending and message receiving, by multiplying, amplifying, transmitting, storing, or assisting with the storage and retrieving of messages, and thereby helping us overcome limits of time, space, and memory.

# EVOLUTION OF COMMUNICATION MEDIA: FROM SMOKE SIGNALS TO THE INTERNET

Our technology for communication has come a very long way in its evolution. It was about 20,000 BCE when early humans first carved symbols on the walls of caves and used drums and smoke to signal one another. Smoke signals and cave drawings served their intended purposes well.

By about 1000 BCE, early hieroglyphic and pictographic drawings had given way to systems of writing that made use of an alphabet (Cherry, 1978; Schement & Stout, 1989). Paper was invented around 100 CE, and the oldest-known printed work is a Sutra printed in Korea in 750 CE. Writing extended the natural human capacity for memory by providing a means for creating lasting and portable messages.

By 1500, Johannes Gutenberg (1398–1468) had completed the printing of a Bible using movable type (see Figure 7.3). Although printing as it is known today began in Germany during the mid-fifteenth century, Chinese, Japanese, and Koreans actually had developed the process much earlier. Printing made it possible to rapidly duplicate and transmit messages. Together, writing and printing had a revolutionary impact on communication and on virtually all facets of life including education, government, commerce, and religion.

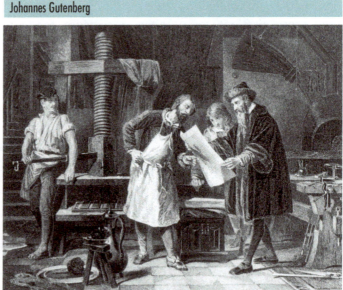

**FIGURE 7.3**

Johannes Gutenberg

© Everett Historical/Shutterstock.com

As we noted in Chapter 2, newspapers appeared in their present-day form in the 1600s. It was during this period that regular mail service was established to link major cities in Europe, and by the 1700s postal services were operating in many countries. The mid-1800s brought the advent of the telegraph and the Morse code, and with them the introduction of electronic media, which greatly increased both *range* (distance) and *immediacy* (shortness of delay between message transmission and message reception).

Prior to Guglielmo Marconi's development in 1895 of the wireless telegraph (or radio, as it is called today), the source and the destination had to be physically connected by wire. With a means for sending coded signals and later voice through the air, many new alternatives became available. These advances paved the way for the introduction of television in the 1930s.

There were a number of other notable advances in the 1800s. In 1866, for example, cable was laid across the seabed of the Atlantic, further extending the capability for rapid message transmission. The telephone—a medium that has come to play an incredibly pervasive role in human communication—was patented during the same period.

The 1950s saw the widespread adoption of television (see Figure 7.4). In 1950, only 10% of U.S. households had television sets; 10 years later that figure had jumped to a remarkable 89%. Communication satellites were developed in the 1960s (Pool, Takaski & Hurwitz, 1984).

In the decade that followed, a number of new communication media became widely available including miniaturized radios, stereophonic audio equipment, home movie systems, photocopiers, and cassette audio recorders.

**FIGURE 7.4**

Before the invention of the remote control, television viewers had to change channels and adjust the volume on the set itself.

© Everett Historical/Shutterstock.com

More recent developments include new and hybrid media such as digital photography, audio and video recording and playback, and the diversified uses and increasing popularity and impact of cellular and wireless telephony, and the Internet. Today satellite systems and networks allow for global subscription radio and television, GPS and mapping systems, and surveillance and defense systems, among others.

In 2014, for example, 90% of adults in the United States had a cell phone, and 58% of them owned a smartphone. Over 40% owned a tablet computer, and roughly 30% an e-reader (Pew, 2014). By the end of 2014, there were nearly 3 billion Internet users, with two-thirds of them living in more highly developed countries. Interestingly, roughly 2.3 billion individuals have broad-band subscriptions internationally, with 55% of these in less developed countries (ITU, 2014).

Can you imagine what it would be like to spend a weekend without your cell phone? A group of Rutgers University students spent an "unplugged weekend" at a camp in a wooded location with surprising results (reported in Lee & Katz, 2014). Although several students felt anxious about not being able to be in constant contact with others, the majority of them reported having "no problem" without their phones and being surprised at how much fun they could have interacting with others face-to-face. As one student commented, "I wondered what it would be like to have no contact with anyone other than who I was with but I loved it and realized you don't need a phone or laptop to have a good time!" One surprising challenge, however, was checking the time since most students rely on their phones instead of wearing wristwatches.

## COMMUNICATION TECHNOLOGY IN CONTEMPORARY LIFE

For the past several decades we have been living in what has been called the *Information Age,* an era when communication technology has become central to nearly all that we do. Our tools for sending, transmitting, and receiving information have always occupied an important place in human activity. Now, more than ever before, communication technology has a pervasive impact on our personal and professional lives, our groups and organizations, our own society, and the world community.

Social media is built on the ideological foundation of Web 2.0, offering platforms for user-generated content intended for sharing within a network or networks. Users dictate both the content that is created (ranging from ideas to pictures and videos) *and* the content that is consumed. This content is generally meant to establish or strengthen connections in a person's network. Facebook, which began in 2004, is currently the most dominant social network in the world with 1.18 billion monthly active users as of June 2015. Other platforms include Instagram, Twitter, Snapchat, Tumblr, and Reddit.

In industry, communication technology plays a vital role in manufacturing, records management, inventory control, among other basic functions, and, in most professional occupational settings, electronic messaging is indispensable to internal business functions and to maintaining contact with employees, customers, and collaborators around the community, the region, and the world.

In the entertainment industry, digitized audio and video, cable television, telecommunications, video-gaming, Internet services, and recording and playback devices have transformed the media landscape.

Communication technology has also become increasingly essential in medicine to aid in diagnostics, patient care, and medical record keeping. They facilitate patient diagnosis, care, and treatment. By means of communication media, medical information can be easily stored and analyzed, and effortlessly moved from one physician or medical facility to another as needed.

Within the news media and the publishing industry, all of the activities associated with information collection, processing, and distribution have been transformed by today's communication technology. Writers and editors have access to a variety of databases to supplement information gathered through interviews and other means. In many cases, printed documents have been replaced, or supplemented by, online documents which are instantaneously available wherever computer connectivity exists.

The Information Age has also had a transformative impact on libraries. The concept of the library as a building where people come to read and check out books and copy articles has given way to the view of a service institution that aims to serve the diverse information needs of its clients. In addition to print materials, patrons at libraries have physical and electronic access to textual databases, voice and video files, and a full range of Internet sources.

Beyond the broad impact on virtually all existing occupations, digital communication media have led to the emergence of a vast number of entirely new jobs in information systems, services, management, and security.

# TECHNOLOGICAL CONVERGENCE

At the heart of these advances is the convergence of media that were once distinct in their forms and uses. Newspapers, for example, historically provided their audience with a summary of daily events. Television, radio, and film were primarily entertainment media. Telephones were used socially and in business contexts, typically as a substitute for short, face-to-face conversations. Today, many of these traditional distinctions are becoming obsolete. Cable television allows us to select shopping, music, religious programming, weather, comedy, movies, and to access the Internet.

Similarly, a computer, tablet, or smartphone connects to the Internet to become a mail system, a newsstand for newspapers and magazines, a game room, a collection of reference books, a casino, a catalogue for consumer goods, a community bulletin board, a job placement agency, an airline reservation service, a place to meet and chat with other people, and a variety of other things.

## Increasing Number of Messages and Media

Each new technological advance, particularly those with the capability of multiplication, amplification, or duplication, brings an increase in the volume of messages and the number of media available to us. Unfortunately, our own ability to select, interpret, and retain this information has not increased as fast as the amount of information available to us has. With access to more media and messages, the problem of information overload—the availability of more messages than can be effectively utilized—becomes more critical. As this occurs, the real challenge facing humans will shift from "how to get it" to "what to do with it." How many emails do we want, or have time to answer? Is there a limit to how much information we can use on any one topic? How many online "friends" can we maintain meaningful relationships with? How many downloaded podcasts can we listen to? How many television shows can we watch? How many websites can we check regularly?

**FIGURE 7.5**

Technology brings people together and keeps them apart.

Schwartz (2005) labels this phenomenon "the paradox of choice." While we often appreciate having numerous products, messages, or websites to choose from, it can be exhausting to find the thing we want (or really need) which leads to poor decision making and often stress (see Figure 7.5).

## New Technology Means More Messages and New Communication Literacy Needs

Because the number of messages and media grows larger while our abilities to use them remain more or less constant, we face major new challenges in information processing. Given the growing imbalance between the array of available messages and the limitations on our ability to process information, it can be argued that we are actually less fully informed about what is available in our environment now than we were before.

It follows that new literacy concepts and skills are required to accommodate these challenges. What are these new literacies? At a minimum, these skills include

- Familiarizing ourselves with available media and assessing their attributes
- Diagnosing our own and others' information needs
- Accessing and retrieving useful and valid information
- Organizing, classifying, and managing information
- Assessing the value and importance of information
- Selecting, ignoring, and resisting messages when they are inappropriate to our needs

## Substituting Communication for Transportation

There has always been an interesting relationship between the functions of transportation technology and communication technology. Even with the earliest media this relationship was apparent. Instead of delivering a message in person, it could be sent on horseback or by ship via courier. It was not necessary to deliver a message personally, if the information could be transported.

Moving messages across time and space can be an effective, efficient, and economical alternative to moving things or people (see Figure 7.6). As Aakhus (2003) notes, in thinking about the fast-paced changes in the area of communication and information technology, the prevailing idea is that "communication is the sharing of minds and that technology should make possible 'perpetual contact' that overcomes time and space barriers" (p. 27).

**FIGURE 7.6**

Technologically mediated shopping can present us with almost limitless choices that may lead to decision fatigue and result in poor choices (Tierney, 2011).

© Tyler Olsen/Shutterstock.com

Today, we think little of online business conferences being held via the Internet with people around the world. A doctor at a hospital can monitor the vital signs of a patient miles away, and, with similar technology, medical personnel have immediate access to current research findings in their efforts to diagnose and treat illness. Lawyers can use specialized databases to search through the equivalent of entire legal libraries to find key cases or legal opinions without leaving their offices. We can navigate our way around traffic jams using apps on our phones. And social media offer seemingly endless possibilities for connectivity among friends, members of clubs, families, business associates, and others.

## Evolving Concepts of Office and Home

With the capabilities of today's communication media, concepts of home and office have become far less distinct than they once were. For most of us, *work* was traditionally a place away from home. For many, work has increasingly becoming less "a place" and more "an activity." The idea of an office filled with people conversing face-to-face about social and business matters is being joined by an understanding of *office* that includes an individual at home in leisure attire, engaged in telework—conducting business via phone, computer, or smartphone.

In discussing how new and converging technology affect people's work lives, Katz (1999) describes first-, second-, and third-order effects. First-order effects consist of the potential for increased productivity and better control over resources—time, people, and dollars. Multitasking, quick response time, mobile access, and better connectivity of all kinds help to make these outcomes possible. Second-order effects include reduced costs of starting new businesses, the potential for economic growth, and, potentially, more efficient and effective relations with clients. Finally, Katz lists organizational control of workers as a third-order effect. Technology makes it easier to track, monitor, and measure productivity and activity—an asset, given some perspectives and purposes, and probably a liability given others.

Technology may allow us to bring our work home with us, but is that always a good thing (see Figure 7.7)? For example, teleworking from home may increase the probability of distractions, decrease social presence (Biocca, Harms & Burgoon, 2003), and perpetuate traditional work and family roles (Sullivan & Lewis, 2002).

**FIGURE 7.7**

How young is too young to bring our technology home to work?

© CroMary/Shutterstock.com

## Increasing Value of Information as a Commodity

The economics of communication and information refers to the *value* associated with communication technology, products, and services. The evidence of value is the willingness of individuals, groups, organizations, and societies to pay for these media and information products or services. Researchers point to an increasing number of people within the United States whose occupational roles involve information production or use; and the production of communication media and messages is central to a great many of the largest and most significant corporations. As communication scholars Schement and Lievrouw (1987) explain:

> Information has been exchanged in the marketplace since ancient times. But before the twentieth century it was rarely sold as a commodity in its own right, and, when it was, it was always treated as an exceptional good. Now it is exchanged as routinely as "ordinary" commodities. (p. 3)

Information products, unlike many other products, can often be easily duplicated and are generally not consumed when they are used. Several pages of an article or a downloaded song can be copied without detracting from the value of the original product. Moreover, a book or CD can be passed along from one person to another, with each person deriving equivalent value. The fact that this is possible is a growing concern to authors, artists, composers, and production and distribution companies. This is not an issue with products like foods or fuels which cannot be easily copied and lose their value as they are consumed.

With the growing popularity of streaming services, we are experiencing what could be called a paradigm shift in which people are not likely to "own anything" anymore. For example, you might share a playlist with someone, but not the actual music artifact (like a record or CD). The change in distribution of information has had a major impact on the concept of ownership with many people taking advantage of the ease of accessing content on the Internet without buying actual artifacts.

Scholar Alfred G. Smith (1974) predicted some years ago that our primary resource would be information. He believed that information would be the primary wealth of individuals, organizations, and nations, and that the prime base of their power would, likewise, become information. Today, information (such as passwords to streaming music or movie accounts) in some sense has indeed become our "wealth."

For individuals, organizations, and societies alike, the potential of the Information Age is most readily available to those who can afford the necessary hardware and software. Because resources are unevenly distributed, advantage goes to those who can afford to acquire these products and services. Thus, it may be argued that rather than narrowing the gap between the information rich and poor, as so many had hoped would happen, advanced technology of the Information Age may further increase that gap.

## Increasing Availability of Synthetic Experience

Communication media often present messages that may be unlike any we experience firsthand. As Funkhouser and Shaw (1990) note:

> Until the nineteenth century, for most people actual experience was limited to events occurring within the "natural sensory envelope"—the limits of the human nervous system to detect physical stimuli, governed by natural, physical processes. (p. 78)

Today, communication media increasingly enable us to experience what may be termed a "synthetic reality." Funkhouser and Shaw (1990) list the following as examples of how media transform events by allowing us to create:

- Altered speeds of movement, either slow or fast motion
- Reenactments of the same action (instant replay)

- Instantaneous cutting from one scene to another
- Excerpting fragments of events
- Juxtaposing events widely separated in time or space
- Shifting points of view, via moving cameras, zoom lenses, or multiple cameras
- Combined sight from one source and sound from another (e.g., background music, sound effects, dubbed dialogue)
- Merging, altering, or distorting visual images, particularly through computer graphics techniques and multiple-exposure processing
- Manufacturing "events" through animations or computer graphics. (p. 79)

Up until a few years ago it would have taken very expensive computers to accomplish all of these transformations. Today we can do much of this on a smartphone (and post it immediately to social media) or with readily available software on our tablets or laptops. Thus, communication media not only extend our capability to experience the realities available to our senses, but actually add a number of "artificial" experiences as well.

## UNDERSTANDING MEDIA INFLUENCE[1]

Communication and information technologies, sometimes referred to by the acronym ICTs, play a very pervasive role in our lives in so many respects, as we have discussed. Their presence is significant in social, economic, political, and educational practices, locally, regionally, nationally, and internationally. Researchers who study ICTs predict that that their presence will only continue to grow (Bannon, 2012; Brahima, 2014).

The popularity and pervasiveness of communication technologies have raised important questions and inspired several models about how people use technologies, how we incorporate technology into our lives, and how these actions influence individual and social behavior (Browning, Sætre, Stephens, & Sørnes, 2008; Hollingshead & Contractor, 2006; Walther, 2011; see Figure 7.8).

**FIGURE 7.8**

Communication technologies are pervasive even in face-to-face working groups.

© Rawpixel/Shutterstock.com

## Cues-Filtered-Out Theories

Early efforts to answer these questions focused on media and what were regarded as their inherent characteristics. Often the goal was to identify and prescribe the best media for particular purposes (Browning et al., 2008; Fulk, Schmitz, & Steinfeld, 1990). Theories that adopt this technology-centered focus, collectively referred to as the cues-filtered-out perspective (Culnan & Markus, 1987), proceed from the premise that face-to-face communication is the ideal form of communication. From that perspective, *mediated communication*—communication where technology is involved—is a limited and restricted form of the process that decreases the availability of social and contextual cues (Baym, 2006; Walther, 2011).

From this point of view, some technologies (like Facetime or Skype) are more like face-to-face communication because they convey more nonverbal information and help users feel more involved with others during interaction. They are said to have higher *social presence.* Other media—those with a reduced capacity for nonverbal communication—are seen as having a lower social presence (Short, Williams, & Christie, 1976; Walther, 2011; Walther & Burgoon, 1992). Lower social presence technologies were considered to be better suited for communication about tasks that do not require much "interpersonal involvement" (Fulk et al., 1990, p. 118), whereas those with a higher social presence were seen as more appropriate for communication involving social and relationship-oriented interaction (Hollingshead & Contractor, 2006; Short et al., 1976).

Another theory that reflected the cues-filtered-out perspective focused on what was termed *media richness* or the capacity of particular media to facilitate timely processing of "rich information." The richness of a medium depended on its ability to provide quick or immediate feedback, convey multiple cues through multiple channels, and support natural language and personally oriented interaction (Daft & Lengel, 1984, 1986; Trevino, Daft, & Lengel, 1990).

Despite the apparent logic and intuitive appeal of the cues-filtered-out perspective, and its continuing influence in the literature, these theories have received inconsistent support when tested in research settings (Fulk et al., 1990; Hollingshead & Contractor, 2006; Taylor, Groleau, Heaton, & Van Every-Taylor, 2000).

## Social Influence Theory

Other research on computer-mediated communication has been critical of reduced-cues theories because of their focus on the objective qualities of particular media. For instance, the *social influence* model emphasized that the processes guiding media choice and use were not born of objectively rational decisions that are devoid of social considerations, but that they were significantly influenced by the attitudes, behaviors, and norms in one's social context (Fulk et al., 1990).

However, critics of the social influence perspective caution that the influence of social and contextual factors on media-related perceptions and behaviors is not unilateral (Contractor & Eisenberg, 1990; Hollingshead & Contractor, 2006). This resonates with recent interest in comprehensive approaches that highlight the emergent and situated communication processes through which context, social actors, and technologies mutually shape one another (e.g., Orlikowski, 2000).

## Adaptive Structuration Theory

Largely consistent with this view is the framework provided by *adaptive structuration theory* (DeSanctis & Poole, 1994; Poole & DeSanctis, 1990). In this perspective, communication technologies are seen as having particular *affordances*. These represent "structural potentials" that can be engaged in various ways—that are realized, adapted, or ignored—depending on the needs and purposes of users (Zhang & Pool, 2007). This framework offers a dynamic perspective that emphasizes the mutually structuring roles of technological affordances, social practices, and contextual dimensions in shaping technological impacts. This perspective has received wide support and has served as the basis for many studies (Hollingshead & Contractor, 2006). It is helpful in explaining why the ways in which technology is eventually used often differ from the expectations and outcomes planned for and expected by designers. A criticism of this approach, however, is its failure to offer precise predictions that can be easily tested through research (Hollingshead & Contractor, 2006).

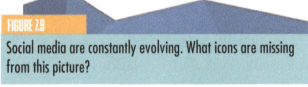

**FIGURE 7.9**

Social media are constantly evolving. What icons are missing from this picture?

Our understanding of media-related behaviors and effects are evolving. Early theories attributed primary control over media choices and outcomes to the inherent characteristics of particular technologies. Those views have given way to perspectives that attribute greater control to individual users and social dynamics. Increasingly popular are theories that acknowledge and underscore the interplay between the embedded affordances of a technology, on one hand, and the individual and social practices that emerge as they are adopted and adapted in the course of interaction (see Figure 7.9).

# MEDIATED COMMUNICATION: A MIXED BLESSING

Mediated communication extends the basic capacities of human communication. We generally think of this expansion in very positive terms, pointing to the capability of media to traverse time and space in a manner and at a pace that would otherwise be impossible. However, mediated communication is a mixed blessing—on the one hand enhancing and enlarging the potential of message sending and receiving, while on the other hand sometimes limiting and constraining communication and human experience.

## Synchronicity

We can think of a continuum of situations in which communication media are involved, ranging from virtually synchronous to extremely asynchronous. At one extreme are communication situations involving media such as books, films, and television programming; at the other are face-to-face interaction, concerts, and events involving "live" media like texting, talk radio, and telephones. Nearer the center of the continuum are email, tweeting, and voice messaging.

Generally speaking, newer media provide greater flexibility in bridging time and space than many of the earlier media.

Compared to face-to-face communication, technologies such as email, texting, and voice mail can be used to either reduce or extend the time lag between when a message is produced and when it is received.

Communication media vary in the extent to which message content and timing are controlled by the source rather than by the user. With mass media such as books, television, newspapers, and magazines, content and timing of production and distribution are source-controlled. Audience members engage in active decision making about whether to give attention to particular mass media offerings and, in many instances, can actively and consciously choose *how* to use the information received. Consumer decisions—as well as letters to the editor and other forms of feedback—have an impact on content, but the influence is delayed and often indirect. In the short-term individuals have no way to interact with or control message content and timing. Such media have limited potential for *interactivity.*

Other media, such as telephones, email, and many computer applications, are more interactive. They permit receivers to exert greater control over the content, timing, and locale. Many can be played at whatever time of day or night we want to listen to them. And we may choose to use them at home, at work, in the car, or while walking or jogging. With some media we can "fast-forward" through selections we don't care for, "pause" for interruptions, and "pause" or "rewind" to repeat segments that we particularly like (see Figure 7.10).

Heeter (1989) provides the following list of dimensions of interactivity that may be used to classify media:

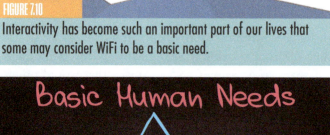

FIGURE 7.10

Interactivity has become such an important part of our lives that some may consider WiFi to be a basic need.

© kirovkat/Shutterstock.com

- *Complexity of choice available.* How much choice users have regarding content and timing of utilization.
- *Effort users must exert.* How the activity required by the user compares to the activity level of the medium.
- *Responsiveness to the user.* How actively a medium responds to users; the degree to which media are "conversational"—that is, operate like human conversations.
- *Monitoring information use.* How able a particular medium is to monitor behaviors of users and adjust its operation based on this feedback.
- *Ease of adding information.* How easily users are able to create and distribute messages for other user audiences. Based on this criterion, broadcast television has very low interactivity, call-in radio has moderate, and computerized bulletin boards have very high levels of interactivity.
- *Facilitation of interpersonal communication.* How difficult interaction is between specific and known interactants. (adapted from pp. 221-225)

## Control of Content

In contrast with the typical face-to-face communication situation, the receiver or audience member in mediated communication often has much less influence on the content and directions of interaction. As suggested previously, this is particularly the case in mass-mediated situations in which the only option available to an audience member who wishes to alter the content of communication is to "turn off" the message—an option that at times we might wish were available in interpersonal situations!

It can also be argued that technologies such as email, texting, voice mail, or traditional written messages actually afford communicators more control. For instance, the receiver of a text message or email has great control over when and how to respond. This attribute helps to explain the popularity of many newer communication technologies.

From a source's perspective, mediated communication situations often afford *more* rather than *less* control. A YouTube video, television program, or written correspondence may be revised many times before being released. In contrast, all face-to-face communication is "live," meaning that messages are produced and transmitted in the same act. There are no opportunities for rewriting, editing, reshooting, retouching, or lip-synching.

## Anonymity

In some mediated communication situations, interactants often have no direct knowledge of one another. In many mass communication situations, for instance, audience members may know the producer, reporter, author, or a celebrity by name but may have little broader knowledge of the individuals involved. Despite this relatively limited information, it is interesting that audience members often think of themselves as "knowing" media personalities. Watching people on reality television is a good example of this since most of the shows are "scripted" in various ways, yet we still think we are watching real interactions and getting to know the people on the show.

The problem of anonymity and depersonalization is particularly apparent from the perspective of mass media sources. If mass communication producers know their audience members at all, it is generally in terms of their aggregate market characteristics such as age, gender, occupation, political affiliation, or brand preferences. In addition, as Rains and Scott (2007) contend, "the growth of mediated communication tools also makes anonymity an increasingly relevant communication concern" (p. 68).

While this limitation may seem to be a liability, there are instances in which mediated communication serves as well as it does for the very reason that interactants do not know one another personally. The success of call-in radio programs can be partly attributed to the anonymity afforded by the medium. People need not identify themselves in order to share their opinions about a controversial topic or seek advice on a personal problem. In such instances, mass communication provides a vehicle for mediated therapeutic communication (Scott, 2013). As Masters (2011) notes:

> Such is the power of anonymity on the web, that it has made it possible for people—some of whom might normally be restricted from communicating with the outside world—to speak without fearing the repercussions of their actions. Actions that could put them in danger if carried out using their real names. Concealing one's true identity online has made it possible for free speech to break through the physical barriers enforced by governments and dictatorships across the world. (n.p.)

Of course, it is important to remember that, in a sense, face-to-face interaction is also often mediated—by makeup, perfume, clothing, furniture arrangement, eyeglasses, scarves, and so on.

## Responsibility and Accountability

The decreased control, anonymity, and depersonalization that sometimes occur in mediated communication situations can foster a sense of detachment, increased passivity, and a decreased sense of responsibility for directing the communication process and its outcomes. To a greater extent than in face-to-face encounters, the sense that we are actively engaged in a human communication act can be lost. Because interactants are removed in time and space from one another, feedback may be delayed or absent, and the dynamic nature of the process is obscured.

## Sense of Place

Scholar Joshua Meyrowitz (1986) began a dialogue regarding electronic technology and one's "sense of place" some years ago. The discussion may have even greater relevance to everyday experience now than it did then. Essentially, the issue is that communication technology—most especially the mobile technologies such as smartphones, laptops, and tablets—allow users to be *physically* in one time or place, but *communicationally* at another point in time or place (see Figure 7.11). To illustrate, you may be sitting on the beach surrounded by sunbathers while talking to a friend miles away. Or you may be traveling in Europe, but using your free time to post pictures to a social media account or to exchange emails with family, friends, or coworkers back home. You might be visiting relatives, but spending much of your time working on a paper that is due when you return from the trip. Or you may be walking down a street while listening to your favorite music.

**FIGURE 7.11**

Technology can transport us to a different time and place. Where do you think he is?

© mimage photography/Shutterstock.com

In these and other such instances, technology quite literally transports a person from the present place and moment to another time and place. No doubt, the ability to personally select the media and messages to which we are is exposed is comforting and probably contributes to our sense of being in control and in familiar circumstances. At the same time, this control and ability to create a personal comfort zone has the potential to lessen the possibility of having novel or unpredictable experiences or of meeting new and unfamiliar people. As the use of portable technologies increases, the possibility of finding ourselves increasingly in the past or future, or somewhere other than where we actually are—rather than in the present moment—seems an increasingly likely prospect and an increasingly interesting topic for reflection.

# COMMUNICATION TECHNOLOGY AND THE QUALITY OF LIFE

## Media Forms

Over the course of human history, the forms of communication media have changed in dramatic, complex ways. Our first messages using communication tools were fashioned from sticks, rocks, smoke, and fire. We have progressed today to the point where we are surrounded by a wide variety of machines and electronic devices that extend our information-processing modalities incredibly. As impressive as these technologies are, there is little doubt that they will continue to evolve in scope and complexity.

As Negroponte (1995) predicted, on-demand information has come to be the expected norm. The realities of the information age include:

- *Place without space.* The limitations of geography have been eliminated in many respects. Our lives depend less and less on being at a particular place at a particular time. For example, our email address and mobile phone number are portable, rather than being in a physical location like postal addresses or land line phones.
- *Being asynchronous.* With asynchronous media, our time-management capacity has greatly increased. We respond to voice messages and email, and watch streaming television programs, when it's convenient for us, rather than when it is convenient for someone else.
- *Demanding on demand.* With new media, it is increasingly possible to shift from "broadcasting" to "broadcatching"—from accepting standardized programming that is broadcast to mass audiences to having programming selected, sorted, and organized in a customized manner that meets our individualized needs. (adapted from pp. 181-191)

# CONCLUSION

For all the obvious changes in the *forms* of our communication media over the years, it is important to question the extent to which their *functions* have changed. There can be little doubt that communication media today are quicker, more flexible, and more powerful than ever before. To what degree, however, have these changes led to an improvement in the quality of human communication or the quality of life? In any given day, how much more do we know as a result of all the technology we have available? Are people more satisfied in their jobs? How much better entertained are we by all the new media? Are we better organized, or happier? Do we have better relationships? Do people understand each other better? Is the promise of improved international relations becoming a reality?

Questions such as these remind us that communication media are only extensions of our own communication abilities and liabilities. They can do little more than transport, store, duplicate, amplify, or display the messages *we* create. The nature and significance of messages and the uses to which they are put will depend, in the final analysis, more on us and less on our media.

# KEY POINTS

After reading this chapter you should be able to:

- Explain the functions and main theoretical perspectives associated with mediated communication
- Analyze the influence and limitations of mediated communication in today's society
- Describe the use and effects of contemporary media tools

# REFERENCES

Aakhus, M. (2003). Understanding information and communication technology and infrastructure in everyday life: Struggling with communication-at-a-distance. In J. E. Katz (Ed.), *Machines that become us: The social context of personal communication technology* (pp. 27-42). New Brunswick, NJ: Transaction.

Bannon D. (2012). *State of the media: The social media report - 2012*. Retrieved from http://www.nielsen.com/us/en/reports/2012/state-of-the-media-the-social-media-report-2012.html

Baym, N. K. (2006). Interpersonal life online. In L. A. Lievrouw & S. Livingstone (Eds.), *The handbook of new media: Updated student edition* (pp. 35-54). Thousand Oaks, CA: Sage.

Biocca, F., Harms, C., & Burgoon, J. K. (2003). Toward a more robust theory and measure of social presence: Review and suggested criteria. *Presence, 12*(5), 456-480.

Brahima, S. (2014). The world in 2014: ICT facts and figures. Retrieved from http://www.itu.int/en/ITU-D/Statistics/Documents/facts/ICTFactsFigures2014-e.pdf

Browning, L. D., Sætre, A.S., Stephens, K. K., & Sørnes, J-O. (2008). *Information & communication technologies in action: Linking theory and narratives of practice.* New York, NY: Routledge.

Cherry, C. (1978). *World communication: Threat or promise? A socio-technical approach.* New York, NY: Wiley.

Contractor, N.S., & Eisenberg, E.M. (1990). Communication networks and new media in organizations. In J. Fulk & C.W. Steinfield (Eds.), *Organizations and communication technology* (pp. 145-174). Newbury Park, CA: Sage.

Culnan, M.J., & Markus, M.L. (1987). Information technologies. In F. M. Jablin & L. L. Putnam (Eds.), *Handbook of organizational communication: An interdisciplinary perspective* (pp. 420-443). Newbury Park, CA: Sage.

Daft, R. L., & Lengel, R. H. (1984). Information richness: A new approach to managerial behavior and organization design. *Research in Organizational Behavior, 6,* 191-233.

Daft, R. L., & Lengel, R. H. (1986). Organizational information requirements, media richness and structural design. *Management Science, 32*(5) 554-571.

DeSanctis, G., & Poole, M. S. (1994). Capturing the complexity in advanced technology use: Adaptive structuration theory. *Organization Science, 5*(2), 121-147.

Fulk, J., Schmitz, J., & Steinfield, C.W. (1990). A social influence model of technology use. In J. Fulk & C.W. Steinfield (Eds.), *Organizations and communication technology* (pp. 117-140). Newbury Park, CA: Sage.

Funkhouser, G. F., & Shaw, E. F. (1990). How synthetic experience shapes social reality. *Journal of Communication, 40*(2), pp. 75-87.

Gumpert, G., & Fish, S. L. (Eds.). (1990). *Talking to strangers: Mediated therapeutic communication.* Norwood, NJ: Ablex.

Heeter, C. (1989). Implications of new interactive technologies for conceptualizing communication. In J. L. Salvaggio & J. Bryant (Eds.), *Media use in the information age: Emerging patterns of adoption and consumer use* (pp. 217-235). Hillsdale, NJ: Lawrence Erlbaum.

Hollingshead, A. B., & Contractor, N. S. (2006). New media and small group organizing. In L. A. Lievrouw & S. Livingstone (Eds.), *The handbook of new media: Updated student edition* (pp. 114-133). London, UK: Sage.

Katz, J. E. (1999). *Connections: Social and cultural studies of the telephone in American life.* New Brunswick, NJ: Transaction.

Lee, S. K., & Katz, J. E. (2014). Disconnect: A case study of short-term voluntary mobile phone non-use. *First Monday, 19*(12). Retrieved from http://firstmonday.org/ojs/index.php/fm/article/view/4935/4183

Masters, A. (2011, September 19). Identity on the Internet: The pros and cons of anonymity. *The Independent* blogs. Retrieved from http://blogs.independent.co.uk/2011/09/19/identity-on-the-internet-the-pros-and-cons-of-anonymity/

Meyrowitz, J. (1986). *No sense of place.* Cambridge, UK: Oxford University Press.

Mobile-broadband penetration approaching 32%. Three billion Internet Users by End of this Year. ITU Press Release. Retrieved from http://www.itu.int/net/pressoffice/press_releases/2014/23.aspx#.U5cI1E1OUqL

Negroponte, N. (1995). *Being digital.* New York, NY: Knopf.

Orlikowski, W. J. (2000). Using technology and constituting structures: A practice lens for studying technology in organizations. *Organization Science, 11*(4): 404-428.

Pew Research Internet Project. Retrieved from http://www.pewinternet.org/fact-sheets/mobile-technology-fact-sheet/

Poole, M.S., & DeSanctis, G. (1990). Understanding the use of group decision support systems: The theory of adaptive structuration. In J. Fulk & C. Steinfield (Eds.), *Organizations and Communication Technology* (pp. 175-195). Newbury Park, CA: Sage.

Rains, S. A., & Scott, C. R. (2007). To identify or not to identify: A theoretical model of receiver responses to anonymous communication. *Communication Theory, 17*, 61-91.

Schement, J. R., & Stout, D. A., Jr. (1989). A time-line of information technology. In B. D. Ruben & L. Lievrouw, *Information and behavior: Volume 3: Mediation, information, and communication* (pp. 395-424). New Brunswick, NJ: Transaction.

Schement, J. R., & Lievrouw, L. (1987). *Competing visions, Complex realities: Social aspects of the information society.* Norwood, NJ: Ablex.

Schwartz, B. (2005). *The paradox of choice: Why more is less.* New York, NY: HarperCollins.

Scott, C. R. (2013). *Anonymous agencies, backstreet businesses, and covert collectives: Rethinking organizations in the 21st century.* Palo Alto, CA: Stanford University Press.

Short, J., Williams, E., & Christie, B. (1976). *The social psychology of telecommunications.* New York, NY: Wiley.

Smith, A. G. (1974). *The cost of communication* (Presidential Address at the International Communication Association annual conference). Abstracted as Smith, A. G. (1975). The primary resource. *Journal of Communication, 25*, 15–20.

Sullivan, C., & Lewis, S. (2001). Home-based telework, gender, and the synchronization of work and family: Perspectives of teleworkers and their co-residents. *Gender, Work & Organization, 8*(2), 123-145.

Taylor, J. R., Groleau, C., Heaton, L, & Van Every-Taylor, E. (2000). *The computerization of work: A communication perspective.* Thousand Oaks, CA: Sage.

Tierney, J. (2011, August 17). Do you suffer from decision fatigue? *New York Times Magazine.* Retrieved fromhttp://www.nytimes.com/2011/08/21/magazine/do-you-suffer-from-decision-fatigue.html

Trevino, L.K., Daft, R.L., & Lengel, R.H. (1990). Understanding managers' media choices: A symbolic interactionist perspective. In J. Fulk & C.W. Steinfield (Eds.), *Organizations and communication technology* (pp. 71-94). Newbury Park, CA: Sage.

Walther, J.B. (2011). Theories of computer-mediated communication and interpersonal relations. In M. L. Knapp and J. A. Daly (Eds.), *The handbook of interpersonal communication* (pp. 443-479). Thousand Oaks, CA: Sage.

Walther, J. B., & Burgoon, J. K. (1992). Relational communication in computer-mediated interaction. *Human Communication Research, 19*(1), 50-88.

Zhang, H., & Poole, M. S. (2007, May). *A multiple case study of media use in workplace virtual teams.* Paper presented at the annual meeting of the International Communication Association, San Francisco, CA.

# ENDNOTE

1. The literature review in this section is based on a draft provided by Sally Abdul Wahab, Rutgers University.

# CHAPTER 8

# THE INDIVIDUAL:
## IDENTITY AND THE SELF

**In this chapter, you will learn about:**
- The role of the information-processing sequence in interpreting verbal and nonverbal messages
- The significance of the symbolic interpretation of our environment in the ways we communicate
- The impact of self-expression, emotions, and self-awareness on our individual identities

## REACTION, ACTION, AND INTERACTION

## COGNITIVE DEVELOPMENT
- Learning
- Characteristics of Personal Representations

## SELF-DEVELOPMENT
- Stress and Growth
- Self-Expression
- Emotional Intelligence

## SELF-AWARENESS

- Self-Reflexiveness and Self-Monitoring
- Self-Talk

## CONCLUSION

## KEY POINTS

# REACTION, ACTION, AND INTERACTION

In previous chapters we discussed nonverbal and verbal communication, message reception and information processing, and communication media and technology in some detail. When we examine each of these, in effect, we "freeze" and dissect the communication process in order to gain a better understanding of its components. The chapters in this section extend this framework to consider the role of communication in the ongoing activities of individuals, relationships, groups, organizations, cultures, societies, and public settings. We begin with a focus on the individual and the role communication processes play in shaping our personal identities and self-concepts.

In the ongoing dynamics of human life, we process visual, auditory, tactile, olfactory, and gustatory messages. We are *reacting* to our environment. We select, interpret, and remember messages, and we use the resulting information as the basis for the decisions that guide our behavior in the short- and long-run. Our decision making occurs in what may be termed an *information-use environment.* We can distinguish four general types of information-use environments (Taylor, 1986).

- *Geographical.* Defined by physical or geographical limits. Examples: a room, building, neighborhood, city, state, region, or country.
- *Interpersonal.* Defined by the presence of other people in face-to-face situations. Examples: ritual greeting situations, riding with others on an elevator, an interview, a conversation, or a date.
- *Group or Organizational.* Defined by the presence of people in a group or organizational unit formed for a specific purpose. Examples: a club, a fraternity or sorority, a religious organization, a corporation, a public institution.
- *Cultural or Societal.* Defined by the presence of people who may be personally unknown to each other, but who are linked by a common cultural, ethnic, or national affiliation. Examples: Latinas, Japanese-Americans, Native Americans, Canadians. (adapted from p. 35)

We carry out decision-making activities in any of these circumstances by employing an *information-use sequence* through which messages are used as the basis for interpretation and action (see Figure 8.1).

In nearly every circumstance, a primary interpretive use of a message is to *describe:* to determine the nature, characteristics, or appearance of an object, situation, or person. Based on our descriptions, *classification* is possible. When we classify, we compare our new observations with information stored from previous experience to see where a person, object, or event "fits."

Through *evaluation* we identify the range of possible relationships between ourselves and the objects, situations, or people in our environment, and determine what, if any, actions or reactions are appropriate and/or necessary.

A fourth step in the message-processing sequence is carrying out particular nonverbal or verbal actions, based on our descriptions, classifications, and evaluations. Then, after *acting,* we often gather information as "feedback" to monitor and assess the impact of those actions. In so doing, we are once again involved in the description, classification, and (re)evaluation and action sequence (see Figure 8.2.).

Let's illustrate this sequence by considering a very simple activity. Imagine for a moment that you have just left a classroom and stepped out into the hallway looking for a place to relax and check your text messages before your next class.

**FIGURE 8.1**

We use messages to which we react to describe, classify, and evaluate the objects, people, and circumstances in our environment. When we act based on our reactions, we create messages, completing the information-use sequence.

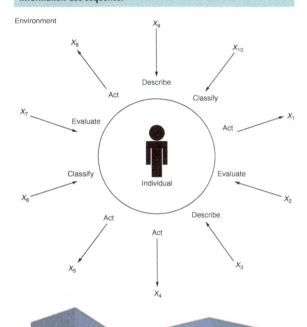

**FIGURE 8.2**

Information-Use Sequence.

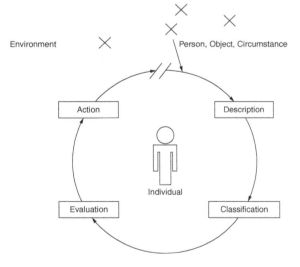

As you begin to move through the hallway, you notice a chair ahead of you. Actually, of course, you don't see a chair in its entirety. Instead, you see a physical object from a particular point of view (see Figure 8.3). Based on the visible characteristics of that object, you infer the existence of portions of it that you cannot see. You may only be able to make out two legs, for instance, connected by what appears to be a one-inch-thick horizontal plane. Given your observation that the object is standing evenly on the floor, and seems similar to other objects in your past experience, it seems reasonable to conclude that there are probably two additional legs which are not visible because of your position relative to the object.

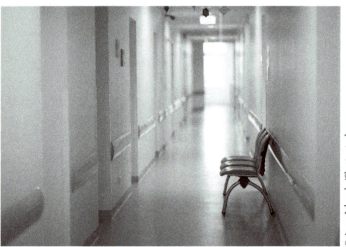

© Anna Jukovska/Shutterstock.com

**FIGURE 8.3**

In observing an object such as a chair, we infer—based on past experience—elements, properties, and characteristics that we often cannot actually see.

As you continue to interpret information, you eventually classify the object as a chair, by which you mean "something to sit on." In the split second that this information-use sequence requires, you observe it, walk over, and sit down, in full confidence that the object will support your weight.

With only a slight change in circumstance, the outcomes of the interpretive process might be quite different. If, for example, the hallway were crowded with people and you were in a hurry, your attention might well be focused on *avoiding* rather than using the chair. In such a situation, the objective would be to maneuver past the object, perhaps without ever giving a thought to it as "something to sit on." The chair would be a "stationary object to be avoided," and you would act to navigate past it.

From the perspective of interpretation, the way we process information—whether about people, circumstances, or objects—is actually quite similar. If you noticed someone walking toward you in the hallway, his or her appearance, expressions, eye movements, actions, or use of time and space would serve as nonverbal message sources in the same way as did the properties of the chair. His or her nonverbal behavior—and verbal behavior if he or she spoke—would serve as the basis for descriptive inferences as to age, gender, race, attractiveness, and perhaps even willingness to engage in interaction.

If, from your description, classification, and evaluation the person seemed friendly, interesting, and receptive, you might exchange glances, smile, or speak. If, however, you were in a hurry to get to your next class, it is likely that you would "make sense of" and relate to the individual in the hallway precisely as you would to the chair in the previous example. He or she would be classified essentially as "an object to be avoided," with the major difference between a person and a chair being that the former is "mobile" and the latter "stationary." Thus, whether the message sources that matter to us in a particular situation are people, objects, or circumstances, we go through a similar process of describing, classifying, evaluating, and then acting. As suggested in this example, because of differing goals, needs, habits, and other factors, the outcomes of this sequence will vary greatly from one situation to another.

When other people are the source of the information being perceived, the process of reacting to them and then acting often gives rise to a sequence of communicative behaviors. In such circumstances the interpretive activities of each person are contingent on the behavior of the other. Through sequential message receiving and sending we *sense, make sense of,* and *act toward* the people, circumstances, and objects in our environment. As we process visual, auditory, tactile, olfactory, or gustatory messages, we are *reacting* to our environment. When we initiate nonverbal and verbal communication, we are *acting.* We are *interacting* when we are involved in message-sending/message-receiving exchanges with others.

# COGNITIVE DEVELOPMENT

As psychologist O. J. Harvey (1963) noted: "That an individual will come to structure or make sense out of a personally relevant situation is one of psychology's most pervasive tenets" (p. 3). We are continuously involved in reacting to, acting toward, and interacting with our environment and the people in it. The sense we make of the situations, people, and objects around us shapes and guides our actions and reactions in the moment. At the same time, we are engaged in a far more subtle activity with major long-term consequences for us. As we routinely process information and develop interpretations, we are also developing internalized representations of our world that allow us to think and comprehend what we experience around us. These personal theories or representations—which are variously called *images, mental models, cognitive maps,* and *semantic networks*—provide our means for relating to the environment and to one another (Boulding, 1963; Budd, 2003; Hunt, 1982).

## Learning

Our images—of chairs, friends and family, and the varying situations we learn to interpret—develop over time in a very complex manner. The process begins early in life. As Delgado (1969) has observed: "The newborn baby is not capable of speech, symbolic understanding, or of directing skillful mobility. It has no ideas, words, or concepts, no tools for communication, no significant sensory experience, no culture" (p. 45). Enabled and limited by the physiological potentialities we inherit (our "cognitive hardware") we begin to learn about our environment and our relation to it and to develop our personalized theories (our "cognitive software"):

> For some time [babies] see just a mass of shifting shapes and colors, a single, ever-changing picture in front of them. . . . The picture . . . is not made up, as it is for us, of many separate elements, each of which we can imagine and name, by itself, and all of which we can combine in our minds in other ways. When we see a chair in a room, we can easily imagine that chair in another part of the room, or in another room, or by itself. But for [babies] the chair is an integral part of the room [they see]. This may be the reason . . . why, when we hide something from a very young [baby], it ceases to exist for [him or her]. And this in turn may be one of the reasons why peek-a-boo games are such fun for small babies to play, and may contribute much to their growing understanding of the world. (Holt, 1983, p. 89)

The infant's awareness of mother, father, food, and objects as potential sources of satisfaction represents perhaps the first elements of the child's lifelong cognitive map-making enterprise. Gradually, the infant's worldview expands to take account of the rapidly changing environment of his or her experience. The fascination and attention to fingers, hands, and mouth widens to toys in and around the crib and to the physical environment itself. The map continues to expand to define more and more detail of the child's room, other rooms in the dwelling, the neighborhood, the community, and, eventually, the country and world. At the same time, the child is developing the verbal and nonverbal communication rules necessary for making sense of and relating to his or her social environment—first family, then friends, relatives, acquaintances, teachers, peers, colleagues at work, and so on.

As children grow, they select, interpret, and retain information, and they begin to learn about the physical and social environment and their relationship to it. The physical and social world provides an extensive menu of message sources, as the developing human individual embarks on a life-long quest to make sense of and cope with the situations he or she encounters (see Figure 8.4).

As suggested earlier, much remains to be learned about the ways in which selected environmental cues are transformed into interpretable information and stored in a way that makes it quickly and easily accessible to us. It is thought by scholars working in this area that much of the information is processed and stored in long-term memory in what cognitive psychologists call a *semantic network*, whereby incoming messages are linked systematically to previously stored information based on common characteristics.

**FIGURE 8.4**

As we respond to the many circumstances, objects, and persons in our environment, we are developing our internalized theories of the world.

A *canary,* for instance, might become significant to an individual through a process of comparing its properties to those of previously observed and classified objects. That it "has wings," "flies," and is "quite small" suggests it is similar to other animals we have learned to call *birds*—about which information has been previously processed and retained. That this *bird* "sings" and is "in a cage in a friend's house," suggests that, while this canary has much in common with other birds, it also is different in some respects. A *canary* is a special kind of bird—a *pet bird.*

As Hunt (1982) explains metaphorically:

> New material is added to this network by being plunked down in a hole in the middle of an appropriate region, and then gradually is tied in, by a host of meaningful connections, to the appropriate nodes in the surrounding network. . . .

> Thus, although remembered information is arranged by categories of subject matter, the arrangement is far less orderly and regular than in reference works or libraries. But also far more redundant: we have many ways of getting to something filed in long-term memory, many cues and routes to the item we are seeking. When no cue or route takes us directly to it, we can guide ourselves to the general area and then mentally run through the items in that area until we come across the one we're looking for. (pp. 107-108)

Our personal theories and representations are the long-term informational consequence of our efforts to adapt to the messages with which we are confronted over the course of our lifetimes. They represent the blending of the many messages to which we have been exposed and the sense we have made of them. They are not simply the result of an accumulation of messages to which we have been exposed (see Figure 8.5), though these messages certainly play an important role (Boulding, 1956).

FIGURE 8.5

Humans interpret, store, and retrieve information according to the associations and meanings the objects, phenomena, and events of their experience have for them.

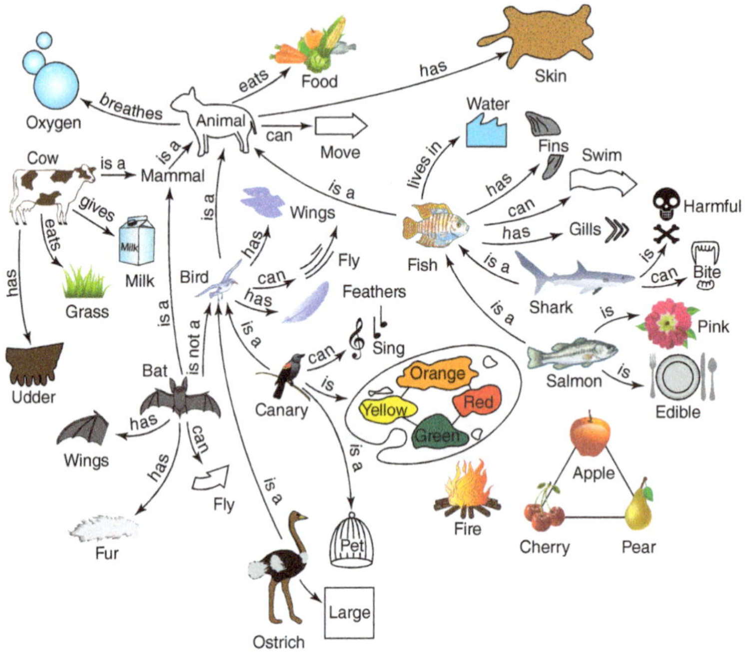

Source: Republished with permission of Taylor and Francis Group LLC Books, from *Cognitive Psychology and Information Processing*, by Roy Lachman, J. L. Lachman, and E. C. Butterfield, copyright © 1979; permission conveyed through Copyright Clearance Center, Inc.

## Characteristics of Personal Representations

Through a subtle self-programming process, as a consequence of communication, we acquire the personal theories and mental models and associations that direct our behavior in any given situation. Whether we are aware of it or not, our mental models and decision rules guide us about what to say, when to say it, how to act in this and that circumstance, how to tell one kind of circumstance from another, what to pay attention to and what to ignore, what to value and what to dislike, what type of people to seek out and which to avoid, what and whom to believe, and so on.

These representations are our means for navigating in our symbolic and physical environments and the basis for our functioning as human beings. They enable us to act and react and to carry our knowledge of our environment forward in time. Without them, each experience would be totally new and potentially bewildering.

The significance of these theories is clear when we consider an illustration such as identifying a chair in the example mentioned earlier or the simple act of putting a key in a lock or opening a door. Our images of keys and doors and our rules for door opening tell us how to locate and use the handle and whether to pull or push the door in order to open it. Without this stored knowledge, each door opening would be a wholly novel and very time-consuming experience.

Models are also invaluable in dealing with interpersonal aspects of our environment. In many cultures, standardized greetings such as a handshake and "Hi, how are you?" and "Fine, thanks, and you?" are easily accomplished. This is the case because we have categorized a particular situation as being like certain other situations in the past, for which we have learned a particular conversational pattern. Our models also guide us in deciding when "Hi! How are you?" is simply a request for a "routine" acknowledgement, or when the person wants more detailed information about our physical or mental health.

In emphasizing the obvious assets and values of our internal theory-building capability, it is quite possible to overlook some of the shortcomings and dysfunctions of this capacity. Primary among these liabilities is the fact that once our internal representations become fairly well defined, they take on an objective quality and sometimes become rigid. Often, they seem so real to us that we lose sight of their representational nature and forget that they are in many senses our own personal creations. We seldom give a second thought, for instance, to whether a paper dollar has buying power or to the meaning of symbols like *dollars*, *dog* or *cat*, *Democrat* or *Republican*, *woman* or *man*. We have so thoroughly internalized our images of *Republicans* or *women* that we may think or behave in ways that suggest these representations are, in fact, precise, complete, objective, and universal descriptions of the people, objects, situations, or ideas which we use for referring to the realities we, personally, have come to know and take for granted.

These kinds of problems come about for various reasons (summarized from Budd, 2003) including:

1. The environment is constantly changing while our representations are relatively fixed.
2. Any representation is necessarily incomplete.
3. Representations are personal and subjective.
4. Representations are social products.
5. Representations are resistant to change.

CHANGING ENVIRONMENT. Like a map and the territory it illustrates, there can never be a point-for-point correspondence between our cognitive map and our environment. General semanticists, who developed the map-and-territory analogy, point out several reasons why this match between our internal maps and external physical and symbolic reality is never complete. The first has to do with the process-like nature of the environment. The environment is ever-changing (Johnson, 1946), but our symbols and symbolic images are not always changing in the same way or at the same rate of speed as the environment. For instance, long after we have moved a clock or wastebasket to a new location, we persist in looking for it where it used to be because of our well-learned maps.

The usefulness of our representations is often time-dependent. Images and models appropriate at one point in time may be useless, even harmful, at other times. For example, we often assume that a GPS system is completely accurate until the voice tells us to turn at a road that doesn't exist or can't find a newly constructed building. The world and the behavior of its inhabitants may change substantially from one time to another, and there is unfortunately no guarantee that our maps will be sensitive to these changes.

**INCOMPLETE REPRESENTATION.** A second reason for mismatches between our maps and the environment is that our representations are always less complete and comprehensive than what they symbolize. Details are invariably left out. Much as a highway map highlights some features of the landscape and ignores others, our personal images are also selective. They are generalizations that categorize or stereotype selected aspects of the environment for our convenience, but in so doing omit any number of details that can limit their accuracy and, therefore, their usefulness (see Figure 8.6).

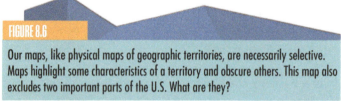

FIGURE 8.6

Our maps, like physical maps of geographic territories, are necessarily selective. Maps highlight some characteristics of a territory and obscure others. This map also excludes two important parts of the U.S. What are they?

© Mahesh Patil/Shutterstock.com

The symbol *dog* that we mentioned earlier illustrates this point. Each person has a different image of the animal to which the word refers. When we think of a dog, our images are based on our own personal experience that bears an arbitrary relationship to the four-legged animal we refer to as *dog*. Further, our personal meaning of *dog* is very likely to be far less comprehensive than the collective standardized definitions of the word. And, of course, if we are very familiar with dog breeding or a fan of dog shows, we use many terms to distinguish various types of *dogs*.

*Stereotypes* tend to reduce individual differences to generalizations about a group in ways that may be damaging to people (Stewart, Cooper, Stewart & Friedley, 2003). In addition, stereotypes generally have an evaluative dimension—they are seen as either negative or positive (Seiter, 1986). For example, the negative stereotypes that women were passive and indecisive were used in the past as an excuse to keep women out of positions of political power. The success of women such as former British Prime Minister Margaret Thatcher, German Chancellor Angela Merkel, and Supreme Court Justices Ruth Bader Ginsberg, Sonia Sotomayor, and Elena Kagan, among many other women leaders, demonstrate the limitations of this stereotype.

PERSONAL AND SUBJECTIVE. As we know, our images develop in our effort to adapt to the situations that confront us in our lives. We are not all confronted with the same situations, and the images and rules we develop as a result of our experiences vary greatly from person to person.

An exchange between two characters in the old yet classic film *Eye of the Beholder* makes this point. The scene takes place on a sidewalk in an urban area. A landlord (Copplemeyer) and his artist tenant (Michael Garrard) gaze across the street at a passing woman:

> *Garrard:* Do you see that woman over there? She isn't real.
> *Copplemeyer:* That woman over there isn't real, huh? I made her up from my imagination?
> *Garrard:* Yes, exactly. One man looks and sees nothing, another looks and falls in love. Today I will put on a canvas what I see in a woman. To me the painting will be as real as that woman. To you it will be only a painting.
> *Copplemeyer:* The painting will be as real as that woman?
> *Garrard:* Yes, Copplemeyer, yes! Do you understand?
> *Copplemeyer:* I understand you are a lunatic!
> *Garrard:* (laughing) You see, Copplemeyer, you prove my point. The man you see in me does not exist. (dialogue from *Eye of the Beholder,* Stuart Reynolds Productions, 1958)

This dialogue clearly illustrates that we each create our own images—and for each of us those images have a tangible and real quality, to the point that we often find it difficult to understand how others might think differently than we do about them.

SOCIAL PRODUCTS. Whether one considers a child striving to make sense of a toy jack-in-the-box, a physicist trying to integrate a new observation into his or her theory, or deciding on a new item of clothing to purchase, the influence of others is unmistakable. From our earliest days, parents, family, friends, and associates—as well as previous generations—play a role in determining the messages and experiences to which we will be exposed and how we will interpret them. Even the language we use is a product of our having developed the necessary knowledge and skills through social learning.

We are influenced not only by these informal, developmental experiences but also by our formal education and training. These social processes direct our attention in a highly selective fashion, highlighting certain phenomena and situations while minimizing others, shaping our representations in a host of subtle and not-so-subtle ways through the course of our lifetime.

For example, many families celebrate religious or civic holidays in ways that have been handed down through several generations. Specific prayers, rituals, customs, decorations, and foods may well be taken-for-granted parts of the tradition. The importance of these traditions for the individuals involved becomes most apparent when couples or friends from different cultural traditions find themselves in a situation where they need to negotiate a way to celebrate a particular event or holiday that "works for" everyone involved.

STABLE AND RIGID REPRESENTATIONS. After our images are fairly well established, new messages generally produce very little fundamental change. After we have developed a preference for one political party, for instance, it is unlikely that a single or even several advertisements or news articles will lead us to change our affiliation. Similarly, once we have decided we don't care for a particular job, television program, or individual, it is seldom the case that any single exposure to potentially contradictory information will change our minds. The action of waves washing against a sandy shoreline provides a useful metaphor. No single wave is likely to have a major impact on the contour of the beach, but the cumulative impact of the action of waves over the course of hours, days, weeks, and months can be very substantial.

MIXED BLESSINGS. Personal representations are mixed blessings. On the one hand, they are invaluable as guides to orient ourselves in what would otherwise seem like a forever new and unpatterned world. On the other hand, our personal representations may also allow us to mislead ourselves because they may not easily accommodate the changing world in which we live, and because they are necessarily incomplete, personal, subjective, socially based, and resistant to change.

Our maps and force of habit tend to guide us toward messages and message sources that are generally consistent with the representations we have developed. In most instances, our tendency is to ignore or distort information that contradicts or disconfirms our image.

Like the scholar who has great difficulty discarding a particular theory or scientific paradigm even in the face of seemingly disconfirming information, we part reluctantly with elements of our personal paradigms—our representations of reality. Nonetheless, in some instances, changes in our models do occur. Sometimes the weight of accumulating evidence, the influence of people who are important to us, or critical incidents in our own lives lead to fundamental changes in our ways of acting, reacting, and interacting. Even a single incident can have a rather dramatic impact. Sometimes, for instance, a car accident, illness, disappointment, or a particular achievement can be a trigger for significant change.

# SELF-DEVELOPMENT

*Becoming* is a term coined by Gordon Allport to capture the dynamic process by which we as humans develop, modify, and refine our personal identity—our "self" and our concept of ourself (Allport, 1955).

We know that our self-development is very much shaped by our earliest interactions with those who care for us as infants and children. For the most part, our caregivers create and control the environment to which we are exposed and with which we must cope. As we grow, our caregivers are our models for how we are to act and how we are to think and feel about ourselves.

According to *social learning theory*, "new patterns of behavior can be acquired through observing the behavior of others" (Bandura, 1971, p. 3). As we grow, the number and diversity of shaping influences increase. As shown in Figure 8.7, encounters with family members are supplemented by face-to-face dealings with peers, and by broadening experiences in relationships, groups, organizations, and society. The impact of these interactions is quite dramatic. We come to use the same slang words and phrases as friends and family members, and we often share their values, opinions, occupational preferences, outlooks, and political preferences. We may adopt similar styles of dress and even develop the same gestures and speech patterns. Some of these shaping influences have a fundamental and lasting impact on our development, others much less so. Communication technologies also play a strong supporting role in our self-development.

An important part of self-development is our self-esteem or sense of self-worth. Self-esteem affects our communication behavior. For example, people with high self-esteem are more flexible in the way they respond to situations (Gudykunst, Ting-Toomey, Sudweeks, & Stewart, 1995). They may be able to cope better with a difficult situation because they are more relaxed and are able to accept themselves as they are.

**FIGURE 8.7**

To a large extent our individual identities and self-concepts are a consequence of having adapted to information from our family and the relationships, groups, organizations, and culture of which we have been a part.

© Flashon Studio/Shutterstock.com

## Stress and Growth

Self-development is an ongoing process of adjusting and readjusting to the many influences, challenges, and opportunities we encounter. As such, it is necessarily a stressful process.

From a biological point of view, the *stress-adjustment cycle* we go through directly parallels that of other living things, whose day-to-day existences are also fraught with continual threats and challenges to their growth and development (Seyle, 1976). However, in terms of the origins of the stress, and the means available for dealing with it, we are quite unlike other animals. Most animals detect and react to threats and challenges in their environment in a direct, reflex-like manner. For instance, when a deer hears a loud noise, it instinctively begins to run away from the source of the noise. It detects a challenge to its well-being, comfort, or safety, and it flees. This instinctive reaction to stressful situations is known as the *fight-or-flight response.*

Human stress is usually the consequence of a second-order information-processing event involving symbolic meaning. Many of the situations that are stressful for us threaten our psychological, rather than physical, well-being. The threat of rejection by a loved one, a heated argument with a colleague, the prospect of failing an important exam, or the pressure of an approaching deadline for an incomplete project are frequently potent stressors for us. Positive events, like marriage, can be stressors, too. These symbolic threats are capable of triggering the same hormonal, muscular, and neural reactions that for other animals are associated only with physical threats to their safety and well-being.

Unlike other animals, we do not generally cope with challenge by physical fleeing or fighting; we have learned that physical combat and running away are not regarded as "civilized" ways for us to deal with problems. Because of this learning, we hold our bodies in check and usually react by "fight" or "flight" only in a symbolic sense. For example, we might spend a large portion of a boring class looking at email or texts and thinking about our plans for the weekend. Although we control our urge to physically flee from the situation, our mind has taken flight.

Though stress and adjustment are normal aspects of human life, evidence suggests that chronic and accumulated stress can have serious physical, as well as emotional, consequences. Research indicates that stress lowers our resistance to illness and can play a contributory role in diseases of the kidney, heart, and blood vessels, as well as contributing to high blood pressure, migraine and tension headaches, gastrointestinal problems such as ulcers, asthma, allergies, respiratory diseases, arthritis, and even cancer (Holmes & Rahe, 1967).

Though there are a number of negative consequences of stress, it is an inevitable part of the process of life and of becoming. It may also be a very positive force in the sense that stress presents opportunities for personal and social growth and change (Ruben, 1978). Ultimately, the consequences of stress for us depend on the ways in which we take advantage—or fail to take advantage—of the opportunities environmental challenges provide.

This duality is expressed clearly by physician M. Scott Peck (2003) in *The Road Less Traveled:*

> What makes life difficult is that the process of confronting and solving problems is a painful one. Problems, depending upon their nature, evoke in us frustration or grief or

sadness or loneliness or guilt or regret or anger or fear or anxiety or anguish or despair. These are uncomfortable feelings . . . often as painful as any kind of physical pain. . . .

Yet it is in this whole process of meeting and solving problems that life has its meaning. . . . It is only because of problems that we grow mentally and spiritually. (p. 16)

*Becoming* is not a passive process. In reacting to, acting upon, and interacting with these influences, we provide the fuel for the becoming process. Each encounter builds on the last, as we negotiate our way through the demands and opportunities around us and as we fashion our identities. In a very real sense, we become what we live. Whatever we are, have been, and will be—whether dominant or submissive, withdrawn or outgoing, self-confident or insecure, rigid or flexible, passive or assertive—is very much influenced by the communication experiences we have had up to that point and the ways we have adapted to them.

## Self-Expression

Although we are discussing the concepts of self-development and self-expression separately, they are inextricably intertwined. Our sense of self is developed in interaction with others; therefore, our ability for self-expression is a crucial component of interpersonal communication. Self-expression is a fundamental facet of human activity. Whether it involves speaking, writing, painting, singing, or engaging in other forms of performance, the process is one of communication.

In a wide range of communication situations, a great deal of our energy is expended not only "making statements," but also "making a statement." "Making statements" serves *instrumental* communication functions. In the case of instrumental communication, we have information we want to convey or receive, and our efforts are directed toward ensuring the clarity of our messages and accuracy of meanings. In contrast, "making a statement" has to do with *expressive* functions of communication. Here, our concerns may be more with impression, tone, and mood.

In his classic book, *The Presentation of Self in Everyday Life,* sociologist Erving Goffman (1959) makes a similar distinction. He notes that there are two kinds of communication: expressions *given* and expressions *given off.* Goffman describes self-expression using a theatrical metaphor in which individuals are actors on a stage, presenting themselves to an audience. In this perspective, people encounter one another in face-to-face engagements and take turns presenting dramas or telling stories to one another. In distinguishing between instrumental and expressive forms of communication, Goffman (1974) notes that:

. . . often what talkers undertake to do is not to provide information to a recipient but to present dramas to an audience. Indeed, it seems that we spend most of our time not engaged in giving information but in giving shows. And observe, this theatricality is not based on mere displays of feelings or faked exhibitions of spontaniety . . . The parallel between stage and conversation is much, much deeper than that. The point is that ordinarily when an individual says something, he is not saying it as a bold statement of fact on his own behalf. He is recounting. He is running through a strip of already determined events for the engagement of his listeners. (p. 508)

Thus, if the goal of instrumental communication is exchanging information, *impression management* is a fundamental function of expressive communication. But it is important to note that expressive communication is not necessarily an intentional process, as suggested by Figure 8.8. Through nonverbal and verbal behaviors, we create the basis for impressions—and form impressions of others—whether we intend for this to occur or not.

Kenneth Burke (1970) believed that people see the world in terms of a drama. He developed the *dramatistic pentad* to analyze the language people use for self-expression. The five elements are:

1. *Scene* (the place where the action occurs). For example, a couple having problems in their relationship might go to a romantic location to see if they can talk about and improve their relationship.
2. *Act* (the action that occurs). For example, there are thousands of videos of animals on the Internet acting in unexpected ways that we find funny.
3. *Agent* (the actor who acts out the action or plot). For example, if you are considered a "take charge" kind of person you are acting as an agent.
4. *Agency* (the tools or means actors use to accomplish their ends). For example, a person may always make a point of complimenting others as a way to maintain friendships.
5. *Purpose* (the reason why people do what they do). For example, people may volunteer at a local

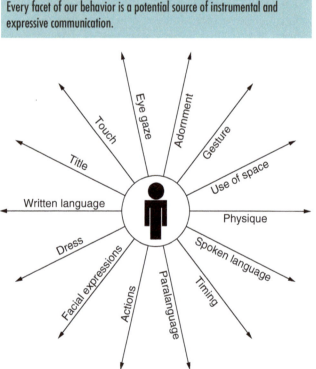

**FIGURE 8.8**

Every facet of our behavior is a potential source of instrumental and expressive communication.

© Kendall Hunt Publishing Co.

charity to help others but also to do something that will look good on a resume. (adapted from Larson, 1995, pp. 134-136)

Burke (1970) argues that people are more likely to use whichever element corresponds to their view of the world. Thus, a person who favors agency, for example, is more likely to argue that a particular restaurant is a good place to eat because it is inexpensive and in a convenient location. A person who focuses on the act might say, "We always eat at the Pizza Palace on Wednesday nights. Why would we go somewhere else?"

It is important to understand our usual mode of self-expression and to determine if we want to modify or alter it to fit the needs or expectations of a particular audience. See Figure 8.9 for an interesting example of self-expression.

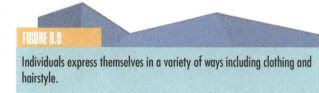

**FIGURE 8.9**

Individuals express themselves in a variety of ways including clothing and hairstyle.

© szefei/Shutterstock.com

## Emotional Intelligence

One of the keys to self-expression is management of emotions—what Goleman (2004) and others refer to as *emotional intelligence or EI*. Most fundamentally emotional intelligence has to do with the way in which we understand, regulate and express our emotional reactions. Goleman (2004) has identified several critical facets of EI:

- *Self-awareness:* the ability to recognize and understand your moods, emotions, and drives, and their effect on others
- *Self-regulation:* the ability to control or redirect disruptive impulses and moods; the propensity to suspend judgment—to think before acting
- *Motivation:* a passion to work for reasons that go beyond money or status; a propensity to pursue goals with energy and persistence

- *Empathy:* the ability to understand the emotional makeup of other people; skill in treating people according to their emotional reactions
- *Social skill:* proficiency in managing relationships and building networks; an ability to find common ground and build rapport. (p. 88)

Emotions often arise through the interpretations we make, and it is through our nonverbal and verbal behavior in social interaction that our orientation toward emotion becomes apparent to others. At the same time, our actions influence others' reactions to us and become critical components in the ongoing development and evolution of relationships—as will be discussed in detail in Chapter 9.

# SELF-AWARENESS

## Self-Reflexiveness and Self-Monitoring

As we discussed previously in this book, the capacity for self-reflexiveness is one of the fundamental characteristics of human communication. Our self-reflexive capability allows us to look upon and analyze ourselves, our thoughts, and our actions. It also permits us to turn our attention inward in order to examine our own communication behavior. Through self-reflexiveness, we can replay and think about our actions, reactions, and interactions. Similarly, we can examine our own self-development and self-expression. In addition, we also can reflect on our interpretive processes, cognitive development, and self-development.

When we engage in any of these forms of self-reflexiveness, we do so by means of *intrapersonal communication*—the processing of messages of which we, ourselves, are the source. By means of intrapersonal communication and self-reflexiveness, we are able to engage in *self-monitoring*—the analysis and adjustment of our actions in order to achieve a particular communication goal (or goals). We are engaged in self-monitoring when we analyze our communication behavior in a public speaking situation, in a job interview, on a date, or in exchanges with family members, friends, and colleagues.

Although we all analyze our communication behavior to some extent, people who are *high self-monitors* are more likely to behave in a way they think is required in a social situation, while *low self-monitors* are more likely to act in a way consistent with their values, attitudes, and beliefs (Gudykunst, Ting-Toomey, Sudweeks, & Stewart, 1995). In each of these cases and so many others, we have one—and often several—communication goals we want to achieve. If we are aware of our goals and understand the nature of communication, we can monitor and adjust our communication behavior, our goals, or both.

Self-reflexiveness can be very beneficial in enhancing our ability to understand and use our communication knowledge. It is this capacity that allows us to make plans and set goals for ourselves. And it is self-awareness and self-monitoring that later allow us to assess our own performance, evaluate it against our goals, and identify ways to improve our performance the next time. This capability can be a mixed blessing, allowing us to recognize and celebrate when our goals are met, yet permitting us to be saddened and dismayed when we feel that they are not achieved.

FIGURE 8.10

The Johari Model

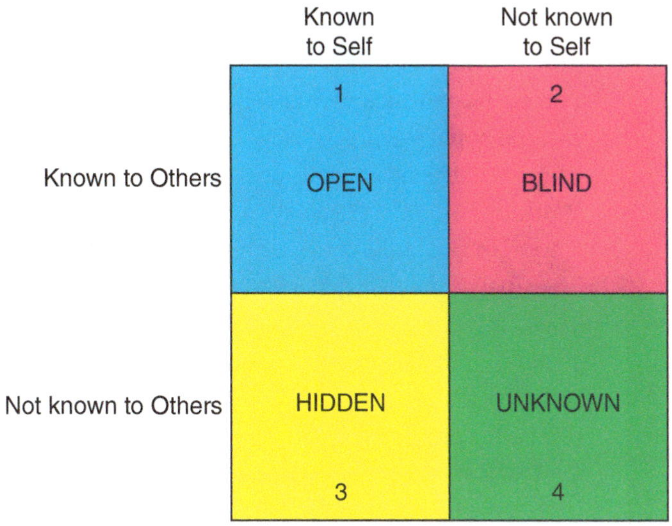

Source: From *Group Processes*, 3rd edition by Joseph Luft. Reprinted by permission of The McGraw-Hill Companies, Inc.

As we noted earlier, it is difficult to discuss self-awareness without referring to interaction with others. One way to think about our understanding of ourself as part of the communication process is by using the Johari window. The *Johari window* provides a useful way to think about the dynamics of self-awareness of behavior, feelings, and motives. Shown in Figure 8.10, the *Johari awareness model* (Luft, 1969), as it is also known, includes four quadrants:

- Quadrant 1, the open quadrant, refers to behavior, feelings, and motivation known to self and others.
- Quadrant 2, the blind quadrant, refers to behavior, feelings, and motivation known to others but not to self.
- Quadrant 3, the hidden quadrant, refers to behavior, feelings, and motivation known to self but not to others.
- Quadrant 4, the unknown quadrant, refers to behavior, feelings, and motivation known neither to self nor to others. (p. 13)

In discussing the model, Luft contends that we should strive to increase self-awareness by reducing the size of Quadrant 2—our blind area. Quadrant 2 is an area of vulnerability in that it includes what others know about our behavior, feelings, and motivation that we are unaware of, or choose to ignore or deny. Decreasing our blind area also has the effect of increasing Quadrant 1—the open area—and this in turn holds promise for improving interpersonal relationships as well as self-awareness. Luft (1969) offers a number of suggestions for how one can enhance self-awareness and change:

1. A change in any one quadrant will affect all other quadrants.
2. It takes energy to hide, deny, or be blind to behavior which is involved in interaction.
3. Threat tends to decrease awareness; mutual trust tends to increase awareness.
4. Forced awareness (exposure) is undesirable and usually ineffective.
5. Interpersonal learning means a change has taken place so that Quadrant 1 is larger, and one or more of the other quadrants has grown smaller.
6. Working with others is facilitated by a large enough area of free activity. It means more of the resources and skills of the persons involved can be applied to the task at hand.
7. The smaller the first quadrant, the poorer the communication.
8. There is universal curiosity about the unknown area, but this is held in check by custom, social training, and diverse fears.
9. Sensitivity means appreciating the covert aspects of behavior, in Quadrants 2, 3, and 4, and respecting the desire of others to keep them so.
10. Learning about group processes, as they are being experienced, helps to increase awareness (enlarging Quadrant 1) for the group as a whole as well as for individual members.
11. The value system of a group and its membership may be noted in the way *unknowns* in the life of the group are confronted. (p. 14)

Self-reflexiveness and self-monitoring provide us with a means of assessing our actions, reactions, and interactions, understanding ourselves, benefiting from experiences, enhancing our interpersonal effectiveness, learning from our failures as well as our successes, and growing as human beings. They can be incredibly powerful tools, providing some of our most important opportunities for applying our understanding of communication and human behavior to the betterment of our own lives (Berquist, 2014).

## Self-Talk

One of the ways to increase self-awareness is to focus our attention periodically on how we talk to ourselves. Many of us spend time analyzing how we talk to others and how they talk to us, but how often do we think about how we talk to ourselves? How do we talk to ourselves when we have failed at something? When we have succeeded? Are we as supportive and forgiving of ourselves as we would be of others?

Self-talk provides clues as to the kind of relationship we have with ourselves (Lederman, 2002). As much as our relationships with others can typically benefit from care and attention, so too can our relationships with ourselves.

# CONCLUSION

We have examined a number of uses and consequences of communication from an individual perspective. By sending and receiving messages, we react to and act toward the people, objects, and events in our environment. It is also through communication that we interact and negotiate meanings with others.

Interpretation is a fundamental process in which communication plays an important role. In making interpretations, we use messages to describe, classify, evaluate, and act in information-rich environments.

Communication is also basic to cognitive development. Through message processing we learn and develop the personalized theories and representations of the world that guide our behavior. These representations have limitations because they may fail to keep pace with changes in the environment. Additionally, they are incomplete, personal and subjective, social products, and stable and sometimes overly rigid.

Becoming is a term coined to refer to the process of self-development. The role of communication in development continues throughout our lives, as we adjust to a variety of individuals, influences, and circumstances.

In the developmental process, we may undergo stress in our efforts to adapt to the challenges and opportunities that present themselves. Many of the stressors to which we react are symbolic and themselves the product of communication. Through communication, we identify these stressors; and message processing is a primary means by which we react to and cope with such circumstances.

Self-expression is a fundamental part of human activity. Whether it involves speaking, writing, painting, singing, or engaging in other forms of performance, the process is one of communication. Communication serves instrumental and expressive functions. Instrumental communication involves conveying information; expressive communication involves impressions.

Self-awareness involves reflecting on and monitoring our own behavior. Awareness involves intrapersonal communication—the processing of messages of which we ourselves are the source. By means of self-reflexiveness and self-monitoring, it is possible to adjust our communication behaviors to achieve particular goals. Analysis of self-talk provides insight into the kind of relationship we have with ourselves. Self-awareness gives us an important opportunity to apply our understanding of communication on our own behalf.

## KEY POINTS

After having read this chapter, you should be able to:

- Describe the information processing sequence through which communication messages are interpreted by individuals
- Analyze the importance of the symbolic messages in our daily interactions
- Explain the impact of self-expression, emotions, and self-awareness in shaping our personal identities and communication style

## REFERENCES

Allport, G. W. (1955). *Becoming*. New Haven, CT: Yale University Press.

Bandura, A. (1971). *Social learning theory*. New York, NY: General Learning Press.

Berquist, W. (2014, December). The new Johari window #2: Models of interpersonal awareness. Retrieved from http://psychology.edu/library/the-new-johari-window-2-models-of-interpersonal-awareness/

Boulding, K. E. (1956). General systems theory—The skeleton of science. *Management Science*, *2*(3), 197-206.

Boulding, K. E. (1963). *The image: Knowledge in life and society*. Ann Arbor, MI: University of Michigan Press.

Budd, R. W. (2003). General semantics. In R. W. Budd & B. D. Ruben (Eds.), *Interdisciplinary approaches to human communication* (2nd ed., pp. 71-93). New Brunswick, NJ: Transaction.

Burke, K. (1970). *A grammar of motives*. Berkeley, CA: University of California Press.

Delgado, J. M. R. (1969). *Physical control of the mind: Toward a psychocivilized society*. New York, NY: Harper & Row.

Goffman, E. (1974). *Frame analysis: An essay on the organization of experience*. Cambridge, MA: Harvard University Press.

Goffman, E. (1959). *The presentation of self in everyday life*. Garden City, NY: Doubleday.

Goleman, D. (2004). What makes a leader? *Harvard Business Review, 82*(1), 82-91.

Gudykunst, W. B., Ting-Toomey, S., Sudweeks, S., & Stewart, L. P. (1995). *Building bridges: Interpersonal skills for a changing world*. Boston, MA: Houghton Mifflin.

Harvey, O. J. (Ed.). (1963). *Motivation and social interaction: Cognitive determinants*. New York, NY: Ronald Press.

Holmes, T. H., & Rahe, R. H. (1967). The social adjustment rating scale. *Journal of Psychosomatic Research, 11*, 213-218.

Holt, J. C. (1983). *How children learn* (rev. ed.). New York, NY: Delacorte Press.

Hunt, M. (1982). *The universe within*. New York, NY: Simon & Schuster.

Johnson, W. (1946). *People in quandaries*. New York, NY: Harper.

Larson, C. U. (1995). *Persuasion: Reception and responsibility* (7th ed.). Belmont, CA: Wadsworth.

Lederman, L. C. (2002). Intrapersonal communication. In J. R. Schement (Ed.), *Encyclopedia of communication and information* (pp. 490-492). New York, NY: Macmillan.

Luft, J. (1969). *Of human interaction*. Palo Alto, CA: Mayfield.

Peck, M. S. (2003). *The road less traveled, 25th anniversary edition*. New York, NY: Simon & Schuster.

Ruben, B. D. (1978). Communication and conflict: A system theoretic perspective. *Quarterly Journal of Speech, 64*(2), 202-210.

Seiter, E. (1986). Stereotypes and the media: A re-evaluation. *Journal of Communication, 36*(2), 14-26.

Stewart, L. P., Cooper, P. J., Stewart, A. D., & Friedley, S. A. (2003). *Communication and gender* (4th ed.). Boston, MA: Allyn & Bacon.

Taylor, R. S. (1986). *Value-added processes in information systems*. Norwood, NJ: Ablex.

# CHAPTER 9

# INTERPERSONAL
## COMMUNICATION AND RELATIONSHIPS

**In this chapter, you will learn:**

- The definitions and key terms associated with interpersonal communication
- The different types of relationships
- The significance of communication in relationship development
- The effects of power and conflict in relationships

## INTERPERSONAL COMMUNICATION AND RELATIONSHIPS

## TYPES OF RELATIONSHIPS

- Dyadic and Triadic Relationships
- Task and Social Relationships
- Short- and Long-Term Relationships
- Casual and Intimate Relationships
- Dating, Love, and Marital Relationships
- Family Relationships

# THE EVOLUTION OF RELATIONSHIPS

- Coming Together Stages
- Coming Apart Stages

# RELATIONAL PATTERNS

- Supportive and Defensive Climates
- Dependencies and Counterdependencies
- Progressive and Regressive Spirals

# FACTORS THAT INFLUENCE PATTERNS

- Stage of Relationship and Context
- Interpersonal Needs and Styles
- Roles and Positional Power
- Conflict

# RELATIONAL COMPETENCE

# CONCLUSIONS

# KEY POINTS

Participation in relationships with friends, family members, intimates, roommates, siblings, employers, and peers plays a central role in our day-to-day interactions. Communication is the basic ingredient in social life and, therefore, an understanding of it can be a very powerful tool for fostering positive and productive relationships of all kinds.

The concepts of *communication* and *relationship* are intertwined in several basic ways. First, as we have seen, one of the most fundamental outcomes of human communication is the development of social units; and no such units are more central to our lives than relationships. Second, our relationships—with parents, relatives, friends, intimates, and colleagues—are essential to our learning, growth, and development. Third, it is within relationships of one sort or another that most of our purposeful communication activities take place.

# INTERPERSONAL COMMUNICATION AND RELATIONSHIPS

What is a relationship? Sometimes the term *relationship* is used generally to refer to other one-to-one social units, such as those composed of a teacher and student, parent and child, employer and employee, or doctor and patient. Sometimes the term *relationship* is used as a way of talking about a friendship we regard as particularly significant. In some instances, *relationship* may refer to emotional or sexual intimacy.

Although most people agree that friendships, intimate arrangements, or other social groupings qualify as relationships, few people would use this term to describe passengers riding on an elevator or strangers passing on a crowded street. From the point of view of communication, however, these also can be thought of as relationships, and analyzing these units provides valuable insights into other, more complex, human relationships.

In the most basic sense, a *relationship* is formed whenever reciprocal message processing occurs: that is, when two or more people mutually take account of and adjust to each other's verbal or nonverbal behavior. This reciprocal message processing, which we can call *interpersonal communication,* is the means through which relationships of all types are initiated, develop, grow, and sometimes deteriorate.

One of the simplest relationships is that created by people passing one another on a crowded sidewalk. In order for two individuals to negotiate past each other without bumping into each other, each must process information relative to the other's presence, location, direction, and rate of movement. The individuals involved must use this information to guide their actions in order to pass without colliding. In this simple situation all the essential elements of any relationship are in operation. In this instance, the communication involved is nonverbal.

A slightly more complex example is provided by people riding on an elevator, as depicted in Figure 9.1. When alone in an elevator, most of us stand to the rear, often in the center. Typically, as a second person enters, we move to one corner or another, leaving the remaining corner for the newly arriving passenger. In so doing, we initiate a simple relationship as we take note of and adjust our behavior—movements, gestures, and position—relative to one another. With little conscious awareness, reciprocal message processing and mutual influence have taken place, as we define and redefine the territory available for our use.

As a third person enters the elevator, further adjustments are likely to occur as the social unit shifts from a two-person relationship to one composed of three individuals. Readjustments of this kind provide observable evidence that reciprocal message processing is taking place and that a relationship has been formed. Again with this example, even though no words were spoken, a relationship is created through nonverbal communication. Unless a conversation ensues, the relationship will be very short-lived, and will terminate as the individuals exit the elevator and end their reciprocal information processing and mutual influence.

Whether our point of reference is strangers passing on the street or an intimate, enduring friendship, the basic dynamics involved in the formation and evolution of relationships are quite similar. In each circumstance, we enter the relationship behaving toward other people on the basis of the personal theories and representations we have acquired through previous experience. As relationships develop, a mutual influence occurs as we adopt or create *joint,* or *relational, communication rules.* These rules guide, shape, and in a sense govern the particular social unit from its initiation through the various stages of development to its eventual termination, in much the same ways as personal representations guide an individual's behavior.

In the case of strangers passing on the street, the information-processing rules the individuals use are relatively simple, and the relationship itself is short-lived. By contrast, intimate relationships between people who have lived or worked together for many years can be exceptionally complex.

© Kendall Hunt Publishing Co.

**FIGURE 9.1**

In a very basic sense, a relationship is formed among passengers on an elevator as the individuals adjust their behavior relative to one another, based on an awareness of one another's presence.

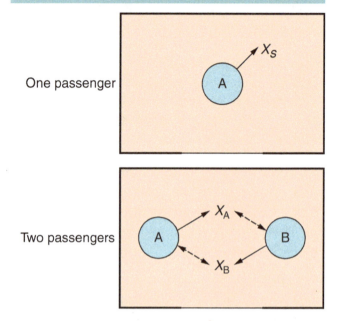

It is important to note that we are unaware of many of the relationships of which we are a part. Very often, we are taking account of and being taken account of, influencing and being influenced, without awareness or intention.

# TYPES OF RELATIONSHIPS

In the remainder of this chapter, the primary focus of our discussion will be on those relationships of which we are aware and which we intentionally form and maintain—relationships where verbal as well as nonverbal communication play fundamental roles. Relationships of this kind can be classified in terms of a number of factors, including the number of people involved, the purpose of the relationship, its duration, and the level of intimacy attained.

## Dyadic and Triadic Relationships

The vast majority of our relationships are *dyads*—two-person units. As children, our first contacts with others are dyadic, and it is not until we reach the age of six to 12 years that we are able to engage in conversation with several people at the same time (Wilmot, 1987). As adults, we are members of a large number of different dyads, such as roommates, best friends, spouses, or co-workers.

As Wilmot (1987) observes, each of the many dyads in which we participate is unique in a number of respects:

1. Every dyadic relationship fulfills particular ends. The functions served by a teacher–student relationship, for instance, are generally quite different from those of a husband–wife relationship; and both are distinct from those served by doctor–patient or employee-employer relationships.
2. Each dyad involves different facets of the individuals who participate in them. The demands placed on an individual as a student in a teacher–student relationship are different from those placed on that same person as a wife in a husband–wife relationship or as a supervisor in a work relationship. No two dyads in which we participate make precisely the same demands on us or present the same opportunities.
3. In any dyad, unique language patterns and communication patterns develop that differentiate that relationship from others. Slang and "in-phrases" among friends, terms of endearment between intimates, and ritualized greetings and workplace jargon among colleagues are the result of these ongoing communication dynamics within relationships.  (adapted from pp. 121-129)

COMPLEXITY. Although the majority of the relationships in which we participate involve two people, we also often find ourselves in social units composed of three or four people, and these relationships may get very complex in terms of the communication patterns that result.

*Triads* (three-person relationships) differ from dyads in several respects, particularly in their complexity. In dyads, reciprocal message processing takes place between two people. With triads, there are six possible message-processing pairings: person 1 with person 2, person 1 with person 3, person 2 with person 3, persons 1 and 2 with person 3, persons 1 and 3 with person 2, and persons 2 and 3 with person 1 (Kephart, 1950).

INTIMACY AND DISCLOSURE. Beyond the increased complexity resulting from more possible pairings, triads differ from dyads in several additional respects. One of these relates to intimacy and the disclosure of personal information.

*Intimacy* is a difficult concept to define. Traditionally, communication scholars have discussed intimacy in terms of amount and depth of self-disclosure. For example, a friendship was seen as intimate if the friends told each other their most personal secrets. More recent evidence suggests that intimacy in relationships results from participating in activities together as well as from disclosing highly personal information (Wood & Inman, 1993). Typically, intimacy develops over time, as a natural part of the communication that takes place between people. Of course, it is possible to have long-term relationships of one kind or another in which personal self-disclosure and intimacy remain quite limited.

Web-based networks like email, websites, and social media afford additional opportunities for personal disclosure. On the one hand, these channels provide alternative means for familiar patterns of disclosure. Additionally, the absence of the immediacy of face-to-face communication, the permanence and broad access to online disclosures, the potential for concealing one's identity in some instances, and opportunities for anonymity in others, certainly have the potential to change the content and extent of disclosure and intimacy (Gibbs, Ellison & Lai, 2011). These are all topics of considerable interest to scholars, policy makers, parents of young users, and the public, generally.

In some dyadic relationship settings, the disclosure of information occurs less naturally. In relationships formed between a person charged with a crime and his or her attorney, for example, the disclosure of what would otherwise be regarded as private information is a component of the interpersonal communication almost from the outset. In this instance, disclosure of personal information is essential to addressing the goals for which the relationship has been initiated.

One of the familiar and also one of the most important examples of this kind of circumstance occurs in interactions between patients and health care providers. Quite often, when patients begin health-related interactions with nurses, therapists, physicians, or other medical providers, they have had little or no communication prior to the encounter. Initially, the relationship between them may be nearly as limited as that between passengers on the elevator. The level of personal disclosure by patients is quickly intensified as patients provide their medical histories on forms they are asked to complete and through questions posed when they interact with health care personnel. Through these communication techniques, patients are required to engage in a level of disclosure that in any other situation would be considered very "unnatural" for a conversation with someone hardly known to the individual and with whom there is little or no relational history (Greene, 2015; Ruben, 1989,

1993). Clearly, in these situations, effective communication and accurate disclosure is essential to diagnosis and treatment, and also can be important in creating a relationship that facilitates future communication and appropriate follow-up (Carpenter & Greene, 2014; Catona & Greene, 2015). Nonetheless, because of the level of "forced" disclosure involved, these situations can be uncomfortable for patients (see Figure 9.2), creating significant interpersonal communication challenges for both the caregiver and the patient (Ruben, 2015).

**FIGURE 9.2**

The type of communication required in health care settings may violate our normal expectations for relationship development.

© Monkey Business Images/Shutterstock.com

For students of communication, reflecting on our patterns of personal disclosure in health care settings or in mediated communication environments—ones where our identities are known as well as those where we are anonymous—can be interesting sources of learning about our own interpersonal communication, including our patterns of disclosure and intimacy in developing relationships.

DECISION-MAKING. In relationships of more than two people, differences of opinion can be resolved by voting to determine the majority opinion. In dyads, negotiation is the only means of decision making available. A further distinction is that triads and larger groups have somewhat more stability than dyads. When only two people are involved in a relationship, either party has the power to destroy the unit by withdrawing. In triads, and in larger social units, the withdrawal of one party may have a marked impact on the unit, but it will not necessarily lead to its termination.

Finally, it is rare that triads operate such that all parties are equally and evenly involved. Typically, at any point in time, two members of the relationship are closer to one another or in greater agreement than the other party or parties. The result is often the formation of coalitions, struggles for "leadership," and sometimes open conflict. Because of this, some authors have argued that there is actually no such thing as a triadic or quadratic relationship, but rather that such units are better thought of as a dyad plus one or as two dyads (Wilmot, 1987).

# Task and Social Relationships

In addition to thinking about relationships in terms of the number of people involved, we can also look at the primary purpose for their formation. Many relationships are developed for the purpose of *coordinated action*—completion of a task or project that one individual could not manage alone. A simple example of this type of relationship is one person holding onto a board while another person saws off a piece.

The relationships created between a taxi driver and passenger or between an athletic trainer and athlete provide other illustrations of two people working together to accomplish a specific task (F. Davis, 1973). Social units composed of employer and employees, leader and followers, physician and patient, teacher and student, therapist and patient, are examples of *task relationships* that play a major role in our lives.

In some situations, accomplishing a task is of secondary importance or perhaps of no significance whatsoever. In such circumstances, *personally* or *socially oriented goals* take precedence. Making a new acquaintance, having coffee with a friend, and spending time chatting periodically with a co-worker during lunch serve a number of important functions, even though they are not essential to the completion of a task. *Social relationships* can provide a means of diversion, recreation, intimacy, or companionship. They may also be a way of avoiding isolation or loneliness, confirming our own sense of worth, giving and receiving affection, or comparing our views and opinions to those held by others (Scott & Powers, 1978).

Individuals may be willing to devote more or less time, energy, and commitment to a relationship, depending on whether they see it as essentially task or socially oriented. As a result, the communication patterns that develop will often vary substantially depending on how the members regard their purpose for participating in a given relationship in the first place (see Figure 9.3).

**FIGURE 9.3**

Friendships serve important functions in our lives.

© Vasilyev Alexandr/Shutterstock.com

# Short- and Long-Term Relationships

Longevity is another factor that has a significant bearing on the nature of relationships. Most of us are engaged in at least several *long-term relationships* with members of our immediate families, relatives, intimates, and friends. We also participate in the formation and/or maintenance of any number of *transitory relationships*—an exchange of smiles and glances while walking down a hallway, a wave and hello to a familiar face in the neighborhood, or an exchange of pleasantries with a clerk in a store.

Between these two extremes are relationships of varying duration. In general, the older a relationship, the more the investment we have made in it, and the greater the investment we are willing to make in order to preserve it. A substantial investment in long-term relationships makes us willing to maintain them with investments that are greater than those we would make in a newly formed relationship.

With short-term relationships there is little history, generally fewer personal consequences should the relationship not progress, and relatively little personal involvement. In such circumstances, we are far less locked into particular identities, and much less constrained by past actions and the images others may have of us. In many instances, short-term relationships can be attractive and functional precisely because they are seen as allowing greater personal flexibility and requiring less investment, commitment, and follow-through (see Figure 9.4).

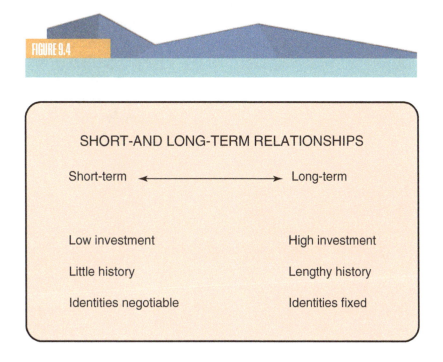

FIGURE 9.4

**SHORT-AND LONG-TERM RELATIONSHIPS**

Short-term ⟷ Long-term

| Low investment | High investment |
| Little history | Lengthy history |
| Identities negotiable | Identities fixed |

# Casual and Intimate Relationships

Relationships can also be characterized in terms of their "depth," or level of intimacy. At one extreme are relationships between acquaintances. At the other extreme are relationships between intimates. Casual relationships between friends and colleagues fall near the center between these two extremes.

In general, relationships between acquaintances are characterized by impersonal and ritualized communication patterns. The following exchange of pleasantries is typical of such relationships:

> *Mateo:* Hello. How are you?
> *Jennifer:* Fine, thanks, and you?
> *Mateo:* Good.
> *Jennifer:* It's a beautiful day today, isn't it?
> *Mateo:* Sure is.
> *Jennifer:* How's the family?
> *Mateo:* Everyone is fine. How's yours?

And so on.

DISCLOSURE. The specifics of the exchange are impersonal and ritualized in the sense that either person could—and probably would—make the same remarks to anyone. There is little that suggests the uniqueness of the relationship to either individual. Further, in such a conversation, there is a lack of *self-disclosure, other-disclosure,* or *topical disclosure* (Greene, 2014; Jourard, 1971; Luft, 1969). That is, neither person is disclosing much information about his or her own opinions or beliefs at other than a surface level, and there is an obvious absence of personal feeling being expressed.

In more intimate relationships, individuals may share some of their private concerns about life, death, illness, and their feelings about other people and themselves. An exchange between people who have attained greater intimacy would contrast markedly with the previous exchange:

> *Mateo:* Hello. How are you?
> *Jennifer:* Not that great, to be honest.
> *Mateo:* What's the matter?
> *Jennifer:* I went for a routine check-up last week, and the doctor doesn't like the look of a spot on my face and thinks it might be cancerous.
> *Mateo:* How serious is it?
> *Jennifer:* They don't know yet. I have to go back for more tests, but I'm really concerned.
> *Mateo:* I don't blame you. Are you comfortable talking about it or would you rather not?

*Jennifer:* I think it would be helpful to me, if it's O.K.

*Mateo:* Of course it's O.K. . . .

And so on.

Contrasted with the earlier example, this exchange is neither ritualized nor impersonal. A high degree of topical-disclosure, other-disclosure, and self-disclosure is involved. The interaction is also distinctive. It seems unlikely that either person would be participating in precisely the same kind of discussion with many other individuals, which suggests the uniqueness of this relationship.

A good deal of research has been conducted on self-disclosure. Findings include:

- Disclosure increases with increased intimacy
- Disclosure increases when rewarded
- Disclosure increases with the need to reduce uncertainty in a relationship.
- Disclosure tends to be reciprocated
- Disclosure is regulated by rules of appropriateness
- Attraction is related to positive disclosure but not to negative disclosure
- Negative disclosure occurs with greater frequency in highly intimate settings than in less intimate ones
- Relationship satisfaction is greatest when there is moderate—rather than a great deal or very little—disclosure  (adapted from Duck & Pittman, 1994; Gilbert, 1976; Littlejohn & Foss, 2011)

Relationships of different levels of intimacy have varying values for us. As Erving Goffman and other writers have noted, the ritualized exchanges that characterize casual acquaintances permit us to maintain contact with a large number of individuals with a minimum of effort and conscious attention. Such exchanges are a way of saying: "Hello, I see you. It seems to me it is worth acknowledging you. I want you to know that. I hope you feel the same way, too." Ritualized conversation is also important because it is generally the first step in developing closer relationships.

Intimate relationships, by contrast, require a substantial investment of time and effort. They can, however, provide opportunities for personal and social growth that may well be impossible to derive in any other way. They afford a context of trust in which individuals can express themselves candidly. Intimate relationships also encourage a greater degree of continuity and honesty than in other relationships, and allow us to openly explore and apply the insights we have gained over a period of time.

Intimate relationships may have physical benefits as well as emotional ones. In his book, *The Broken Heart: The Medical Consequences of Loneliness,* James Lynch (1979) cites research that indicates that the absence of intimate relationships can have negative medical consequences. More recent research supports the finding that "loneliness matters" in important ways. For example, people who are lonely may have physical consequences such as high blood pressure and cardiovascular disease that lead to a decreased life span (Hawkley & Cacioppo, 2010). This research vividly underscores the critical role of intimate relationships in having healthy lives.

Research suggests that having a relationship with a pet may serve many of the same beneficial roles as human interactions in times of stress, providing not only a source of companionship but also an aid to health and relaxation. Headey (2003) notes that pet ownership is associated with better physical and psychological health including fewer doctor visits. And many of us "talk" to our pets. At least half of adults and 70% of adolescents who own pets report that they confide in them (Frumkin, 2001). Pet behaviors such as seeming attentive, interested, and loyal are many of the characteristics we value in friends and human companions. These behaviors may give us a sense of security and reassurance and confirm our sense of self-worth.

## Dating, Love, and Marital Relationships

Communication obviously plays a very important role in dating, love, and marital relationships. The initial attraction and encounters that lead to dating, love, and marriage begin as casual contacts and develop through stages of increasing intimacy. As Thomas (1977) explains:

> Talking is one of the primary activities marital partners engage in together and most couples spend enormous amounts of time talking to each other. Communication between marital partners is vitally important for individual wellbeing and mutual harmony. It reflects difficulties and strengths in the marriage and in other areas of life, and sets the stage for future marital satisfaction or discord. (p. 1)

Communication researcher Michael Beatty (1986) points out that early in the development of dating and love relationships, couples often overlook or avoid discussions of potential problems and conflicts. They may assume that conversing about problems and the expression of conflict or anger will necessarily be destructive. As difficulties become great, pressure to address these issues increases. Couples lacking a tradition of disclosure and openness in dealing with one another and their relationship may decide that breaking up is the only logical alternative. Increasing attention is being devoted to turbulence in relationships with the goal of better understanding its origins, situations where its emergence is likely, and strategies for addressing the challenges that it presents. Some studies focus specifically on the relationship turbulence associated with life transitions such as those often associated with courtship, marriage, becoming parents, military deployment and reintegration upon return to the United States, and parents becoming "empty nesters" when their children leave home (Estlein & Theiss, 2014; Nagy & Theiss, 2013; Solomon & Knoblock, 2004; Theiss, Estlein & Weber, 2013; Theiss & Koblock 2014; Theiss & Solomon, 2006).

Researchers have suggested that couples who are willing and able to talk with one another about their relationship, its transitions, and its problems may achieve more satisfying and effective relationships (Beatty, 1986; Knoblock, Solomon & Theiss, 2006). Through conversation:

- Partners are able to anticipate or deal with potential problems at an early stage.
- Partners have the benefit of knowing how each other perceives and feels about the relationship, its development, and each other's contribution to it.
- Partners have the opportunity to work together to meet challenges and solve problems.
- Partners can monitor the relationship, and that process will provide an additional source of intimacy and commonness between them.

## Family Relationships

Families (and our images of families) are based on, formed, and maintained through communication. Family members and family relationships simultaneously influence and are influenced by each other (Vangelisti, 2004).

Historically, families have been defined from three perspectives: structural, psychosocial task, and transactional (Koerner & Fitzpatrick, 2004). *Structural* definitions are based on the presence or absence of certain family members (for example, parents and children) and distinguish between families of origin, families of procreation, and extended families. *Psychosocial task* definitions are based on whether groups of people accomplish certain tasks together (for example, maintaining a household, educating children, and providing emotional and material support to each other). *Transactional* definitions are based on whether groups of intimates through their behavior generate a sense of family identity with emotional ties and an experience of a history and a future.

Koerner and Fitzpatrick (2004) explain that some families exhibit what they term a *conversational orientation*, creating an atmosphere in which all family members are encouraged to voice their opinions about a wide range of topics. These families believe that open and frequent sharing of information is essential to an enjoyable and rewarding family life. Families exhibiting a *conformity orientation* create a communication climate that is characterized by homogeneity of attitudes, values, and beliefs. This type of orientation is usually associated with a more traditional family structure.

Differences in these orientations result in four different types of families (Koerner & Fitzpatrick, 2004):

- *Consensual* families are high in both conversation and conformity orientation. Their communication is characterized by an interest in open communication and exploring new ideas as well as a desire to preserve the existing hierarchy within the family.

- *Pluralistic* families have a high conversation orientation and low conformity. They are more likely to engage in open, unconstrained discussion among all family members about a variety of topics.
- *Protective* families are low on conversation orientation and high on conformity orientation. Their communication is more likely to emphasize parental authority with parents believing they should make all the decisions for their children.
- *Laissez-faire* families are low in both conversation and conformity orientations. They have relatively little interaction among family members. Parents exhibit relatively little interest in their children's decisions and do not appear to value communicating with them. (adapted from pp. 185-186)

The relationship between family communication and media is highly interdependent and complex. Wilson (2004) reminds us how family life may be organized, structured, and defined in part by media, particularly television. In many families, the arrangement of furniture, meal times, and even conversations are structured around television. Mass media, social media, tablets, and smartphones have the potential to enhance family interaction if they bring families together in a shared social space and promote togetherness. On the other hand, as seems often to be the case depending on the way communication media are used (see Figure 9.5), such media may promote independence and reinforce the separateness of individual identities and interests of family members (O'Keeffe & Clarke-Pearson, 2011).

**FIGURE 9.5**

Media may enhance or complicate family communication.

© Robert Kneschke/Shutterstock.com

# THE EVOLUTION OF RELATIONSHIPS

Whether relationships are dyads or triads, task or socially oriented, short- or long-term, casual or intimate, the dynamics by which they are initiated, develop, and eventually deteriorate and terminate are quite similar in terms of communication (Knapp & Vangelisti, 2009; Mongeau & Henningsen, 2008).

The process is described as being motivated by the needs of the individuals involved to *reduce uncertainty* about one another by gaining knowledge of one another (Berger & Calabrese, 1975), through *social exchange,* to develop a progressive sense of what will be potentially gained or lost by furthering the relationship (Thibaut & Kelly, 1959), and through *social penetration* occurring through increasing verbal and nonverbal communication and self-disclosure (Altman & Taylor, 1983).

Communication theorists Mark Knapp and Anita Vangelisti (2009) have proposed that relationships "come together" and "come apart" in stages (see Figure 9.6). These stages can be described as follows:

**FIGURE 9.6**

**A Model of Interaction Stages**

| Process | Stage | Representative Dialogue |
|---|---|---|
| | Initiating | "Hi, how ya doin'?" |
| | Experimenting | "Oh, so you like to ski...so do I." <br> "You do! Great. Where do you go?" |
| Coming Together | Intensifying | "I..I think I love you." <br> "I love you too." |
| | Integrating | "I feel so much a part of you." <br> "Yeah, we are like one person. What happens to you happens to me." |
| | Bonding | "I want to be with you always." <br> "Let's get married." |
| | Differentiating | "I just don't like big social gatherings." <br> "Sometimes I don't understand you. This is one area where I'm certainly not like you at all." |
| | Circumscribing | "Did you have a good time on your trip?" <br> "What time will dinner be ready?" |
| Coming Apart | Stagnating | "What's there to talk about?" <br> "Right. I know what you're going to say and you know what I'm going to say." |
| | Avoiding | "I'm so busy, I just don't know when I'll be able to see you." <br> "If I'm not around when you try, you'll understand." |
| | Terminating | "I'm leaving you...and don't bother trying to contact me." <br> "Don't worry." |

Knapp, Mark L.; Vangelisti, Anita L., *Interpersonal Communication and Human Relationships, 6th Edition,* © 2009. Reprinted by permission of Pearson Education, Inc., New York, New York.

# Coming Together Stages

INITIATING.  The initial stage in the formation of any relationship involves *social initiation* or *encounter*. In this phase, two or more people take note of and adjust to one another's behavior. Often the initial messages to which the individuals adjust are nonverbal—a smile, glance, handshake, movement, or appearance. If the relationship continues, progressive reciprocity of message processing occurs. One person notices the other's actions, position, appearance, and gestures. The second person reacts, and those reactions are noted and reacted to by the first person, whose reactions are acted on by the second person, and so on.

During the early stages of a relationship, the individuals involved operate in terms of the personal theories, representations, and communication habits they bring with them from previous experiences. As interpersonal communication progresses, each begins to acquire some knowledge of the other's ways of sensing, making sense of, acting, and reacting. Gradually, through combination, recombination, blend, mutation, compromise, and unspoken negotiation, the joint rules by which their particular relationship will operate begin to emerge.

As we encounter another person and initiate a relationship, we have two concerns—being perceived positively by the other person and evaluating the other person. Most people want to be perceived by others as worthy human beings, and, therefore, we try to act in a manner we believe will be seen favorably by the other person. Most people going for a job interview, for example, will not bring a bottle of soda to drink during the interview. In general, a person who brings soda to an interview is likely to be perceived as someone who does not understand—or will likely not conform to—the culture of a workplace. We make evaluations in a similar manner in other types of relationships, as well.

EXPERIMENTING.  The second stage of relational development, *experimenting*, picks up shortly after the initial encounter, as the participants begin exploring the relationship potential of the other person and the possibility of further pursuing the relationship. In this phase we gather information about the other person's style, motives, interests, and values. This knowledge serves as the basis for assessing the merits of continuing the relationship.

This stage may be characterized by small talk, but the importance of this talk is anything but small. All relationships begin with the participants trying to find out information about each other. Beyond observing what a person looks like from the outside, we need to know what the person is like "on the inside" in order to

**FIGURE 9.7**

Relationship stages are reflected in nonverbal as well as verbal behavior patterns.

© karelnoppe, 2014. Shutterstock, Inc.

feel comfortable talking about topics of more depth than the weather or the score of the last football game. Sometimes this conversation is difficult because we really don't know what the other person likes to talk about. Sometimes this conversation is formalized, as in a job interview in which the interviewer has a set list of questions to ask of each applicant, or in an examination at a doctor's office that involves a specific list of questions in order to make a diagnosis.

Although exploration may be hard work, it is often enjoyable to get to know another person and to hear what he or she has to say about particular topics. Future conversations get easier as we learn more about people and get to know their likes and dislikes better.

**INTENSIFYING.** If the relationship progresses, it moves into the intensifying phase (Knapp & Vangelisti, 2009). In reaching this level, the participants have arrived at a decision—which they may or may not verbalize—that they wish the relationship to continue. As the relationship progresses, they acquire a good deal of knowledge about each other and, at the same time, create a number of joint rules, a shared language, and characteristic relational rituals. A relationship at this stage may stall, deteriorate, or continue to develop (see Figure 9.7).

At this stage of a relationship, people often consider themselves "close friends." People at this stage are more likely to share deeper secrets (such as their fear of failure or past drug use), to use more personal terms or nicknames for each other, and to develop symbols that have a private meaning. For example, items that were purchased by the couple (like a favorite lamp or chair) or events that were shared (like getting soaked in a rainstorm while waiting for a bus) are used as the basis for intimate conversations (Baxter, 1987). Relationships may also be intensified through nonverbal communication.

**INTEGRATING.** Should the relationship progress further, some formal, symbolic acknowledgement binding the individuals to one another is common. In the case of a love relationship, the formal bonding may take the form of engagement or wedding rings (see Figure 9.8). With an individual being hired for a job, the employee and employer may sign a contract. Where two people are entering a business partnership, the relationship may be formalized by ratifying legal agreements.

**FIGURE 9.8**

**Symbols and rituals are important signs of relational bonding.**

During this stage, the individuals advance in their joint creation of relational rules, including the development of shared symbols and preferred and characteristic patterns of conversing. The meanings of these verbal and nonverbal behaviors become standardized. Over time, the relationship develops a distinctiveness that distinguishes it in subtle and not-so-subtle ways from the many other relationships in which the individuals have been involved before.

BONDING. *Bonding* is a very important stage in any relationship. This is the stage in which people announce to the world that they are committed to each other. This commitment may be indicated nonverbally (for example, with an engagement ring) or by referring to a person in a different way (for example, "this is my fiancé").

Although the beginning of this process may be very exciting (such as planning a wedding or getting a first job), the relationship can develop repetitive communication patterns. These patterns may be positive or negative. For example, some couples may enjoy greeting each other in the same way every day when they return from work ("So how was your day?") while others find that they have the same fight ("Why are you always late?") over and over again.

## Coming Apart Stages

DIFFERENTIATING. With the passage of time, people inevitably grow and develop, creating pressure for change on the other person in the relationship, as well as on the relationship itself. As a consequence, a need for redefining some of the joint rules of the relationship often arises. There are many classic illustrations of these types of situations: perhaps a teenager no longer wants to be so closely supervised by his or her parents, a spousal relationship is strained when one spouse is having trouble at work or an employee wants more independence on the job than when first hired. In each instance, changes in the individuals and circumstances create turbulence and place strains on relationships and on the accepted and often difficult-to-change rules and patterns that have developed.

Sometimes differentiating is a very gradual, natural, and easily manageable part of the evolution of a relationship. In other instances, when change is too rapid or extreme, or resistance too great, a deterioration process begins. The couple who fights about one partner's chronic lateness may resolve their difficulties by agreeing to meet in a location in which the prompt partner can do something while waiting for the other person. An employer with an employee who is chronically late may file a formal reprimand and warn the person that his or her job is in jeopardy if the behavior does not change.

CIRCUMSCRIBING. People in a relationship may begin more and more to "go their own ways" physically and symbolically. Things that once were shared no longer are. Words or gestures that once mattered no longer do. Once-glowing prospects for the future at a particular job become blurred and faded. Rules that grew naturally in a love relationship during its development now seem confining and are followed with resignation.

In this stage, communication may be restricted to "safe areas" or topics that are guaranteed not to start a conflict (Knapp & Vangelisti, 2009, p. 44). Couples may act social and friendly in public but return to silence when they are at home.

STAGNATING. Relationships that are stagnating have ceased to progress. People may avoid talking about anything because they believe all conversations will lead to fighting about something. Once a relationship has reached this point, it is quite likely that it is headed for dissolution, since the behaviors of each person come to make less and less difference to the actions and reactions of the other.

AVOIDING. People in the stagnating stage are usually in the same physical environment, but once the avoiding stage begins, as the name implies, the participants do everything they can to be apart from each other. Typical communication can be direct (e.g., "Please don't call me anymore. I just don't want to see or talk to you.") or more indirect (e.g., consistently being late for appointments or beginning an interaction with "I can't stay long") (Knapp & Vangelisti, 2009, p. 45).

TERMINATING. Relationships may take a very long time to reach this stage or may terminate much more quickly. In a long-term relationship, physical separation and the dissolution of any legal or contractual obligations are the final steps in the often-painful process of terminating a relationship.

It is important to remember that relationships do not necessarily move through these stages in an orderly way. They may stall in any one stage, back up and go forward again, or stop at one point for an extended period of time.

# RELATIONAL PATTERNS

As relationships evolve, characteristic communication patterns develop. These relational patterns are the result of joint rules that have developed between the people involved. In this section, we will briefly consider four of the most common of these communication patterns: (1) supportive and defensive climates; (2) dependencies and counter-dependencies; (3) progressive and regressive spirals; and (4) self-fulfilling and self-defeating prophecies. The following descriptions are adapted from Gibb (1961); Watzlawick, Beavin, and Jackson (1967); and Wilmot (1987).

## Supportive and Defensive Climates

The orientations of individuals within relationships and their patterns of communicating with one another create a climate of communication. Climates and individual behaviors can be characterized along a continuum from highly *supportive* to highly *defensive*. For example:

"I appreciate how understanding you were last night when I was upset."
"Do you have to criticize and judge everything I do?"
"I wish you would appreciate me more."
"It seems as though you find fault with me no matter what I say or do."
"You're being so defensive!"

Each of these statements is a comment on how supportive or defensive the speaker perceives another person—and the relationship overall—to be at a particular point in time.

There are a number of communication behaviors (adapted from Beebe & Masterson, 1986; Gibb, 1961) that tend to create and maintain defensive climates within relationships including:

- *Evaluating:* Judging others' behavior
- *Controlling:* Striving to control or manage others' behavior
- *Developing strategy:* Planning techniques, hidden agendas, and moves to use in relationships like playing a game
- *Remaining neutral:* Remaining aloof and remote from others' feelings and concerns
- *Asserting superiority:* Seeing and expressing yourself as more worthy than others
- *Conveying certainty:* Assuming and acting as though you are absolutely certain in your knowledge and perceptions

In contrast, the following behaviors (adapted from Beebe & Masterson, 1986; Gibb, 1961) are seen as contributing to a supportive climate:

- *Describing:* Describing rather than judging or evaluating the other person's behavior
- *Maintaining a problem orientation:* Focusing on specific problems to be solved
- *Being spontaneous:* Dealing with situations as they develop, without a hidden agenda or "master plan"
- *Empathizing:* Looking at things from the other person's viewpoint
- *Asserting equality:* Seeing and presenting yourself as equal to others
- *Conveying provisionalism:* Maintaining a degree of uncertainty and tentativeness in your thoughts and beliefs

## Dependencies and Counterdependencies

The dynamics of dependency and counterdependency are prevalent in many relationships at various points in time. A *dependency relationship* exists when one individual in a relationship who is highly dependent on another for support, money, work, leadership, or guidance generalizes this dependency to other facets of the relationship.

The classic example of this kind of relational dynamic develops between children and their parents or, in some cases, between therapists and their patients (Carkhuff & Berenson, 1977). In both instances, one person has particular needs or goals that are being met by the others in the relationship. The dependent pattern may become more generalized, so that one person comes to rely on the other in circumstances that are unrelated to the original basis for dependency. When this occurs, a dynamic is set in motion that can have far-reaching impact and consequences for the individuals as well as the relationship. Whether people are discussing politics, sex, or religion, whether they are trying to decide where to eat or where to live, the dependent person comes to take cues from the other, on whom he or she has learned to rely, as the following conversation might suggest:

*Alicia:* I think we should order a pizza for lunch. How does that sound?
*Maria:* Fine.
*Alicia:* Come to think of it, I'm really not in the mood for pizza. How about Chinese?
*Maria:* Sure, that sounds great, too.

In other relationships, or in the same relationship at other points in time, the dependency is in the opposite direction. In these circumstances, one individual relates to the other not as a dependent but, instead, as a *counterdependent*. While the dependent individual complies with the other person in the relationship across a wide range of topics, the counterdependent person characteristically disagrees, as the following scenario illustrates:

*Alicia:* I think we should order a pizza for lunch. How does that sound?
*Maria:* I'm tired of pizza.
*Alicia:* How about Chinese?
*Maria:* That's no better. I was thinking of a getting a salad.
*Alicia:* OK. There's a new place that delivers really good salads.
*Maria:* It's really not worth all this time deciding what to eat. Let's just order pizza and be done with it.

In the first circumstance, we can assume that whatever Alicia suggests, Maria would follow. In the second, it seems likely that whatever Alicia suggests, Maria will disagree.

As dependencies and counterdependencies become a habitual way of relating, they guide, shape, and often overshadow the specific content of conversation. Eventually, at the extreme, the content of what the individuals say comes to have little impact on the dynamics. When person A says "yes," person B agrees. Or, when A says "no," B consistently disagrees.

## Progressive and Regressive Spirals

When the actions and reactions of individuals in a relationship are consistent with their goals and needs, the relationship progresses with continual increases in the level of harmony and satisfaction. This circumstance can be described as a *progressive spiral.* In progressive spirals, the reciprocal message processing of the interactants leads to a sense of positiveness in their experiences. The satisfaction each person derives builds on itself, and the result is a relationship that is a source of growing pleasure and value for the participants.

The opposite kind of pattern can also develop, in which each exchange contributes to a progressive decrease in satisfaction and harmony. In these circumstances—*regressive spirals*—there is increasing discomfort, distance, frustration, and dissatisfaction for everyone involved. Perhaps the simplest example of a regressive spiral is provided by an argument:

> *Anna:* Will you try to remember to do the dishes tomorrow morning before you go to work?
> *Abbas:* You know I get really sick of your nagging all the time!
> *Anna:* If you were a little more reliable and a little less defensive, we might not need to have these same discussions over and over again.
> *Abbas:* You're hardly the one to lecture me about memory or defensiveness. If you remembered half the things you've promised to do, we would have a lot fewer arguments. It's your defensiveness, not mine, that causes all of our problems. . . .

Like dependencies, spirals often take on a life of their own, fueled by the momentum they themselves create. What begins as a request to do the dishes can easily become still another in a string of provocations in a relationship where regressive spirals are common. And, by contrast, "Hi, how are you?" can initiate a very positive chain of events in a relationship characterized by frequent progressive spirals.

Over time, the spirals that characterize any relationship alternate between progressive and regressive. However, in order for a relationship to maintain strength, momentum, and continuity, the progressive phases must outweigh and/or outlast the regressive periods.

## FACTORS THAT INFLUENCE PATTERNS

We have looked at the role communication plays in the evolution of relationships and the patterns that develop within them. In this section, we will focus on the factors that influence these patterns. A number of elements have an impact on interpersonal communication. Particularly important are stage and context of interaction, interpersonal needs, and style, power, and conflict.

## Stage of Relationship and Context

Communication patterns in a relationship vary greatly from one stage to another. Naturally, people meeting each other for the first time interact in a different manner than people who have lived together for several years. The nature of interpersonal patterns also varies depending on the context in which conversation is taking place. People meeting in a grocery store are quite likely to act and react differently to one another than if they are talking at a party or at a business meeting. Together, these two factors account for much of the variation in the patterns of communication within relationships.

## Interpersonal Needs and Styles

Beyond the rather direct and obvious impact of stage and context, the interpersonal needs and styles of the people involved represent other influences on communication within relationships.

Often noted as especially important in this way are our interpersonal needs for *affection, inclusion,* and *control.* In his classic work, William Schutz (1968) has suggested that our desires relative to giving and receiving affection, being included in the activities of others and including them in ours, and controlling other people and being controlled by them are very basic to our orientations to social relations of all kinds.

We each develop our own specific needs relative to control, affection, and inclusion. The particular profile of needs we have, and how these match with those of other people, can be a major determinant of the relational patterns that result. For instance, we could expect that one person with high needs for control and another with similarly strong needs to be controlled would function well together. The former would fall comfortably into a dominant leadership role, while the latter would be very willing to follow. If, on the other hand, two people who work or live together have similarly high (or low) needs for control, one might predict a good deal of conflict (or a lack of decisiveness) within the relationship (see Figure 9.9).

FIGURE 9.9

Some people demonstrate a higher need for control in relationships than others.

© bikeriderlondon/Shutterstock.com

Interpersonal *style* also plays a key role in shaping the communication patterns that emerge in relationships. As discussed earlier, some people are more comfortable operating in an outgoing, highly verbal manner in their dealings with others, while others characteristically adopt a more passive and restrained interpersonal style, due either to preference or apprehension about speaking in social situations. Those who use a more outgoing style deal with their thoughts and feelings in a forthright, assertive manner (Anders & Tucker, 2000; Bower & Bower, 1991). If they want something, they ask for it. If they feel angry, they let others know. If they feel taken advantage of, they say so. If they don't want to comply with a request, they have little trouble saying "no!"

In contrast to an externalizing style of interpersonal communication, the internalizing style involves "absorbing" the verbal and nonverbal messages of others, giving the outward appearance of acceptance, congeniality, and even encouragement, regardless of one's thoughts or feelings (Ruben, 1982, 2006). For any of several reasons, people who are prone to use the internalizing style often "bottle up" thoughts, opinions, and feelings. If they are angry, it is seldom apparent from what is said. If they disagree, they seldom say so. If they feel taken advantage of, they may allow the situation to continue rather than confront it openly.

Though few of us use either style exclusively, we often favor one approach over the other in the majority of our dealings with people; and, depending on the style of the people with whom we are in a relationship, this factor alone can become a primary influence in shaping our interactions and our relationships, as is suggested in the following conversation:

> *Tom:* Georgia, you wouldn't mind taking me home tonight after work, would you? I know I impose on you a lot, but Mary needed the car again today, and I know you're the kind of person who doesn't mind helping out now and then.
> *Georgia:* Well, I was going to go shopping tonight, but if you have no other way, I guess I could take you.
> *Tom:* Hey thanks, Georgia. I was sure I could count on you. How are things anyway? Really busy, I'll bet. Hey, listen, I'd better get back to work. I'll meet you by your car at 5:30. Thanks again.

Tom's externalizing style, in combination with Georgia's internalizing style, will no doubt be critical factors in defining many of the interactions that take place between them.

## Roles and Positional Power

Interpersonal communication within relationships is also shaped by the distribution of power and influenced by roles. Where one individual is employed by the other, for instance, the relationship is *asymmetrical,* or uneven, in terms of the actual power each has in the job situation (Watzlawick et al., 1967). The employer can exercise more control over that facet of their relationship—so long as the other person does not quit—simply as a consequence of the uneven control over resources and decision making.

There are many similar situations where asymmetries affect interpersonal communication. The relationship between a therapist and a patient, a teacher and a student, a parent and a child, or a supervisor and supervisee are among the most common examples. In each, one member of the relationship occupies a role or position of power which can be expected to have a substantial impact on the interpersonal communication patterns that develop.

In peer-to-peer, colleague-to-colleague, or other relationships of this type, there is the potential for symmetry. Where this possibility exists, interpersonal communication creates any of a number of patterns, and the influence and dependencies that result will be a consequence of the communication rather than of preexisting power or role relationships.

## Conflict

The presence of *conflict*—"an incompatibility of interest between two or more people giving rise to struggles between them"—can have a major impact on communication dynamics (Simons, 1974, pp. 177-178). Sillars suggests that when people are involved in conflict situations they develop their own personal theories to explain the situation. These theories, in turn, have a great influence on how interactants deal with one another. There are three general communication strategies used in conflict resolution:

- *Passive and indirect strategies.* Avoiding the conflict-producing situation and people
- *Distributive strategies.* Maximizing one's own gain and the other's losses
- *Integrative strategies.* Achieving mutually positive outcomes for both individuals and the relationship (adapted from Sillars, 1980, p. 188)

## RELATIONAL COMPETENCE

Being competent in interpersonal communication involves applying an understanding of communication and interpersonal relationships to everyday life. The goal is to use our knowledge to increase interpersonal satisfaction and effectiveness from our own perspective, as well as from the perspective of those with whom we interact (Spitzberg & Cupach, 1984).

Self-awareness in relationships can contribute to interpersonal communication competence. Noted psychologist Carl Rogers (1961) offered the following personal observations on therapeutic relationships, which can be applied in many other types of relationships as well:

- In my relationships with persons I have found that it does not help, in the long run, to act as though I were something that I am not.
- I find I am more effective when I can listen with acceptance to myself, and can be myself.
- I have found it of enormous value when I can permit myself to understand another person.
- I have found it enriching to open channels whereby others can communicate their feelings, their private perceptual worlds, to me.
- I have found it highly rewarding when I can accept another person.
- The more I am open to the realities in me and in the other person, the less do I find myself wishing to rush in to "fix things."
- Life, at its best, is a flowing, changing process in which nothing is fixed. (adapted from pp. 16-27)

Empathy and respect for other people's opinions, knowledge, and perspectives generally enhance communication, and attention to listening, careful observation, and thoughtful interpretation are vital to communication competence in relationships. Every person reacts to a situation in his or her own way; some people are more interpersonally sensitive than others. The following guidelines can be helpful in establishing and maintaining satisfying relationships (Beebe & Masterson, 1986):

- Try to determine your listening objectives.
- Try not to be distracted by an emotion-arousing word or phrase.
- Adapt to the speaking situation.
- Practice your listening skills.
- Listen to the total person—both the verbal and nonverbal channels.
    (adapted from pp. 211-214)

## CONCLUSION

In this chapter, we have examined communication in relationships. We discussed a number of ways of thinking about and characterizing relationships, and explored common communication patterns that can occur. Communication plays a central role in the development and evolution of all human relationships. Relationships also provide perhaps the most important context in which we attempt to use our communication abilities to achieve particular goals and meet particular needs.

In the most general sense, a relationship exists whenever there is reciprocal message processing—when two or more people react to one another's verbal and nonverbal behavior. It is by means of interpersonal communication that relationships are initiated, develop, grow, or deteriorate.

Intentionally established relationships can be considered from several perspectives: whether they are dyadic or triadic; whether they are task-oriented or social in purpose; whether they are short- or long-term; whether they are casual or intimate. We also have discussed dating, love, and marital relationships.

Relationships progress through a series of relatively predictable stages, beginning from an initial social encounter, progressing to stages of increasing interaction and joint rule creation. Many relationships involve some formalized acknowledgement of their status, such as marriage or a legal business contract. A relationship may stall in one of these stages, back up and go forward again, or stop and remain in one stage for an extended period of time.

Over time, communication patterns develop in relationships. Often these dynamics take the form of defensiveness or supportiveness, dependencies or counterdependencies, progressive or regressive spirals, or self-fulfilling or self-defeating prophecies. These dynamics can have a far more significant impact on the form and development of patterns in relationships than does the content of interaction.

A number of factors, such as stage and context, interpersonal needs and style, distribution of power, and the presence of conflict, play a role in facilitating the development of particular patterns.

## KEY POINTS

After having read this chapter, you should be able to:

- Define interpersonal communication
- Explain the different types of relationships
- Analyze the key stages of a relationship
- Describe the meaning of interpersonal competence from a communication perspective

# REFERENCES

Altman, I., & Taylor, D. A. (1983). *Social penetration: The development of interpersonal relationships.* New York, NY: Irvington.

Anders, S. L., & Tucker, J. S. (2000). Adult attachment style, interpersonal communication competence, and social support. *Personal Relationships, 4,* 379-389.

Baxter, L. A. (1987). Symbols of relationship identity in relationship cultures. *Journal of Social and Personal Relationships, 4,* 261-280.

Beatty, M. J. (1986). *Romantic dialogue: Communication in dating and marriage.* Englewood, CO: Morton.

Beebe, S. A., & Masterson, J. T. (1986). *Family talk: Interpersonal communication in the family.* New York, NY: Random House.

Berger, C. R., & Calabrese, R. J. (1975). Some explorations in initial interaction and beyond: Toward a developmental theory of interpersonal communication. *Human Communication Research, 1*(2), 99-112.

Bower, S. A., & Bower, G. H. (1991). *Asserting yourself: A practical guide for positive change* (updated ed.). Reading, MA: Addison-Wesley.

Carkhuff, R. R., & Berenson, B. G. (1977). *Beyond counseling and therapy* (2nd ed.). New York, NY: Holt, Rinehart & Winston.

Cacioppo, J. T., et al. (2002). Loneliness and health: Potential mechanisms. *Psychosomatic Medicine, 64*(3), 407-417.

Carpenter, A., & Greene, K. (2014). Online health information exchange and privacy. In T. Thompson & J. G. Golson (Eds.), *Encyclopedia of health communication* (pp. 978-981). Thousand Oaks, CA: Sage.

Carpenter, A., & Greene, K. (2014). Disclosure: Family health history. In T. Thompson & J. G. Golson (Eds.), *Encyclopedia of health communication* (pp. 342-345). Thousand Oaks, CA: Sage.

Catona, D., & Greene, K. (2015). Self-disclosure. In C. R. Berger & M. E. Roloff (Eds.), *International encyclopedia of interpersonal communication.* Hoboken, NJ: Wiley-Blackwell.

Davis, F. (1973). The cabdriver and his fare: Facets of a fleeting relationship. In W. G. Bennis, D. E. Berlew, E. H. Schein, & F. I. Steele (Eds.), *Interpersonal dynamics: Essays and readings on human interaction* (pp. 417-426). Homewood, IL: Dorsey.

Duck, S. (1982). A topography of relationship disengagement and dissolution. In S. Duck (Ed.), *Personal relationships 4: Dissolving personal relationships* (pp. 1-30). New York, NY: Academic Press.

Duck, S., & Pittman, G. (1994). Social and personal relationships. In M. L. Knapp & G. R. Miller (Eds.), *Handbook of interpersonal communication* (2nd ed., pp. 676-695). Thousand Oaks, CA: Sage.

Estlein, R., & Theiss, J. A. (2014). Inter-parental similarity in responsiveness and control and its association with perceptions of the marital relationship. *Journal of Family Studies, 20,* 239-256.

Frumkin, H. (2001). Beyond toxicity: Human health and the natural environment. *American Journal of Preventive Medicine, 20*(3), 234-240.

Gibb, J. R. (1961). Defensive communication. *Journal of Communication, 11*(3), 141-148.

Gibbs, J. L., Ellison, N. B., & Lai, C. H. (2011). First comes love, then comes Google: An investigation of uncertainty reduction strategies and self-disclosure in online dating. *Communication Research, 38*(1), 70-100.

Gilbert, S. J. (1976). Empirical and theoretical extensions of self-disclosure. In G.R. Miller (Ed.), *Explorations in interpersonal communication* (pp. 197-216). Beverly Hills, CA: Sage.

Greene, K. (2014). Disclosure: Providers and patients. In T. L. Thompson & J. G. Golson (Eds.), *Encyclopedia of health communication* (pp. 348-352). Thousand Oaks, CA: Sage.

Hawkley, L. C., & Cacioppo, J. T. (2010). Loneliness matters: A theoretical and empirical review of consequences and mechanisms. *Annals of Behavioral Medicine, 40*, 218-227.

Headey, B. (2003). Pet ownership: Good for health? *MJA Open: Journal of the Australian Medical Association, 179*, 460-461.

Jourard, S. M. (1971). *The transparent self* (rev. ed.). New York, NY: Van Nostrand Reinhold.

Kephart, W. M. (1950). A quantitative analysis of intra-group relationships. *American Journal of Sociology, 55*, 544-549.

Knapp, M. L., & Vangelisti, A. L. (2009). *Interpersonal communication and human relationships.* Boston, MA: Pearson.

Knobloch, L.K., Solomon, D.H., & Theiss, J.A. (2006). The role of intimacy in the production and perception of relationship talk within courtship. *Communication Research, 33*(4), 211-241.

Koerner, A. F., & Fitzpatrick, M. A. (2004). Communication in intact families. In A. L. Vangelisti (Ed.), *Handbook of family communication* (pp. 177-195). Mahwah, NJ: Lawrence Erlbaum.

Littlejohn, S. W., & Foss, K. A. (2011). *Theories of human communication* (10th ed.). Long Grove, IL: Wadsworth.

Luft, J. (1969). *Of human interaction.* Palo Alto, CA: National Press Books.

Lynch, J. J. (1979). *The broken heart: The medical consequences of loneliness.* New York, NY: Basic Books.

Mongeau, P., & Henningsen, M. Stage theories of relationship development. In Braithwaite, D. O., & Baxter, L. A. (Eds.). *Engaging theories in interpersonal communication: Multiple perspectives* (pp. 363-375). Thousand Oaks, CA: Sage.

Nagy, M. E., & Theiss, J. A. (2013). Applying the relational turbulence model to the empty-nest transition: Sources of relationship change, relational uncertainty, and interference from partners. *Journal of Family Communication, 13*, 280-300.

O'Keeffe, G. S., & Clarke-Pearson, K. (2011). Clinical report—The impact of social media on children, adolescents, and families. *American Academy of Pediatrics, 127*(4), 800-804.

Rogers, C. R. (1961). *On becoming a person: A therapist's view of psychotherapy.* Boston, MA: Houghton Mifflin.

Ruben, B. D. (1982). Communication, stress, and assertiveness: An interpersonal problem-solving model. In J. W. Pfeiffer & J. E. Jones (Eds.), *The 1982 annual handbook for group facilitators.* La Jolla, CA: University Associates.

Ruben, B. D. (1989). The health caregiver-patient relationship: Pathology, etiology, treatment. In E. B. Ray & L. Donohew (Eds.), *Communication and health: Systems and applications* (pp. 51-68). Hillsdale, NJ: Lawrence Erlbaum.

Ruben, B. D. (1993). What patients remember: A content analysis of critical incidents in health care. *Health Communication, 5*(2), 99-112.

Ruben, B. D. (2006). *Organizational developmental series: The communication style inventory (CSI): A guide to social and professional competence.* Washington, DC: National Association of College and University Business Officers.

Ruben, B. D. (2015). Communication theory and health communication practice: The more things change, the more they stay the same. *Health Communication,* 1-11. Available online: November 2014. http://dx.doi.org/10.1080/10410236.2014.923086

Schultz, W. (1968). *The interpersonal underworld.* Palo Alto, CA: Science and Behavior Books.

Scott, M. D., & Powers, W. G. (1978). *Interpersonal communication: A question of needs.* Boston, MA: Houghton Mifflin.

Sillars, A. L. (1980). Attributions and communication in roommate conflicts. *Communication Monographs, 47,* 180-200.

Simons, H. W. (1974). The carrot and stick as handmaidens of persuasion in conflict situations. In G. R. Miller & H. W. Simons (Eds.), *Perspectives on communication in social conflict* (pp. 172-191). Englewood, NJ: Prentice Hall.

Solomon, D. H., & Knobloch, L. K. (2004). A model of relational turbulence: The role of intimacy, relational uncertainty, and interference from partners in appraisals of irritations. *Journal of Social and Personal Relationships, 21*(6), 795-816.

Spitzberg, B. H., & Cupach, W. R. (1984). *Interpersonal communication competence.* Beverly Hills, CA: Sage.

Theiss, J. A., Estlein, R., & Weber, K. M. (2013). A longitudinal assessment of relationship characteristics that predict new parents' relationship satisfaction. *Personal Relationships, 20,* 216-235.

Theiss, J. A., & Knobloch, L. K. (2014). Relational turbulence during the post-deployment transition: Self, partner, and relationship focused turbulence. *Communication Research, 41,* 27-51.

Theiss, J.A., & Solomon, D. H., (2006). A relational turbulence model of communication about irritations in romantic relationships. *Communication Research, 33*(5), 391-418.

Thomas, E. J. (1977). *Marital communication and decision making: Analysis, assessment, and change.* New York, NY: Free Press.

Thibaut, J. W., & Kelley, H. H. (1959). *The social psychology of groups.* New York, NY: John Wiley.

Vangelisti, A. L. (2004). *Handbook of family communication.* Mahwah, NJ: Lawrence Erlbaum.

Watzlawick, P., Beavin, J. H., & Jackson, D. D. (1967). *Pragmatics of human communication.* New York, NY: Norton.

Wilmot, W. (1987). *Dyadic communication* (3rd ed.). New York, NY: Random House.

Wilson, B. J. (2004). The mass media and family communication. In A. L. Vangelisti (Ed.), *Handbook of family communication* (pp. 563-593). Mahwah, NJ: Lawrence Erlbaum.

Wood, J. T., & Inman, C. C. (1993). In a different mode: Masculine styles of communicating closeness. *Journal of Applied Communication Research, 21,* 279-296.

# CHAPTER 10

# GROUP
# COMMUNICATION

**In this chapter, you will learn about:**

- The definitions and rationale of group membership
- The different types of groups and the responsibilities of individual group members
- The stages of group development and the importance of leadership
- The decision-making process in a group setting
- The responses to group conflict

## GROUPS: THE PREDICTABLE REALITIES

## WHY PEOPLE JOIN GROUPS

## TYPES OF GROUPS

- Task and Social Dimensions
- Contrived and Emergent Groups

## ROLES AND RESPONSIBILITIES

- Task-Oriented Roles
- Group-Building and Support Roles
- Individualistic Roles

# LEADERSHIP

- Functions of Leadership
- Approaches to Leading and Leadership

# GROUP DEVELOPMENT

- Group Communication Networks
- Stages of Development
- Culture: Symbols, Rules, and Codes
- Group Initiation and Socialization

# GROUP DECISION MAKING

- Consensus
- Compromise
- Majority Vote
- Arbitration

# GROUP COHESIVENESS

- Symptoms of Too Little Cohesiveness: Boredom and Indifference
- Symptoms of Too Much Cohesiveness: The Groupthink Syndrome

# CONFLICT IN GROUPS

# MEDIATED GROUPS

# CONCLUSION

# KEY POINTS

Each of us spends a great deal of time in groups of various kinds—families, peer groups, clubs, work groups or teams, religious groups, and other face-to-face and mediated groups. As we shall see, the communication process is essential to the formation of groups and is essential to every facet of their functioning.

Groups are social systems made up of people who come with their own unique orientations—perspectives, goals, needs, values, experiences, styles, and motivations. For groups to be effective in fulfilling their varying purposes, the diverse orientations of members must be focused, channeled, and coordinated.

Groups differ from relationships in terms of the number of people involved, the purposes for which they are formed, the resources available for decision making, and the complexity of the communication dynamics. Compared to dyadic relationships, the presence of additional people and the potential for increased communication is, on the one hand, a very positive characteristic of groups. Increased size means that there are additional people to address issues, undertake projects, solve problems, engage in social interaction, and share in other responsibilities necessary for effective group functioning. On the other hand, the larger size also leads to problems associated with providing ample opportunities for participation, achieving agreement on goals, ensuring information is available to all group members, defining roles and responsibilities, providing appropriate leadership, and creating cohesiveness and unity while benefiting from the diverse array of resources and perspectives of individual members. (See Table 10.1)

**TABLE 10.1**

**Characteristics of Groups: Consequences of Size**

| Benefits | Costs |
|---|---|
| Additional Members to Assist with Activities | Effort Needed to Develop Consensus on Goals |
| | Effort Needed to Keep Members Informed |
| Additional Members to Participate in Decision Making | Effort Needed to Include Members |
| | Effort Needed to Counteract Pressures Toward Conformity |
| Additional Resources for Problem Solving | Effort Needed for Leadership |

# GROUPS: THE PREDICTABLE REALITIES

Consider the following scenario:

You're enrolled in a course that requires a group project as a significant component of the course. During the first class, groups of eight members each were randomly formed by the instructor, and your group has decided that its first meeting will be next week at 9:00 PM at the Student Center. The goal for the first meeting will be to decide on the topic for your group's project. You have been giving this a good deal of thought during the past week, and have come up with what you think is an excellent idea—a project focusing on homelessness as a national and community problem.

You arrive for the meeting at 9:00 PM and see five members of your group who have also arrived at the designated meeting place. You introduce yourselves and exchange pleasantries.   It's now 9:10 PM, and two members are still missing so the six of you decide to have some coffee as you wait for the others to arrive. It's now 9:20 PM, and it's still just the six of you.  After some grumbling about the missing group members, a decision is made to get started with the meeting.

You begin with a review of the assignment on the syllabus. You decide to put forth your idea for a project. One other member of the group voices support, and a second offers what you take to be an affirming nod, but says nothing. You continue to expand on why you think this would be an excellent topic, hoping that your additional comments will broaden enthusiasm within the group for the idea.

As you're wrapping up your comments, a seventh member of your group arrives, and offers apologies for being late—it seems he ran into a friend just outside the Student Center and got wrapped up in a conversation. He introduces himself, and others introduce themselves to him.  You're in a quandary at this point. Do you present your project idea again from scratch for the new person? You realize that this would probably bore the others, but you do want to gain his support, and you're still not sure where some of the others in the group stand on your proposal. You decide on a short recap. The student who just arrived looks a bit confused as you're describing your idea and has no visibly discernible reaction.

One of the two group members who has been silent up to this point begins to speak and offers up an idea for a different project, one that would focus on bullying in high schools. Another person who has yet to speak nods vigorously in affirmation as the idea is presented and offers comments of support for the idea when the speaker has finished. You comment that this is certainly an important topic, but you express concern that this subject has already been covered so much in the media that it might seem a bit boring to the class and the instructor. The recently arriving student offers an affirming nod. The student who presented the bullying idea says she doesn't really see that as a problem. Others say nothing. They give no indication how they feel about the relative merits of the two ideas, nor do they seem to have alternative suggestions.

It's now 9:50 PM, and the eighth member of the group arrives with an explanation for her tardiness that involves difficulty finding a parking place and then having no money for the meter, having to find somewhere to get change, and so on. You find yourself tuning out in annoyance, and the faces of others reveal an equal level of frustration.

After a quick round of introductions again, the person advocating the bullying idea starts to do a recap of the group discussion beginning with a spirited summary of her idea and a somewhat less enthusiastic recounting of your proposal.

At this point, one of the students who has been quiet says she will need to leave in 10 minutes, and two others say they will also have to leave soon, to which the student who just arrived says that maybe she shouldn't have spent all that time trying to park if the meeting is going to end so soon.

Someone asks if there are other project ideas that should be considered, and some unfocused discussion follows. Seeing that the group is unlikely to reach a decision tonight—certainly not the one she had hoped for—the bullying proposer suggests that the group schedule a follow-up meeting for later in the week and urges everyone to think about the issue of a topic in the meantime. Someone asks when the meeting will be, and several possibilities are offered but none seem to work for everyone. "We can work it out via email," offers another group member and suggests that everyone exchange email addresses before you leave, which you do. And with that, the first meeting comes to an end.

Unfortunately, this kind of group dynamic is not all that unique. Even in this rather "simple" situation, many of the complexities of group life reveal themselves (Bormann & Bormann, 1996). The task here is fairly straightforward, and the individuals would seem to have common reasons for membership and a collective desire to succeed in the task and the course. Nonetheless, these eight individuals bring widely ranging perspectives and experiences, differing levels of preparation and motivation, and their own communication skills and styles. As in many such situations, the structure of the group, the approach to the task, and the roles members will play must all be negotiated through communication, and the processes through which these negotiations take place are seldom simple.

While there is no magic formula for assuring that groups emerge and run smoothly, there is no question that knowledge of the factors involved and of the dynamics at play, combined with an understanding of and skill in communication, can be of great assistance in facilitating these outcomes. In the pages ahead, we explore all of these themes.

# WHY PEOPLE JOIN GROUPS

People join groups to pursue individual needs in a social context. Groups assist people in meeting a number of goals such as completion of tasks, socializing and companionship, support for personal development or change, spiritual growth, and economic gain (see Figure 10.1). A number of factors go into individual decisions as to which groups to join, among them are (adapted from Wilson, 2005, pp. 140-143):

- Attraction to others in the group
- Attraction to the group's activities
- Attraction to the group's goal
- Attraction to being affiliated with the group
- Attraction to needs outside the group

**FIGURE 10.1**

Studies of seating patterns in groups suggest that people who sit in positions A, C, and E are more vocal contributors to discussions than people in positions B or D (Knapp & Hall, 2002). Often, people with more dominant personalities tend to choose the high participation positions while others, who prefer to avoid high levels of participation, avoid them.

© cherezoff/Shutterstock.com

# TYPES OF GROUPS

## Task and Social Dimensions

Often, the primary objective for a group relates to the completion of a task or job. Examples are organizing a social event, building a house, or carrying out community service projects. There are several types of task-oriented groups (adapted from Pavitt & Curtis, 1994, p. 30):

- *Duplicated activity group:* Each member does the same job. Examples: All members plant trees or prepare letters for mailing.
- *Assembly line group:* Each member works on a different part of the task. Examples: Some members dig holes, others plant trees, and others water and clean up; or some members fold letters, others add the stamps, and others stuff and mail.
- *Judgmental, problem-solving, and decision-making group:* Members of the group identify and choose among possible answers, strategies, or options. Examples: A group decides how many and what kind of trees to plant, where to plant them, and plans the planting process.

In other groups, the primary goal is to facilitate members achieving personally or socially oriented goals, such as interpersonal support, encouragement, and diversion. Social clubs and discussion groups are examples.

To a greater or lesser extent, most groups serve a combination of task-, personally, and socially oriented goals. Even in what might seem to be a very task-oriented group, such as a work group on an industrial assembly line, personal and social goals, such as creating positive feeling toward members of the group and its activities, are often important as well. This is especially the case if members of a task group will need to work together for some period of time. In such cases, good morale may enhance productivity, and, conversely, poor morale can undermine it. A task orientation is necessary to carry out group activities; positive personal and social outcomes encourage full participation and positive feelings among members toward the group and one another.

## Contrived and Emergent Groups

Some groups are *emergent.* These groups form naturally out of the spontaneous activities of individuals. Acquaintances who become friends and begin to go places and do things with one another provide an example of an emergent group.

More often groups are *contrived*—intentionally formed for specific purposes (Thayer, 1968). Contrived groups typically have specific, stated goals or objectives, such as to complete a class project, to share professional interests, to help members quit smoking, or to support a political candidate.

Sometimes groups that are initially emergent shift to contrived, such as when acquaintances decide to form a club or work groups; the reverse also occurs where "spin-off" or secondary groups emerge from what were initially contrived groups.

## ROLES AND RESPONSIBILITIES

In emergent groups, member roles and responsibilities develop primarily as the result of informal, often unverbalized, negotiation, as illustrated in Figure 10.2. In larger and more formal groups, individual roles and responsibilities may be made explicit. In clubs, for instance, the responsibilities and duties of officers, committee members, and other positions are generally detailed in written bylaws or a constitution. And in work groups or teams, the mission, goals, time constraints, and resources available may be specified.

**FIGURE 10.2**

Membership in various groups can be an important part of our lives.

© CristinaMuraca/Shutterstock.com

In a now classic article on group roles, Benne and Sheats (1948) outlined three types of member roles that develop in groups over the course of time: (1) roles related to the completion of the task, (2) roles related to building and supporting the group, and (3) individualistic roles. They identified a number of specific roles within each of these categories including:

## Task-Oriented Roles

- *Initiator-contributor:* Suggests or proposes new ideas or changed ways of regarding the group problem or goal
- *Information-seeker:* Asks for clarification of suggestions made in terms of their factual adequacy and for authoritative information and facts pertinent to the problem being discussed
- *Opinion-seeker:* Asks for clarification of the values pertinent to what the group is undertaking, of values involved in a suggestion made, or of values in alternative suggestions

- *Information-giver:* Offers facts or generalizations which are "authoritative" or relates his or her own pertinent experience to the group problem
- *Opinion-giver:* States his or her belief or opinion pertinent to a suggestion made or to alternative suggestions
- *Elaborator:* Spells out suggestions in terms of examples, offers a rationale for suggestions previously made, and tries to understand how an idea or suggestion would work out if adopted by the group
- *Coordinator:* Shows or clarifies the relationships among various ideas and suggestions, tries to pull ideas and suggestions together, or tries to coordinate the activities of various members of subgroups
- *Orienter:* Defines the position of the group with respect to its goals by summarizing what has occurred, points to departures from agreed-on directions or goals, or raises questions about the direction the group discussion is taking
- *Evaluator-critic:* Subjects the accomplishment of the group to some standard or set of standards of group functioning in the context of the group task
- *Energizer:* Prods the group to action or decision, attempts to stimulate or arouse the group to "greater" or "higher quality" activity
- *Procedural-technician:* Expedites group movement by doing things for the group—performing routine tasks such as distributing materials or managing objects for the group (e.g., rearranging the seating)
- *Recorder:* Writes down suggestions, makes a record of group decisions, or writes down the results of the discussion

## Group-Building and Support Roles

- *Encourager:* Praises, agrees with, and accepts the contributions of others
- *Harmonizer:* Mediates the differences between other members, attempts to reconcile disagreements, relieves tension in conflict situations through jesting
- *Compromiser:* Operates from within a conflict by offering a compromise, admitting a mistake, or moving toward another position
- *Gatekeeper/expediter:* Attempts to keep communication channels open by encouraging or facilitating the participation of others or by regulating the flow of communication
- *Standard setter:* Expresses standards for the group to attempt to achieve in its functioning or applies standards in evaluating the quality of group processes
- *Group observer:* Keeps records of various aspects of group process and feeds such data with proposed interpretations into the group's evaluation of its own procedures
- *Follower:* Goes along with the movement of the group, more or less passively accepting the ideas of others, serving as an audience in group discussion and decision making

## Individualistic Roles

- *Aggressor:* May work in many negative ways, including deflating the status of others, expressing disapproval of the values, acts, or feelings of others, attacking the group or the problem it is working on, joking aggressively, or showing envy toward another's contribution by trying to take credit for it
- *Blocker:* Tends to be negative and stubbornly resistant, disagreeing and opposing without or beyond reason, and attempting to maintain or bring back an issue after the group has rejected it
- *Recognition seeker:* Works in various ways to call attention to himself or herself, including boasting, reporting on personal achievements, acting in unusual ways, or struggling to prevent being placed in an "inferior" position
- *Self-confessor:* Uses the audience opportunity the group setting provides to express personal, nongroup-oriented "feeling," "insight," or "ideology."
- *Dominator:* Tries to assert authority or superiority by manipulating the group or certain members of the group
- *Help seeker:* Attempts to call forth "sympathy" responses from other group members or from the whole group
- *Special interest pleader:* Speaks for the "small business owner," "commuter students," "the grass roots" community, the "soccer mom," "labor," and so on, usually cloaking his or her own prejudices or biases in the stereotype which best fits his or her individual need

## LEADERSHIP

No doubt the role that receives the most attention in any discussion of groups is that of the leader. The basic role of a leader is to coordinate the activities of group members so that they contribute to the overall goals and general adaptability of the group. While leadership roles are generally assumed to relate to completion of a task, many leaders are also adept at assuming group-building and support roles.

In small groups of four or fewer people, patterns of leadership are likely to emerge as a result of the needs, preferences, expertise, prior experience, and communication styles of the people involved. Leadership may well be a subtle, even unnoticeable, aspect of the group's operation. In such cases, leadership may be shared or rotated, with little or no overt discussion about the role—or about who is or is not serving in that capacity at a particular point in time. In such instances, not only may leadership functions be shared and rotated, but followership roles of various kinds—equally critical to group effectiveness—may also be shared and rotated. Followership is equal in importance to leadership, because without willing followers there can be no effective leaders—in fact, leadership is as much defined by the willingness of others to follow as it is by the knowledge, skills, and initiative taken by those who we think of as leaders (Ruben, De Lisi & Gigliotti, 2016), as illustrated in Figure 10.3.

In larger groups, particularly those which function over longer periods of time and perform specific tasks, leadership is an essential, formalized, and often highly visible element in the day-to-day and long-term functioning of the group. Leaders in such groups may be selected—or elected—through a formalized process. However leaders are chosen, a wide range of responsibilities may be associated with the role; and however group roles and responsibilities are defined, communication plays a predictably central role in the process.

**FIGURE 10.3**

Leaders need followers to be effective.

© Golden Pixels LLC/Shutterstock.com

## Functions of Leadership

Explicit leadership activities as well as more informal and subtle social influence dynamics occur through nonverbal and verbal communication. As mentioned previously, the basic facilitative functions of leadership fall into two categories: (1) group task-achievement functions, and (2) group-building and support functions. Note that the following list of components of these functions (adapted from Baird & Weinberg, 1981, p. 214) has a good deal in common with the list of common group roles we discussed earlier in this chapter. In the case of leaders, these functions encompass the sense of responsibility not only for one's own actions and activities, but also for the group as a whole.

Group Achievement Functions

- Informing
- Planning
- Orienting
- Integrating
- Representing
- Coordinating
- Clarifying
- Evaluating
- Stimulating

Group Maintenance Functions

- Promoting participation
- Regulating interaction
- Promoting need satisfaction
- Promoting cooperation
- Arbitrating conflict
- Protecting individual rights
- Providing exemplary behavior
- Assuming responsibility for group failure
- Promoting group development

## Approaches to Leading and Leadership

Effective leaders help groups clarify purposes and aspirations, develop plans and and goals, and coordinate actions and activities. Leaders may take a personal and directive approach to the execution of their responsibilities or responsibilities can be shared among members of a group. Where the directive, centralized style is selected, the term *autocratic* is often used to describe the leadership pattern. For example, if a number of members aren't able to attend a meeting, or voice no preference, a leader who exercises an autocratic style may elect to make the decision unilaterally that this year the group will do a service project for senior citizens instead of collecting money to help children with cancer.

When leadership responsibilities are shared, the style is described as *democratic* or *participatory.* This type of leadership approach encourages members of a group to become involved in decision making, and transparency is valued when it comes to sharing information needed for decisions. Moreover, democratic leadership makes it possible for members to play an active role in defining their roles and responsibilities. A third approach to leadership, *laissez-faire,* is a "hands-off" style in which little authority is exercised by a leader to direct activities, establish procedures, or encourage formalized systems of participation by group members.

Which approach is preferable? Based on studies comparing leadership styles and their effects, it was first thought that the democratic style was superior in terms of group productivity and morale. Certainly the connotation of "democratic" suggests that that would be the case. However, further research confirmed that some groups function very well with more authoritarian leadership. Examples are military groups, surgical units, and athletic teams. A reasonable conclusion is that there is no ideal leadership style for all groups and circumstances; rather, the appropriateness of a particular style depends on the nature and purpose of the group, individuals involved, and various other factors (Northouse, 2013).

As this discussion illustrates, there are a variety of points of view as to what constitutes effective leadership, and how good leaders acquire the capabilities that are necessary to be successful (Ruben, 2006).

**GOOD LEADERS ARE BORN.** The classic view was that "good leaders are born not made." This idea assumes that leadership qualities—or the absence thereof—are an inherent part of a person's personality. In this way, either we possess or do not possess leadership qualities.

**GOOD LEADERS ARE DEVELOPED.** An alternative view, one that is now far more widely accepted than the previous perspective, is that good leaders develop as a result of their experiences. In this perspective, acquiring the capabilities for effective leadership is a matter of learning and internalizing appropriate capabilities. The assumption is that leadership skills can be learned by anyone, and as a result there are no inherent limitations on who can become an outstanding leader.

**GOOD LEADERS ARE DEFINED BY CONTEXT.** The contextual approach views leadership as the result of individual abilities (inherited plus learned), the purposes of the group, pressures put on the group from outside, and the way members in the group talk, work, or relate to one another.

Bormann and Bormann (1996) offer the following description of this approach to leadership:

> The contextual view recognized that some people learn to play the game of "being leader" and that they tend to have certain opening moves that they use in starting the game whenever they join a new work group. To some extent, the way they try to be leader depends upon what they think about the group. They do not approach the squad at basic training in the army with the same expectations that they do a peer discussion group. . . . Such an explanation provides a more complete view of leadership than do either the trait approach or the one-best-style approach. It includes the idea that leaders are to some extent "born," but it also suggests that potential leaders can acquire skills and improve talent. (pp. 105-106)

We will be discussing specific leadership theories in greater detail in Chapter 11. What's important to take away from this discussion is that there are various ways of thinking about how leaders come to be effective and what effectiveness in leading groups actually involves. These perspectives need not be seen as mutually exclusive. It's likely the case that most students of leadership would now reject the great-leaders-are-born perspective, particularly when stated in the extreme. Individual talents and predispositions are understood to play a role in how we learn, who we become, and what capabilities we develop. More important are our experiences—the role models we have around us and the informal and formal learning that takes place as we participate in and observe leaders of various kinds in the various social settings in which we are engaged over the course of our lifetimes. The contextual approach emphasizes the importance of the setting, group purpose, leadership style, the composition of the group, and the relationships among members.

No matter which leadership perspective you prefer, it is important to remember that:

- Leadership is enacted through communication
- Leaders must continually analyze and refine the procedures and practices of their groups to maintain viability in a complex, changing environment
- A key to successful leadership is the ability to coordinate diverse groups of people working on differing tasks in a changing and often unstable environment  (adapted, in part, from Barge, 1994)

# GROUP DEVELOPMENT

## Group Communication Networks

We noted earlier that, in terms of communication, the increased number of individuals in groups is a mixed-blessing. In this section, we will explore this idea and some of the implications involved in more detail.

In a two-person relationship, there is the possibility of only one reciprocal communication linkage. With three interactants, there are six possible message-processing linkages: Person A with Person B, Person A with Person C, Person B with Person C, Persons A and B with Person C, Persons A and C with Person B, and Persons B and C with Person A. When we consider the possible interpersonal linkages in a group of four members, there are 25 potential communication relationships! The addition of just one more person creates the potential for 19 additional communication linkages (Kephart, 1950).

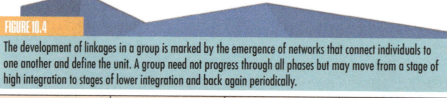

FIGURE 10.4

The development of linkages in a group is marked by the emergence of networks that connect individuals to one another and define the unit. A group need not progress through all phases but may move from a stage of high integration to stages of lower integration and back again periodically.

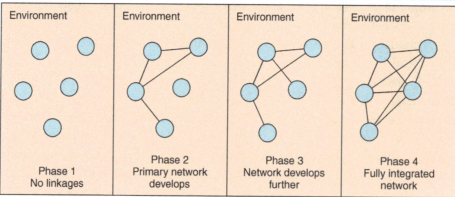

© Kendall Hunt Publishing Co.

FIGURE 10.5

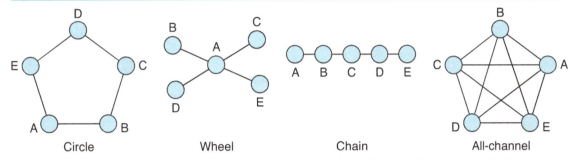

In studies of common group communication networks, such as those shown here, centralized networks (like the "wheel") contributed to rapid performance, but the error rate was high. Low centralization (such as provided in the "circle") was found to be associated with a high degree of individual satisfaction. Researchers also noted that being in a key position in a network, one requiring that information be channeled through one individual, led to information "overload."

Circle      Wheel      Chain      All-channel

Source: Harold J. Leavitt, "Some Effects of Certain Communication Patterns on Group Performance," *Journal of Abnormal and Social Psychology*, 46, (1951), pp. 38–50; M. E. Shaw, "Some Effects of Unequal Distribution of Information Upon Group Performance in Various Communication Nets," *Journal of Abnormal and Social Psychology*, 49, (1954), pp. 547–553. © Kendall Hunt Publishing Co.

In groups that are emergent, reciprocal message-processing linkages or *networks* develop naturally, often spontaneously. Networks begin to form as individuals meet and get to know each another. With the passage of time, the network becomes well-developed as all members of the group participate in interactions. Theoretically, as shown in Figure 10.4, the network will evolve to include all group members, at least minimally.

In actual practice, a number of patterns are possible, as shown in Figure 10.5. In the *circle* network, each group member interacts with two other people. Person A interacts with Person B and Person E, Person B with Person A and Person C, and so on. The *wheel* configuration describes a situation in which all messages flow through one individual—Person A. Person A interacts directly with all members of the group, but none of the others interact directly with one another. In a *chain,* members interact in a serial, straight-line manner. The *all-channel* pattern denotes a network in which each member of a group sends messages to, and receives messages from, every other member. In any group, some linkages in networks are utilized more and others less; some people become central to the network, others peripheral; still others may become isolated from others in the network. And, clearly, patterns change over time.

## Stages of Development

Studies of the development of task-oriented groups suggest that they move through four phases. One of the most popular ways to label these stages is: forming (learning about each other), storming (challenging each other), norming (working with each other), and performing (working as one) as displayed visually in Figure 10.6 (Tuckman, 1965).

© Robert Blaga/Shutterstock.com

**FIGURE 10.6**

**Stages of Group Development**

Another description of these stages uses the following labels (Fisher, 1970; Fisher & Ellis, 1990) as illustrated in Figure 10.7:

- Orientation phase
- Conflict phase
- Emergence phase
- Reinforcement phase

The first stage, *orientation,* consists of getting acquainted, expressing initial points of view, and forming linkages relative to the task at hand. In the early phases of a group's work, the discussion tends to focus on "small talk," such as the weather, the setting, circumstances that brought the people together, goals of the group, and so on.

As the group proceeds to work on its task, roles and responsibilities are contemplated and differences of opinion generally emerge. During what is termed the *conflict* phase, the expression of differing points of view often leads to polarization. Gradually, accommodations

**FIGURE 10.7**

**Communication linkages in group development**

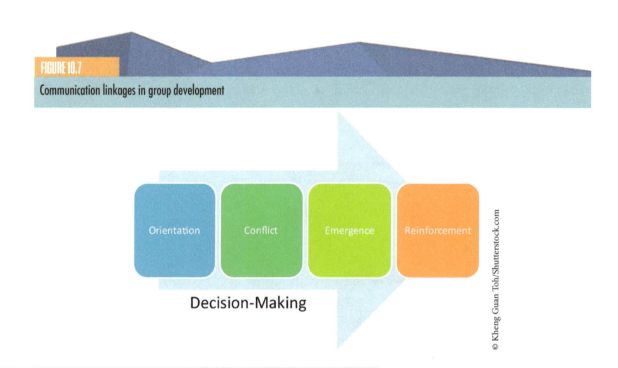

© Kheng Guan Toh/Shutterstock.com

are made among members and subgroups with differing viewpoints, as the group begins to take on an identity of its own in the *emergence* phase. As the group's project nears completion, cooperation among individuals in the network increases, as does support for—and *reinforcement* of—the group's solution (Poole & Roth, 1989). These stages are general descriptions of the development of a group. Not all groups follow these stages in precisely this order. Studies suggest that many groups may not proceed in this orderly fashion at all (Fisher, 1970; Littlejohn & Foss, 2011). Sometimes groups move from one stage to another and then back again. Nevertheless, whether or not a particular group follows this model, this sort of typology helps us to understand the nature of group process.

A number of factors influence the dynamics of groups as they evolve. Among these are: the amount of structure within the group; the time available to the group for completion of the task; the group size; the group members' attitudes and feelings about the task, topic, and one another; and the nature of the task (Wilson, 2005). The following task characteristics are particularly important to a group's progress (adapted from Shaw, 1986):

- *Task difficulty:* The amount of effort required to complete the job
- *Solution multiplicity:* The number of reasonable alternatives available to solve the problem
- *Interest and motivation:* Interest generated by the task
- *Cooperation requirements:* The degree to which cooperation by group members is necessary to complete the task
- *Familiarity:* The extent to which the group has had experience with a particular task

## Culture: Symbols, Rules, and Codes

As networks develop and groups move through various stages of development, symbols, rules, and codes of various types emerge and become standardized through communication, as shown in Figure 10.8. The process creates the group's *culture*.

Every group has its own culture and its unique symbols, rules, and codes.

© bikeriderlondon/Shutterstock.com

**FIGURE 10.8**

Through their verbal and nonverbal behavior, individuals collectively create the groups to which they belong and the cultures, symbols, rules, jargon, and other conventions characteristic of each. Once created, the culture of the group "acts back upon" its members. Over time, individuals are greatly influenced by the group, and in turn they collectively create the group.

These serve to contribute to the group's identity and provide a basis for a sense of commonality among members.

Some aspects of group culture develop naturally, as with slang phrases among members of a club or social group, or informal "dress codes" in a peer group. In other instances, symbols, rules, and codes result from systematic efforts by members of a group. In such cases, symbols and rules are created to give the group an identity, to differentiate it from others, or to identify or differentiate a particular group from a larger unit of which it is a part. The decorated jackets of sorority members serve this function, as do stylized handshakes or team names and logos.

Culture plays a pervasive role in the dynamics of groups. It provides members of a group with a sense of individual and collective identity and contributes to the development of order, structure, and cohesiveness in the overall operation of the system.

Deal and Kennedy (1982) observed major corporations and developed a description of elements of culture that can be applied to groups as well as to large organizations. Their research identified values, heroes, and rites and rituals as common characteristics of all organizational cultures.

*Values* are the basic concepts and beliefs of a group. They form the heart of a group's culture and establish the standards of achievement. Core values embody what is important to a group. Values serve as guides for individual behavior, and members are recognized and rewarded for actions and activities that are consistent with those principles. For example, a working group that places great value on customer service, courtesy, and individualized customer care will be more likely to reward employees who provide that type of service than employees who want to serve the highest number of customers in the shortest amount of time.

Cultures and groups also have *heroes* who personify and exemplify characteristics that are central to the aspirations of a group. Heroes, whether real or fictitious, serve as role models for group members to follow. Heroes may be individuals who are noted for their achievements, were foundational to the history of the group, led a successful mission of one kind or another, or overcame major personal or professional impediments.

*Rites and rituals* are the routines and accepted practices within a group. These activities may consist of nothing more significant than everyone in a group shaking hands and introducing themselves at the beginning of a meeting or they may be elaborate, formal ceremonies associated with initiation or religious events. Rites and rituals serve to communicate and reinforce the purposes, aspirations, and values of a group. Although some rites and rituals are traditional and sustained over time, others are modified or evolve over time to reflect changes in group or societal attitudes.

## Group Initiation and Socialization

Becoming a member in any group involves an initiation and socialization into the cultural and communication patterns of the group. Our initiation as members of various groups begins during our earliest years within a family. As a child, a good deal of learning, accommodation, and fitting in is required. We must learn the family's rules as to what to do, when to do it, what to say, and where to say it. Later, as we engage with others in neighborhood groups, peers groups, athletic teams, and community groups, the socialization processes continue—sometimes in quite subtle ways. Entry into certain clubs, fraternal orders, and religious groups makes this process of fitting in a very explicit part of the initiation of a new member into the unit. Even in those social and work groups where there is no formal apprenticeship, internship, or trial period, the individual must come to terms with the group's rules and realities in order to be accepted and to function effectively as a member.

Acquiring membership in a group requires adjustment to the cultural patterns through communication. In most cases, there will be opportunities, initially and more so over time—to change a group's culture. Compared to entering a relationship, however, becoming a member of a group can be a less active, less creative, more accommodating—and sometimes a more frustrating—process than becoming part of a relationship.

# GROUP DECISION MAKING

One of the core activities of any group is decision making. Decisions range from simple and straightforward questions such as where to go for dinner or when to hold a meeting, to more complex and entangled questions about group policy and priorities. Rules that guide decision making in small, informal groups emerge naturally as members spend time with one another. In larger, more structured groups, decision-making sessions are generally convened and given a specific name—*meetings*. During meetings, the behaviors of group members typically follow a number of reasonably well-defined rules, some emerging spontaneously, with others following group traditions, formalized bylaws, or parliamentary procedure.

When we think about decision making, we generally focus our attention first on *what* decisions are made. *How* decisions are made, however, is often equally important. Issues related to the "what" relate to the *products* of group decision making. Issues related to the "how" a group makes decisions have to do with the group decision-making *process*.

Various decision-making methods are available; and each has pluses and minuses in terms of the quality of the product and process. A decision made by a knowledgeable leader for the group may be a better decision than one less-informed members would reach through discussion and compromise.

However, because they allow everyone the opportunity to play a more active part in the process, discussion and compromise are likely to result in better feelings and greater commitment to the decision by members. Ideally, decision making should be undertaken in a way that provides the best outcomes in terms of both the decision-making product and process. Thinking back to the beginning of this chapter, and the example of the group trying to select an appropriate class project, provides a good example.

It may be that a single individual is most informed about a topic being considered and is, therefore, arguably the most appropriate one to make the decision about the direction the group should take, and perhaps the best suited to oversee the work of the group going forward. The *product* of such a decision might be very valid and reasonable, but a *process* in which one person imposes their judgment and their directive role on the group will likely be troubling to various group members. The result would likely undermine group support for the selected project and also for the leader. The need to balance attention to products of decision making and the processes involved is yet another complexity that confronts leaders and others engaged in group activities.

Groups must engage in a number of steps to make effective decisions (Hirokawa, 1988). Among the important considerations are:

1. The group must come to understand the nature of the dilemma they face.
2. Group members must agree on the requirements for an acceptable solution.
3. The group must come up with a range of realistic alternative proposals for solutions.
4. The group needs to thoroughly and accurately assess the positive consequences of each alternative proposal.
5. The group must thoroughly and accurately assess the negative consequences of each alternative proposal. (Pavitt & Curtis, 1994, p. 283)

There are a number of methods by which groups can make decisions, among them: consensus, compromise, majority vote, decision by leader, and arbitration (Wilson, 2005). The example at the beginning of this chapter involving the class project can be used to illustrate how each of these decision-making methods might be employed.

## Consensus

*Consensus* refers to a process which requires that a group arrive at a collective decision with which all members genuinely agree. For example, through discussion, it might eventually become apparent that every member of a group could accept the idea of doing a project on homelessness, bullying, or another subject. Discussion would continue until a consensus is reached, at which time the group would have made its decision and would be ready to undertake this kind of project.

## Compromise

*Compromise* is a process of negotiation and give-and-take to arrive at a position that takes account of—but may not be completely consistent with—the preferences of individual members. For example, some members of the group might want to focus on homelessness, while others favor a project on bullying. Through discussion and compromise, the group could decide to undertake a project that included dimensions of both—perhaps harassment and abuse of the homeless.

## Majority Vote

*Majority voting* is a method for arriving at group decisions mathematically. A decision is made when it is supported by a majority of members. In very formal groups, there may be a specific definition for majority (for example, 50% of the members plus one or two-thirds of the people attending a meeting). In our example, four members vote in favor of a project on homelessness, and two want to focus on bullying. Two have no preference. The vote is four to two in favor of a homeless project, and the decision is made.

## Arbitration

Agreement through a process of formal negotiation between parties unable to reach a decision by other means is called *arbitration.* For example, assume that even after several meetings and extensive discussion the two suggested themes—homelessness and bullying—are still under consideration. Both have supporters, and neither group wants to yield their position. Discussion and a trial vote reveal that there is a four to four split, with no one willing to change his or her position. An imposed decision risks permanently alienating members. One solution would be to meet with the instructor and ask for help in resolving the impasse.

More often than not, arbitration is used in conflicts between, rather than within, groups—for instance, a deadlock between labor and management over terms of a contract. These groups may also have very specific rules for arbitration.

## GROUP COHESIVENESS

*Cohesiveness* refers to group loyalty (Bormann & Bormann, 1996). A cohesive group is one in which members have a "team spirit" and are committed to a group's well being.

The relationship between cohesiveness and performance is important in any group. It is through communication that cohesiveness—or the lack of it—is fostered. Moreover, the presence or absence of cohesiveness influences the patterns and quality of communication within a group. As suggested earlier, when present, cohesiveness also encourages task and social dimensions of productivity and good morale (adapted from Bormann & Bormann, 1996, p. 124):

- Cohesive task groups are more productive. They do more work because members work cooperatively, distribute the workload well, and use time efficiently.
- Cohesive groups have higher morale because their members value and feel like they are a part of the group. Members pay attention to, appreciate, spend time and effort with one another, and share success as well as failure.
- Cohesive groups have efficient and effective communication because channels are open. Members are present, receptive, and committed to ensuring the communication necessary to promote productivity and high morale.

Various techniques are available to promote group cohesiveness including:

- Increasing the amount of communication among members
- Giving a group an identity and emphasizing it; talking about the group as a group
- Building a group tradition by recognizing special dates or occasions
- Emphasizing teamwork and striving to increase the attractiveness of participation in the group
- Encouraging the group to recognize good work
- Setting clear, attainable group goals
- Providing rewards for the group
- Treating members like people worthy of respect and dignity, not like parts in a machine (adapted from Bormann & Bormann, 1996, pp.137-139 and Pavitt & Curtis, 1994, pp. 96-97)

## Symptoms of Too Little Cohesiveness: Boredom and Indifference

There are a number of symptoms and consequences of low cohesiveness (Bormann & Bormann, 1996). These include a lack of member involvement, the absence of enthusiasm, and minimal question asking. Meetings are quiet, even boring, with members behaving in a polite but apathetic manner. Even important decisions are handled routinely, and the prevailing sentiment is best expressed as "Let's get this over with."

# Symptoms of Too Much Cohesiveness: The Groupthink Syndrome

Cohesiveness and loyalty to the group can have a down side. In *Groupthink,* Irving L. Janis explains that decision-making groups can actually be *too* cohesive (Janis, 1982; Littlejohn & Foss, 2011). Within highly cohesive groups, pressure to agree with the group can become very powerful. A *norm,* or accepted standard, of avoiding disagreement may develop. The group can be so cohesive and team-oriented that opinions that contradict the majority view may go unverbalized and/or be inadvertently overlooked. The *groupthink syndrome* occurs because members place great value on loyalty and being a team player. One of the characteristics of groupthink that makes it particularly troublesome is that the process often occurs without the awareness of the participants.

GROUPTHINK WARNING SIGNS. The presence of certain factors signals the potential for groupthink. These include (Wilson & Hanna, 1986):

- *Overestimation of the group's power and morality:*  Assuming the group is not accountable to others and that it is pursuing the morally correct course of action
- *Closed-mindedness:*  Ignoring or distorting alternative viewpoints
- *Pressures toward conformity:*  Subtle and not-so-subtle influence toward agreement among group members and lack of willingness to acknowledge or discuss differences of opinion  (pp. 272-273)

Consequences of groupthink may include: an incomplete survey of alternatives and options, failure to examine risks of preferred choices, failure to reappraise initially rejected alternatives, poor information search, selective bias in processing information at hand, and failure to work out contingency plans (Wilson, 2005).

Extreme pressure toward group loyalty and being "team players" can stifle dissent and critique—both of which can play essential parts in creativity and quality decision making. Some techniques that can be used to lessen the likelihood of the groupthink syndrome include (Janis, 1982; see also discussion in Littlejohn & Foss, 2011):

- Leaders can encourage members to be critical.
- Leaders can avoid stating their own preferences and expectations at the outset.
- Members of the group can discuss the group's deliberations with trusted associates outside the group and report back to the group on their reactions.
- Experts can be periodically invited to meetings and should be encouraged to challenge the views of group members.
- A member who is articulate and knowledgeable can be appointed to the role of devil's advocate, with the task of looking for alternatives, questioning the group's direction, and assuring that possible objections are considered.
- Leaders can allocate time during each meeting to review minority, opposing, or alternative points of view.

# CONFLICT IN GROUPS

At various stages in the development of any group, conflict is inevitable. The conflict may have to do with disagreements over a group's goals, member roles or responsibilities, decision making, resource allocation, group dynamics, relationships among particular individuals, or any of a number of other factors.

Conflict is not inherently a problem. In fact, while the experiencing of conflict is generally unpleasant, we know that without conflict, quality, diversity, growth, and excellence may be diminished for individuals, relationships, or groups. Thus, the goal is not necessarily to eliminate conflict. Rather, the objective in any situation should be to better understand conflict, to be able to identify its origins, to be able to determine its potential for making a positive contribution, and to be able to resolve or manage it productively.

A number of approaches have been developed to analyze and resolve conflict within groups. One interesting approach classifies conflict based on two dimensions: *assertiveness*, or behaviors intended to satisfy our own concerns, and *cooperativeness*, or behaviors intended to satisfy the concerns of others (see Figure 10.9). Considered in combination, these two dimensions describe five different styles of conflict (adapted from Folger & Poole, 1984 and Ruble & Thomas, 1976):

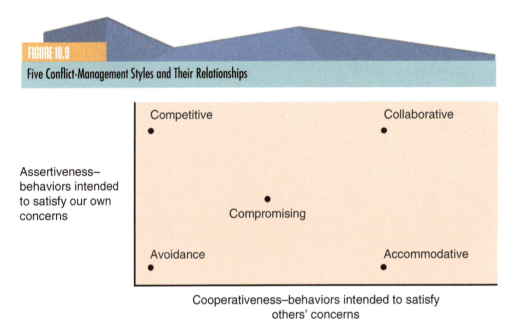

**FIGURE 10.9**

**Five Conflict-Management Styles and Their Relationships**

Source: Reprinted from *Organizational Behavior and Human Performance,* Vol. 16, No. 1, by Thomas L. Ruble and Kenneth W. Thomas, "Support for a Two-Dimensional Model of Conflict Behavior", pp. 143-155, Copyright © 1976, with permission from Elsevier.

1. *Competitive style:* High in assertiveness and low in cooperativeness. Example: the tough competitor who desires to defeat others—a "fight orientation."
2. *Accommodative style:* Low in assertiveness and high in cooperativeness. Example: the easygoing, undemanding, and supportive follower.
3. *Avoiding style:* Low in assertiveness, low in cooperativeness. Example: the low-profile, indifferent, group isolate—a "flight orientation."
4. *Collaborative style:* High in assertiveness, high in cooperativeness. Example: the active, integrative problem solver.
5. *Compromising style:* Moderate in assertiveness, moderate in cooperativeness. Example: the "meet-you-half-way" or "give-up-something-to-keep-something" approach.

This framework is useful for understanding origins of conflict within groups. Moreover, it suggests how certain styles and strategies can be helpful in resolving and managing conflict.

# MEDIATED GROUPS

Task and social groups are formed and evolve online as well as in face-to-face settings. Members of a community group may hold weekly virtual meetings to exchange local information and develop strategies for action. A group of engineers from throughout the country may regularly "meet" through video-conferencing. Or, high school friends may organize through social media to plan a reunion.

As discussed in Chapter 7, communication media make it possible for groups to transcend the limitations of both space and time—meeting virtually at times and places that are convenient for individuals scattered across the state, the country, or the globe. Increasingly, social media are offering a great many new opportunities for creating, maintaining, and supporting groups through virtual communication. See Figure 10.10 for some interesting findings about virtual communication in groups.

# CONCLUSION

We spend a great deal of time in groups of various kinds—participating in clubs and associations, attending community or religious functions, working at our jobs, and taking part in social activities. The groups in which we participate over the course of our lifetime create a wide range of demands and opportunities for us; and, in the process of adjusting to these, we develop, change, and grow.

As with relationships, groups are created and maintained by people engaged in reciprocal message processing. Groups differ from relationships in terms of the number of people involved, available resources, and complexity. Groups are created to serve a number of goals and purposes. Some groups serve primarily task-oriented functions and emphasize performance. Others stress personally or socially oriented functions and morale. Most groups are concerned with both types of goals. Groups may be contrived or emergent. In small social units, group communication networks evolve naturally. In larger and more formalized groups, networks are often purposefully established to regulate the flow of information.

Groups move through a series of stages as they evolve. The dynamics involved depend on a number of factors, including the difficulty of the task, number of alternative solutions to the task, and interest created by the task. Groups develop a culture—their own symbols, rules, and codes.

**FIGURE 10.10**

In recent years, innovative technologies have enabled a number of non-traditional ways of leading. One of the more interesting new challenges in leadership occurs when leaders are physically distant from their subordinates. The leader may be located in New Jersey but the employees may work in China and Peru. In this case, the distance between them is one of both physical geography and time.

If you've ever been in a long-distance romantic relationship, you know that distance can sometimes pose challenges to a relationship. Similarly, physical distance can affect manager-employee relationships in various ways. Trust might be challenged; cross-cultural communication issues may surface; and distanced employees may feel "cut off" from those at corporate headquarters.

Communication researcher Stacey Connaughton has discovered that, as long as distanced employees believe they have access to their leader (through mediated channels or face-to-face), physical distance does not appear to affect their job satisfaction or satisfaction with their distanced leader.

© Vert Aleksey/Shutterstock.com

The major activity of some groups is decision making, and a number of methods are available for doing this. Roles and responsibilities also are central to the functioning of groups. In smaller groups, roles and definitions of responsibility evolve naturally. Some roles are related to task completion. Others have to do with team building and support; still others are individualistic. In larger, more structured groups, roles and responsibilities are often formal rather than informal, created rather than natural, explicit rather than implicit. Leadership accomplished through communication is basic to groups of all kinds.

Cohesiveness is an important factor in group functioning. It is important for productivity, morale, quality decision making, and effective communication. The groupthink syndrome occurs when members—often unknowingly—become preoccupied with maintaining cohesiveness within a group. Conflict is an inevitable, and often productive, aspect of group functioning.

Mediated communication allows us to participate in groups even if the members are not in the same location. Technology such as the Internet allows group members to overcome barriers of time and space.

## KEY POINTS

After having read this chapter, you should be able to:

- Identify the different types of groups and the pros and cons of joining one
- Describe the responsibilities of the group members and the role of the group leader
- Analyze the stages of group development
- Explain the process of group decision making
- Appreciate the responses to group conflict and associated conflict styles

## REFERENCES

Baird, J. E., Jr., & Weinburg, S. B. (1981). *Group communication: The essence of synergy* (2nd ed.). Dubuque, IA: Brown.

Barge, J. K. (1994). *Leadership: Communication skills for organizations and groups.* New York, NY: St. Martin's Press.

Benne, K. D., & Sheats, P. (1948). Functional roles of group members. *Journal of Social Issues, 4,* 41-49.

Bormann, E. G., & Bormann, N. C. (1996). *Effective small group communication* (6th ed.). Edina, MN: Burgess.

Deal, T. E., & Kennedy, A. A. (1982). *Corporate cultures: The rites and rituals of corporate life.* Reading, MA: Addison-Wesley.

Fisher, B. A. (1970). Decision emergence: Phases in group decision-making. *Speech Monographs, 37*(1), 53-66.

Fisher, B. A., & Ellis, D. G. (1993). *Small group decision making and the group process.* New York, NY: McGraw-Hill.

Folger, J. P., & Poole, M. S. (2012). *Working through conflict: Strategies for relationships, groups, and organizations* (7th ed.). Glenview, IL: Scott, Foresman.

Hirokawa, R. Y. (1988). Group communication and decision-making performance: A continued test of the functional perspective. *Human Communication Research, 14*(4), 487-515.

Janis, I. L. (1982). *Groupthink: Psychological studies of policy decisions and fiascos* (2nd ed.). Boston, MA: Houghton Mifflin.

Kephart, W. M. (1950). A quantitative analysis of intragroup relationships. *American Journal of Sociology, 55*(6), 544-549.

Knapp, M. L., Hall, J. A., & Horgan, T. G. (2013). *Nonverbal communication in human interaction* (8th ed.). Belmont, CA: Wadsworth.

Littlejohn, S. W. , & Foss, K. A. (2011). *Theories of human communication* (10th ed.). Long Grove, IL: Wadsworth.

Northouse, P. G. (2013). *Leadership theory and practice* (7th ed.). Thousand Oaks, CA: Sage.

Pavitt, C., & Curtis, E. (1994). *Small group discussion: A theoretical approach* (2nd ed.). Scottsdale, AZ: Gorsuch Scarisbrick.

Poole, M. S., & Roth, J. (1989). Decision development in small groups IV: A typology of group decision paths. *Human Communication Research, 15*(3), 323-356.

Ruben, B. D. (2006). *What leaders need to know and do: A leadership competencies scorecard.* Washington, DC: National Association of College and University Business Officers.

Ruben, B. D., De Lisi, R., & Gigliotti, R. A. (2016). *Guide for leaders in higher education: Core concepts, competencies and tools.* Sterling, VA: Stylus.

Ruble, T. L., & Thomas, K. W. (1976). Support for a two-dimensional model of conflict behavior. *Organizational Behavior and Human Performance, 16,* 143-155.

Shaw, M. E. Scaling group tasks: A method for dimensional analysis. *JSAS Catalog of Selected Documents in Psychology, 8,* M.S. 294.

Thayer, L. (1968). *Communication and communication systems in organization, management, and interpersonal relations.* Lanham, MD: University Press of America.

Tuckman, B. W. (1965). Developmental sequence in small groups. *Psychological Bulletin, 63*(6), 384-399.

Wilson, G. L. (2005). *Groups in context: Leadership and participation in small groups* (7th ed.). Boston, MA: McGraw-Hill.

# CHAPTER 11

# ORGANIZATIONS

**In this chapter, you will learn about:**

- The ways that communication is used in organizations
- The evolution of key organizational theories
- The role of leadership in organizations
- The structure of formal and informal communication networks in the workplace
- The variables that affect and contribute to the culture of an organization

## COMMUNICATION AND ORGANIZATIONS

## ORGANIZATIONAL PURPOSES, PLANS, AND GOALS

## ORGANIZATIONAL THEORIES

- Scientific Management
- Human Relations
- Systems
- Quality
- Innovation and Employee Engagement

# ROLES AND RESPONSIBILITIES

# LEADERSHIP

# COMMUNICATION NETWORKS

- Network Functions
- Network Size
- Internal Networks: Message Flows within Organizations
- External Networks: Relating to Other Organizations and Publics
- Mediated Communication Networks
- Organizational Communication Networks in Action

# ORGANIZATIONAL CULTURE

- Origins of Organizational Cultures
- Functions of Organizational Cultures
- Assimilation, Socialization, and Innovation in Organizations

# ORGANIZATIONAL CLIMATE

# ORGANIZATIONAL DIVERSITY

# CONCLUSION

# KEY POINTS

# COMMUNICATION AND ORGANIZATIONS

We spend a significant amount of our time in organizations—attending school, working, and participating in professional, religious, political, health, civic, and other organizations. Organizations come in all shapes and sizes. Some are small, others are very large; some are informal, and others are formal. Some have a very public presence; others conceal their identities (Scott, 2013). We look to these various organizations for fulfillment of personal, social, occupational, religious, and financial needs.

While organizations have many different forms, all have a good deal in common in terms of communication. It is through communication that organizations emerge and evolve. It is also communication which makes possible the coordination of individual members' actions and activity without which social organization of any kind would be impossible.

Communication is also essential to the day-to-day functioning of organizations. It is through communication that members of organizations: (1) coordinate activities; (2) establish purposes, plans, and goals; (3) delineate the roles and responsibilities; (4) establish and maintain leadership; (5) create information networks; (6) develop and maintain the organizational culture and climate; and (7) benefit from diversity in all its forms. In this chapter, we will examine each of these organizational dynamics and their relationship to communication.

## ORGANIZATIONAL PURPOSES, PLANS, AND GOALS

Organizations may serve any number of purposes. Sometimes, particularly in the case of small and more informal organizations, those purposes are unstated. More often, organizations are created for specific, often explicitly stated, reasons.

In the case of more formalized organizations, their purpose or reason-for-being is referred to as the organizational *mission*. Some organizations are formed with a primary mission related to the manufacturing and marketing of consumer goods—producing automobiles, computers, or cell phones, for instance. In other organizations, the purpose relates to creating a service. Hotels, hospitals, schools, or libraries are examples of this type of organization. Some organizations that create products or services have the aim of generating profits; others are formed to provide services to their members, a community, or the public, and profitability is not a component of their mission. Organizations operate in the business sector, in education, health care, and government, as well as in social settings—and while each sector and each organization is unique, having a purpose is common to all.

*Plans* specify the means through which an organization carries out its mission and pursues its aspirations (often, called a *vision*) and the *goals* that make these accomplishments possible (Tromp & Ruben, 2010).

Within most organizations—more so than in relationships or groups—the mission, aspirations, plans, and goals are purposefully established and formally documented. This is not to say that organizational purposes, plans, and goals are rigid and constant over time (see Figure 11.1). They can and do evolve. In fact, to be successful and to sustain themselves over the long term, organizations must engage in continual review and improvement and, at times, more formalized and fundamental planned change efforts, as internal, marketplace, and other circumstances warrant (Lewis, 2011; Ruben, 2013).

Communication plays an important role in all of these processes. Communication is the process through which a mission, vision, plans, and goals are initially shaped, and it is also the means through which members of the organization discuss, debate, and ideally come to a shared perspective on these purposes and directions as circumstances change. To a large extent, the more carefully developed and implemented these communication efforts are, the more shared commitment and motivation there will be among those whose support is critical to the organization's success, adaptability, and sustainability.

**FIGURE 11.1**

What are this organization's purpose, plans, and goals?

© RobMarmion/Shutterstock.com

# ORGANIZATIONAL THEORIES

A number of "schools of thought" as to the nature of organizations have been advanced over the years. Each school reflects the way scholars and practitioners think about organizations and how they work, the role of leaders, the motivations that guide organizational members, and a variety other facets of organizational life.

## Scientific Management

The *scientific management* approach to organizational behavior is arguably the first widely acknowledged theory—actually a collection of theories—about how organizations function. The most visible figure in the field was Frederick W. Taylor (1865–1915), whose 1911 book, *Scientific Management*, embodied the philosophy and theory of the approach. In Taylor's (1911) view, people in organizations are seen as being motivated primarily by tangible and material rewards. By implication, maximum productivity is presumed to be achievable by employees who are clear on what they are to do and to whom they are responsible, and who are financially rewarded for their work.

Essentially, the scientific management school views the organization as a *machine* (see Figure 11.2). Like a machine, an organization is seen as being effective to the extent that it runs efficiently. Workers are the vital cogs in the organizational machine and are understood to be motivated primarily by financial considerations. The task of a manager is to engineer work and the workplace environment in order to achieve maximum productivity and profitability through the use of formal authority and formal, downward channels of communication.

© Sergey Nivens/Shutterstock.com

**FIGURE 11.2**

The scientific management approach values efficiency and machine-like productivity.

A clear and specific organizational structure, job specialization, fair rewards, defined rules, and distinct lines of responsibility and authority are regarded as basic. The primary purpose of communication, in this school of thought, is to provide information to employees that will clarify the tasks they are to perform and to reward them monetarily based on their accomplishments.

## Human Relations

What has come to be referred to as the *human relations school* of organizational behavior set forth a more social view of work life. Chester Barnard's 1938 book, *The Functions of the Executive,* was a major impetus for this perspective, as were the well-known Western Electric Company, Hawthorne Works studies that focused on working conditions, morale, and productivity.

In the Hawthorne studies, researchers F. J. Roethlisberger and William J. Dickson (1938) set up experimental work rooms and groups to study the impact of such factors as the length of the work day, the length of the work week, and the introduction of breaks during the day. Much to their surprise, they found that regardless of what specific changes they introduced into the experimental environment—whether they shortened or lengthened working hours, days, or weeks, for instance—worker productivity improved. Every change they made in the environment seemed to increase productivity. By the end of the two-year study, efforts to account for the increased productivity led to an examination of every imaginable explanation including environmental factors, worker fatigue and monotony, wage incentives, method of supervision, and even temperature, humidity, and seasonal variation.

Ultimately, the researchers concluded that differences in productivity were not due to specific changes in the work environment, but that the greater productivity resulted from the positive interpersonal relationships and unusual level of supervisor attention present in the experimental group at every phase of the research. The experiment had fostered closer working relations and had established greater confidence and trust in the supervisors than were present in the normal work situation.

If the *machine* is the image that best captures the thinking of scientific management, the *family* serves a comparable function for the human relations approach. Organizations are seen as effective when they address worker needs, build trust, and encourage collaboration. In this perspective, workers are thought to be motivated primarily by the desire for job satisfaction, recognition, attention, and participation in decision making. Managers, accordingly, strive to create a supportive, open, and trusting workplace climate where employees collaborate, are appreciated, and feel valued (Rogers & Rogers, 1976). This view provides a much less mechanistic approach to human behavior in organizations. Instead, people are seen as being motivated by social, as well as economic, goals. Workers are thought to be most highly motivated when they are socially involved with colleagues and when they have been involved in making decisions that affect them.

In this school of thought, communication is seen as a crucial process for facilitating social interaction and participation—the sense of family. Achieving these objectives is regarded as the primary function of management.

## Systems

*Systems theory* emphasizes the way in which systems maintain themselves through ongoing interactions between their parts and their environments (Ruben & Kim, 1975; Thayer, 1968). In the systems perspective, individuals, relationships, groups, and organizations are seen as interacting with and dependent on one another and their environment (Miller, 1965; von Bertallanffy, 1968).

Communication is the process through which organizations emerge and evolve and the basis upon which organizations and other systems relate to their surroundings and to one another. People are seen as being shaped by the organization, and, simultaneously, organizations are seen as being influenced by the behavior of the people, relationships, and groups that compose them—in what is referred to as a *mutually causal process* (Ruben & Kim, 1975; von Bertalanffy, 1968).

Organizations are *complex systems* (Thayer, 1968). Within any organization, there are any number of smaller work units—essentially, organizations in their own right—whose mission, aspirations, and goals must also be created, maintained, and coordinated with one another and with the organization as a whole. Workers, and the units of which they are a part, are viewed as components of the organizational system, and information flow and feedback within and among these subsystems is understood to be necessary to the adaptability of the individuals, their units, and the organizations as a whole in their marketplace environment.

Communication connects the components of complex organizations and is essential to information gathering and dissemination as well as decision making and guidance of the system as a whole in its efforts to adapt to its environment. In this perspective, managers must ensure that communication and information systems serve to facilitate effective interaction, coordination, and adaptability. More generally, the task of managers is to create and guide organizational systems so that they are open and responsive to the needs and opportunities of the environment.

## Quality

The *quality school*, which became popular in the late 1980s, builds on previous schools of thought in interesting ways. Following the traditions of scientific management, the control of quality of products and services and the idea of continually striving to improve work processes and procedures are basic to this framework. Reflecting the perspectives of the systems school, the quality approach regards organizations as effective when they are responsive to the demands and opportunities of the environment—specifically to customers, clients, patients, students, patrons, and other key groups the organization exists to serve. And, consistent with the views of the human relations approach, the quality approach sees workers as seeking involvement, collaboration, and the opportunity to do high quality work—and recognizes the value to the organization and its culture when these outcomes occur.

Rather than viewing the organization as a *machine,* a *family,* or a *system,* the dominant metaphor for theorists concerned with quality in organizations is *team.* Managers are viewed as *coaches* who coordinate worker expertise and marketplace information to assess, meet, and exceed the product and/or service expectations of the individuals and groups served by an organization and its products or services.

Among the noted contributors to the development and popularization of the quality approach are Walter Shewhart, W. Edwards Deming, Joseph Juran, and Phillip Crosby (Lewis & Smith, 1994). Walter Shewhart, often referred to as the father of the quality approach, developed theories and techniques for preventing variability in manufacturing processes through statistical process control techniques. W. Edwards Deming is best known for his contributions to Japanese industry, in which he served as an advisor as a part of the post–World War II reconstruction effort (see Figure 11.3). His impact was substantial, and the Japanese named their most prestigious quality award, the Deming Prize, in his honor.

Another name associated with the quality school is Joseph Juran, who emphasized the importance of continuous improvement and attention to consumers. In his view, *quality* should be defined in terms of the customers' perceptions of the suitability of a product or service (Lewis & Smith, 1994). Phillip Crosby has also played an important role in popularizing the quality approach. He developed the Quality College in 1980, where an estimated five million people have attended courses (Lewis & Smith, 1994).

Among the corporations to pioneer the quality approach were organizations like Motorola, AT&T, Xerox, Proctor & Gamble, IBM, Ford, Disney, Federal Express, General Motors, and Johnson & Johnson. Studies indicate that more than three-fourths of the corporations in the United States implemented quality programs aimed at enhancing competitiveness, operational efficiency, productivity, cost-effectiveness, customer responsiveness, employee involvement, and ultimately market and financial position (Lewis & Smith, 1994). Then, following the lead of corporations, many health care and educational organizations sought to apply quality concepts and values within their specialized contexts.

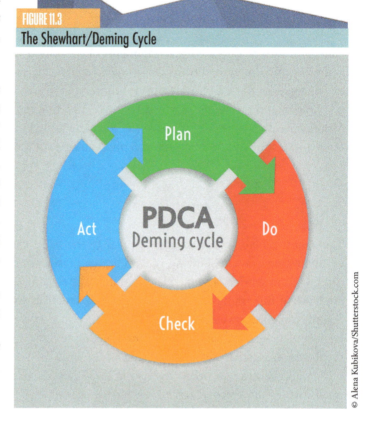

© Alena Kubikova/Shutterstock.com

**FIGURE 11.3**

**The Shewhart/Deming Cycle**

The quality school of thought places great emphasis on understanding and addressing the needs and expectations of *customers* and *stakeholders*—individuals and groups for whom an organization provides products or services and/or on whose assessment of the quality of these activities the support and reputation of the organization depends (Ruben, 1995, 2016). Within the quality framework, these stakeholders are variously called *customers, clients, constituencies, consumers, publics, audiences, beneficiaries,* or *users* (see Figure 11.4). The importance of focusing on the perspectives of these groups has been essential to sustainability in the business world and has become increasingly important in education and health care, where the key "customer" groups include specialized groups such as students, parents, the public, patients, insurance companies, state and federal governments, and others. Although these groups may not fully fit the traditional definition of "customers," understanding, reconciling, and addressing their various needs and perspectives has become a central concern within the education and health care communities.

Organizational assessment and continuous improvement are fundamental concepts in the quality school of thought. Fundamentally, *assessment* is a strategy for evaluating the performance of an organization in relation to the expectations of its various stakeholders and the organization's mission and vision.

Congress passed the Malcolm Baldrige National Quality Improvement Act in 1987; the Act was designed to enhance the competitiveness of U.S. businesses. In 1999, the Act was expanded to include health care and educational organizations; and in 2007 nonprofit/government organizations were included. The purpose of the program is to: (1) identify and recognize role-model businesses; (2) establish criteria for evaluating improvement efforts; and (3) disseminate and share best practices (NIST, 2015). Organizations interested in being considered for recognition as an organization that subscribes to the precepts of the quality school complete a comprehensive self-study and submit an application. Baldrige Awards are given in various categories at the national level and in many state programs as well.

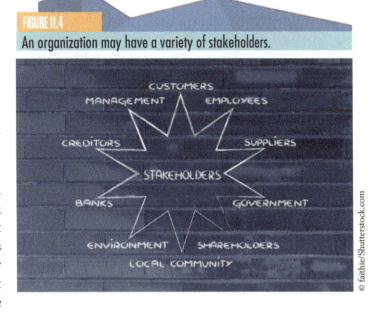

© faithie/Shutterstock.com

**FIGURE 11.4**

**An organization may have a variety of stakeholders.**

*Quality improvement* involves working collaboratively within an organization—often in teams—to continually improve organizational performance. Various tools are used by these teams, including Business Process Reengineering and Six Sigma, which are popular approaches that provide detailed analysis, measurement, and refinement of the way work procedures and processes are performed. Typically, teams are composed of a small number people with a broad base of knowledge and experience with the areas being addressed and who are committed to work collaboratively with the guidance of a group facilitator to identify and eliminate gaps and waste and to increase effectiveness and efficiency. Before embarking on an improvement project, team members receive specialized training in the tools they will use in analysis and improvement.

## Innovation and Employee Engagement

In recent years, what might be called an "innovation and employee engagement school"—which integrates many elements from the previous schools—has been gaining in popularity (Hamilton, 2015). Increasingly, today's organizations are focusing attention on both innovation *and* employee engagement to promote growth and financial strength. Many organizations are continuing efforts on work process analysis, measurement, and improvement techniques and teams. However, increasingly, these efforts have become more selective, focusing on priority areas and providing training for employees who will take part in specific projects, rather than for all employees (as was originally the case in some organizations).

Shifts are also taking place in how improvement is approached. While the quality approach placed great emphasis on unit-based teams to pursue incremental and continuous improvement goals, many organizations are seeking more dramatic and radical changes—changes in structure and technology that are disruptive of current organizational patterns and practices (Christensen, 2013; Christensen & Overdorf, 2000). Not long ago, for example, the "core business" of bookstores, video stores, record stores, and newsstands was the dissemination of information and entertainment. Because of marketplace disruptions, many of these businesses no longer exist or they have found it necessary to radically change their mission, vision, plans, and goals by replacing them with new collaborations, mergers, structural reorganizations, and interdisciplinary ventures designed to better anticipate the changing environment as well as to make use of new communication technologies.

Anticipating dramatic changes in the marketplace, and the mix of new products and services, requires organizational *innovation*—to identify and implement transformative, radical, "out of the box" approaches, with the goal of moving the organization in new, adaptive, and creative directions. Innovation is thought to benefit greatly from the engagement of members of an organization—the corporation, health care organization, or educational institution, for example—in active reflective, planning, and communication processes to answer questions such as the following (Ruben, 2014):

- In what ways are we unique as an organization?
- What are our core competencies?
- What are our core product lines, programs, or services that are our strengths?
- Are there product lines, programs, or services that we should consider discontinuing?
- How can we innovate in ways that will leverage our strengths, core competencies, and uniqueness to solidify our standing, status, and future?

# ROLES AND RESPONSIBILITIES

The foregoing review of schools of thought about organizations is useful in a number of respects. Among other benefits, the review calls attention to roles and responsibilities within organizations and how these concepts have evolved over time.

In any organization, the completion of a product- or service-oriented mission requires a *division of labor*—the partitioning of the larger tasks into smaller parts and the delineation of departments and, within them, individual roles. A *role* is a set of behaviors—a job to be done, a position to be filled, or a function to be carried out.

In relationships and groups, the roles individuals play—and their responsibilities to others in the social unit—generally evolve quite naturally out of the interactions among members as the unit develops. In these instances, the process of role delineation is informal, as in study groups or high school cliques. In larger organizations, the division of labor among working units and individualized role definitions are more formalized. Typically, individual roles and responsibilities are formally delineated through "job titles," "hiring policies," "job descriptions," and "promotion and termination procedures."

Fundamental aspects of departmental and role relationships—the ways in which work units are related to one another—are also formalized in most organizations. Formal organization charts, such as the one shown in Figure 11.5, portray these relationships. They indicate a *chain of command* and *reporting lines*—who reports to whom.

**FIGURE 11.5**

**A formal organizational chart.**

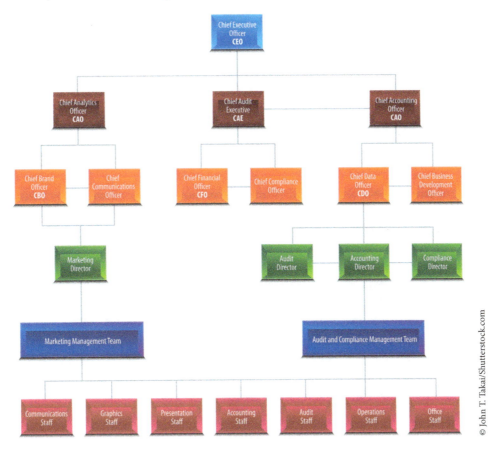

© John T. Takai/Shutterstock.com

# LEADERSHIP

Some authors make a distinction between the concepts of management and leadership (Kotter, 1990; Northouse, 2016). When this distinction is made, *management* is generally used to refer to the vast array of duties associated with keeping an organization running smoothly on a day-to-day basis. Many of these responsibilities—including issues related to personnel, finance, the physical plant, and the like—can seem rather repetitious and routine. These are the responsibilities that "keep the trains running on time" and tend not to be the creative and dynamic activities that come to mind when conjuring up the goings on in the corner executive floor of a corporation, the president's office of a university, or the administrative suite in a major hospital system. When we think of the work of senior administrators, we often tend to glamorize the role and focus on the inspirational, vision-setting activities that motivate and guide an organization into new and uncharted waters, deciding "where the train routes should be" or perhaps developing altogether new modes of transportation.

But are these sets of activities really mutually exclusive or does one person often engage in both kinds of activities in his or her role in an organization? Over time, people find themselves engaging in both management and leadership functions which are vital to organizational effectiveness, efficiency, innovation, and sustainability (Northouse, 2016).

This discussion is a part of the larger question: What is leadership? Despite a wealth of research done on the topic, James MacGregor Burns (1978), an important figure in modern leadership studies, concludes that "Leadership is one of the most observed and least understood phenomena on Earth" (p. 2).

Bass' (1990) handbook is an especially useful resource in understanding the development and advancement of research on leadership. He argues that, "The study of leadership rivals in age the emergence of civilization which shaped its leaders as much as it was shaped by them. From its infancy, the study of history has been the study of leaders – what they did and why they did it" (p. 3). With these deep historical roots, leadership has long been a subject of great interest to people interested in communication in organizations.

Definitions of leadership have evolved to meet the unique needs of particular scholars and settings. In fact, as Stogdill (1974) indicates, "There are almost as many different definitions of leadership as there are persons who have attempted to define the concept" (p. 7). Capturing the many dimensions of leadership with enough precision *and* flexibility is challenging. According to Ruben (2006), the array of competencies associated with leadership includes analytic competencies, personal competencies, communication competencies, organizational competencies, and positional competencies. Ideally, leaders are able to perform well in all of these areas.

Attempting to find agreement in the myriad definitions of leadership, Northouse (2016) identifies the following common themes found in the literature:

- Leadership is a process
- Leadership involves influence
- Leadership occurs in groups
- Leadership involves common goals (p. 6)

Northouse (2016) goes on to define leadership as "a process whereby an individual influences a group of individuals to achieve a common goal" (p. 5). If leadership is understood to be a process of social influence, it would seem that communication could contribute meaningfully to both the study and practice of leadership. It is also important to point out that the communication processes involved in social influence are two-way. That is, leaders influence members of a group or organization, and these members also have an influence on leaders and leadership through their willingness to support, follow, and/or comply. As we noted in Chapter 10, without willing followers, there can be no leadership (Ruben, De Lisi, & Gigliotti, 2016).

Recognizing the centrality of communication in leadership studies, Hackman and Johnson (2013) posit the following definition of leadership: "Leadership is human (symbolic) communication that modifies the attitudes and behaviors of others in order to meet shared group goals and needs" (p. 11). Leaders may take on a number of different identities in the life of an organization depending on the context and situation, including: storytellers, agents of change, counselors, spokespeople, visionaries, impression managers, and cheerleaders. As leaders enact these roles in an organization, a basic understanding of the needs of the group, organization, network, and environment may ultimately influence the effectiveness of the enterprise. Whatever forms and directions leadership efforts take, communication is always at the core of the process (see Figure 11.6).

As the context for leadership has evolved, so have the theoretical approaches to understanding leadership (Hackman & Johnson, 2013; Northouse, 2016). The major approaches to leadership include:

- *Trait approach:* Assumes that leaders embody innate leadership qualities
- *Situational approach:* Suggests that the traits needed for effective leadership vary based on the situation

**FIGURE 11.6**

Some of the components of effective leadership.

© Dusit/Shutterstock.com

- *Functional approach:* Emphasizes behaviors that contribute to effective leadership
- *Relational approach:* Highlights the interdependence of leaders and followers
- *Transactional approach:* Emphasizes stability in organizational life, with a particular focus on organizational operations and supervision
- *Transformational approach:* Focuses on the ability of leaders to create change in the lives of the people they lead

In the context of organizations and leadership, it is also important to acknowledge the ways in which leadership communication reflects one's perspective on organizations. To some, the art of communication is considered to be the art of leadership, for example, since leadership, as a process, relies on communication (Witherspoon, 1997). This process is understood to be both transmissional and meaning-centered, whereby the leader accomplishes goals and frames experiences for members of the organization through discourse (Fairhurst & Connaughton, 2014).

As indicated in the first chapter, communication is seen as a process through which people create and use information to relate to the environment and to one another. Leaders gather, create, interpret, and shape information and create messages to inform, coordinate, or persuade others. Through efforts to "manage meaning," leaders endeavor to shape the experiences and actions of their followers (Alvesson, 2002). In this sense, it is through the act of communication that leadership itself becomes possible.

History provides a wealth of examples of effective and ineffective leaders. In most cases, the success or failure of these leaders depends on their ability to connect with others through verbal and nonverbal communication. The communication process through which connections are formed and maintained is one of mutual influence. As noted previously, leaders influence members of a group or organization, and these members also have a defining influence on leaders and leadership action through their willingness to follow, validate, support, or endorse those actions—or their failure to do so (Ruben, De Lisi, & Gigliotti, 2016).

# COMMUNICATION NETWORKS

## Network Functions

As with relationships and groups, organizations have their origins in *communication networks*— reciprocal message processing linkages. From the perspective of an organization, the functions of communication networks include:

- Providing the means for coordinating the activities of individuals, relationships, groups, and other subunits within the organization

- Providing mechanisms for directing the activities of the organization as a whole
- Facilitating the exchange of information within the organization
- Ensuring the flow of information between the organization and the external environment in which it exists

## Network Size

One important differentiating characteristic of organizations is size. We have seen from previous discussions that an increase in the number of individuals in a social unit dramatically increases the number of reciprocal communication linkages that are possible and necessary to connect the people involved. This is a problem of major proportions within large organizations.

In small groups, little needs to be done to formalize communication networking. People can generally talk to whomever they wish, about whatever they wish. When a group gets together, whatever happens, happens. In organizations, given the incredibly large number of potential two-person linkages, formalization of face-to-face and mediated communication networks is essential (see Figure 11.7).

## Internal Networks: Message Flows within Organizations

**Downward Message Flows.** Generally speaking, formalized lines of information that flow within

**FIGURE 11.7**

The chart at the top depicts the *formal organization* and *chain of command* within a typical hierarchical company. The drawing underneath illustrates the *communication network* among members of the company. Within the company, there are four *cliques*—subsystems of individuals who interact with one another relatively more than with others. There is also an *isolate* (11), an *isolated dyad* (21 and 22), and a *liaison* (1)—an individual interlinking various cliques.

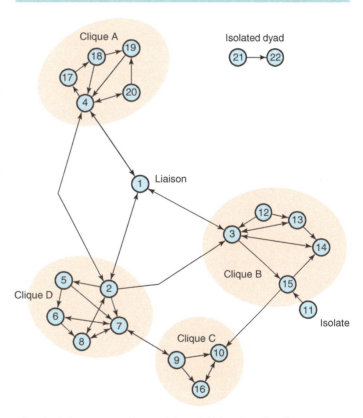

organizations correspond closely to the lines of authority. The most familiar pattern of formalized information flow is from management to employees—from a supervisor to a supervisee.

In such circumstances, messages flow "downward" from people in positions of relatively greater authority to others in the organization who report to them—directly or through intermediaries. Messages transmitted downward generally serve one or more of the following functions (Pace, 1983):

- Specifying a task to be performed
- Providing instructions about how to perform a task
- Providing information about the reason for a particular task that needs to be performed
- Providing information about organizational policies or practices
- Providing information about an employee's performance
- Providing information about the organization and its mission

**UPWARD MESSAGE FLOWS.** Messages channeled from supervisees to supervisors—from individuals in organizational groups, departments, or divisions to people occupying managerial roles—represent what is called an *upward message flow.* Upward communication has several functions, including (Pace, 1983):

- Providing input for decision making
- Advising about supervisees' information needs
- Providing information regarding supervisees' level of receptivity to information, satisfaction, and morale
- Providing a potentially constructive outlet for grievances and complaints
- Allowing superiors to assess the effects of previous downward communication
- Helping supervisees cope with problems and facilitating their involvement

**HORIZONTAL MESSAGE FLOWS.** What are often called *horizontal communication networks* refer to linkages that connect individuals at the same level of authority within an organizational group, department, or division. Functions of horizontal information sharing include (Pace, 1983):

- Coordinating planning and execution of tasks
- Providing for collective problem solving
- Facilitating common understanding
- Resolving differences
- Developing supportive and productive work relationships

**INFORMAL MESSAGE FLOWS.** Aside from the formalized, intentionally designed linkages, other *informal* or *emergent networks* inevitably develop among individuals and subunits in any group or organization. These informal networks—which include the *grapevine*—serve to link individuals to one another in much the same way as do formal networks. Unlike their formalized counterparts, however, informal linkages come into being primarily because of the personal and social needs of the members.

Sometimes informal communication networks correspond closely in structure to the formal systems. For instance, a supervisor and his or her subordinates may regularly have lunch together and discuss personal and professional matters. Often, formal and informal networks are very different. A grounds supervisor may ride to work with an administrative assistant to the vice president for operations, for instance. In any case, informal networks established between employees in different departments, through social media, on the golf course, or on the way to and from work, are important channels within any group or organization. These networks have a substantial impact on both the content and flow of messages in the more formalized networks.

Informal networks have a variety of characteristics.  In general, they:

- Are face-to-face
- Are less constrained by organizational and political restraints
- Move messages rapidly
- Tend to be more the result of the situation than the people or their roles
- Tend to develop more often within organizational workgroups, departments, or divisions than between them
- Generally transmit information that is accurate, though often somewhat incomplete, leading to misinterpretation (adapted from Davis & O'Connor, 1977)

**FIGURE 11.8**

Holacracy is new way of thinking about the organizational structure. In holacracies, authority is distributed to self-organized teams, and decisions are made locally.  Unlike traditional organizations' structures, the CEO follows the same "rules" as everyone else in the company (http://www.holacracy.org).

© Rawpixel/Shutterstock.com

# External Networks: Relating to Other Organizations and Publics

### Inflow: Research and Surveillance.

All groups and organizations depend on various constituencies, stakeholders, or *publics,* in the larger environment for their survival.

Volunteer groups rely on contributors, business organizations on consumers and the government, hospitals on patients and physicians, advertising agencies on their clients and the public, newspapers on their subscribers and advertisers, and so on. *External networks* connect the organization with these publics and to the larger environment.

External networks also enable the system to gather information from the environment. Through market research, monitoring and analysis of various information sources, and direct surveillance of competitors and other environmental factors, organizations receive information necessary to identify and respond appropriately to environmental change, threat, opportunity, or challenge.

**OUTFLOW: ADVERTISING, MARKETING, AND PUBLIC RELATIONS.** External networks are also used to provide external publics with information that members of the group or organization think desirable, proper, or necessary. The terms *advertising, marketing,* and *public relations* refer to activities that involve the transmission of messages into the environment with the goal of informing and systematically influencing these publics and possibly engaging them in dialogue.

## Mediated Communication Networks

In most organizations, internal face-to-face interaction is supplemented (and sometimes replaced by) mediated systems. This is true in internal networks which utilize social media, email, and text messaging, and in external networks where websites, cell phones, FAQs (frequently asked questions), and other mediated systems are increasingly used to facilitate regular, efficient, and hopefully effective and satisfying contact with key external stakeholder groups.

## Organizational Communication Networks in Action

In the ongoing dynamics of organizational communication, networks seldom operate in the straightforward, rational, predictable manner one might infer from a description of possible types of networks and directions of message flow. In actuality, the functioning of communication networks is exceptionally complex, often unpredictable, sometimes uncontrollable, and frequently chaotic.

In any organization, messages are being sent simultaneously in a variety of directions using face-to-face and mediated communication. In such circumstances, "breaks" in the network, distortion, contradiction, and confusion inevitably occur—they are more the rule than the exception. And, as in other communication situations, the messages a manager or a subordinate thinks he or she is sending in an email or through face-to-face conversation is often quite different than the meaning others derive from those messages. Furthermore, the sheer size of an organizational network and the distance between the top and bottom levels of the hierarchy intensify problems. Distance generally increases the likelihood of information loss, distortion, and the possibility of distrust and suspicion.

Given the complexity and array of challenges associated with information flow in organizations, difficulties are inevitable, leading to this cautionary list of principles put forth by organizational scholar Osmo Wiio (summarized in Locker & Kienzler, 2013, p. 14):

- Communication usually fails, except by accident.
- If a message can be interpreted in several ways, it will be interpreted in a manner that maximizes the damage.
- There is always someone who knows better than you what you meant by your message.
- The more we communicate, the worse communication succeeds.

Clearly, the complexity of organizational networks and that of the communication process combine to make organizations one of the most challenging contexts for those interested in studying or applying an understanding of the nature of communication and its impact on human behavior.

# ORGANIZATIONAL CULTURE

As interaction takes place through the networks of any organization, verbal and nonverbal behavior patterns develop and become routinized. Over time, they become important social realities for an organization—what can be called an organization's "culture." An *organizational culture* is the sum of its symbols, events, traditions, standardized verbal and nonverbal behavior patterns, stories, rules, and rituals that give the organization its character or "personality."

**FIGURE 11.9**

Through their verbal and nonverbal behavior people collectively create the organizations to which they belong and the symbols, events, standardized verbal and nonverbal behavior patterns, stories, rules, rituals, and other conventions characteristic of the organization.

© Syaheir Azizan/Shutterstock.com

## Origins of Organizational Cultures

Organizational cultures grow out of the communication activities of individual members. Though organizational cultures are the products of human communication, they can take on an objective quality and "act back on" individuals within an organization (see Figure 11.9).

Symbols are one important element of the culture of many organizations. Trademarks, buildings, office furnishings, and uniforms are examples of symbols that are often visible facets of an organization's culture. Sometimes organizational symbols develop naturally, as with informal dress codes among employees of a company. In other instances, symbols—trademarks or slogans, for instance—are purposefully developed to enhance an organization's identity and actively promoted as part of the organization's branding efforts.

Space is another important organizational symbol. In many organizations, rules are developed for use in allocating space to employees, such that the location, size, and decor of an employee's office or workspace reflect his or her position. Larger, more elaborately furnished and decorated offices go to individuals of a higher rank within the organization. Lesser officials may have smaller, modestly decorated offices; people at still lower levels may have no private workspace, separated from one another by portable partitions or bookcases and file cabinets. For reasons that may make little sense to an outsider, carpeting in a vacated office might be ripped up and thrown away, rather than being left for a new occupant whose rank within the organization would not merit carpeted floors. These actions are regarded as necessary to preserve the culture.

As more employees telecommute (work at home or take their offices with them on the road), organizations are adapting their spaces. Some organizations have eliminated most or all individual offices and have replaced them with large areas that contain desks, telephones, data ports, and other office equipment that are shared by people who only occasionally are physically present at the office or work at home most days. For these organizations, virtual connectivity is increasingly a necessary and accepted alternative to co-located communication. Variations are substantial from one organization to the next, and, with advances in technology that allow many workers to perform their duties virtually anywhere, symbolic dimensions of "office space" are becoming somewhat less important in many organizations.

The language used to talk about an organization is also a reflection of and, at the same time, an influence on its culture (Modaff, Butler, & DeWine, 2011). Organizations in which people talk about promotions in terms of sports metaphors like "fighting one's way to the top" or "last man standing" are likely to have quite different cultures than ones where promotions are described in terms of "members of a family working together to help each other succeed."

Organizational stories are another important facet of an organization's culture (Schein, 2010). Most organizations have a collection of favorite stories about notorious past and present personnel, organizational achievements or failures, and memorable moments in the life of the organization. For example, one employee might relate a story about "the guy who tried to negotiate his way to a higher salary a few years back by boasting to management of an offer from another company. Management wished him luck in his new job and asked him how soon he would be leaving." Or: "Let me tell you about the security guard who asked the president for an ID. She was promoted for taking company security so seriously." Implicit in these stories are statements about organizational values, ethics, management practices, and other facets of life in the organization. Through stories and storytelling, organizational cultures are transmitted from one generation of employees to another.

## Functions of Organizational Cultures

Organizational cultures play a central and pervasive role in the dynamics of organizations of all kinds (Deal & Kennedy, 2000), and they serve many important communication functions for those who create and participate in them, including:

- Providing people with a sense of individual and collective identity
- Contributing to the establishment of structure and control
- Aiding with the introduction of members to the customs and traditions of the organization
- Fostering cohesiveness among members of the organization

## Assimilation, Socialization, and Innovation in Organizations

Becoming a member of an organization requires an initiation into its culture through processes referred to as *socialization* and *assimilation.* Even in organizations with no formal apprenticeship or internship, any employee must come to terms with an organization's culture to be accepted and to function effectively. Formal communication networks play a role in this process, but informal networks are often even more essential to "learning the ropes" (see Figure 11.10).

**FIGURE 11.10**

As part of the expression of an organizational culture, employees may be required to dress alike.

© michaeljung/Shutterstock.com

Within any organization—or relationship, group, or society—there is a tension between influences that contribute to cultural stability and continuity and those that contribute to cultural innovation and change. Stability within organizations is fostered when members carry cultural traditions forward with them in time. Yet, innovation and change call for—and are often triggered by—departures from tradition. Sometimes innovations are introduced intentionally, as discussed previously. At other times, change happens by accident because of the way individuals cope with and internalize (or fail to internalize) the culture of the organization. Cultural continuity and cultural innovation are, thus, countervailing forces; both are necessary to the survival and prosperity of organizations over time.

# ORGANIZATIONAL CLIMATE

Climate is another aspect of organizations in which communication plays a direct role and one which is closely related to culture. An organization's *climate* is the atmosphere or tone members of the organization experience as they go about their daily routines. Climates are created through communication. In turn, climates influence organizational members and are perpetuated through organizational communication processes. Even as consumers, we may have a sense that not all organizations—department stores, hospitals, or schools, for instance—feel the same although their product or service may be similar. Often, differences in the feeling we get are a reflection of differences in the organizational climates, which were created and maintained through communication.

In very general terms, we can talk about climates being positive or negative (Falcione & Kaplan, 1984). Positive—supportive—climates have been described as having the following characteristics:

- Supportiveness of supervisor–subordinate communication
- Perceived quality and accuracy of downward communication
- Perceived openness of the supervisor–subordinate relationship
- Opportunities [for] and degree of influence of upward communication
- Perceived reliability of information from subordinates and coworkers (p. 296)

Studies show that where supportive climates exist, job satisfaction is high and productivity may improve as well (Falcione & Kaplan, 1984). Generally speaking, a positive climate and high levels of satisfaction will be reflected in the positive treatment of clients and consumers, as well as colleagues.

Organizational climates, whether positive or negative, are often self-perpetuating. Individuals tend to be attracted to—and selected to participate in—organizations in which members share their values, needs, attitudes, and expectations. Individuals with incompatible orientations are less likely to stay, or they may not be retained by the company even if they do initially affiliate themselves.

# ORGANIZATIONAL DIVERSITY

In the last decade, the growth of the U.S. population has slowed and therefore the number of individuals entering the U.S. labor force has declined. Predictions are that the next 10 years will see a slowly growing, but aging and far more ethnically diverse labor force (Bureau of Labor Statistics, 2013). From 1980 to 2020, the white working-age population is expected to decline from 82% to 63%, while the total "minority" portion of the workforce is projected to double (increasing from 18% to 37%), and the Hispanic/Latino population is expected to triple (increasing from 6% to 17%) (National Center for Public Policy and Higher Education, 2005). By 2022, women are projected to represent almost half (47%) of the labor force (Bureau of Labor Statistics, 2013). In addition, the percentage of women who are managers has been increasing steadily (U.S. Census Bureau, 2010).

Gotsis and Kortezi (2015) note that important dimensions of diversity in organizations include those that are more obvious to others (e.g., age, gender, race, and ethnicity) as well more subtle dimensions that are not directly observable (e.g., educational level, financial status, social class, religion, and sexual orientation, among others). Changes in workforce diversity have important implications for organizations and present increased opportunities for communication (Stewart, 1997; 2001).

Diversity expert Barbara Walker (1991) observes that: (1) people work best when they feel valued; (2) people feel most valued when they believe that their individual and group differences have been taken into account; (3) the ability to learn from people regarded as different is the key to becoming fully empowered; and (4) when people feel valued and empowered, they are able to build relationships in which they work together interdependently and synergistically.

Many of the diversity initiatives undertaken by organizations involve communication principles including encouraging mentoring, providing cultural awareness training, and facilitating successful interpersonal interactions among people from diverse backgrounds (Kulik & Roberson, 2008).

A classic survey of 4,191 employees from three organizations by Brinkman (1992) identified seven issues of importance when considering diversity in the workplace:

- *Climate:* What are employee perceptions about an organization's ability to embrace diversity?
- *Hiring practices:* Are particular people excluded from an organization?
- *Promotion practices:* Are diverse people being promoted and welcomed into managerial-level jobs?
- *Training and development:* What is the amount and type of training and help offered to employees?
- *Equity and fairness:* Is there a general sense of fairness and respect in the organization?
- *Visible commitment:* Is there a commitment to diversity reflected by gender and minority/nonminority ratios, recognition for achievements, and other visible and tangible signs?
- *Politics in the workplace:* Is there a perception that favoritism toward particular types of people exists? (pp. 1-2)

Organizations that score positively in each of these areas are more likely to be places that welcome and benefit from a more diverse work force. Organizations that ignore these problem areas are not dealing effectively with diversity in their work force.

Diversity presents any number of communication challenges but also many communication opportunities. In meeting the needs of a diverse market, valuing diversity within the organization and beyond makes it possible to benefit fully from the changing realities of our multicultural society.

# CONCLUSION

Communication, as we have seen, is as essential to the emergence of organizations as it is for the development of individuals, relationships, and groups. Without message processing, even the simplest coordination between individuals would be impossible. In small organizations with a dozen people and large enterprises of several thousand employees, communication is critical to defining goals, delineating individual roles and responsibilities, controlling the organization's operations, establishing networks, and creating the organization's culture and climate.

A goal is the objective a system is designed to achieve. It is the benchmark against which the effectiveness, success, viability, and adaptability of the system can be assessed. Organizations are formed with product- or service-oriented goals. A division of labor and a delineation of roles are needed to achieve these goals. A role is a set of defined behaviors—a job to be done, a position to be filled, or a function to be carried out. Relationships between roles may be indicated by reporting lines and formal organizational structure.

Organizational systems need a control mechanism for planning, decision making, financial oversight, monitoring operations, coordinating activities, and evaluating organizational functioning. These are management functions. The way in which they are carried out in an organization depends on the prevailing view of the nature of human behavior in organizations. The scientific management, human relations, systems, quality, and innovation and employee engagement views provide different ways of thinking about organizational behavior, management, and communication functions.

Communication networks serve important functions within organizations. Formal message flow through networks in an organization may be downward, upward, or horizontal. Informal networks are also basic to organizations. External networks link an organization to its environment. Face-to-face networks in organizations are increasingly supplemented by mediated communication. In the ongoing dynamics of organizational communication, networks seldom operate in the straightforward, rational, and predictable manner suggested by descriptions of the types of networks and the direction of message flow.

Leadership is a process of social influence that occurs within a group context and involves goal attainment. Over the years, the study of leadership has focused on various approaches including trait, situational, functional, relational, transaction, and transformational. It is also important to remember the role of followers in the leadership process.

Organizational cultures emerge over time as a result of interactions among organization members. An organization's culture is the sum of its symbols, events, standardized verbal and nonverbal behavior patterns, stories, rules, and rituals that give the organization a character or personality.

Communication also results in the creation of organizational climates. A climate is the atmosphere or tone experienced by members of an organization as they go about their daily routines.

Diversity is one of the major opportunities facing contemporary organizations.

## KEY POINTS

After having read this chapter, you should be able to:

- Analyze the role of communication in organizations
- Identify the main organizational theories and their associated effects on communication
- Describe the roles and characteristics of organizational leaders
- Explain the importance of formal and informal organizational networks
- Articulate the characteristics of an organizational culture

## REFERENCES

Alvesson, M. (2002). *Understanding organizational culture*. Thousand Oaks, CA: Sage.

Barnard, C. I. (1938). *The functions of the executive*. Cambridge, MA: Harvard University Press.

Bass, B. M. (1990). *Bass & Stogdill's handbook of leadership: Theory, research, and managerial applications (3rd ed.)*. New York, NY: Free Press.

Brinkman, H. (1992, April). Key issue of the 1990s: Workforce diversity. *Team Works*, pp. 1-2.

Bureau of Labor Statistics. (2013, December). Labor force projections to 2022: the labor force participation rate continues to fall. Retrieved from http://www.bls.gov/opub/mlr/2013/article/labor-force-projections-to-2022-the-labor-force-participation-rate-continues-to-fall.htm

Burns, J. M. (1978). *Leadership* (1st ed.). New York, NY: Harper & Row.

Christensen, C. M. (2013). *The innovator's dilemma: When new technologies cause great firms to fail.* Boston, MA: Harvard Business Review Press.

Christensen, C. M., & Overdorf, M. (2000, March-April). Meeting the challenge of disruptive change. *Harvard Business Review*, pp. 67-76.

Davis, W. L., & O'Connor, J. R. (1977). Serial transmission of information: A study of the grapevine. *Journal of Applied Communication Research*, 5(2), 61-72.

Deal, T. E., & Kennedy, A. A. (2000). *Corporate cultures: The rites and rituals of corporate life.* New York, NY: Basic Books.

Fairhurst, G. T., & Connaughton, S. L. (2014). Leadership: A communicative perspective. *Leadership*, 10(1), 7-35.

Falcione, R. L., & Kaplan, E. A. (1984). Organizational climate, communication, and culture. In R. N. Bostrom (Ed.), *Communication yearbook 8* (pp. 285-309). Beverly Hills, CA: Sage.

Gotsis, G., & Kortezi, Z. (2015). *Critical studies in diversity management literature: A review and synthesis.* New York, NY: Springer.

Hackman, M. Z., & Johnson, C. E. (2013). *Leadership: A communication perspective* (6th ed.). Long Grove, IL: Waveland Press.

Hamilton, D. (2015). Personal correspondence.

Kotter, J. P. (1990). *A force for change: How leadership differs from management.* New York, NY: Free Press.

Kulik, C. T., & Roberson, L. (2008). Common goals and golden opportunities: Evaluations of diversity education in academic and organizational settings. *Academy of Management Learning & Education, 7*(3), 309-331.

Lewis, L. K. (2011). *Organizational change: Creating change through strategic communication.* Malden, MA: Wiley-Blackwell.

Lewis, R. G., & Smith, D. H. (1994). *Total quality in higher education.* Delray Beach, FL: St. Lucie Press.

Locker, K., & Kienzler, D. (2013). *Business and administrative communication* (10th ed.). New York, NY: McGraw-Hill.

Miller, J. G. (1965). Living systems: Basic concepts. *Behavioral Science, 10*(3), 193-237.

Modaff, D. P., Butler, J. A., & DeWine, S. A. (2011). *Organizational communication: Foundations, challenges, and misunderstandings* (3rd ed.). Boston, MA: Pearson.

National Center for Public Policy and Higher Education. (2005, November). *Policy alert.* Retrieved from http://www.highereducation.org/reports/pa_decline/decline-f1.shtml

NIST. (2015). Baldrige performance excellence program. Retrieved from http://www.nist.gov/baldrige/

Northouse, P. G. (2016). *Leadership: Theory and practice* (7th ed.). Thousand Oaks, CA: Sage.

Pace, R. W. (1983). *Organizational communication: Foundations for human resource development.* Englewood Cliffs, NJ: Prentice-Hall.

Roethlisberger, F. J., & Dickson, W. J. (1939). *Management and the worker.* Cambridge, MA: Harvard University Press.

Rogers, E. M., & Agarwala-Rogers, R. (1976). *Communication in organizations.* New York, NY: Free Press.

Ruben, B. D. (1995). The quality approach in higher education. In B. D. Ruben (Ed.), *Quality in higher education* (pp. 1-34). New Brunswick, NJ: Transaction Books.

Ruben, B. D. (2006). *What leaders need to know and do: A leadership competencies scorecard.* Washington, DC: National Association of College and University Business Officers.

Ruben, B. D. (2013). *Understanding, planning, and leading organizational change.* Washington, DC: National Association of College and University Business Officers.

Ruben, B. D. (2014). *Excellence in higher education: A framework and tool for continuous improvement and innovation.* Poughkeepsie, NY: Marist College Press.

Ruben, B. D., De Lisi, R., & Gigliotti, R. A. (2016). *Guide for leaders in higher education: Core concepts, competencies and tools.* Sterling, VA: Stylus.

Ruben, B. D., & Kim, J. Y. (1975). *General system theory and human communication.* Rochelle Park, NJ: Hayden Books.

Schein, E. H. (2010). *Organizational culture and leadership: A dynamic view* (4th ed.). San Francisco, CA: Jossey-Bass.

Scott, C. R. (2013). *Anonymous agencies, backstreet businesses and covert collectives: Rethinking organizations in the 21st century.* Stanford, CA: Stanford University Press.

Stewart, L. P. (1997). Facilitating connections: Issues of gender, culture, and diversity. In J. M. Makau & R. C. Arnett (Eds.), *Communication ethics in an age of diversity* (pp. 110-125). Urbana, IL: University of Illinois Press.

Stewart, L. P. (2001). Gender issues in corporate communication. In D. J. Borisoff & L. P. Arliss (Eds.), *Women and men communicating: Challenges and changes* (2nd ed., pp. 171-184). Prospect Heights, IL: Waveland.

Stogdill, R. M. (1974). *Handbook of leadership: A survey of theory and research.* New York, NY: The Free Press.

Taylor, F. W. (1911). *The principles of scientific management.* New York, NY: Harper & Row.

Thayer, L. O. (1968). *Communication and communication systems.* Homewood, IL: Richard Irwin.

Tromp, S., & Ruben, B. D. (2010). *Strategic planning in higher education: A guide for leaders.* Washington, DC: National Association of College and University Business Officers.

U.S. Census Bureau. (2010). *Women in the workplace.* Retrieved http://www.census.gov/newsroom/pdf/women_workforce_slides.pdf

von Bertalanffy, L. (1968). *General system theory: Foundations, development, applications..* New York, NY: G. Braziller.

Walker, B. A. (1991). Valuing differences: The concept and a model. In M. A. Smith & S. J. Johnson (Eds.), *Valuing differences in the workplace* (pp. 7-16). Alexandria, VA: American Society for Training and Development.

Witherspoon, P. D. (1997). *Communicating leadership: An organizational perspective.* Boston, MA: Allyn & Bacon.

# ENDNOTE

1.  The review and summary of leadership theories provided in this section was drafted by Ralph Gigliotti, Graduate Fellow, Center for Organizational Development and Leadership, Rutgers University.

# CHAPTER 12

# CULTURES
## AND SOCIETIES

**In this chapter, you will learn about:**

- The definitions of culture
- The relationship between culture and communication
- The stages of cultural adaptation
- The characteristics of international communication

## THE NATURE OF CULTURE

## THE RELATIONSHIP BETWEEN COMMUNICATION AND CULTURE

## CHARACTERISTICS OF CULTURE

- Cultures Are Complex and Multifaceted
- Cultures Are Invisible
- Cultures Are Subjective
- Cultures Change Over Time
- A Word of Caution

## THE ROLE OF MEDIATED COMMUNICATION

# CULTURAL ADAPTATION

- Stages of Cultural Adaptation

# INTERCULTURAL COMMUNICATION

- National and International Networks

# SOCIETIES (COMPLEX CULTURAL AND COMMUNICATION SYSTEMS)

# INTERNATIONAL COMMUNICATION: THE GLOBAL VILLAGE—FACT OR FICTION?

- Complexities Abound

# CONCLUSION

# KEY POINTS

Cultural issues that have always been of interest to travelers and scholars have taken on a new importance in recent years for people in the United States and for others around the world. Differences in language, religion, dress, and names, which may have drawn little attention previously, have become vitally important symbols in communication and information processing. In the absence of specific knowledge about a person's background or nationality, assumptions, misperceptions, misunderstandings, and cultural stereotyping can occur. For example, consider the following:

- A woman wearing a *hijab* is asked if she has any relatives who are terrorists
- A political candidate talks about building a wall between the United States and Mexico
- A male student from Colombia makes a female teacher feel uncomfortable because he stands "too close" to her when he is asking her about changing his grade
- A person giving a speech assumes that everyone in the audience who is Black is African American
- An American visiting another country decides to dress up for Halloween only to discover that a zombie costume scares people who don't celebrate the day by wearing costumes

In this chapter, we will examine the nature of culture and how it influences and is influenced by communication. In addition, we will look at the nature of intercultural communication and its central role in contemporary life.

# THE NATURE OF CULTURE

*Culture*, like *communication*, is a familiar word to most people. Partly because of this familiarity, the term is used in a number of different ways. The most common usage is as a synonym for country or nation. If we are in the United States and come across several people talking in a language other than English we may think that they are "from another culture," meaning, in this case, that they seem to be from another country. At other times, the term is used to refer to desired qualities or attributes. For instance, someone who has poor table manners or lacks knowledge of classical music might be described as "uncultured"—meaning unrefined, uneducated, or unsophisticated.

To those who study human behavior, *culture* has a more precise definition. It is not regarded as something people have (or do) or something that is positive or negative. In fact, culture is not a thing at all, in the sense that it is an object that can be touched, physically examined, or located on a map. Rather it is an idea or a concept, first described by E. B. Tylor in 1871 as "that complex whole which includes knowledge, belief, art, morals, law, custom, and any other capabilities and habits acquired by . . . member[s] of society" (quoted in Wolfgang & Ferracuti, 1982, p. 95). From the point of view of communication, *culture* can be defined as the complex combination of common symbols, knowledge, folklore, customs, language, information-processing patterns, rituals, habits, and other behavioral patterns that link and give a common identity to a particular group of people at a particular point in time (see Figure 12.1).

**FIGURE 12.1**

A variety of verbal and nonverbal message sources provide visible traces of culture that confront individuals within societies.

© PEPPERSMINT/Shutterstock.com

© Boris Stroujko/Shutterstock.com

© Paul D. Smith/Shutterstock.com

© YURY TARANIK/Shutterstock.com

Hall (1976) conceived of culture as an iceberg in which behaviors and some beliefs are the tip of the iceberg, i.e, they are observable, but the majority of values and thought patterns are not observable and, therefore, are hidden from view. He believed that active participation in a culture was necessary to understand other people and that their values and thought patterns could only be revealed if a person spends time interacting with people from another culture. More contemporary commentators have rejected the iceberg metaphor since it does not capture the idea of coordinating action and meaning. As Bennett (2013) contends:

> Comparing culture to an iceberg floating in the sea implies that culture is an actual thing. The 10% above the water is really visible to everyone who looks in that direction, and the 90% below the water is both real and dangerous, since it can sink the unwary sojourner.
>
> The metaphor does not in any way imply that culture is a process of coordinating meaning and action—rather, it implies that culture is an entity with mysterious unknown qualities. (n.p.)

## THE RELATIONSHIP BETWEEN COMMUNICATION AND CULTURE

Let's examine the concept of culture and its relationship to communication in more detail. First, it is important to recognize that all social systems—relationships, families, groups, organizations, and societies—develop and maintain cultures (Thayer, 1968). And they do so through communication.

In each relationship, for instance, a *relational culture* emerges naturally over time. As we discussed in earlier chapters, couples may have songs, memorable places, dates of special significance, unique terms of endearment, and shorthand verbal and nonverbal codes—such as phrases or gestures that have a unique meaning. Each of these has a particular meaning and significance because of a shared and distinctive communicative history.

The same process occurs in groups and organizations, though a larger number of people are involved. As communication networks emerge and evolve, shared patterns and realities develop. In each, as we have seen, particular words or phrases, approaches to leadership, norms of behavior, or conventions of dress emerge as a result of communication and mutual adaptation of the members.

Societies, which we will discuss in more detail later in this chapter, are larger and more complex social systems, yet the same communication dynamics are at work.

The symbols of a society are perhaps the most visible signs of culture. Symbols are basic to the culture of each society. Spoken and written language are the most basic cultural elements, but other symbols have similar importance. Particular objects, places, people, ideas, documents, songs, historic events, monuments, heroic figures, architectural styles, and even folktales may be important to a culture.

**FIGURE 12.2**

**Flags are societal symbols.**

As illustrated in Figure 12.2, every country has a distinctive national flag. Yet, if we analyze the flags in terms of physical characteristics such as their form, overall size, composition, and weight, most are really quite similar. Composed of pieces of cloth that vary from one another in little more than color, flags play important symbolic roles in human affairs. They mark territories, represent particular geographic locations, symbolize political or religious ideologies, and provide a symbol of commonality and unity for the residents of the territories they symbolize.

In addition to flags, in most societies particular statues, places, people, documents, and symbols have special meanings, and their shared appreciation unites members of the culture in a common identity. While the specific elements of culture vary from one society to another, the linking and collective identity functions they serve are comparable within all societies.

Within societies, as in other social systems, communication is the means through which individuals create, share, and perpetuate culture. Shared verbal and nonverbal communication patterns, orientations toward ethnicity, politics, courtship, child rearing, religion, and other facets of social life also become a part of the culture of a society.

Cultures—whether of relationships, groups, organizations, or societies—serve several common functions related to communication (Kim, 1999; Orbe, 1997; Tanno & Gonzalez, 1998) including:

- Linking individuals to one another
- Creating a context for interaction and negotiation among members
- Providing the basis for a common identity

Clearly, the relationship between culture and communication is complex. On the one hand, cultures are the by-products of the communication activities that take place in relationships, groups, organizations, and societies. Indeed, were it not for our human capacity for symbolic language, we would be unable to develop a common culture. And without communication and communication technology it would be impossible to pass along the elements of our culture from one place to another and from one generation to the next. On the other hand, our individual communication preferences, patterns, and behaviors are by-products of cultures and the ways we adapt to the cultural demands and opportunities we encounter over the course of our lifetimes.

As much as it is accurate to say that culture is defined, shaped, transmitted, and learned through communication, the reverse is equally correct (Hall, 1976). In effect, then, there is a reciprocally influencing, or reciprocally defining, relationship between human communication and culture. Through communication we shape our cultures, and, in turn, our cultures shape our communication patterns. As Marshall McLuhan (1964) noted: "We shape our tools and thereafter our tools shape us." We can apply this idea to the relationship between the communication process, through we which shape our culture, and the ways in which our culture shapes us through communication.

# CHARACTERISTICS OF CULTURE

The idea of culture and its relationship to communication can be made clearer by discussing the following common characteristics of cultures: (1) cultures are complex and multifaceted, (2) cultures are invisible, (3) cultures are subjective, and (4) cultures change over time.

## Cultures Are Complex and Multifaceted

The complexities of culture are most apparent, and potentially most problematic in terms of communication, at the level of societies. Here, language differences are often involved along with fundamental issues such as social customs, family life, dress, eating habits, class structure, political orientation, religion, customs, economic philosophies, beliefs, and value systems.

Particular cultural elements such as these do not exist in isolation but, instead, influence one another in a number of subtle ways. For example, the values of a societal culture have an impact on economics and vice versa, and both influence and are influenced by social customs, religion, and family life. Consider this illustration: The tendency toward large families in some cultures is explained not only by custom but also by economics, religion, health, and the level of technology. In an agrarian society where infant mortality is high due to disease and poor health conditions, having many children also may be seen as desirable since they can provide help with duties necessary to the survival of the family. In a number of countries, the decreasing size of families is also influenced by many of these same cultural factors, including economics, customs, available technology, social conditions, and evolving gender attitudes.

If we examine the verbal and nonverbal communication patterns in any culture, the same pattern of complexity and association is apparent. Greeting forms, gestures, conversational topics and formats, dress, language habits, courtship practices, eye-contact preferences, uses of space, orientations toward time, gender roles, orientations toward elders, and attitudes toward work all influence and are, in turn, influenced by a variety of cultural dimensions.

In Saudi Arabia, for example, religion, tradition, and law prescribe very different public roles for women and men. For example, women are not allowed to drive or ride bicycles, usually wear a full-length covering called an *abaya*, and may need to be accompanied by a male relative to eat in particular restaurants. Cultures change, however, and while Saudi society remains differentiated by gender in many ways, a number of major changes have been introduced in recent years. The country has opened its first co-educational university in the multi-cultural city of Jeddah, more women are working in hospitals, women can now vote, and plans call for women to be eligible to run as candidates in local elections in 2015 (*Aljazeera*, 2013).

While every culture is unique in many respects, it is also possible to identify general patterns of similarity and difference. In terms of orientation toward communication practices, cultures can be described in terms of three general aspects: high and low context, individual and collective orientation, and monochronic and polychronic perspective toward time (Hall & Hall, 1990).

HIGH AND LOW CONTEXT CULTURES. Hall and Hall (1990) define *context* as "information that surrounds an event; it is inextricably bound up with the meaning of that event" (p. 6). They indicate that cultures of the world—and the communication practices of individuals within those cultures— range from *high* to *low context*. According to Edward Hall:

> A high context (HC) communication or message is one in which *most* of the information is already in the person, while very little is in the coded, explicit, transmitted part of the message. A low context (LC) communication is just the opposite; i.e., the mass of the information is vested in the explicit code. (quoted in Hall & Hall, 1990, p. 6)

In Japanese, Arab, and Mediterranean cultures, for example, there is an extensive overlapping of personal, social, and work relationships. Because of these overlapping communication networks, in high-context cultures such as these many everyday communication activities do not require much background information. The people who work together spend so much time together socially and in family activities that they are very well-informed about many aspects of one another's lives. Thus, when they talk, much can be taken for granted because of the rich communicative history of their relationships. Hall and Hall (1990) contrast such cultures with low-context groups (such as North Americans, Germans, Swiss, Scandinavians, and other northern Europeans) who tend to compartmentalize their personal relations, work relationships, and other aspects of their lives. Interactants within high- or low-context cultures have few problems interacting with one another.

People from high-context cultures rely more on nonverbal cues and on what they know about a person's background to guide them through a conversation, while people from low-context cultures are more likely to ask the other person direct questions about their experiences, attitudes, and beliefs (Gudykunst, 2003). However, conversations across context types can become quite problematic, as when a Westerner and a Middle Easterner meet for the first time to engage in negotiations or to conduct business.

**INDIVIDUAL AND COLLECTIVE ORIENTATION.** Feelings of responsibility toward the group is a feature of cultures that may vary from intense concern about the group's welfare and perceptions to a primary emphasis on the importance of individuals and their desires. Simply put, in individualistic cultures, the individual's goals are of prime importance, while in collective cultures, the group's goals are more important (Gudykunst, 2003; Hall & Hall, 1990).

The United States is an example of a relatively individualistic culture. Competition is encouraged, and people are expected to be responsible for their own actions. Success is typically defined in terms of individual accomplishment—"working one's way up the ladder." When people are asked what they do for a living, the response usually begins with a job title (e.g., "I'm a real estate agent"), followed by a description of their work responsibilities (e.g., "I specialize in selling high value commercial properties").

In Japan, traditionally a more collectively oriented culture, things are quite different. People are responsible to and for the entire group and are expected to adhere to group values and rules. Japanese people responding to the question "What do you do for a living?" more likely begin by explaining where they work and only then describe what they do, reflecting the greater importance attached to the work of the group than to personal accomplishments.

**MONOCHRONIC AND POLYCHRONIC TIME.** Time—a dimension of importance in many communication situations—is particularly vital to understanding cultures and differences between them. Hall and Hall (1990) distinguish between two orientations to time: monochronic and polychronic. *Monochronic time* describes the orientation of people who pay attention to, and do, one thing at a time. *Polychronic* refers to people who attend to and do many things at once.

In monochronic cultures, time is thought of as a commodity, as something to be counted, managed, allocated, and spent. Monochronic time is divided quite naturally into segments to be scheduled. In a monochronic system, a schedule or agenda becomes extremely important, as does completing tasks in a timely manner. In these cultures, people talk about time as though it were money, as something that can be "spent," "saved," "wasted," and "lost" (Hall & Hall, 1990). Whereas scheduling, attention to time management, and the compartmentalization of personal and work-related activities are important in monochronic cultures, people in polychronic cultures have a much more fluid approach to such matters. Life in the United States—especially business life—clearly exemplifies the monochronic orientation, which is also a part of the cultures of Switzerland, Germany, and

Scandinavia. In contrast are time-flexible Mediterranean or South American cultures (Hall & Hall, 1990). People from monochronic cultures may get frustrated dealing with people from polychronic cultures and vice versa. For example, a North American businessperson attending a conference in Spain may expect the meetings and meals to begin and end at the times printed on the schedule. When the lunch that was scheduled to begin at noon doesn't start until 1:00 or 1:30, the attendees from polychronic cultures may seem unconcerned. Those from monochronic cultures experience the "delay" as a problem and are likely to become agitated.

Differences between high- and low-context and monochronic and polychronic cultures are useful for characterizing cultures and also help to explain some of the problems that occur in intercultural communication, a topic we will discuss in more detail later. Figure 12.3 provides an interesting perspective on this issue.

## Cultures Are Invisible

Most of what characterizes the culture of a relationship, group, organization, or society is as invisible to the people it envelops as the air that surrounds them. For each of us, our culture—and its

### FIGURE 12.3

Cultural variations in orientation to time, pace of life, or, as it is sometimes referred to, tempo, are topics of both practical and theoretical interest. How does one study these differences systematically? Robert Levine uses three interesting, naturalistic methods that involve comparing measures of three types across cultures. First, he measures the amount of time it takes for a random sample of pedestrians to walk 60 feet. Second, he observes a sample of postal workers and measures the amount of time it takes for them to transact a request for stamps. Third, he measures the accuracy of 15 randomly selected bank clocks in the downtown area of a city as a way of assessing the concern with accuracy of timekeeping within the culture. The three measures are then combined to provide an overall pace-of-life score. Based on these scores, Switzerland, Ireland, Germany, Japan, and Italy, in that order, were the fastest-paced cultures of the 31 cultures he studied, and Mexico, Indonesia, Brazil, El Salvador, and Syria the slowest. The United States and Canada ranked in the middle at fifteenth and sixteenth, respectively

Levine found that five factors accounted for the overall pattern of differences between faster-and slower-paced cultures, health of a culture's economy, degree of industrialization, size of population, climate, and cultural orientation toward individualism–collectivism. In general, wealthier, more industrialized, more densely populated, cooler, and more individualistic cultures were more fast-paced.

Levine used a similar research method to study 36 cities within the United States, and, not surprisingly, found a number of differences. In addition to measuring walking speed, he also measured bank teller transaction speed, talking speed, and the percentage of people wearing wrist watches. Seven of the top ten most fast-paced cultures were in the Northeast—with Boston, Buffalo, and New York City ranking at the top of the list. Six of the ten slowest-paced cities were in California, and two were in Tennessee. The three slowest were Los Angeles, Sacramento, and Shreveport, LA.

Source: Robert Levine, *A Geography of Time*. New York, NY: Basic Books.

© blvdone/Shutterstock.com

many influences—is so subtle and pervasive that it often goes unnoticed. It's there now, it's been there as long as anyone can remember, and few of us have reason to think much about it.

In many parts of North America, the English language is taken for granted by most people as are a number of nonverbal conventions. For instance, many business colleagues think little about a quick handshake greeting, intermittent eye glances, and two-and-a-half to four feet of space separating interactants when they first meet. In a similar way, we take for granted the many relational, group, and organizational cultures that guide and shape our lives. The romantic glances and expressive touch between intimates and the conventions of dress and jargon in our various groups and organizations become natural behaviors to the people involved.

Sometimes we do become aware of the existence and nature of our cultures. When this occurs, it generally happens in one of three ways: (1) violation of a cultural convention, (2) cross-cultural contact, or (3) scholarly analysis.

VIOLATION OF A CULTURAL CONVENTION. When someone within a culture violates taken-for-granted cultural practices or standards, it tends to attract attention. In the case of the customary handshake ritual, for instance, we think little about it unless our expectations are violated. If, when you meet a person for the first time, he or she refuses to take your hand or has an exceptionally overpowering grip, you are likely to take note. And how would you feel if someone reached out to shake hands in the middle of a long conversation? We have a similar reaction when a new acquaintance stares incessantly or stands five or more feet from us during casual conversations. As with so many other facets of our lives, we have been learning the cultural conventions for greeting and conversing with each other since we were children; and we generally think nothing about these conventions unless or until they are violated.

The same process occurs in cultures or relationships. Perhaps the most striking example happens when a person in a romantic relationship "senses that something is wrong" because the other person doesn't look at him or her "the way he or she is used to" or no longer seems to "joke around" in the usual way. When our expectations are violated, we realize at some level of awareness that we have acquired a number of patterns, customs, habits, and meanings which we simply take for granted.

There is, however, no evidence that "exposure equals competence" (Brinkmann & van Weerdenburg, 2014, p. 128). In other words, merely spending time in another country does not make us more interculturally competent communicators, but having friends from other cultures does (Brinkmann & van Weerdenburg, 2014).

CROSS-CULTURAL CONTACT. The second way in which we can be alerted to the presence and impact of our culture is when we encounter people from another culture and observe major differences between their behavior and our own (see Figure 12.4). To many Europeans, men kissing one another on the cheek as a greeting goes unnoticed, while this gesture often startles North Americans. The

Japanese habit of closing the eyes when concentrating on a question may be quite unnerving to a Canadian businessperson who has no idea how to interpret the action.

Travel—domestic and especially international—is certainly a powerful way to increase our awareness of cultural differences. Given the communication technology available today, we can also "travel the world" via the Internet and learn a great deal about other cultures.

SCHOLARLY ANALYSIS. The third way we can become aware of our culture is through studying our own or others' descriptions of it. Nonfiction and fiction books can provide us with a great deal of information about our own and other cultures. Reading the vast scholarly literature on cultural differences and similarities also contributes to our knowledge and understanding.

## Cultures Are Subjective

Because we have grown up with and take our cultures so much for granted, we are largely unaware of their subjective nature. To the people involved, aspects of culture are rational and make perfect sense, although they may not seem that way to "outsiders." We may easily

**FIGURE 12.4**

We judge the quality of our relationships through culturally learned communication behaviors.

© Photodiem/Shutterstock.com

© Jason Stitt/Shutterstock.com

come to assume that things are the way they "should be"—intermittent glances during casual conversation, shaking hands as a greeting, waving to an acquaintance, and so on.

A good example of this kind of assumption making is provided by colors. Obviously, red is red, and orange is orange. And we all know that red is *not* orange, right? The taken-for-granted language we use to describe color and the ways we categorize and perceive color around us may vary considerably from one culture to another. We seldom think about the fact that divisions of the color spectrum are arbitrary, as are their labels. People in language communities that have not been as influenced by Western culture divide the color spectrum differently. For example:

> The Himba tribe from northern Namibia . . . does not classify green and blue separately, the way Westerners do, but it does differentiate among various shades of . . . green. And when tested, members of the tribe . . . readily distinguish among greens that tend to look the same to Western eyes.
>
> While the English language has 11 separate color categories—red, green, blue, yellow, black, white, grey, pink, orange, purple and brown—the Himba have only five. (Newton, 2012).

Examples like this help to remind us that the cultural patterns, codes, and realities we take for granted are not necessarily "true" or "right."

A more theoretically appropriate view is that our cultures are the way they are because we and our ancestors created them in particular ways. We have come to accept their correctness in the same way that other people have come to accept the rightness of their cultures—through communication.

## Cultures Change over Time

Cultures and subcultures do not exist in a vacuum. We carry the influence of these cultures with us as we participate in any number of relationships, groups, and organizations. As we as individuals change, we provide an impetus for the change of cultures of which we are a part. In this sense we are each agents of cultural change.

In addition to natural, evolutionary cultural developments that inevitably occur, other cultural changes occur in a more intentional revolutionary way. In recent years, for example, concerned African Americans, Latinos, women, LGBTQ people, and physically challenged individuals have focused attention on discriminatory conventions and practices that have become a part of our society's culture. Efforts by members of these groups (and their allies) have not only accelerated and directed cultural developments within the society as a whole but have undoubtedly had an impact on the cultures of relationships, groups, and organizations, as well.

## A Word of Caution

Efforts to identify and classify cultures based on an analysis of the identification of similarities and differences among them has a long academic tradition. The results of this research are helpful for understanding the nature of culture, cultural difference, and the processes through which cultures develop and evolve (Kim, 1999). This kind of research can also have a very practical value for those seeking to understand and function effectively in particular cultures or in cross-cultural settings in general.

In undertaking this kind of analysis, and in using the information which results, there is the very real danger of cultural stereotyping (which in the extreme can result in "racial profiling")—a practice of adopting and sometimes acting on unfounded generalizations about people from particular national, regional, religious, ethnic, or other groups. It is important to remember that what can be said about a group never fully applies to the individual people who comprise it. In our efforts to classify and understand the commonalities within other cultures, we would do well to remind ourselves of the incredible diversity that we find within our own culture and the many subcultural groups within it and to recognize that a similar degree of diversity exists in other cultures and subcultures, as well.

## THE ROLE OF MEDIATED COMMUNICATION

Many institutions within society contribute to the creation, perpetuation, and evolution of culture. Families play a very basic part in this process, as do places of worship, schools, corporations, the government, and the business community. Mediated communication also plays an indispensable role.

Mediated communication extends our creating, duplicating, and storing capabilities. Our technology broadens the pool of messages available in common to individuals. Some of these mediated messages relate to our relational, group, and organizational cultures. Texting, email, and photographs serve this purpose for relationships, in much the same way that social media, printed constitutions, badges, and emblems serve this function for groups. Websites, posters, brochures, and newsletters, similarly, contribute to and reflect the culture of organizations. At the societal level, the cultural contribution of mediated communication is immense. Mass media institutions such as newspapers, radio, television, books, and film have long played a fundamental role in packaging and transmitting cultural information, as do libraries and museums (Budd & Ruben, 1988; Hunt & Ruben, 1992; Schiller, 1989). The Internet and social media now have a central role in contributing to these cultural dynamics, too.

As we will discuss in the next chapter, political communication, advertising, and public relations also contribute to our cultural information base. Advertisements for commercial products promote our market-based economic system and urge us to become consumers. Sporting events provide another interesting illustration of the ways in which mediated and mass communication can serve as a carrier of cultural messages. Even video games provide implicit cultural messages. Games that have a reset button that allows players to start over without any consequences or a pause control that allows them to take a break from a particular game and return later are luxuries that aren't available in everyday encounters.

Mass communication also plays a role in commercializing cultural symbols. Not only people (for example, Beyoncé, Taylor Swift, Martha Stewart, or Alexander Wang), but also fictional characters (such as Big Bird, Spiderman, or Mickey Mouse) are commercialized through mass communication. So, too, mass communication is essential in the commercialization of places, for example, Disney World, Central Park, Cancún, Las Vegas, New York, and Paris.

Mediated messages are a kind of cultural mirror, combining with the messages of face-to-face communication to provide a menu and an agenda of concerns, issues, values, personalities, images, and themes that occupy a central role in the symbolic environment to which individuals must adapt. In this way, mediated communication plays a fundamental role in the socialization process of the individual and in so doing contributes at the same time to the stability and order of social systems (Duncan, 1985).

## CULTURAL ADAPTATION

Adapting to a culture occurs through communication and social influence. It involves learning appropriate personal representations, maps, rules, and images of the relationships, groups, organizations, and society of which we are members (see Figure 12.5).

Most of the learning is natural and inevitable. We would learn to speak our native language by listening to people talking, for example, whether we were ever formally taught it or not. We absorb cultures—become Koreans, Kenyans, Italians, Syrians—with virtually no effort or awareness on our part that it is happening. Even less obviously, we adapt to and absorb the cultures of relationships, groups, and organizations in which we become involved. We take on the cultural conventions of our friends, family, ethnic groups, religious orientations, professions, and society with little effort on our part.

Cultural adaptation also involves active persuasion, as with the education provided by family members, religious institutions, and schools aimed at providing the knowledge, values, and rules that others deem necessary.

Because we tend so easily and so thoroughly to adapt to our own cultures, it is often a difficult and stressful matter to readjust to others. Newly retired, divorced, or widowed people, for instance, often find the adjustment to the cultures of their new situation extremely difficult. Adjusting to the subculture of a prison often presents the same problems; and, once this adjustment has taken place, readjustment upon release to the culture of the world outside the prison can be even more difficult.

These kinds of adjustments can result in what has been called *culture shock*—feelings of helplessness, withdrawal, paranoia, irritability, and a desire for a home, among other symptoms (Koester, 1984). Initially, culture shock was thought to be a disease—a form of mental illness exhibited by people who were suddenly transplanted from one geographic location to another (Foster, 1962). This perspective has been replaced by the idea that culture shock is a feeling of dis-ease which results from the "reduced ability to interact within the social and communication structure of the different society" (Barna, 1976, p. 4). According to Barna (1976), people who are experiencing culture shock are not able to be good communicators since they are distracted by "internal noise" and aren't able to pay adequate attention to the messages they are sending or receiving (p. 14). Suggestions for avoiding culture shock include learning as much as you can about the culture you are going to enter, exposing yourself to different types of people and worldviews so that listening to others becomes interesting instead of threatening, and becoming secure in your own identity.

**FIGURE 12.5**

Intercultural communication scholar Young Yun Kim reminds us that millions of people change homes each year, crossing cultural boundaries. Immigrants and refugees resettle in search of a new life, side by side with temporary sojourners finding employment overseas as artists, musicians, writers, accountants, teachers, and construction workers. As well, diplomats and other governmental agency employees, business managers, Peace Corps volunteers, researchers, professors, military personnel, and missionaries carry out their work overseas for varying lengths of time. Individuals such as these are the contemporary pioneers venturing into an unfamiliar terrain where many of the "business-as-usual" ways of doing things lose their relevance. Even relatively short-term sojourners, such as exchange students, must be at least minimally concerned with building a healthy functional relationship to the host environment in ways similar to the native population. As they confront their predicaments and actively engage in new learning, they are embarking on a gradual, long-term process of growth beyond their original cultural perimeters. As we undertake this project of cross-cultural adaptation, we are also embarking on a path of personal development—one in which we stretch ourselves out of the familiar and reach for a deepened and more inclusive understanding of human conditions, including our own.

© Blend Images/Shutterstock.com

## Stages of Cultural Adaptation

There have been numerous attempts to describe and delineate the stages of cultural adaptation (Kealey, 1978; Kim, 1988; Ward, Bochner & Furaham, 2001). These researchers suggest that there are generally four phases (illustrated in Figure 12.6):

1. Phase 1 is a "honeymoon" period during which people adjusting to a new culture are excited by the novelty of the people and new surroundings or situations.

2. Phase 2 is a period in which fascination and novelty often turn into frustration, anxiety, and even hostility, as the realities of life in an unfamiliar environment or circumstance become more apparent.

3. Phase 3 marks the beginning of the readjustment process, as people begin to develop ways of coping with their frustrations and the challenge of the new situation.

4. In Phase 4, the readjustment continues. During this period, several outcomes are possible. Many people regain their balance and comfort level, developing meaningful relationships and an appreciation of the new culture. Other people are unable fully to accept the new culture but find a way to cope with it adequately for their purposes. A third response is simply to find a way to "make the best of it," though with substantial personal discomfort and strain. Some people are unable to reach even this level of adjustment and find their only alternative is to retreat from the situation.

When a person is adjusting to the culture of a new society thousands of miles from home, where the geography, climate, rituals, customs, religious observances, lifestyles, daily practices, and languages are unfamiliar, cultural adaptation may be a very intense and stressful experience.

The same dynamics of adaptation occur in more common circumstances. Any time we move from one area to another, enter a new relationship, start a new job, move in with new roommates, or find ourselves in a novel situation, we are likely to go through these same stages of adaptation as the adjustment to new people, new expectations, new symbols, and new cultural realities takes place.

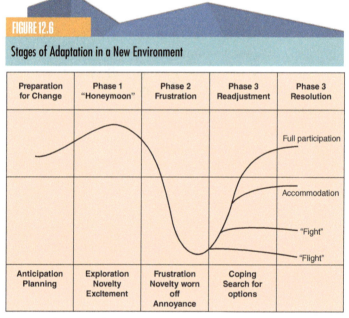

FIGURE 12.6

Stages of Adaptation in a New Environment

| Preparation for Change | Phase 1 "Honeymoon" | Phase 2 Frustration | Phase 3 Readjustment | Phase 3 Resolution |
|---|---|---|---|---|
| | | | | Full participation |
| | | | | Accommodation |
| | | | | "Fight" |
| | | | | "Flight" |
| Anticipation Planning | Exploration Novelty Excitement | Frustration Novelty worn off Annoyance | Coping Search for options | |

Source: Based on review of literature on stages of adaptation presented in *Adaptation to a New Environment*, by Daniel J. Kealey (Ottawa, Canada: Canadian International Agency, Briefing Centre, 1978).

Often, the initial enthusiasm in a new country, community, job, organization, relationship, or situation gives way to frustration, disappointment, and even some degree of depression, as it becomes apparent that the new situation is not all we had imagined it would be. Gradually, we begin to adapt, as we revise our expectations, develop new understanding, and apply the skills necessary to cope with the new relationship, group, organization, or circumstance. In some instances, we adjust fully. In others, we give the appearance of fitting in but never really become comfortable.

## INTERCULTURAL COMMUNICATION

Understandably, the topic of intercultural communication has become a very popular area of study and practice in recent years. Many writings in the field are dedicated to providing an overview of theory and research in the area (e.g., Gudykunst & Kim, 2003; Lustig & Koester, 2015; Samovar, Porter, McDaniel, & Roy, 2015; Ting-Toomey & Chung, 2012).

What, exactly, is intercultural communication? Whenever we interact with someone from another culture, we are engaged in *intercultural communication.* Given our definition of culture, this means that every communication situation is intercultural to some degree. In any communication situation, each person brings unique symbols, meanings, preferences, and life experiences that reflect the many cultures of which he or she has been a part of over the course of his or her lifetime.

As we meet new people, we are in the process of negotiating the beginnings of new relationships and relational cultures. From the first moments of contact between two people, we begin a process of intercultural communication, mutual exploration, negotiation, and accommodation. At the instant we take notice of another person, we don't know whether we have similar knowledge levels, backgrounds, orientations toward time, political philosophies, gestural patterns, greeting forms, religious orientations, or even a common language capability. And we don't know whether or not we have had similar experiences in previous relationships, groups, or organizations, but in any event those previous experiences and the associated cultures provide the guide for these new encounters.

As we interact, we use communication to reduce our uncertainty about the situation and the people involved (Gudykunst & Kim, 2003). We talk and listen to one another. We take account of appearance, dress, adornments, posture, and walk. Gradually, we begin to acquire information that helps us to determine what we have in common and where we differ. As the process continues, the pool of common information available to us grows steadily and with it the possibilities of which we are becoming a part.

While the process may sound quite simple, the complexities and potential challenges are substantial—the greater the cultural gap, the greater the complexity and challenge.

Every communication situation is somewhat intercultural in the sense that no two people have precisely the same cultural backgrounds. The greater the difference in cultural backgrounds, the greater the communication challenge, and the less likely that "message sent" will equal "message received." However, some situations in which we assume that there are no major cultural differences—for instance, both people were raised in the United States and speak English as their first language—can still present major intercultural challenges as a result of differing family, religious, ethnic, occupational, or geographic influences.

Brinkmann and van Weerdenburg (2014) offer a model that they call the Intercultural Readiness Check (IRC) which includes four competencies that they believe are necessary for effective communication across cultures: (1) intercultural sensitivity, (2) intercultural communication, (3) building commitment, and (4) managing uncertainty (see Table 12.1). Although this model was designed for work teams, it can be applied in interpersonal and group contexts as well.

Researchers (Gudykunst & Kim, 2003; Kim, 1988; Ruben, 1978, 2015; Ruben & Kealey, 1979) have identified and discussed a number of potentially important components of intercultural communication competence—many of which apply to communication competence within our own cultures, too. These include:

- Respect for people whose behaviors and cultures differ from our own
- Ability to accept the relativity of one's own view of "right" and "wrong"
- Willingness to acquire knowledge of others' cultures
- Empathy for others' situations
- Sensitivity to cultural differences in language, conversational rules, and nonverbal behavior
- A nonjudgmental approach to different cultural patterns
- Tolerance for new and ambiguous situations
- Self-awareness

# SOCIETIES (COMPLEX CULTURAL AND COMMUNICATION SYSTEMS)

A *society* is a complex social system composed of a large number of diverse, geographically dispersed, and mutually dependent people, groups, and organizations in pursuit of interrelated goals. Societies—like other social systems—are created, defined, and maintained through communication.

## National and International Networks

Two types of communication networks are basic to the functioning of a society: (1) national networks and (2) international networks. *National networks* are the pathways *within* a society that

Ursula Brinkmann and Oscar van Weerdenburg, *Intercultural Readiness*, published 2014, Palgrave MacMillan. Reproduced with permission of Palgrave MacMillan.

**TABLE 12.1**

The four IRC competencies and their facets.

| INTERCULTURAL SENSITIVITY | |
|---|---|
| The degree to which we are actively interested in other people's cultural backgrounds, their needs and perspectives. | |
| **Facet 1: Cultural Awareness** | **Facet 2: Attention to Signals** |
| The ability to see our own interpretations, norms and values as culture-specific and to consider different cultural perspectives as equally valid. | The extent to which we seek information about others' thoughts and feelings by paying attention to verbal and nonverbal signals when interacting with them. |
| **INTERCULTURAL COMMUNICATION** | |
| The degree to which we actively monitor how we communicate with people from other cultures. | |
| **Facet 1: Active Listening** | **Facet 2: Adapting Communicative Style** |
| The degree to which we are mindful when communicating with others, and pays due attention to their expectations and needs. | The degree to which we adjust how we communicate in order to fine-tune a message in line with cultural requirements. |
| **BUILDING COMMITMENT** | |
| The degree to which we actively try to influence our social environment, based on a concern for relationships and integrating people and concerns. | |
| **Facet 1: Building Relationships** | **Facet 2: Reconciling Stakeholder Needs** |
| The degree to which we invest in developing relationships and diverse networks of contacts. | The degree to which we seek to understand the interests of different stakeholders, and can create solutions to meet these needs. |
| **MANAGING UNCERTAINTY** | |
| The degree to which we see the uncertainty and complexity of culturally diverse environments as an opportunity for personal development. | |
| **Facet 1: Openness to Cultural Diversity** | **Facet 2: Exploring New Approaches** |
| The degree to which we are willing to deal with the added complexity of culturally diverse environments. | The degree to which we are stimulated by diversity as a source of learning and innovation, and risks trying out new ideas. |

connect individuals, groups, and organizations to one another (see Figure 12.7). The functions served by these networks include:

- Providing societies with access to the information necessary to identify and adapt to the needs and challenges of the environment and the world community
- Providing the means through which information is conveyed among members of a society
- Facilitating the coordination of often-diverse activities of individuals, groups, and organizations within a society
- Supplying the channel through which collective decisions are made and implemented

In a democratic society, many of the critical linkages in the national network are provided by people elected by or chosen to represent a particular group or organization. Members of a community select people to represent their concerns and points of view to other groups at a regional or state level. At a still higher level, representatives from regions, states, and other groups and organizations join together to pool information, discuss common concerns, set priorities, and make decisions for the society as a whole.

This process of collaboration and collective decision making results in the creation of recommendations, policies, and laws. Information about these deliberations and their outcomes is then distributed to members of the society using a variety of pathways. Internet sites and social media play an increasingly important role in this regard, contributing to the role traditionally played by news media and public affairs programming, political communication, campaigning, government publications, websites, and other mass communication channels in combination with interpersonal communication. Collectively, these national networks create what Karl Deutsch (1966) termed the "nerves of government." Besides national networks that are so essential to the functioning of a society, *international networks* are also extremely important. These transnational networks are linkages *between* societies.

Interpersonal contact by tourists, diplomatic personnel, and representatives to the United Nations and other international agencies plays an important role in linking societies to one another. Other pathways are those created through international news and entertainment programming, sports and cultural exchanges, international banking transactions, governmental propaganda, and intelligence operations. The role of social media and the Internet have been remarkably pervasive in creating international networks that are contributing to what is quite literally a global village.

**FIGURE 12.7**

**National and International Networks**

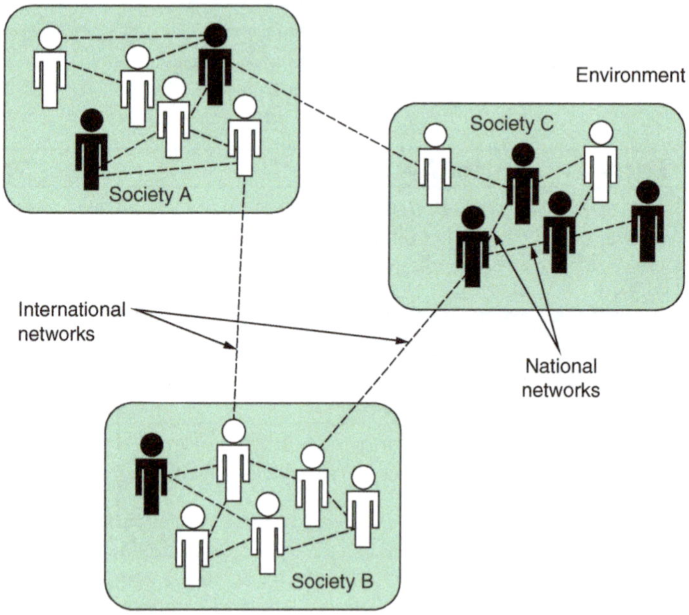

© Kendall Hunt Publishing Co.

# INTERNATIONAL COMMUNICATION: THE GLOBAL VILLAGE—FACT OR FICTION?

One of the most widely read scholars to offer predictions of the future of technology and international communication was Canadian scholar and educator Marshall McLuhan (1964), who pointed optimistically to a future in which citizens of the world would be linked together in a "global village." His 1960s vision of a massive network in which individuals in all societies would be connected through communication has turned out to be a remarkably accurate portrayal of the technologically connected world in which we live.

## Complexities Abound

The recognition that global information sharing is indeed a reality raises new questions as to whether a global village is desirable in all respects. Indeed, some scholars have suggested that some of the barriers being diminished through information and communication technology may be quite important to maintain. Detractors contend that continuous communication across cultural boundaries contributes to a homogenizing effect and fear that valued distinctions between cultures or societies will diminish. People who see this blurring of differences as threatening to the distinctiveness of a particular relationship, group, organization, culture, or society may actively resist intercultural communication and change.

It is also argued that economic dependency on countries that produce communication hardware has implications for dependency on these same providers for content and programming—provided primarily by English-speaking organizations. For example, in 2014 *NCIS* was the most-watched television drama in the world (Kissell, 2014). What would people from other countries who have little contact with people from the United States think if this television program was their primary source of cultural information?

This potential for economic and cultural control raises fundamental questions. Is it possible for an individual, organization, or society to be dependent on others economically and technologically but be uninfluenced by their cultural messages? Or does control of communication media, products, and services imply cultural influence and dependency? Clearly, the challenge is to reap the benefits of global communication without sacrificing individual and cultural integrity and independence in the process.

Another important issue has to do with the nature of communication as it relates to predictions about improvements in international cooperation and understanding. While we can certainly think of many situations where increased communication has contributed to improved intercultural and international relations, we can also identify perhaps as many circumstances where more communication seems to have led to a deterioration in relations. While we could question the quality and effectiveness of the message sending and receiving associated with these circumstances, it is clear that communication was present, though shared understanding often was not.

These concerns remind us that more communication media, networks, messages, and services alone provide no guarantee of improved international understanding or cooperation. We have certainly come to recognize that the capability of communication and the sharing of a common symbolic environment do not automatically lead to shared or converging ways of thinking or behaving, common value orientations, or similar information processing patterns for the people involved.

In all fundamental respects, a war, an argument, or a divorce is as much a product of communication as is peaceful coexistence, a reconciliation, or a marriage. Occasionally, negative outcomes develop because of a lack of a common base of information or reciprocal message processing. More often, however, these results occur because of the *presence* rather than *absence* of communication. As we know, even when two people are confronted by the same messages, their ways of selecting, attaching meaning and significance, and retaining information may inhibit—or even preclude—the chance for mutual understanding, agreement, or convergence. For example, the problem of human rights in many countries of the world does not seem to be the result of a breakdown in reciprocal message processing. Virtually all of us have access to messages relative to the problems of human rights and some awareness of the problem. But access to and awareness of messages are not necessarily good predictors of whether and how the messages will be attended to, interpreted, or used.

The area of international communication and relations provides a vivid example of a fundamental communication insight—more message sending doesn't necessarily make things better. This is an important idea with profound implications for understanding the complexity of communication in relationships, in general, and in international affairs more specifically.

# CONCLUSION

From the point of view of communication, culture can be defined as the complex combination of common symbols, knowledge, folklore conventions, language, information-processing patterns, rules, rituals, habits, lifestyles, and attitudes that link and give a common identity to a particular group of people at a particular time.

All social systems—relationships, groups, organizations, and societies—develop and maintain cultures through communication. The symbols of a society are among the most visible signs of culture. Cultures link people to one another, provide the basis for a common identity, and create a context for interaction and negotiation. The relationship between culture and communication is reciprocally defining: Through communication we shape our cultures and, in turn, our cultures shape our communication patterns.

Cultures are complex and multifaceted, invisible, and subjective; and cultures change over time. We become aware of cultures through violations of cultural conventions, cross-cultural contact, and scholarly analysis.

Mediated communication plays an important role in the creation and maintenance of cultures. By extending our capacity to create, duplicate, and store messages, our technology broadens the pool of information available in common to people in relationships, groups, organizations, and societies. The cultural information base of a society consists of news, information, and entertainment programming. Mediated messages are a kind of cultural mirror, combining with the messages of face-to-face communication to provide an agenda of concerns, issues, values, personalities, and themes that occupy a central role in the symbolic environment to which individuals must adapt.

Adapting to a culture is a natural process of developing appropriate personal theories, representations, maps, and images of the cultures of which we are members. Because we adapt to our own cultures so easily and thoroughly, it is frequently a difficult and stressful matter to adjust to others' cultures, perhaps resulting in what has been called "culture shock."

We are engaged in intercultural communication when we interact with people from other cultures. Every communication situation involving someone we don't know well is intercultural to some degree. As we meet new people, we negotiate the beginnings of new relationships and new relational cultures.

A society is a complex social system composed of a large number of diverse, geographically dispersed, and mutually dependent people, groups, and organizations in pursuit of common goals. Societies are created, defined, and maintained through communication among the people who compose them. Societies operate by means of national and international networks. These networks provide the means through which information is conveyed among members of a society, facilitate the coordination of diverse activities within a society, and supply the channel through which collective decisions are made and implemented.

In the short run, at least, the presence of communication and commonly available messages are not necessarily more likely to produce convergence than divergence, love than hate, understanding than misunderstanding, peace than war. In the long run, we can be more hopeful that the ever-increasing pool of shared messages—along with common needs and goals—will lead to an increasingly predictable and shared understanding of world cultures. And, while simply increasing the number of communication situations provides no guarantee of improved world relationships, efforts to improve communication competencies, such as listening, empathy, and respect, and others discussed previously, can certainly help to bridge the gap.

## KEY POINTS

After having read this chapter, you should be able to:

- Define the term culture from a communication perspective
- Explain the characteristics of culture
- Analyze the stages of cultural adaptation and the role of communication in responding to cultural change
- Articulate the importance of international communication in today's world

## REFERENCES

Aljazeera. (2013, February 19). Saudi women take seats in Shura council. Retrieved http://www.aljazeera.com/news/middleeast/2013/02/2013219201637132278.html

Barna, L. M. (1976). How culture shock affects communication. *Communication, 5*(1), 1-18.

Bennett, M. (2013, May 10). Culture is not like an iceberg. *ICL Blog.* Retrieved from http://www.afs.org/blog/icl/?p=3385

Brinkmann, U., & van Weerdenburg, O. (2014). *Intercultural readiness: Four competencies for working across cultures.* New York, NY: Palgrave Macmillan.

Budd, R. W., & Ruben, B. D. (Eds.). (1988). *Beyond media: New approaches to mass communication* (rev. ed.). New Brunswick, NJ: Transaction.

Bureau of Naval Personnel. (1973). *Overseas diplomacy: Guidelines for United States Navy.* Washington, DC: U.S. Government Printing Office.

Deutsch, K. W. (1966). *The nerves of government: Models of political communication and control.* New York, NY: Free Press.

Duncan, H. D. (1985). *Communication and social order.* New Brunswick, NJ: Transaction.

Foster, G. (1962). *Traditional cultures: The impact of technological change.* New York, NY: Harper and Row.

Gudykunst, W. B., & Kim, Y. Y. (2003). *Communicating with strangers: An approach to intercultural communication* (4th ed.). New York, NY: McGraw-Hill.

Hall, E. T. (1959). *The silent language.* New York, NY: Doubleday.

Hall, E. T. (1976). *Beyond culture.* Garden City, NY: Anchor Press/Doubleday.

Hall, E. T., & Hall, M. R. (1990). *Understanding cultural differences: Germans, French, and Americans.* Yarmouth, ME: Intercultural Press.

Hunt, T., & Ruben, B. D. (1992). *Mass communication: Producers and consumers.* New York, NY: HarperCollins.

Kealey, D. J. (1978). *Adaptation to a new environment.* Ottawa, Canada: Canadian International Development Agency, Briefing Centre.

Kim, Y. Y. (1988). *Communication and cross-cultural adaptation.* Clevedon, UK: Multilingual Matters.

Kim, Y. Y. (1999). Unum and pluribus: Ideological underpinnings of interethnic communication in the United States. *International Journal of Intercultural Relations, 23* (4), 591-611.

Kissell, R. (2014, June 11). "NCIS" has become world's most-watched TV drama. *Variety.* Retrieved from http://variety.com/2014/tv/news/ncis-most-popular-drama-in-worldwatched-tv-drama-1201218492/

Koester, J. (1984). Communication and the intercultural reentry: A course proposal. *Communication Education, 33*(3), 251-256.

Lustig, M. W., & Koester, J. (2015). *Intercultural competence* (7th ed.). Boston, MA: Pearson.

McLuhan, M. (1964). *Understanding media: The extensions of man.* London, UK: Routledge & Kegan Paul.

Newton, M. (2012, September 4). It's not easy seeing green. *The New York Times.* Retrieved from http://6thfloor.blogs.nytimes.com/2012/09/04/its-not-easy-seeing-green/

Nimmo, D. D., & Combs, J. E. (1983). *Mediated political realities.* New York, NY: Longman.

Orbe, M. P. (1997). *Constructing co-cultural theory: An explication of culture, power, and communication.* Thousand Oaks, CA: Sage.

Ruben, B. D. (1978). Human communication and cross-cultural effectiveness. *International and International Communication Annual, 4,* 95-105.

Ruben, B. D. (2015). Intercultural communication competence in retrospect: Who would have guessed? *International Journal of Intercultural Relations, 48,* 22-23.

Ruben, B. D., & Kealey, D. J. (1979). Behavioral assessment of communication competency and the prediction of cross-cultural adaptation. *International Journal of Intercultural Relations, 3*(1), 15-47.

Samovar, L. A., Porter, R. E., McDaniel, E. R., & Roy, C. S. (2015). *Intercultural communication: A reader* (14th ed.). Boston, MA: Cengage.

Schiller, H. I. (1989). *Culture inc.: The corporate takeover of public expression.* New York, NY: Oxford University Press.

Tanno, D. V., & Gonzalez, A. (Eds.). (1998). *Communication and identity across cultures.* Thousand Oaks, CA: Sage.

Thayer, L. (1968). *Communication and communication systems: In organization, management and interpersonal relations.* Homewood, IL: Irwin.

Ting-Toomey, S., & Chung, L. C. (2012). *Understanding intercultural communication* (2nd ed.). New York, NY: Oxford University Press.

Ward, C., Bochner, S., & Furaham, A. (2001). *Psychology of culture shock* (2nd ed.). New York, NY: Routledge.

Wolfgang, M. E., & & Ferracuti, F. (Eds.). (1982). *The subculture of violence: Toward an integrated theory in criminology.* Beverly Hills, CA: Sage.

# PUBLIC
# COMMUNICATION

Communication occurs in a number of contexts and forms. In this chapter, we focus on communication that takes place in public—including public speaking, mass communication, political communication, public relations, and advertising. As will become apparent, if it is not already, public communication plays a critical role in creating and disseminating the messages that are central to our activities as individuals and in relationships, groups, communities, organizations, and societies.

## WHAT IS PUBLIC COMMUNICATION?

## THE ROLE OF PUBLIC COMMUNICATION

# UNDERSTANDING PUBLIC COMMUNICATION

- The Speech
- The Presentation

# UNDERSTANDING MASS COMMUNICATION

- Production, Distribution, and Consumption
- Information Products and Services
- The Audience
- Four Basic Functions of Mass Communication
- Political Communication
- Public Relations
- Advertising
- Broader Functions of Public and Mass Communication

# THE EFFECTS OF PUBLIC AND MASS COMMUNICATION

- The Communicator/Producer Perspective
- The Audience/Consumer Perspective
- Uses and Gratifications
- Integrating Perspectives

# CONCLUSION

# KEY POINTS

# WHAT IS PUBLIC COMMUNICATION?

The term *public* communication can be contrasted with interpersonal, group, or organizational communication. These latter forms of communication are generally more private and personal. Public refers to situations in which messages are created and disseminated to a *relatively* large number of receivers, in a setting that is *relatively* impersonal. Public speaking, concerts, theater, and public debates are examples of public communication. Communication involving mass media such as newspaper and magazine articles, television programs, podcasts, movies, and various forms of advertising are also examples.

The term *relatively* is italicized in this definition in the previous paragraph because what is "public" and what is not is often a matter of degree. When, for example, does communication between individuals in a group or organization qualify as public communication? Most of us would agree that when three or four people who know each other well speak to each other it is certainly interpersonal or perhaps group communication, but not public communication. On the other hand, we would get little disagreement that, if the message were presented to 250 people at an annual meeting of a division of an organization or a professional association, it would be "public communication." But what if the communication event consisted of prepared and rehearsed remarks (perhaps via webcast or email) to 5, 10, 25, or 50 people, who didn't know each other all that well? At what point does the situation become "public" communication? It is our view that there is no magical threshold test for when a communication situation is and when it is not public communication. However, there are some general guidelines which are helpful in differentiating these situations from others.

Public communication situations tend to be characterized by:

- An audience. Generally, a large number of people are involved in the event, so much so that a communicator tends to think of intended receivers in aggregate terms—as an audience rather than as individuals. Giving a speech to a class would fit the definition, while rehearsing a speech in front of your roommates would not.
- Impersonality. The source often does not know all the participants personally, and this lack of knowledge, the situation, and the number of people involved make it difficult for a communicator to send "personalized" messages. Even though a speaker may know some receivers very well, he or she may not be able to acknowledge or make use of this knowledge and must instead use a "to whom it may concern" approach.
- Planned, predictable, and formal. The public communication process is planned, predictable, and/or formalized. The physical setting in which an event (a public speech or network news program) takes place may be arranged in a particular way (e.g., seating or layout of a setting) and may follow a predetermined agenda.
- Source control. The source has disproportionate control over determining what messages are created and disseminated. For example, the speaker sets and manages the agenda and determines the content (see Figure 13.1).
- Limited interactivity (feedback). Audience members have limited means of reacting to the source or his or her message and have little ability to shape the course of the communication event. "Negotiation" of the content does not occur in the sense we're used to experiencing in interpersonal or most group settings. In most mass communication situations, the message sender and the act of message sending is separated from the message receiver and the act of receiving in time, space, or both, often making interaction and feedback difficult. Often the feedback a speaker receives is too delayed to alter the source's current content. If, during a speech, a speaker notices that half the audience is yawning, the speaker can adapt and liven up the material. If, however, an audience member does not appreciate the sexist

nature of a television's reporter's language, then he or she could post a comment online and hope that the reporter will receive the message and care enough to try to prevent future occurrences of such language. In an interpersonal context, this delay would not occur, and a speaker could almost instantly amend his or her language to best suit the audience.

- **SOURCE CENTRALITY.** The source has easy and direct access to all receivers, but receivers may not have the same access to one another. For

**FIGURE 13.1**

Public communication often takes place in formal, carefully arranged settings.

example, a politician speaking on television addresses all members of the viewing audience; however, members of the audience cannot address one another. Of course, social media are breaking down some of these barriers with technology such as live tweeting.

# THE ROLE OF PUBLIC COMMUNICATION

Although the differences between public communication and other forms of communication are sometimes a matter of degree, these forms and contexts of communication are important to understand in their own right precisely because of the characteristics listed above: (1) a large number of people are typically involved in the audience; (2) the communication event is planned, relatively predictable, formal, and impersonal; (3) the source exercises great control over message content, with little opportunity for interaction with or among recipients; and (4) in the case of mass communication, media are involved that tend to further extend the reach of human communication and their role in shaping our cultures (see Figure 13.2). In addition to the familiar public and mass communication channels, many institutions within society contribute to the creation, perpetuation, and evolution of culture. Schools play a very basic part in the creation, distribution, and sharing of culture, as do churches, governments, and the business community.

# UNDERSTANDING PUBLIC COMMUNICATION

One of the most common public communication events is the public speech. It is important to remember in a public communication context that both the speech and its presentation can and should be considered separately. Obviously, the speech does not exist apart from its presentation. From a practical point of view, however, preparing a speech and preparing a presentation are separate phases of a public communication situation.

## The Speech

Preparation for a speech falls into four general categories (adapted from Bradley, 1991; Lucas, 2012):

**FIGURE 13.2**

Health communication researcher Itzhak Yanovitzky has found that many public health communication campaigns influence the behavior of target audiences indirectly by promoting change in public health policy (e.g., laws mandating stiffer penalties for drunk driving, increasing taxes on tobacco products, and banning smoking in public parks). These policies change society's views of a particular behavior (e.g., making smoking less socially acceptable) and result in changes in individuals' behavior.

© Winning7799/Shutterstock.com

1. **PREPARING TO CREATE THE SPEECH.** This step involves:
   - Discovering ideas and evidence
   - Gathering and organizing information
   - Assessing the audience
   - Analyzing and focusing the topic
   - Developing a thesis
   - Reaching conclusions
2. **DRAFTING THE SPEECH.** At this point, public communicators try to give a structure and form to their presentation. This step involves creating introductions and conclusions, using evidence to support major conclusions, developing and placing specific examples, and developing visual aids.
3. **REVISING.** This step may involve major changes to the presentation. In this step, the communicator pays particular attention to structure, logic, evidence, examples, and further

development. The speaker must make sure that he or she has given the audience what they need to be informed, persuaded, or for other intended communication goals to be realized.

4. **EDITING.** This step consists of fine-tuning. During this stage the speaker pays particular attention to mechanics such as transitions between major points, delivery and appearance, citing sources, and presentation style.

## The Presentation

Preparing the presentation consists of the following four stages:

1. The first and most important activity is *preparing the speech,* as described previously. Once this is done, preparation for the presentation can begin.

2. *Rehearsal.* The public communication event (for example, a speech, a concert, a play) should be rehearsed. Depending on the formality of the situation, a dress rehearsal may be held that includes simulating the situation as closely as possible. Anyone who has ever participated in a wedding rehearsal knows how important it is to completely prepare for the event so that everyone knows his or her role. Less formal events call for rehearsals that help plan the timing of the event or speech and familiarize speakers with the setting and any technology to be used in the presentation.

3. Advanced preparation includes *developing flexible presentation strategies* (such as changes in the length of the presentation or additional visual aids) that can be used as necessary to react to feedback from the audience. For example, if an audience seems confused by a presentation, the effective public communicator is ready to explain major points in more detail or to provide additional examples. If the audience appears bored or already familiar with some of the ideas being presented, a good speaker will condense parts of the presentation or vary his or her vocal tone, speak directly about issues of concern to the audience, or use more interesting visual aids to win back the attention of the audience.

4. *Other presentation elements* such as clothing need to be attended to before a public communication event. Dress is an important unifying force for audiences and speakers. Politicians often wear caps with particular insignias to indicate that they identify with their audience. This type of nonverbal cue signifies the message, "I'm one of you." On other occasions, the public communicator may want to distance himself or herself from the audience. Religious leaders often wear different clothing while conducting services in order to reinforce their roles as spiritual advisors.

Although we have discussed these steps as if they were sequential, in reality the sequence may be adjusted based upon the circumstances.

## Audience Analysis and Adaptation.

Effective public communication always involves consideration of the audience. Simple demographics are the most basic information that is necessary to find out about an audience. For example, people of any age may be interested in learning about a new technique for fly fishing if they are fishing enthusiasts. On the other hand, it would be unwise to speak about casino gambling to a group of people who do not gamble because of their religious beliefs. The importance of any given demographic factor varies depending on the speaker and the topic of the speech.

Some demographic features that may be important in planning a public presentation include age, gender, race, ethnicity, religion, socioeconomic status, country of origin, educational level, language spoken at home, sexual orientation, gender identity, and geographical location.

**FIGURE 13.3**

Ida B. Wells (1862–1931) was an investigative journalist who delivered public speeches in the United States and Europe on civil rights and women's suffrage. She was one of the founders of the NAACP.

IDA B. WELLS.

© Everett Historical/Shutterstock.com

A good speech is adapted to a particular audience to the degree that the speaker would have to change it (by modifying examples or word choice, for example) for another audience. If a speaker can deliver a speech to another audience without making any changes, the speech is not specific enough for the intended audience.

**Developing a Purpose and a Thesis.** As we discussed earlier, one of the major differences between public communication and interpersonal communication is that public communication usually has a predetermined purpose established by the communicator. In arriving at the purpose, a communicator needs to answer three general questions with respect to the potential audience for the message (Lucas, 2012):

- To whom am I speaking?
- What do I want them to know, believe, or do as a result of my speech?
- What is the most effective way of composing and presenting my speech to accomplish that aim? (p. 98)

In interpersonal communication, ideas may be presented spontaneously without much advance preparation. In a public communication event, a great deal of time is usually devoted to advance thinking about who the audience is, what we want them to gain from listening to us, and what strategies will best accomplish these goals.

One of the ways in which public communicators clarify the purpose for their speeches is through the development of a thesis. The *thesis* of a speech is the one main definite idea to which all others are subordinated. If we think of the topic of the speech as a question, then the thesis is the answer to that question. It is a specific statement of purpose.

Effective theses are (McCrimmon, 1974):

1. RESTRICTED. A good thesis limits the scope of what can be discussed in detail in the time allotted to a speech. For example, trying to describe the changing roles of women on television in the last two decades in five minutes would be extremely ambitious. A 20-minute speech on the changing role of the main characters in a specific program would be a more restricted and reasonable idea.
2. UNIFIED. A thesis should present one dominant idea. There may be more than one idea a communicator wants to convey, but they should all be unified by some other idea. For example, an effect may have more than one cause so that a speaker may need to discuss three causes, but these causes are united under a single common theme.
3. PRECISE. In a good thesis, a restricted, unified idea is presented with clarity. There should only be one possible interpretation. There is no place for ambiguous or vague language (e.g., "voting for this candidate will make all the difference") or clichés (e.g., "time will tell," "opposites attract," or "every cloud has a silver lining") in an effective thesis. (adapted from pp. 16-18)

Without an effective thesis we often end up treating the entire subject area as a thesis and rambling around purposelessly. We may be providing accurate information to the audience, but it has no clear point. In addition, we have no criteria for selecting and ordering material so we leave ourselves open to the audience asking, "What is the point of this?" Effective public communicators always ask themselves, "What exactly about my subject is the point?" When listening to public presentations, we can judge their effectiveness using these criteria to examine the thesis presented.

MAKING AN ARGUMENT. Making an argument, or *persuasion,* is an attempt to win over or convince an audience to agree with a particular position or to pursue some course of action. There are two general approaches to making an argument: *emotional appeals* which produce belief and *reasoned appeals* which produce conviction. For example, a speaker who graphically describes the aftermath of an accident that resulted from drunk driving is using emotional appeals to persuade an audience not to drink and drive. A speaker who presents numerous facts demonstrating the negative consequences of credit card debt is using reasoned appeals to persuade an audience not to abuse their credit cards.

There are many techniques that are used in efforts to persuade audiences, for example (Bradley, 1991; Kearney & Plax, 1996):

- Using repetition
- Associating one's claim with something already thought of positively by the audience or associating opposing claims with something already thought of negatively by the audience
- Purposely omitting relevant information
- Using emotional, connotative language
- Using emotional appeals such as guilt, fear, or love (see Figure 13.4)
- Appealing to human needs such as the need for ego gratification, reassurance of worth, emotional and physical security, love, creative outlets, power, roots, or immortality
- Creating cognitive dissonance by presenting inconsistent ideas
- Arguing from ethos, or the source's credibility
- Appealing to cultural values
- Using content appeals based on reasoning and evidence

While persuasive public communicators may make use of some or all of these approaches, effective and ethical persuasion should be based heavily on content appeals using reasoning and evidence. Except with hostile audiences in cases in which the goal is to change the direction of already held attitudes, content appeals should be balanced with controlled emotional and other appeals as long as those appeals work within the structure of the argument. With hostile audiences speakers need to be as unemotional as possible, because any emotion aroused in the audience will intensify

**FIGURE 13.4**

Using emotional appeals in a speech may be effective in changing your audience's attitudes, but such appeals don't give them any information to use if they are confronted later by someone arguing the opposite point of view.

© Peshkova/Shutterstock.com

already held attitudes. Unless the goal is to reinforce these pre-existing attitudes, all content appeals should use two-sided arguments in which the speaker both provides positive arguments for his or her claims and raises and refutes strong arguments for opposing claims.

Public communicators can develop effective arguments by following these suggestions:

- Make limited claims
- Avoid overstatement, including words such as *never*, *always*, or *everyone*
- Be open about uncertainties
- Control tone—especially avoid over-emotionalism
- Avoid frequent or heavy use of sarcasm
- In addition to using solid reasoning and credible evidence, use devices to keep the audience's attention and sympathy (e.g., intelligent use of understatement, overstatement, metaphor, allusion, humor, or controlled emotions is effective)
- Be sure to produce a clear, logical structure for the presentation with a clear purpose at all points

**USE OF EVIDENCE.** Evidence to support an argument consists of a series of reasons or facts, details, examples, references, and quotations. Facts do not speak for themselves; they only speak for those who know how to use them, to put them in a strategic place, and to explain their significance. It is important for a speaker to choose a thesis based on an examination of evidence rather than choosing the evidence to support the thesis. Evidence should be used wisely. There is no need to use evidence to support statements that you can reasonably expect an audience to accept without support. Statements that are needed to make a persuasive point, however, should be supported.

An easy way to check if evidence is necessary is to use a three-level pyramid structure with your thesis at the peak as the first level. At level two, put those statements which, if accepted, would persuade an audience to accept the thesis. At level three, provide evidence for all level two statements that members of the audience might hesitate to accept (Jensen, 1981; Larson, 1995). Little time has to be spent giving evidence to support level three statements, which ought to be non-controversial facts.

**VISUAL AIDS.** There are four types of visual aids that help public communicators convey their messages to large audiences:

1. The *actual object* being talked about (e.g., a person giving a presentation on dog grooming might demonstrate on a real dog)
2. A *model* of the object (e.g., demonstrating on a toy dog)
3. *Mediated objects* (e.g., using pictures or videos of dogs being groomed)
4. *Mediated models* (e.g., charts or diagrams with information on appropriate methods of dog grooming)

Visual aids function to add interest to a presentation by giving the audience something to examine. They may also clarify what the speaker is saying by providing a visual illustration of the points being made. In addition, visual aids like PowerPoint, Keynote, or Prezi can jog a speaker's memory and be used as visual "notes."

There are several guidelines for preparing effective visual aids:

- *Make them visible.* It is frustrating for an audience to be shown a visual aid that is not easily visible. Good public communicators make sure their visual aids are large enough to be seen. Remember that a slide that looks good on a computer screen may not show up effectively when projected to a large auditorium.
- *Make them simple.* Avoid too much detail to keep the visual aid from being confusing. Omit information that is not directly relevant to your thesis.
- *Make them complete.* Although it is important to make visual aids simple, it is also important to present all the needed visual information. Don't leave out important information or the audience may be confused.
- *Make them appropriate.* Good visual aids fit the purpose, tone, and content of the presentation. If the speech is a serious one designed to persuade an audience not to drink and drive, demonstrating a drinking game would not be appropriate, but explaining how much alcohol is in a particular drink would be.
- *Make them communicative.* Good visual aids add something to the speech. Speakers use them because they have a purpose, not just for appearances.
- *Make them relevant.* It is important to display a visual aid only when you are talking about the subject and remove it as soon as you have moved on to another point. If you have finished speaking about methods of dog grooming and are now talking about how much to charge, for example, it will distract the audience if you still have a picture of a dog on display (see Figure 13.5).

**FIGURE 13.5**

Having too many things to look at during your presentation is distracting for your audience.

© Andresr/Shutterstock.com

**MEDIATED PRESENTATIONS.** Access to technology and the Internet has contributed to an increased use of mediated presentations. Examples of mediated public speaking include: producing a presentation as part of a course requirement and sharing it online; completing a job interview via Skype or another mediated software; or using a videoconferencing platform (e.g., Adobe Connect, GoToMeeting) to deliver a presentation to a client located across the world (Fraleigh & Tuman, 2014). The preparation principles discussed earlier in this chapter are certainly applicable to a mediated presentation. However, presenters in a mediated speech should also carefully consider and plan for the effective set-up and operation of the necessary technology and hardware (e.g., camera, recording software). In addition, in almost all cases of mediated presentations, the speaker will face a *virtual audience.* This means that an effective mediated presentation should be designed to appeal to audience members who are in different locations from the speaker and, in the best case scenario, can only be seen via a camera window.

**COMMUNICATION APPREHENSION.** Communication apprehension, anxiety before and during a public communication event, is a natural part of the public communication experience. Almost everyone feels anxiety when speaking or performing in front of a large audience. In fact, some communication scholars have argued that a slight degree of anxiety leads to better performances because people who do not feel any anxiety may fail to adequately prepare for a public communication event and, therefore, not perform to the best of their abilities. Thus, controlled anxiety may be desirable for effective performance.

The normal range of communication apprehension can be controlled by several techniques (adapted, in part, from Bradley, 1991, pp. 33-38):

- *Attitude:* Face each public communication opportunity as a challenge to get a message to a large audience and not as an insurmountable obstacle.
- *Experience:* The more experience a person has in public communication situations, the easier it is to face the next situation.
- *Preparation:* Never attempt to "just wing it" during a public communication event. Even speeches that seem totally spontaneous may have been thought out far in advance. Obviously, it is impossible to have a comment memorized for every public situation we might ever face, but some type of advance preparation will improve our performance in almost any type of public or mediated event.
- *Gestures:* Often gestures that are appropriate for interpersonal communication situations "get lost" in a public communication context. Effective public communicators learn to modify or enlarge their natural repertoire of gestures to reach a larger audience. Gestures can often be an effective way to manage our anxiety by using extra energy that otherwise might get transformed into nervous habits like excessive blinking or gripping the podium too tightly (see Figure 13.6).

- *Remembering that most physiological reactions are not perceived by the audience:* It is important to remember that the audience rarely perceives the anxiety a public communicator may feel. Even when they do, signs of slight anxiety such as a wavering voice or shaking hands will usually be perceived with empathy and not criticism.
- *Talking to the audience as individuals, not just as a group:* Mild anxiety can often be managed by addressing remarks to individual members of the audience. Talking directly to several people makes a public communication situation seem more interpersonal in nature. It is often easier to think about the individual people in an audience and their opinions rather than to try to address the group as a collective.

Making eye contact with individuals in an audience can often help to allay anxiety. Many people become anxious when talking to a group, but their anxiety is lessened when they begin to "talk to" particular people in the audience. Receiving individual feedback instead of just seeing a sea of faces is often enough to turn an anxiety-provoking public communication event into a more pleasant, rewarding experience.

*Recognizing that audience members usually are friendly and want the speaker to succeed:* Most audiences are composed of individuals who would like the speaker to do a good job. Audiences are rarely openly hostile to a speaker. Knowing that the audience is on the speaker's side can help an individual to be a more effective speaker. Sometimes, however, we know that the audience disagrees with us. This often occurs in a persuasive speaking situation when we are trying to convince an audience to change their attitudes. Nevertheless, even if the audience is antagonistic toward a speaker's opinion or point of view, audience members still want the speaker to give a good presentation.

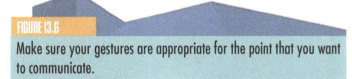
FIGURE 13.6

Make sure your gestures are appropriate for the point that you want to communicate.

© geliatida/Shutterstock.com

# UNDERSTANDING MASS COMMUNICATION

Mass communication is an extension of public communication. Particularly where traditional mass media are involved, the informative, persuasive, or entertaining messages of public communication efforts can be amplified, multiplied, duplicated, and distributed far beyond the context of a lecture hall or concert with the aid of communication technology.

As with public communication, mass communication is generally a more formalized, planned, and purposeful process than face-to-face communication. To a greater extent than in many other contexts of communication, economic considerations also are important. The production of news or television programming, advertisements, and political campaigns are extremely expensive undertakings. Developing websites and maintaining a social media presence also involve expenses. And, as we shall see, questions of social impact are also important when one considers mass communication because of the potential for the rapid and widespread distribution of messages made possible by traditional and new media.

## Production, Distribution, and Consumption

The Industrial Revolution (about 1760 to 1840) began an age in which the mass production, distribution, and consumption of *manufactured goods* was central to the economic and social fabric of our society. In a similar way, the communication revolution has brought us to an age in which the basic commodity is *information*. Mass communication organizations produce, distribute, and market information products and services (Hunt & Ruben, 1993; Ruben, Reis, Iverson & Hunt, 2010). The P-I-C framework (illustrated in Figure 13.7) includes the following components:

- *Production* refers to the creation, gathering, packaging, or repackaging of information.
- *Information production and distribution* from the point where messages are created to the point where they are available to consumers. The movement may occur immediately, as with a live television broadcast, or it may involve substantial time delays, as with magazines, books, films, or recorded programs.
- *Consumption* refers to the uses, impacts, and effects that mass communication can have for a single individual, relationship, group, organization, or society. Examples include: being informed, entertained, persuaded, educated, amused, motivated, or deceived. For a society, the influences of mass communication may be social, political, cultural, economic, or technological.

**FIGURE 13.7**

**Model of Mass Communication**

**P Production** → **I Information Products and Services** → **C Consumption**

**Description:**
Mass communication organizations create and distribute information products and/or services

**Organizations:**
- Television networks
- Newspaper publishers
- Movie producers
- Magazine publishers
- Book publishers
- Record companies
- Advertising agencies
- Public relations firms
- Libraries
- Museums
- Information services
- Etc.

**Description:**
Information products and/or services are distributed to an audience

**Products/Services**
- Television programs
- Newspapers
- Movies
- Magazines
- Books
- Record/tapes
- Ads
- Public relations campaigns
- Documents
- Exhibits
- Research reports/databases
- Etc.

**Description:**
Information products and services compete for the attention of, acceptance by, and use by audiences

**Audiences:**
- Individuals
- Couples, families, co-workers, etc.
- Groups
- Organizations
- Societies

**Uses/Impact:**
- Information
- Entertainment
- Persuasion
- Education
- Diversion
- Motivation
- Deception
- Socialization
- Etc.

The economic relationship between consumers and producers may be direct, indirect, or a blend of the two. In the case of films or purchased downloads, for example, consumers directly underwrite production and distribution costs through their purchases. Network television and commercial radio producers and distributors are supported by advertisers who want to gain access to the consumers of those mass communication products. In such instances, consumers provide indirect financial support for production and distribution each time they purchase an advertiser's product. With newspapers and magazines, cable and satellite radio and television, and many Internet services, the economic link between consumers and producers is partially direct—through payment of subscription charges or provider connection fees. It is also partially indirect—through the purchase of advertisers' products.

## Information Products and Services

*Information products* are collections of messages—textual, visual, or vocal—organized in a particular way for a particular purpose or for use by a particular audience. Information products include not only news but also entertainment, public relations and advertising, computerized databases, even museum exhibits or theatrical performances.

*Information services* are activities associated with the preparation, distribution, organization, storage, or retrieval of information. Information services include news or editorial research, public relations consulting, and electronic information delivery.

## The Audience

The term *audience* refers to the group of individuals who have the potential for being exposed to and using an information product or service. In the terminology of information science, the audience is the *user group.*

Traditionally, when talking about mass communication, the word *audience* evoked an image of a large, diverse group of viewers or readers all being exposed to the same information at more or less the same time and all unknown to the information producers. However, newer communication technologies make it easier to direct messages to specific segments of a mass audience, all of whom may not be watching or listening at the same time. This view of "audience" does not presume that the user group must be of a specific size, nor be particularly diverse, nor that all of its members are exposed to the same information at the same time, nor that members of the group are unknown to the information producers. More basic is the requirement that the information product involved must have been purposefully produced and distributed by an organization for a particular constituency (Pavlik & McIntosh, 2015). A network television program fits this definition, as does an online video for a corporation, a church website, or a museum exhibit.

This approach to mass communication takes account of:

- Traditional mass media and newer communication technologies
- Convergence among once distinct mass communication media, products, and services
- Interactive capabilities of many mass media
- Active decision-making roles played by mass communication producers *and* consumers
- Complex individual, social, economic, and cultural dynamics that contribute to the interplay between mass communication producers and consumer groups
- General and specialized mass communication producers, products, services, and consumer groups

# Four Basic Functions of Mass Communication

Mass media and mass-mediated communication serve a number of functions. Sociologist and mass communication scholar Charles Wright (1986) describes four of these functions: surveillance, correlation, socialization, and entertainment (adapted from pp. 14-22):

SURVEILLANCE. Media provide a constant stream of news-related messages that enable audience members to be aware of developments in the environment that may affect them. *Surveillance* may consist of a warning function, alerting members of the audience to danger—a hurricane or a terrorist alert, for example.

Mass-mediated communication also serves a *status conferral function;* individuals, organizations, and issues that are reported on by mass media tend to be seen as significant by members of the audience. Additionally, mass-mediated communication serves an *agenda-setting function* in that it helps to set the public agenda as to issues, individuals, and topics of concern to mass media audience members.

CORRELATION. Mass media serve to interrelate and interpret information about the events of the day. The *correlation function* serves to help audience members determine the relevance that surveillance messages have for them.

SOCIALIZATION. Partly as an extension of the surveillance and correlation functions, mass-mediated communication socializes individuals for participation in society. Mass media provide common experiences and foster shared expectations as to appropriate and inappropriate behaviors. Mass-mediated communication also plays a central role in the transmission of cultural heritage from generation to generation.

ENTERTAINMENT. Mass media are a pervasive source of mass entertainment and provide the basis for diversion and release for audience members.

Wright's functions of mass communication can be observed in the fields of political communication, public relations, and advertising. In those three key applications of public communication we can observe a number of common concepts that we have discussed in this book including the use of symbolic messages, the effects of persuasion, and the importance of mediated communication.

# Political Communication

The field of political communication is multidisciplinary and draws on research from scholars in the areas of political science, communication, and mass media. Perloff (2014) defines political communication as:

the process by which language and symbols employed by leaders, media, or citizens, exert intended or unintended effects of the political cognitions, attitudes, or behaviors of individuals or on outcomes that bear on the public policy of a nation, state, or community. (p. 30)

This definition leads to the specification of five main characteristics—political communication (Perloff, 2014):

- Is a process
- Relies on words and symbols
- Involves three main players (political elites, media, citizens)
- Can have intended or unintended effects
- Can have influence at the micro (individual thoughts and behaviors) and macro (public opinion and policy) levels (adapted from pp. 30-33)

The availability and access to modern mass communication technologies have resulted in an increased focus on political communication messages and the variety of influences they may have. It is increasingly the case that political campaigns at the national level cannot be successful without a consistent and strong social media presence.

## Public Relations

The formal study of *public relations (PR)* is a relatively recent phenomenon despite the fact that from a practical standpoint evidence of PR can be traced back to events

**FIGURE 13.8**

Lucy Stone (1813–1893) delivered her first public speech on women's rights in 1847 at a time when many people considered it inappropriate for women to speak in public. For a time, she appeared at her public lectures wearing the controversial "Bloomer dress" (long pants topped by a shorter skirt).

© Everett Historical/Shutterstock.com

like the Boston Tea Party in 1773. In 2012, the Public Relations Society of America (PRSA) adopted the following definition:

> Public relations is a strategic communication process that builds mutually beneficial relationships between organizations and their publics. (PRSA, 2015).

According to PRSA, there are three key aspects associated with this definition: (1) *process* which illustrates the dynamic nature of the communication processes that take place during a public relations campaign; (2) *relationships* which highlights the importance of the connection on behalf of the public relations official or agency; and (3) *publics* which refers to the target audiences of a public relations message and can be either internal (within the organization, e.g., employees) or external (outside the organization, e.g., government officials).

The basic functions of public relations include activities such as community relations (e.g., organizing an event for the community which is sponsored by the organization and securing adequate media coverage of it), government affairs (lobbying the government/elected officials to act favorably on legislation that would be favorable to a specific industry sector), and crisis communication (responding effectively to a crisis faced by an organization). Regardless of the public relations function that is applicable to an organization or scenario, the goal of a PR practitioner is always the same: portray the company/client in the best possible light. Given that goal, spin tactics or spin control (where events and actions are given an alternate or better interpretation during interactions with media representatives and the associated publics) are key to successful public relations.

## Advertising

The entertainment function of mass communication as described by Wright (1986) is best illustrated through contemporary modes of advertising. Advertising today is a multibillion dollar global industry. One notable trend in this industry is the increase in mobile and online ads. The ability to skip commercials in a television show through the use of DVRs and a shift to mobile media consumption through the use of social media networks have resulted in advertisers finding alternate ways to deliver their messages including through online and mobile media platforms. According to a report from the Interactive Advertising Bureau, Internet advertising revenue in 2015 reached $13.3 billion just in the United States alone (IAB, 2015).

Regardless of the delivery method of the advertisement, the goal is always the same: highlight the unique selling proposition (especially for product-based ads). The unique selling proposition is the concept or idea that makes the advertised product different from similar ones within the same industry. Through the use of verbal and nonverbal messages, advertisers attempt to produce effective persuasion. But what is the point at which an advertisement moves from persuasion to deception? The pros and cons of advertising have been extensively debated over the years. Proponents of advertising highlight the information and entertainment functions of the advertising industry, whereas critics point to the deceptive aspects of commercial advertising and the likelihood of creating false needs for unnecessary products.

Identifying ethical advertising as a tool of public communication is not an easy process. For example, how would you feel if your instructor ended each class session with the following statement: "This lecture is brought to you by company XYZ." Would it make a difference if, in exchange for listening to that statement, you were offered high-tech technology in your classroom including seating with individual monitors and an outlet to charge your phone or laptop?

## Broader Functions of Public and Mass Communication

**PACKAGING AND DISTRIBUTION OF CULTURE.** In any society, mass communication institutions package and distribute the cultural knowledge base. This knowledge base consists of news and entertainment programs, public relations, and advertising, along with other information products and services provided by libraries, museums, theme and amusement parks, cable and satellite services, software producers, computer services, art galleries, sports, and even shopping malls (Hunt & Ruben, 1993).

Mass media such as newspapers, television, and film have long played a fundamental role in packaging and transmitting cultural information. However, when we think more broadly, we realize that many other organizations whose primary function is not mass communication in the usual sense of the term also serve these same functions.

**POPULARIZING AND VALIDATING FUNCTION.** While the concept of a cultural information base may seem abstract, its consequences are not. Through mass communication, concepts of what is real and make-believe, or right and wrong, are distributed from place to place and from generation to generation and, in the process, are popularized and sanctioned. News, entertainment, sports, and advertising programming tell us stories about people and how they live, provide insights into how people think, and portray the consequences of particular behaviors. In subtle ways, they provide lessons about relationships, family life, war, crime, music, religion, and politics. Whether the topic is sex, violence, fitness, drugs, or racial issues, they contribute to the visibility, currentness, and validity of the topics they address.

**NEWS AND INFORMATION.** Sometimes intentionally, but more often unintentionally, news and informational programming have the effect of popularizing and validating particular concerns and ideologies (ways of thinking) by focusing on some while ignoring others. Even interviews and public opinion polls contribute to the popularity and legitimacy of certain issues through the choices that information producers make. Interviews and polls, for example, deal with particular topics and questions. Many topics are available, but only some are included. To ask respondents their opinions on environmental pollution, the actions of a local political figure, or a government policy is to state by implication that these are important topics of the day. Their importance is further underscored when the results of the poll are published. These selected topics are given a visibility and legitimacy that is not afforded to other topics of perhaps equal significance but which were not selected for examination.

Mass communication news and informational programming contributes to the popularization and legitimation of culture through the selection of what is and what is not "news." For example, the selection and repeated rebroadcasting of particular images, events, or excerpts from a political speech elevate the visibility, permanence, and significance that are associated with these sights or "sound bites." Mass communication also contributes to the cultural agenda by the interpretation (or lack of interpretation) of news events and through the way "causes" and "effects" are implied.

ENTERTAINMENT AND ADVERTISING. Entertainment programs contribute to the web of culture, often in subtle ways. They provide commentary on how people should live, look, think, talk, and relate to others. Advertisements also provide strong cultural messages regarding economics and consumption. In other words, they urge us to become consumers. Encouraging consumption is a universal theme in advertising and many kinds of promotion. However, rarely is the message "We want you all to get out there and buy goods and services whether you need or can afford them" made explicit. One area where this theme *is* apparent is in advertising for credit cards. Direct mailings and "take an application" posters urge college students "to establish your credit now" and assure that "you have been pre-approved" or that the bank will "say yes" when you apply. The implicit economics lesson is a simple one: It is important to be a consumer, it is necessary to establish credit—the sooner the better—and it is good to use credit cards to make purchases.

SPORTS: HEROES AND VILLAINS. Sporting events provide another interesting illustration of the ways in which mass communication serves as a carrier of cultural messages. Nimmo and Combs (1983), in their book *Mediated Political Realities,* discuss how sports programming prepares viewers for political participation in society. Sporting events, particularly when distributed by mass media, are presented as suspense-filled contests with heroes and villains. They present a story of the "triumph of justice or the intervention of fortune, . . . heroic deeds and untimely errors, dramatic climaxes, and the euphoria of the victors along with the gloom of the vanquished" (p. 126) Sports commentators contribute further to the melodramatic nature of sports by introducing rivalries and quarrels among players, salary and contract disputes, fights and fines, winning and losing, romance and death. Sporting events teach about playing by the rules, losing gracefully, sportsmanship, competition, and persistence.

These themes influence the way other facets of life are viewed. Media coverage of politics or criminal trials, for example, often places more emphasis on rules, tactics, and "spin" strategies than on issues of right or wrong, guilt or innocence.

### Video and Computer Games: Control and Consequences.

Video games—another somewhat less obvious form of mass communication—also provide implicit cultural messages (see Figure 13.9). Trees, people, houses, animals, and other cars buzz back and forth across the road in front of your metallic red Lamborghini as you screech around the turns. Suddenly a bike pulls out in front of you and you are forced to swerve off the road into a ditch, where your car crashes into a brick wall and blows up. Is this a problem? Not if the press of a button brings you back to the start of the track in the same shiny car—and this is exactly how things work in the world of video-gaming. One of the strongest messages that video games send is immortality and the possibility to redo what went wrong without consequence (R. Ruben, 1989) since you can always hit the "restart" button and characters are reborn

**FIGURE 13.9**

Research shows that children who play video or computer games for an average of an hour or less per day are more social and satisfied with life than children who don't play these games at all. But the positive effects disappear if children play such games for more than an hour a day (Przybylski, 2014).

© Kamira/Shutterstock.com

Not only is violence in these types of entertainment media prominent and often graphic, it has increased dramatically and continues to do so (Anderson & Dill, 2000). When video games first appeared in the 1970s, they contained simple and apparently harmless content, such as the wildly popular *Pong*. In the 1980s, games like *Pac-Man* and *Donkey Kong* became dominant. In the 1990s, with the decline of arcades and the increasing popularity of home consoles, more violent video games became popular, including *Mortal Kombat*, in which realistic human fighters battle to the death. Today, with games such as the *Grand Theft Auto* series and *The Last of Us,* the level of violence has increased substantially. However, long-term studies have not demonstrated the influence of video game violence on societal violence (Ferguson, 2015).

### Commercializing Function.
Mass communication often plays a role in giving commercial value to and helping to sell particular cultural symbols. In this sense, mass communication institutions are part of the cultural industry, which UNESCO (United Nations Educational, Scientific and Cultural Organization; unesco.org) describes as an industry involved in the large-scale production, reproduction, storage, or distribution of cultural goods and services.

Herbert Schiller (1989), a communication and culture scholar, writes that increasingly:

> cultural creation has been transformed into discrete, specialized forms, commercially produced and marketed. Speech, dance, drama (ritual), music, and the visual and plastic arts have been vital, indeed necessary, features of human experience from earliest times. What distinguishes their situation in the [present] . . . era are the relentless and successful efforts to separate these elemental expressions of human creativity from their group and community origins for the purpose of *selling them* to those who can pay. (pp. 30-31)

Mass communication plays a major role in the commercialization of celebrities, brand names, art objects, music, and other elements of culture. This is especially obvious in areas where the popularization of particular individuals through public and mass communication has given great value to them, their names, and anything associated with them. One example is the endorsement of clothes or other products by actors or sports figures. Commercialization also takes place when a celebrity's name is added to products, services, or ideas as a way of enhancing their value or marketability. Ironically, public and mass communication play a role in giving celebrities commercial value and are then used to enhance and market the value of products or services they endorse.

SOCIAL CONTACT AND SENSE OF COMMUNITY. Mass communication consumption can serve as a substitute for human contact, helping individuals avoid isolation and loneliness. As noted by Kubey and Csikszentmihalyi (1990):

> Those who lack structured interactions with other people due to unemployment, divorce, widowhood, personality factors, or declining health are more likely than others to turn to television for companionship, information, and escape. Older people who are widowed and/or retired, for example, are among the heaviest television viewers. (p. 168)

Interactive media may be seen as serving mass communication and interpersonal communication functions at the same time.

Mass communication gives people a sense of community and connection to others. It can also provide a stimulant to interaction to the extent that we share the same interests as other information consumers. Reading celebrity news online, attending a particular concert, watching a popular television series, or viewing a football game may facilitate interaction by providing topics for conversation.

In general then, mass communication plays a major role in the production and distribution of social realities. In our society, and in most others, the mass media are the major providers of standardized messages regarding people, products, situations, and events—messages that often have a major influence on the understandings, knowledge, and images members of the audience develop.

# THE EFFECTS OF PUBLIC AND MASS COMMUNICATION

In general terms, there are two ways of thinking about public and mass communication effects. One focuses on the communicator, the message, and the technology. The second emphasizes the audience members.

## The Communicator/ Producer Perspective

The communicator/producer-centered approach sees the source, message, technology, information products, and services as controlling influences on audience members. This way of thinking is suggested by statements such as "His speeches and media campaign made him a winner," or "Decaying morals within society are a consequence of increasing sexuality in public communication, television, records, and music videos." Each statement implies a *causal relationship* between public and mass communication on the one hand and individual, group, or societal behavior on the other.

**FIGURE 13.10**

Media scholar Joseph Turow reminds us that media companies are usually in business to make money from the materials they produce and distribute, which is another characteristic that sets them apart from such communication activities as gossip among friends and construction of an Internet site by a class. But, by surrounding huge populations with words, sounds, and images, media firms go beyond mere money making. They contribute to the notions people carry in their heads about what society is like, how they fit in, and what power they have to change things for the better.

© elder nurkovic/Shutterstock.com

## The Audience/Consumer Perspective

*Consumer* approaches emphasize the role audience members play in public and mass communication outcomes. While most communicator/producer theories may portray audience members as *passive* and *controlled*, the audience/consumer perspective emphasizes their *active* and *controlling* role. This way of thinking is implied in the statement, "When I hear a political speech filled with oversimplification and generalization, I just tune it out," or "Today's audience members are sophisticated enough to enjoy all forms mediated entertainment without being adversely influenced."

The tension between views of mass communication as highly influential (those emphasizing source/producer influences) and those which view audience members as more powerful (emphasizing the consumer perspective) is ongoing. Do violent movies cause people to develop violent tendencies or do individuals' needs for violence lead them to watch (and producers, therefore, to continue to create) violent programs? As we have seen earlier, attempting to explain communication outcomes in a one-way, cause-and-effect manner (as is characteristic of the S → M → C → R = E paradigm) may underestimate the fundamentally interactive, mutual influences that systems theorists believe are fundamental to communication. The systems framework implies that outcomes (or effects) are the result of interactions that take place over time between the individual and his or her physical and social environment.

## Uses and Gratifications

The foundation of the consumer approach to mass communication theory comes from a tradition called "uses and gratifications," originally advanced by Katz, Blumler, and Gurevitch (1974):

> [The uses and gratifications approach] . . . views members of the audience as actively utilizing media contents, rather than being passively acted upon by the media. Thus, it does not assume a direct relationship between messages and effects, but postulates instead that members of the audience put messages to use, and that such usages act as intervening variables in the process of effect. (p. 12)

This perspective views audience behavior as being guided by the pursuit of particular goals and needs. One of the particular benefits of the uses and gratifications approach is that it provides a generalized way of thinking about mass communication "effects." That is, rather than viewing mass communication and its effects as a unique and specialized form of human communication, mass communication outcomes are seen as arising from interactions between individuals and the environment, in the same manner as in interpersonal, group, organizational, and other settings. As Littlejohn and Foss (2011) put it: "Audience members are largely responsible for choosing media to meet their own needs, and media are considered to be only one factor contributing to meeting needs" (p. 351).

*Dependency theory* extends the core concepts of the uses and gratifications approach and helps to reconcile this view with earlier theories that envisioned mass media as extremely powerful in bringing about effects in the audience members (Ball-Rokeach & DeFleur, 1976; DeFleur & Ball-Rokeach, 1989). Dependency theory suggests that audience members do rely on media to meet their needs, but they come to depend on some media more than others and, moreover, their dependence on media both influences, and is influenced by, their needs and uses. Thus, some individuals may depend largely on particular mass media for their information on current events (such as television), while others may meet their needs for diversion and entertainment using other media (such as the Internet). Depending on the choices made by members of the audience, particular media will become more important and influential, while others become less so. The dependency model also suggests that in times of societal change and conflict, audience members are more likely to question social institutions and their own beliefs and, in such circumstances, the importance of mass media increases for audience members (Littlejohn & Foss, 2011).

## Integrating Perspectives

Both the communicator/producer and audience/consumer perspectives are valuable to understanding the dynamics of public and mass communication. Communicator-oriented approaches remind us that public and mass communication sources play an important and influential role in our lives through the creation, packaging, commercialization, validation, and distribution of the information that fills our environment—information we must organize ourselves in order to function.

Consumer-oriented theories stress the role individual audience members play in explaining the impact of mass communication. They emphasize the significant role of individual needs and uses, attitudes, and beliefs in the dynamics of message reception. In so doing, they remind us that as consumers we play an active role in the communication process and in determining its effects.

How can these two perspectives be integrated? Consider the following analogy: "High-powered sports cars cause accidents." It is true that high-powered sports cars are involved in a number of accidents—more accidents than cars lacking such power. Are the cars themselves to blame? Would we eliminate all these accidents if we stopped producing fast cars? To what extent are the drivers to blame?

A person can certainly speed and drive recklessly in a Ferrari. The car *is* designed for high performance. But these same behaviors are also possible in a Honda Civic, if a driver chooses to *use* it in these ways. However, we can't take this argument too far; without a car, after all, there can be no speeding or reckless driving. We might, therefore, want to conclude that in any given instant a high-powered sports car *contributes to,* but does not itself *cause,* accidents. Thus, accidents are the result of particular *patterns of consumption in relation to product characteristics and availability.*

If we think of public—and particularly mass—communication, the case of high-powered cars provides a helpful analogy because it involves a relationship between technology and human behavior. As with cars and drivers, it seems reasonable to assume that communication technologies and products facilitate but are seldom the sole cause of audience behavior. Generally, the effects that occur between public and mass communicators and consumers are *mutually causal* or *mutually controlling.*

As in the Ferrari example, the influences of public and mass communication result from *both* (1) the availability of particular messages and technologies with particular characteristics and capabilities and (2) the uses to which audience members attend to, interpret, remember, and use those messages.

Thus, the "effects" of public and mass communication are the result of particular *patterns of message reception in relation to characteristics and availability of messages and technology.* Communicators, messages, and technologies play an important role in defining, influencing, and shaping the available options, direction, and limits of those uses. As audience members we influence the impact of public and mass communicators, individual and institutional, through the choices we make—to attend or not, buy or not, read or not, listen or not, watch or not, and so on. Over the long term, these choices influence what is made available to us through public and mass communication, which in turn influences the range of choices we have available.

# CONCLUSION

Public and mass communication play a critical role in creating and disseminating messages. Public and mass communication refer to situations where messages are created and disseminated to a *relatively* large number of receivers, in a setting that is *relatively* impersonal. Public speaking, theater, and public debates are examples of public communication. Communication involving mass media such as newspaper and magazine articles, television programs, and advertising are examples of mass communication. The term *relatively* is italicized, because what is "public" or "mass" and what is not is often a matter of degree.

The public speech is one common example of public communication. The speech and its presentation should be considered separately. Developing a speech falls into four general categories: preparation, creating the speech, revising, and editing. The presentation consists of preparing the speech, rehearsal, developing presentation strategies, and other presentational elements. Audience analysis and adaptation, developing a purpose and a thesis, making an argument, the use of evidence, visual aids, and communication apprehension are all important considerations in understanding the dynamics of public communication.

Mass communication is an extension of public communication involving technology. Key considerations in the process include: production, distribution, and consumption; information products and services; and the audience. Four basic functions of mass communication are: surveillance, correlation, socialization, and entertainment. Broader functions of mass communication include: the packaging and distribution of culture; the popularizing and validating function; the commercializing function; and social contact and sense of community.

In general, there are two ways to think about public and mass communication effects. One emphasizes the role played by the communicator/producer; the other the role played by the audience/consumers. Both perspectives are valuable for understanding mass communication and can, and should, be integrated for a comprehensive view of the process.

As producers of public communication and consumers of mass media, we have a number of responsibilities. Perhaps the most important of these is to behave ethically. It is easy to see why ethical behavior is so important for public speakers. As speakers, we must always try to present the most accurate information that is available to us. Outright lies and even stretching the truth are not acceptable in a public context. In fact, speaking ethically enhances one's credibility. It is well known that speakers who present information that is contradictory to their point of view and who then effectively refute this information are more persuasive than speakers who ignore opposing arguments.

Today's information-rich environment is providing more opportunities for unethical behavior using technology. For example, it is very easy to send a potentially harmful message to thousands of people via Facebook. Some people pass along obscene or offensive messages. While we have the right to view all of the information that is available to us on the Internet, we do not have the right to consciously inflict harm on others. It is every person's responsibility, ultimately, to make sure that his or her messages are not inappropriate or harmful to others.

To become more effective consumers and producers of public or mediated messages, we should expose ourselves to a variety of media and to a variety of products in these media. There is a wealth of information available today in mediated formats, but much of it is repetitious and designed to appeal to a mass audience. Unfortunately, the plot of the latest reality show or action/adventure movie is much like the plot of last year's big hit of the same genre. It is important to seek out alternative mediated messages to expand our knowledge about the role of communication in the contemporary world. For example, look for films directed by African-American or women directors. Listen to college radio stations or National Public Radio. Read magazines designed for audiences interested in particular topics such as politics, hobbies, or self-development. Go to museums that contain collections focused on unfamiliar topics. All of these experiences improve our own ability to communicate by enhancing our personal experiences of the world and helping us to understand others' experiences of it.

# KEY POINTS

After having read this chapter, you should be able to:

- Define public communication
- Analyze the main functions and applications of public communication in contemporary society
- Describe how political communication, public relations and advertising represent the basic functions of mass communication
- Evaluate the effects of public communication in today's world

# REFERENCES

Anderson, C. A., & Dill, K. E. (2000). Video games and aggressive thoughts, feelings, and behavior in the laboratory and in life. *Journal of Personality and Social Psychology, 78*(4), 772-790.

Ball-Rokeach, S. J., & DeFleur, M. L. (1976). A dependency model of mass-media effects. *Communication Research, 3*(1), 3-21.

Blumler, J. G., & Katz, E. (1974). *The uses of mass communication: Current perspectives on gratifications research.* Beverly Hills, CA: Sage.

Bradley, B. E. (1991). *Fundamentals of speech communication: The credibility of ideas* (6th ed.). Dubuque, IA: Wm. C. Brown.

DeFleur, M. L., & Ball-Rokeach, S. J. (1989). *Theories of mass communication* (5th ed.). New York, NY: Longman.

Ferguson, C. J. (2015). Does media violence predict societal violence? It depends on what you look at and when. *Journal of Communication, 65*, 193-212.

Fraleigh, M. D., & Tuman, S. J. (2014). *Speak up: An illustrated guide to public speaking* (3rd ed.). Boston, MA: Bedford/St. Martins.

Hunt, T., & Ruben, B. D. (1993). *Mass communication: Producers and consumers.* New York, NY: HarperCollins.

Jensen, J. V. (1981). *Argumentation: Reasoning in communication.* New York, NY: D. Van Nostrand.

Katz, E., Blumler, J., G. & Gurevitch, M. (1974). Uses of mass communication by the individual. In W. P. Davidson & F. T. C. Yu (Eds.), *Mass communication research: Major issues and future direction* (pp. 11-35). New York, NY: Praeger.

Kearney, P., & Plax, T. G. (1996). *Public speaking in a diverse society.* Mountain View, CA: Mayfield.

Kubey, R., & Csikszentmihalyi, M. (1990). *Television and the quality of life: How viewing shapes everyday experience.* Hillsdale, NJ: Lawrence Erlbaum.

IAB. (2015, June 11). U.S. Internet ad revenues reach historic $13.3 billion in Q1 2015. Retrieved from http://www.iab.net/about_the_iab/recent_press_releases/press_release_archive/press_release/pr-061115#sthash.CymlzN3K.dpuf

Larson, C. U. (1992). *Persuasion: Reception and responsibility* (6th ed.). Belmont, CA: Wadsworth.

Littlejohn, S. W., & Foss, K. A. (2011). *Theories and human communication* (10th ed.). Long Grove, IL: Wadsworth.

Lucas, S. E. (2012). *The art of public speaking* (12th ed.). New York, NY: McGraw-Hill.

McCrimmon, J. M. (1974). *Writing with a purpose.* Boston, MA: Houghton Mifflin.

Nimmo, D., & Combs, J. E. (1983). *Mediated political realities.* New York, NY: Longman.

Pavlik, J. V., & McIntosh, S. (2015). *Converging media: A new introduction to mass communication.* New York, NY: Oxford University Press.

Perloff, M. R. (2014). *The dynamics of political communication: Media and politics in the digital age.* New York, NY: Routledge.

Przybylski, A. K. (2014). Electronic gaming and psychosocial adjustment. *Pediatrics, 134*(3), 716-722.

PRSA. (2015). What is public relations? Retrieved from http://www.prsa.org/aboutprsa/publicrelationsdefined/#.Va1WOvmrFfY

Ruben, R. (1989). Lessons of videogaming. Unpublished paper, Rutgers University.

Ruben, B. D., Reis, R., Overson, B. K., & Belmas, G. (2010). *Mass communication: Producers and consumers* (2nd ed., customized version). Dubuque, IA: Kendall-Hunt.

Schiller, H. I. (1989). *Culture, Inc.: The corporate takeover of public expression.* New York, NY: Oxford University Press.

Wright, C. R. (1986). *Mass communication: A sociological perspective* (3rd ed.). New York, NY: Random House.

# INDEX

NOTE: Page references in *italics* refer to figures and photos.

## A

Westley and MacLeans model of communication, *32,* 32–33
communicator perspective, 352
community, mass communication as substitute for, 351
competence, relational, 241–242
compliance-gaining, 127–129
compromise, in groups, 267
computer games, 350, *350*
Comte, August, 8
conflict
    conflict phase in group development, *262,* 262–263
    in groups, 270–271, *271*
    in relationships, 241
conformance, 118–119
Connaughton, Stacey, 272
Conrad, D., 4
consensual families, 229–230
consensus, in groups, 266
consistency, 128
consumption
    consumer perspective and mass communication, 352–353, 354–355
    of mass communication, 342–343, *343*
context
    high and low context cultures, 309–310
    interacting and, 64
    perception and information processing, 162, *163*
contrived groups, 253–254
control
    interpersonal needs and, 239
    verbal/nonverbal communication and, 76
control of content, mediated communication and, 186–187
conversational orientation, 229
cooperativeness, 117, 270–271
coordinated action, 224
Corax of Syracuse, 23
correction channel, 32
correlation, mass communication and, 345
cosmetic surgery, 81, 86
counterdependency relationship, 236–237

courtship, as life function of communication, 52, *52*
covert rules, language and, 75–76
credibility, 159
Crosby, Phillip, 281–282
cross-cultural contact, 312–313
Csikszentmihalyi, M., 351
cues-filtered-out theories, 183
cultures and societies, 303–327. *see also* nonverbal communication
    characteristics of culture, 308–315, *311, 313*
    communication as essential to, 16–17
    cultural adaptation, 316–319, *317, 318*
    culture, overview, 63–64
    in group development, *263,* 263–264
    intercultural communication, 319–320
    international communication, 323–324
    nature of culture, 304–305, *305*
    organizational culture, *293,* 293–296, *295*
    overview, 304
    public and mass communication functions for, 348
    relationship between communication and culture, 306–308, *307*
    role of mediated communication in, 315–316
    societies as complex cultural and communication systems, 320–322, *321, 322*
customers, quality theory about, 282

## D

Dance, Frank, 14
dating relationships, 228–229
Deal, T. E., 264
decision making
    in groups, 265–267
    by individuals, 223
decoding, 104–105
defensive climate, of relationships, 235–236
Delgado, J. M. R., 197–198
Delia, J. G., 130

delivery, of message, 160

Deming, W. Edwards, 281

Deming cycle, *282*

democratic leadership, 258

dependency relationship, 236–237

dependency theory, 353

description, 195

Deutsch, Karl, 322

Dickson, William J., 279

differentiating stage of relationships, *231*, 234

disclosure, 222–223, 226–227

discovered actions, nonverbal communication and, 89

Disney, 282

distant (facial) display, 90–91

distribution

    mass communication, 342–343, *343*, 348

    of message, 171

diversity, in organizations, 297–298

division of labor, 284–285

dramatistic pentad, 208–209

dress, nonverbal communication and, *86*, 86–87, *87*

Durkheim, Emile, 8

dyadic relationships, 221–223

## E

Eastern Communication Association, 28

Ekman, P., 80, 91

Ellsworth, P. C., 80, 81

emergence phase, in group development, *262,* 262–263

emergent groups, 253–254

emotion

    emotional appeal, 23, 337, *337*

    emotional intelligence, 209–210

    facial expression and, 80, *81*

encoding, 104–105

entertainment, mass communication and, 345, 349

environment

    adapting to, 17–18

    changing, 201–202

    environmental influences, 160–163, *162, 163*

    individuals' reaction to, 194–197, *195, 196*

episodic memory, 146–147

ethics, 65

evaluation, 195

evidence, in speeches, 338

experience, 153, *153*

experimenting stage, of relationships, *231,* 232–233

external networks, of organizations, 291–292

eye gaze

    eye contact, 81–83

    pupil dilation, 84

## F

facial expression, 73, *79,* 79–84, *80, 81, 84*

family relationships

    culture and, 308

    interpersonal communication and, 229–230

Federal Express, 282

feedback, 331–332

Festinger, Leon, 163

fight-or-flight response, 206

Fiske, J., 106

Fitzpatrick, M. A., 229

flags, symbolism of, 307, *307*

Ford Motor Company, 282

Foss, K. A., 353

Frazer, Sir James George, 9

free speech, anonymity and, 187

friendship

    friendship/liking principle, 158

    social relationships and, 224, *224*

    verbal communication and, 128

Friesen, W. V., 80, 91

Frisch, Karl von, 54

functional approach, to leadership, 288

*Functions of the Executive, The* (Barnard), 279

Funkhouser, G. G., 181

# G

gender
- culture and, 309
- language and, 119–122, *122*

General Motors, 282

generation of meaning, 106

gestures
- as nonverbal communication, 88–91, *89, 91*
- for public speaking, 340–341, *341*

Gibb, J. R., 235

Ginsberg, Ruth Bader, 203

global village, 323–324

goals
- organizational, 277–278, *278*
- perception and information processing, 149–151, *150*
- personal or socially oriented, 224

Goffman, Erving, 207–208, 227

Goleman, D., 209–210

Gorgias of Leontini, 23

Gotsis, G., 297

Greece (ancient), communication theory and, *24,* 24–25, *25, 26*

greetings, 90

Grice, H. Paul, 117

group communication, 247–274
- characteristics of groups, 249, *249*
- communication as essential to groups, 16–17
- conflict in groups, 270–271, *271*
- group cohesiveness and, 267–269
- group decision making, 265–267
- group development and, 260–265, *261, 262, 263*
- leadership and, 256–260
- mediated groups, 271
- overview, 250–252
- reasons people join groups, 252
- roles and responsibilities, *254,* 254–256
- seating patterns in groups, *252*
- technology and, *272*
- types of groups, 253–254

*Groupthink* (Janis), 269

groupthink syndrome, 269

growth, self-development and, 205–207

Guerrero, L. K., 74

guide sign, 90

Gurevitch, M., 353

gustatory messages, *49,* 51

Gutenberg, Johannes, *174*

# H

habit, 153, *153*

Hackman, M. Z., 287

hair, nonverbal communication and, 85, *85*

Hall, E. T. (Edward), 93, 306, 309–310

Hall, J. A., 79–80

Hall, M. R., 309–310

haptics, 92

Harvey, O. J., 197

Hawthorne studies (Western Electric Company), 279–280

Headey, B., 228

Heeter, C., 186

Heider, Fritz, 163

hemispheric specialization, nonverbal communication and, 77

hierarchy of needs, 148–149, *149*

high context culture, 309–310

high self-monitors, 210

holocracy, *291*

home, concept of, 179–180

Homer, 22

Hopper, Grace, *35*

Hopper, T., 86

horizontal message flow, 290

Hovland, Carl, 29

human communication
- as open system, 48
- as unique, 56–57, *57*

human relations school of organizational behavior, 279–280

Hunt, Morton, 145, 164, 199

# I

IBM, 282

identity. *see also* individuals
  common identity, 17
  defined, 204–205
  free speech and anonymity, 187
  gender and, 119, 122
  hierarchy of needs and, 148
  identity confusion, 53
  principle of nonidentity, 114
  social identity, 86–87
  social influence and, 130
imitated actions, nonverbal communication and, 89
impression management, 208
inclusion, 239
inconvenience (facial) display, 90
indifference, in groups, 268
individuals, 193–275. *see also* interpersonal
      communication and relationships
  cognitive development of, 197–204, *199, 200,*
      *202*
  communication as essential to, 16
  identity (self), defined, 204–205
  individualistic roles in groups, 256
  individual orientation and culture, 310
  as message senders/receivers, 58
  reaction, action, interaction, and, 194–197, *195,*
      *196*
  self-awareness of, 210–212, *211*
  self-development of, 204–210, *205, 208, 209*
inevitability, 66
informal message flow, 290–291
information
  as commodity, 35, 180–181
  Information Age, 34–36, *35,* 176–177
  informational influence, 131
  information processing (*see* perception and
      information processing)
  information-use environment, 194
  information-use sequence, 195, *195*
  mass communication and, 342–343

mass communication and information
      products, *343,* 343–344
  public and mass communication, 348–349
inherited actions, nonverbal communication and, 89
initiating stage, of relationships, *231,* 232
initiation, in groups, 265
innovation
  innovation and employee engagement school
      of organizational communication,
      283–284
  organizational culture and, 295–296, *296*
inoculation, 129
integrating stage, of relationships, *231, 233,* 233–234
intensifying stage, of relationships, *231, 233, 233*
intent, 14, 159–160
intentionality, 73
interaction
  individuals and, 194–197, *195, 196*
  interaction stages of relationships, *231,* 231–235
  limited, in public communication, 331–332
Interactive Advertising Bureau, 347
interactiveness, 117–118
interactivity, of mediated communication, 185–186,
      *186*
intercultural communication, *317,* 319–320. *see also*
      cultures and societies
Intercultural Readiness Check (IRC), 320, *321*
interdisciplinarity, 1940s-1960s, 28–29
internal networks, in organizations, 289–291
international communication, 323–324. *see also*
      cultures and societies
International Communication Association, 29
international networks, 320–322, *322*
interpersonal communication and relationships,
      217–246
  evolution of relationships, *231,* 231–235, *232,*
      *233*
  factors influencing relationship patterns, 238–
      241, *239*
  interpersonal needs and styles, 239–240
  overview, 218
  relational competence, 241–242

organizational communication and, *293*

overview, 71–72

similarities to verbal communication, *73*, 73–75

space (proxemics) and, *93*, 93–95, *94*

time (chronemics) and, 95–97

touch (haptics) and, 92

normative influence, 131

Northouse, P. G., 286, 287

novelty, perception/information processing and, *156*, 156–157

# O

office, concept of, 179–180, *180*

olfactory messages, *49*, 51

open systems, 48

organization, perception/information processing and, 156

organizational communication, 275–301

communication as essential to, 16–17

communication networks and, 288–293, *289, 290*

leadership and, 286–288, *287*

organizational climate and, 296

organizational culture and, *293*, 293–296, *295*

organizational diversity and, 297–298

organizational purposes, plans, goals, 277–278, *278*

organizational theories, 278–284, *279, 282, 283*

overview, 276–277

roles and responsibilities, 284–285, *285*

orientation phase, in group development, 262, *262*

origin, 154–155

outcomes, 15

overt rules, language and, 75–76

# P

packaging, public communication and, 348

paradox of choice, 178

paralanguage, 77–79

parent-offspring relations, as life function of communication, *52*, 53

participatory leadership, 258

patterns, relational, 235–242, *239*

Patterson, M. L., 72

Peck, M. Scott, 206

peer pressure, 160

people, as message senders/receivers, 58

perception and information processing, 137–167. *see also* individuals

as active and complex process, 163

interpretation, 144, *144*

message and information influences, 153–157, *156, 157*

overview, 138–142

receiver influences, 147–153, *148, 150, 152, 153*

retention (memory), 144–147

selection, *142*, 142–144

source influences, 157–160

technological and environmental influences, 160–163, *162, 163*

Perloff, M. R., 345

permanence, of symbols, 60

*Personal Influence* (Katz, Lazarsfeld), 32

personal representations, 200–204, *202*

personal space, *93*, 93–94

personal theories, about communication, 10–11, 13

persuasion

argument in speeches, 336–338

compliance-gaining and, 127–129

early communication theory and, 23

media influence and, *182*, 182–184

social influence and, 130–131

verbal communication and, 127–131

verbal/nonverbal communication and, 74–75

Peters, J. D., 38

Pfau, M., 129

phonological characteristics, gender and, 121

physical attraction, 158–159

physical characteristics, perception/information processing and, 155

physical environment, 94–95, *95*

physique, 85–86

plans, organizational, 277–278, *278*

Plato, 23, 24

pluralistic families, 230

point of view, 15

political communication, 345–346

polychronic time, 310–311, *311*

portability, of symbols, 60

positional power, in relationships, 240–241

power

    perception and information processing, 160

    positional power in relationships, 240–241

presentation, preparing, 334–335

*Presentation of Self in Everyday Life, The* (Goffman),
        207–208

principle of non-allness, 114

principle of nonidentity, 114

principle of self-reflexiveness, 114–115

printing press, advent of, 174, *174*

private status, public *versus,* 76

problem solving, 38

process, of communication. *see* communication
        process

Proctor & Gamble, 282

producer perspective, 352

production

    mass communication, 342–343, *343*

    of message, 171

profiling, caution about, 315

progressive spirals, 238

Protagoras of Abdera, 23

protective families, 230

protowords, 108

proxemics, *93,* 93–95, *94*

proximity, perception/information processing and,
        157–158

PRSA (Public Relations Society of America), 347

psycholinguistic approach, to language, 108

psychological task definitions, 229

public communication, 329–358

    defined, 330–332, *332*

    effects of mass communication and, *352,* 352–355

mass communication, 342–351, *343, 346, 350*

    role of, 332

    understanding, *333,* 333–341, *335, 337, 339, 341*

*Publick Occurrences Both Foreign and Domestick,* 27

public relations

    as external organizational network, 292

    overview, 346–347

Public Relations Society of America (PRSA), 347

pupil dilation, 84

purpose, organizational, 277–278, *278*

# Q

quality, theories about, 281–283, *282*

Quality College, 282

*Quarterly Journal of Public Speaking,* 28

*Quarterly Journal of Public Speech,* 28

question asking, gender and, 120

Quintilian, 23, 24

Quintus Serenus Sammonicus, 111

# R

radio, advent of, 175

Rains, S. A., 187

Rapoport, A., 114

reaction, 194–197, *195, 196*

reasoned appeals, 337

receiver influences, 147–153, *148, 150, 152, 153*

reception, 172

reciprocity, 127

regressive spirals, 238

reinforcement phase, in group development, *262,*
        262–263

relational approach, to leadership, 288

relational culture, 306

relationships

    communication as essential to, 16

    culture and, 311–313, *313* (*see also* cultures and
        societies)

    defined, 219–220, *220*